Berlin and the BBC

Berlin and the BBC

A Century of Sound and Vision

Edited by

Patrick Major
Miles Taylor

ISBN 978-3-11-130205-8
ISBN 978-3-11-130250-8 (PDF)
ISBN 978-3-11-130278-2 (E-PUB)
DOI https://doi.org/10.1515/9783111302508

Library of Congress Control Number: 2026937139

Bibliographic information published by the Deutsche Nationalbibliothek
The Deutsche Nationalbibliothek lists this publication in the Deutsche Nationalbibliografie; detailed bibliographic data are available on the internet at http://dnb.dnb.de.

De Gruyter and Walter de Gruyter GmbH are part of De Gruyter Brill.
www.degruyterbrill.com

Questions about General Product Safety Regulation: productsafety@degruyterbrill.com

Cover illustration: A native Berliner, Marlene Dietrich (1901–92) performed songs for the BBC Allied Expeditionary Forces Programme during the Second World War © BBC

Contents

Foreword

I was 100 years old in 2022! Or at least that's how it felt – as my whole year was consumed with marking the BBC's centenary, the first public service broadcaster ever to celebrate a century of continuous broadcasting.

Obviously, a big focus for me was the UK, paid for as the BBC is by its nation of licence fee payers. So I explored the BBC as a voice of nationhood, as an institution and blueprint of public service broadcasting, and of course as a trigger for citizen memory – where were you when Neville Chamberlain announced "this country is at war with Germany", when Queen Elizabeth was crowned, when Radio 1 hit the airwaves? But this extraordinary conference gave us the BBC centenary with a difference. The focus of the city of Berlin liberated rich reflection and revelation; cultural conversation and contrast; incisive analysis and a probing dynamism.

There were seismic moments and structures to orientate ourselves around – WW2 and then the creation of German broadcasting, the building of the Berlin Wall and then its eventual fall. As author John le Carré said "I saw the Wall go up when I was 30 and saw it come down when I was 60". In between was a world of differences, of post-Cold War Utopian possibilities. And sometimes we were up close and personal. BBC Correspondent Vernon Bartlett memorably interviewing Adolf Hitler, observed he had "a moustache which is wider than it used to be, so that it is no longer possible to compare the Chancellor with Charlie Chaplin". And sometimes we had the long view: the constant interrogation of archives that relate the city's history to *now* and then now and then a different *now* again.

There was cultural curiosity too, as Nick Kenyon reminded us how music can on occasion rise above politics – just a few yards away from where the seminar took place Leonard Bernstein redefined Beethoven's Ninth and Schiller's text as a hymn of universal freedom. And there were personal narratives, from the Beats to Bowie, the latter writing "I couldn't have written things like *Low* and *Heroes* if it hadn't been for Berlin". And a questioning about how to define contemporary culture, in this case Berlin's famous techno scene, without falling into a distancing fossilisation.

Finally, the correspondents roundtable left us with an accumulation of rich and valuable testimonies. From the initial perspective voiced by many of their BBC masters that Berlin (and by inference Germany) "is a worthy story, an economic story... but it tends to be boring" to the sense of Berlin as an engine of the future of Europe and beyond.

 | HTTPS://DOI.ORG/10.1515/9783111302508-203

A huge thank you to everyone who brought their insight and illumination to this wonderful round table and to Miles Taylor and his team for organising it. As the writer Rory McLean wrote: “To me Berlin is as much a conceit as a reality. Why? Because the city is forever in the process of becoming, never being”.

Robert Seatter

Preface

This volume is derived from a conference hosted in November 2022 by the Großbritannien-Zentrum/Centre for British Studies, Humboldt-Universität zu Berlin. Marking the centenary of the British Broadcasting Corporation, the essays investigate the unique relationship between the BBC and the city of Berlin. International scholars from media and film studies, musicology and contemporary history together with news correspondents past and present assess how German culture and history, filtered through the experiences of Berlin, featured in the programmes and reporting of the BBC over a period of one hundred years.

Founded in 1922, the BBC developed strong and influential connections with Germany from the start, focused particularly on Berlin. Germany pioneered radio technology in the 1920s, and the British regarded the principal Berlin radio networks as model examples to follow. The first Director-General of the BBC, John Reith, wanted to broadcast "high" culture to British radio audiences. Berlin orchestral music was frequently selected for the early live performances of the BBC. By the 1930s, special BBC correspondents were reporting from Berlin. The BBC in Berlin contributed to British attitudes towards the Third Reich, notably through its coverage of appeasement policy and the 1936 Olympic Games in the city. During the Second World War, the BBC developed its German Service aimed at listeners across German-speaking regions, but with much of the content derived from and focused on Berlin. And after 1945, the BBC set up its operations in the occupied part of the city, becoming a key institution in the cultural politics of the Cold War, both westward-facing, in transmitting news and features from West Berlin to British and world listeners (and later TV viewers), and also GDR-centred with the continuing activity of the BBC German Service. The fall of the Berlin Wall in 1989 and the reunification of Germany in 1990 were hugely significant moments for the BBC, with more radio and TV programmes and news items devoted to Berlin and its redevelopment in the 1990s and 2000s than other news organisations.

As one of the few international cultural institutions present in the city throughout the Weimar years, the onset of the Third Reich, the era of divided Germany through to the reunification and the return of the capital to the city, the BBC is a potentially revealing case-study of how British-German relations changed over time. This volume aims to create a fuller understanding of how German culture has been presented to English-speaking audiences, and conversely how British national identity and memory has been formed by images and stereotypes of Germany.

 | HTTPS://DOI.ORG/10.1515/9783111302508-204

We are grateful to the following organisations for supporting the original conference and for their assistance with the compilation of this volume: the BBC Photo Library, the British Embassy Berlin, the Deutsch-Britische Gesellschaft, the Deutsche Forschungsgemeinschaft, the Museum für Kommunikation (Berlin), and the BBC Written Archives Centre. All BBC copyright content is reproduced courtesy of the British Broadcasting Corporation (all rights reserved).

Patrick Major
Reading
Miles Taylor
Berlin
November 2025

Figures

 | HTTPS://DOI.ORG/10.1515/9783111302508-205

Notes on Contributors

Katya Adler
BBC Europe correspondent.

Frank Bösch
Director of the Center for Contemporary History and Professor of German and European 20th Century History, University of Potsdam.

Chris Bowlby
former BBC correspondent and producer.

Ben Bradshaw
formerly MP for Exeter and former BBC Berlin correspondent.

Mark Brayne
former BBC Berlin correspondent.

Mark Fenemore
former Senior Lecturer in Modern European History, Manchester Metropolitan University.

Sheer Ganor
Assistant Professor of History, University of Minnesota, Twin Cities.

Heather Gumbert
Associate Professor of History, Virginia Polytechnic Institute and State University, Blacksburg.

Jenny Hill
former BBC Berlin correspondent.

Frank Jahn
ARD London correspondent.

 | HTTPS://DOI.ORG/10.1515/9783111302508-206

Nicholas Kenyon
Opera Critic *The Telegraph*, former Controller BBC Radio 3 (1992–98), Director BBC Proms (1996–2007), and former Managing Director of the Barbican Centre, London (2007–21).

Kate Lacey
Professor of Media History and Theory, University of Sussex.

Patrick Major
Professor of Modern History, University of Reading.

Joseph Oldham
Former Associate Professor in Mass Media and Communication, British University in Egypt, Cairo.

Emily Oliver
Independent Researcher (Magdalen College School), Oxford.

Beate Peter
Assistant Professor of Cultural Sociology, University of Groningen.

Vike Martina Plock
Professor of Modern Literature and Culture, University of Exeter.

Johannes Riedel
Editor, Deutsche Welle TV, formerly Editor BBC World Service, London.

Robert Seatter
former Head of BBC History.

Will Studdert
Senior Research Fellow, Universität Hamburg.

Miles Taylor
Professor of British History & Society, Centre for British Studies, Humboldt-Universität zu Berlin.

Toby Thacker
formerly Senior Lecturer in Modern European History, Cardiff University.

CHAPTER 1

Introduction

Patrick Major and Miles Taylor

1 Sounds of War: Berlin between the BBC and the Propaganda Ministry

When the BBC was founded on 18 October 1922, Britain and Germany had recently emerged from a conflict that had perfected mass, kinetic killing, but was still grappling with the ethereal world of radio which would help decide the next war. Battleships at Jutland had communicated partly by signal-light; trench officers by field telephone, but wireless delivery of the human voice was still experimental technology. Britain had developed the telegraph in the 1830s, and the first news ticker – Wolffs Telegraphisches Bureau – was founded in Berlin in 1849, two years before London's Reuters. With cross-Channel, then transatlantic submarine cables in 1851 and 1866, the English-speaking world could now reach the Prussian capital almost instantaneously. But still all that telegraphs could relay were mute impulses. Telephony advanced matters in the 1870s, when the human voice could be transponded by microphone into a signal and de-coded at the far end through a speaker. But telephones still required lines. In the late 1880s Heinrich Hertz proved the existence of electromagnetic waves, and in 1901 the British-based Italian physicist Guglielmo Marconi achieved the first transatlantic transmission, bouncing radio waves off the ionosphere to defeat the curvature of the earth. Crucially, wireless allowed Imperial Germany to leapfrog the emerging Anglophone monopoly on cable. In 1903 Berlin's rival firms Siemens and AEG founded a new joint subsidiary, Telefunken, heavily subsidised by government. A giant 200m radio mast arose at nearby Nauen, which by 1914 could transmit up to 3,000 miles, well within range of the USA and, not coincidentally, of the U-boats soon to be patrolling the North Atlantic. "Elektropolis" Berlin was becoming a high-tech player in Germany's *Weltpolitik* (Tworek 2019, 45–69).

The main radio users in the First World War were specialists and enthusiasts. By the 1920s, however, radiophonic developments were creating a viable mass medium for domestic, peacetime consumption. Although the BBC had started in 1922 as a hotchpotch of private ventures, by 1927 the Company had become a firmly established Corporation with a royal charter. In the eyes of its founder, Sir John Reith, public service broadcasting was to operate for the

 | HTTPS://DOI.ORG/10.1515/9783111302508-001

general good, not commercial gain. It was not like America. But radio was all the rage everywhere. In 1926 a new Radio Tower was erected in Berlin's Westend. Standing almost 150m high, it remained the capital's tallest structure for over forty years. By the 1930s the new medium's success was being cemented in other flagship buildings. From 1931 to 1933, the Reich Broadcasting Company erected its Haus des Rundfunks, an art deco shrine to radiophonics designed by Hans Poelzig, with perfect acoustics throughout (Kowalke 2016). Meanwhile on an oval plot of land in London's W1A, BBC Broadcasting House was being built by Val Myer, completed in 1932. Its minimalist curves in sheer Portland stone, converging on a "prow" at the entrance, as well as "porthole" windows along its top deck beneath aerial masts, reminded one observer of a "petrified dreadnought" (Hines 2008, 41). But the BBC motto was distinctly unwarlike: "Nation Shall Speak Peace Unto Nation"; and as a symbol of Anglo-German cooperation, its first magnetic, steel-tape recording equipment, the Blattnerphone, was made in Germany. Nation also played music unto nation. Amongst the first live transmissions from Berlin to Britain, were performances by the Berlin Philharmonic, concert orchestras from the city, and Weber's *Der Freischütz* from the Berlin State Opera (*Radio Times*, 1929; *Radio Times* 1932a; *Radio Times* 1932b).

Broadcasting House was perhaps deliberately constructed away from Fleet Street, the traditional home of the British press. It is easily forgotten today that early broadcasting suffered from an inferiority complex towards the print media. Scooping the press was actively discouraged. Newspapermen had the ear of government and vast circulations. Yet under "appeasement" policy Whitehall and Fleet Street were at pains not to antagonise National Socialist Germany. As Miles Taylor shows in chapter 1 the BBC had their own agent of appeasement in Vernon Bartlett, who broadcasted from Berlin, as well as other European cities between 1928 and 1933. Similarly other foreign correspondents such as the *Daily Express*'s Sefton Delmer cultivated the NSDAP leader in return for exclusives, reporting a communist rather than Nazi threat during Weimar's street-fighting years. (As poacher-turned-gamekeeper, the buccaneering Delmer was later entrusted with Britain's wartime black propaganda against Germany, including the clandestine radio station Soldatensender Calais – Pomerantsev 2024, 154–64.) Less cosily, the *Daily Mail*'s Rothay Reynolds reported from Berlin for almost the entire interwar period, whereas the *Manchester Guardian*'s Frederick Voigt decamped in 1933, following death threats (Wainewright 2017, 112–13). Yet it was *The Times*' Norman Ebbutt who was prepared to stick his neck out furthest, reporting Nazi lawlessness, only to have his copy watered down by London. After ten years in the German capital, he was expelled as *persona non grata* in August 1937, suffering a career-ending stroke a month later aged just 43 (McDonough 1992, 419–20). Radio broadcasting did steal a march over print journalism in 1936, with the BBC on hand to transmit coverage of Olympic Games, hosted in Berlin, an event infamously turned into a Nazi spectacle. BBC reporters such as Harold Abrahams, Olympic champion of 1924, did their best to ignore the pomp and concentrate on the sport (Socolow 2016, 131–66).

Another correspondent developing a distaste for what he called the "gangster world" of Nazism was the young Hugh Carleton Greene (1910–87), whom readers will encounter throughout this volume. In 1934 this 6'6", somewhat inscrutable Englishman was posted to Berlin by the *Daily Telegraph*, becoming chief correspondent in May 1938. He witnessed the Night of the Long Knives and Austria's *Anschluß*, documenting the Nazi regime's consolidation, while never forgetting the oppositional voices within. He saw his future third wife, Tatjana Sais, for the first time, onstage at Berlin's Katakombe cabaret, and frequented the all-night Taverne *Stammtisch*, where foreign correspondents rubbed shoulders with Gestapo agents, whether they knew it or not (Raleigh 1941, 113–27). In 1939 Greene, too, was expelled in reprisal for British deportations of Nazi journalists, but five years honing his German stood him in good stead as the soon-to-be head of the BBC German Service. He went on to be Director-General in the 1960s, becoming one of the most influential figures in BBC history. "Berlin may have meant and done things to many people", wrote his biographer, "but it *made* Hugh Greene." (Tracey 1983, 58)

Upon the outbreak of hostilities, British foreign correspondents could no longer correspond, relying on heavily chaperoned American colleagues to cover Berlin until they too had to leave after Pearl Harbor (Heinzerling and Herschaft 2024, 81–193). War also witnessed sweeping changes to broadcasting: the BBC suspended its infant television service and regional radio, replacing it with a national BBC Home Service. Soon after, the Empire Service became the Overseas Service. Broadcasting House itself was sandbagged and painted in green camouflage. Famously, at 8.05pm on 15 October 1940 it was hit by a Luftwaffe time-delayed bomb, crashing through several floors and killing seven, before audibly exploding during the 9 o'clock news. Newsreader Bruce Belfrage, now covered in soot and plaster, dusted himself down, kept calm and carried on. The war was crucial to the BBC myth of unflappability.

As well as trying to keep up home morale, the BBC had to decide what to tell the British public about the Germans. Entente propaganda from the First World War, full of lurid tales of "Hunnish" atrocities in Belgium, was now viewed as discredited. The Nazi party itself was still fair game. A radio docudrama series, *Shadow of the Swastika*, using sound effects for added immediacy, was aired in 1939–40, giving the unpleasant facts about Hitlerism so recently suppressed under appeasement (Goody 2020). But where did "ordinary Germans" figure in this demonology – accomplices or hapless bystanders? Despite prime minister Neville Chamberlain's initial distinction between Nazi state and German people, from 1940 under Winston Churchill there was an increasing tendency to conflate the two, and to attack the German "character" (Nicholas 1996, 154–60). This bordered on "Vansittartism", named after the senior British diplomat whose *Black Record* (Vansittart 1941) vilified all Germans as inherently warlike and expansionist, a kneejerk view which has lodged deep within the British populist psyche.

The greatest changes to the wartime BBC came in the realm of foreign broadcasting. State-to-state broadcasting gave rise to what is now called public diplomacy (Ribeiro and Seul 2015). Traditional diplomacy had operated at government-to-government level, but now individual citizens could be targets in the soft-power plays of another state. Prompted by Mussolini's launch of Radio Bari in 1934, aimed at the British Middle East, the BBC had set up its first foreign-language Arabic Service in January 1938, followed by a Spanish and Portuguese Service in March, geared towards Latin America. More followed, as country after country fell to the Wehrmacht and its far-eastern Axis ally, Japan, in the early 1940s. By 1945 the BBC was broadcasting in 45 languages! The World Service, as it was rebranded in 1965, would not have existed without the galvanising effect of the Second World War (Webb 2014, 13).

Back in 1938 other pioneering foreign-language broadcasting was aimed much closer to home, brought to a head by the Sudeten Crisis. In late September, at government request, the BBC hurriedly improvised a new European Service, consisting of French, Italian and German broadcasts to relay Chamberlain's "peace in our time" messages direct to Continental listeners. At the same time, the Foreign Office (FO) entered into a gentleman's agreement with the Corporation to monitor output for fear of jeopardising Anglo-German relations (Seul 2015; Short 1989). Despite the BBC charter proclaiming its journalistic independence, the hidden hand of government was to flex itself in years to come, forcing out two directors-general in 1987 and 2004. On the eve of war, however, there was patriotic consensus that the BBC should operate close to government. When appeasement was finally abandoned after Germany occupied Prague in March 1939, a BBC German Service proper was established. After an interlude with Air Ministry intelligence, Hugh Greene, late of the *Telegraph*'s Berlin desk, was appointed to run it in October 1940. Although initially housed in Broadcasting House, after being bombed out and temporarily billeted in Maida Vale, all the European services were moved to Bush House on London's Strand in early 1941. This was to remain the home of all external broadcasting for the next 70 years.

Bush House was rather an outlier, institutionally if not geographically. Greene and the "Bushmen", many seconded from the armed forces, viewed career BBC officials at Broadcasting House as bureaucratic and "stuffy" (Tracey 1983, 75). This was a prejudice perhaps shared by George Orwell, a scriptwriter there in 1942, who supposedly based *Nineteen Eighty-Four*'s Room 101 – the space where victims confront their worst nightmares – on one of its conference rooms. Bush House, by contrast, was semi-detached by virtue of its special relationship with government, under the protecting but controlling hand of the FO's troubleshooter Ivone Kirkpatrick. (The BBC's external services were paid for by the FO, not the licence fee.) The Political Warfare Executive was also brought under the same roof, its German section head, the impulsive Richard Crossman, quite unlike the less voluble, but equally determined Hugh Greene, who tussled, too, with his nominal European Service boss, Noel Newsome. Greene preferred to tell straight news to Germany, despite the succession of early British defeats. Only honesty would generate trust. The BBC played a long game of establishing credibility, not just with home audiences, but with the enemy too. Greene was also prepared to differentiate between "bad Nazis" and "good Germans", driving wedges between NSDAP and Wehrmacht, while Newsome espoused a more blanket anti-Germanism (Newsome 2019, 258–75). But it was testament to the BBC German Service's internal democracy that it thrashed out its editorial differences in daily morning conferences, in marked contrast to Goebbels' weekly press conferences at the Propaganda Ministry, which were mere dictation exercises.

Britain's chronic lack of linguists meant heavy reliance on exiles from across Europe, making Bush House something of a melting-pot. The biographies of the antifascist Austro-German diaspora have been collectively curated in Charmian Brinson and Richard Dove's invaluable yearbooks, one of which is devoted to the BBC German Service (Brinson and Dove 2003). Native speakers were not generally allowed on the microphone themselves; as part of its "white" propaganda, the BBC preferred recognisably British German-speakers, such as Lindley Fraser, Marius Goring and Patrick Gordon Walker. They adopted a softly-softly, indirect approach. "The BBC's German broadcasting must aim at stimulating doubt among the confident and at encouraging defeatism and irritation with the regime in the apathetic", stipulated a 1940 memorandum on approaches to German listeners. "In other words it must operate by sapping, not by frontal attacks." (Mansell 1982, 150) Whereas other BBC European Services, such as the Italian, may have broadcast to armed resistance movements, and occasionally called for action, even there "the antifascist cause was not a British priority" (Lo Biundo 2022, 192). By 1945 Allied strategy had long since abandoned 1940's "detonator concept", of fomenting mass insurrection on the Continent.

Many of the German-speaking artists and performers, some from the Weimar avant-garde, would have liked the German Service to be "artier", teasing BBC colleagues that Britain was the "land without music". One of these may have been the German Jewish composer, Berthold Goldschmidt, revisited here by Nicholas Kenyon. Another exiled musician, Hermann Meyer, who tried to interest the BBC in futuristic "radio music", but ended up giving talks on early music, is discussed by Toby Thacker. (See chapters 4 and 8 respectively.) Classical playlists were laden with hidden meanings. The Reichssender beamed Beethoven and Wagner at the Anglophone world, conducted by the Berlin Philharmonic's Wilhelm Furtwängler; the BBC broadcast back music banned under the Nazis, by Jewish composers such as Mahler and Mendelssohn. Yet Humphrey Jennings' 1942 documentary *Listen to Britain* showed a country still at ease imbibing "Aryan" German classics. In the postwar ruins of Berlin, classical music remained a cultural battleground, as the Soviets and the West competed to be the curators of "true" German *Kultur* (Anderton 2019).

Axis programming also understood mass appeal. Soldatensender Belgrad, entertaining the Afrika Korps, avoided spoken-word formats in favour of popular music, including the haunting wartime anthem "Lili Marleen". Starting as a German hit sung by Lale Andersen, it even received fan mail from homesick Allied POWs. "Practically all our troops in the Middle East habitually listen to Axis radio in preference to the BBC", complained one BBC Cairo controller. "Cut the talk. … Give us straight music" (cited in: Leibovitz and Miller 2009, 118). Despite BBC rumour-mongering that Andersen was now incarcerated in a camp (she had indeed fallen foul of the regime), the solution was to re-record with English lyrics. "Lili Marlene" was then sung by Vera Lynn and more famously by Marlene Dietrich, who also serenaded the Allied Expeditionary Force in 1944 from behind the iconic BBC microphone. In chapter 6 Emily Oliver explores other popular musical wars of the ether.

"Lili Marleen/Marlene" was a reminder of the double-edged dangers, and opportunities, of mass communication. The very unintelligibility of its German lyrics encouraged Allied troops to make up their own as an early form of meme, including the famous "D-Day Dodgers" lament, mocking the British establishment (Jackson 1979, 55–62). But would radio humour travel as well, or simply rebound? Just as the Home Service had comedies such as *It's That Man Again*, poking fun at "Funf" the bungling Nazi spy, the German Service did selectively deploy humour. If not quite as contagiously lethal as Monty Python's "Funniest Joke in the World" (BBC1, 5 October 1969), the British sense of humour could be weaponised. Yet an important element of audience psychology was that German listeners should not become the butt of jokes, but feel able to laugh along at Nazi officialdom. These comedies have been analysed both collectively (Moorehead 2016) and individually: *Kurt und Willi* (Taylor 2006), the party functionary and his hapless visitors; *Private Hirnschal* (Naumann 1983, 121–68), the dim-witted soldier writing home to his wife; and the garrulous *Frau Wernicke* (Hughes 2013), Berlin housewife extraordinaire. Wernicke is also tackled here by contributors Vike Plock, analysing her *Berliner Schnauze* – a cousin of Cockney humour – and Sheer Ganor, who traces the real-life Jewish German actress behind the character, Annemarie Hase, and her awkward re-integration into postwar Germany (see chapters 5 and 7).

As has become evident, the Axis did not just sit back and passively submit to Britain's sonic attacks. The mass-produced, bakelite *Volksempfänger* was a deliberately long- and medium-wave receiver only, with poor reception for Allied broadcasts; only those with money for higher-spec, shortwave sets could hear foreign programming properly. Nevertheless, each new radio carried a cardboard tag, warning of the penalties for *"Schwarzhören"* or illicit listening. In September 1939, the Third Reich promulgated an Emergency Radio Decree, criminalising the listening to, and dissemination of, foreign broadcasts. But this did not stop some Germans doing precisely that. The repetition of oppositional views heard on the BBC in the company of others *could* have serious consequences if denounced. It has been estimated that one to three million Germans in a population of eighty million may have listened to the BBC during the war (Plock 2021, 238). Berlin prosecutions under the Radio Decree went from just 21 in 1942, to 38 in 1943, before jumping to 60 in 1944 (Hensle 2003, 334–35). Involving custodial senses, and very rarely even the death penalty, these may have been the tip of an iceberg, but they are still tiny figures. Although it is highly problematic to trace the exact provenance of views heard over the airwaves, a significant proportion must have originated from the BBC.

Yet Berlin talked back. The Propaganda Ministry had its counterpart to the German Service. The Reichssender had started broadcasting in English as early as 1933, targeting not only Britain, but also the crucial American audience, a significant part of which, especially in the Upper Midwest, was German by extraction. International broadcasting was still technically challenging, requiring short-wave, high-powered transmitters. In 1935 a large 100,000kW mast was erected at Zeesen, just south-east of Berlin, followed by Deutschlandsender III in 1939, a 337m colossus at Herzberg, the tallest structure in Europe, second only to the Empire State Building. But what of the people behind the microphones? The Propaganda Ministry appeared more relaxed than London about allowing enemy nationals on air. William Joyce, alias

"Lord Haw-Haw", became the most notorious renegade British voice on the airwaves. His activities are well documented (Cole 1964; Selwyn 1987; Holmes 2016, 182–98), as well as his resonance back in Britain, which was not quite as negligible as British propaganda made believe (Doherty 2000). Joyce, living with his wife in Berlin-Westend, was one of a hundred British expatriates broadcasting for the Reichssender or monitoring BBC output to Germany (Keene 2008). This rogues' gallery included disgraced ex-British army officer Norman Baillie-Stewart, who had been imprisoned in the Tower of London for espionage (Murphy 2003, 50–60); John Amery, narcissistic playboy son of a British Cabinet minister, who soon became an alcoholic liability (Weale 2001, 93–225); and "Dolly" Eckersley, ex-wife of the BBC's former chief engineer, who worked as a continuity announcer, while 17-year-old son James read the news (Cullen 2021).

This community of collaboration – some convinced fascists, others victims of circumstance – was working for a steadily losing cause. In August 1943 Berlin's broadcasting facilities were evacuated to Zeesen, due to the growing bombing threat. (Baillie-Stewart's Berlin house was indeed flattened in 1944.) Little did Britain's expats know that they were at times only a few miles from another group of broadcasting émigrés working for the other side. A select band of Jewish-German volunteers were flying above them for the RAF, on so-called "ABC" missions, blocking Luftwaffe night-fighter controllers by broadcasting on the same frequency from miniature airborne studios. 17 such specially adapted Lancaster aircraft were shot down during the air Battle of Berlin in 1943/44 (Sugarman 2001, 192). In chapter 3, Patrick Major explores the messages broadcast to the British public to explain the controversial "area bombing" of the Reich and its echo in British public opinion, as well as the BBC's historic war reports recorded live over the Reich capital. As the war reached its endgame, the BBC's War Reporting Unit, landing soon after D-Day, covered the advance across France, into the Low Countries and ultimately into heart of the Reich itself. London was coming to Berlin.

2 Visions of Division: The BBC in Cold War Berlin

Unconditional surrender in 1945 changed everything. Berlin was no longer Reich capital – there was no longer a Reich – but the seat of Allied military government under an occupation of unknown duration. Germany was divided into four zones, and Berlin four sectors: US, UK, USSR and French, but the island city lay deep within the Soviet Zone, 110 miles from the "mainland" British Zone to the west. As part of the quadripartite machinery, a British

Control Commission for Germany was installed in the former German Labour Front buildings at Fehrbelliner Platz. The British garrison headquarters and Secret Intelligence Service (SIS) station moved into the Olympic Stadium complex in Charlottenburg. On today's Theodor-Heuss-Platz, other facilities occupied the Deutschlandhaus and neighbouring Amerikahaus, home of Germany's embryonic television studios. Now renamed "Summit House", its NAAFI (Navy, Army and Air Force Institutes) canteen brought the blessings of British cuisine – the legendary *Berliner Currywurst* was concocted from ingredients bartered here. Yet by 1949 the city had split into two, with two city halls, two police forces. The eastern half claimed to be "Capital of the German Democratic Republic", an entity the West refused to recognise; the western half went into a Cold War limbo, a semi-detached *Land* of the new Federal Republic of Germany.

Whereas life under West Germany's *"Wirtschaftswunder"* gradually normalised, the Cold War frontline in Berlin remained volatile and austere: Hugh Greene referred to Berlin as the "ugliest capital in Europe" (Greene 1945). Even such mundane issues as transport and power supply could be flashpoints. Broadcasting was a crucial component of the Allies' denazification and re-education programmes. Although the Haus des Rundfunks sat squarely in the British Sector, the Russians who had captured it in April 1945 refused to leave, using it for their own broadcasting. The "squatting" of the building lasted months, then years, provoking a siege involving power-cuts, barbed-wire and round-the-clock military police patrolling. Meanwhile the Russians gutted the studios within, leaving just a shell when the British finally took charge in 1956 (Bauernfeind 2010, 90–95). In the long interim, the western Allies were forced to seek broadcasting alternatives. Initially, the BBC shared space at Lancaster House, at Fehrbelliner Platz in Wilmersdorf, the headquarters of the British occupying force. The Americans set up their own Rundfunk im amerikanischen Sektor (Radio in the American Sector or RIAS) in 1946, initially operating from the Reich Post Office building, but swapped in 1948 for the former IG Farben offices in Berlin-Schöneberg (Galle 2003, 110–24). It was rumoured that the newly founded CIA was behind much of RIAS, which became a special target of the eastern intelligence services. It was here that East Berlin strike leaders headed on the eve of the June 1953 uprising, and where the announcement of a general strike was broadcast (Schlosser 2015, 75–105).

Hamburg, not Berlin, was the focus of British postwar media reconstruction. In April 1945 its studio, where an inebriated William Joyce had made his valedictory broadcast, was announced to be under new management by BBC correspondent Wynford Vaughan-Thomas. Joyce was subsequently captured, tried at the Old Bailey, and hanged as a traitor in January 1946, the same month Hugh Greene arrived in Hamburg to oversee the new Nordwestdeutscher Rundfunk. As Frank Bösch shows in chapter 10, his mission was to model NWDR on the BBC. However, West Berlin's central position made it an irresistible platform for broadcasting into surrounding East Germany by the back door. NWDR consequently maintained an outside Funkhaus in Berlin-Schöneberg at Heidelberger Platz, served by a VHF antenna in Ruhleben (Dovifat 1970). And while the BBC German Service continued broadcasting from London's Bush House, focusing on re-education and projection of British values, it also maintained a BBC Berlin office at Savignyplatz close to the Bahnhof Zoo. Before the Wall, visitors from both halves of Berlin could easily drop in here or to the British Information Centre on the Kurfürstendamm. The Exhibition Grounds by the Radio Tower also held annual shows partly designed to attract East German footfall, allowing the BBC, along with the later British Council, to greet Anglophiles from behind the Iron Curtain.

In 1949 the BBC German Service added an East Zone Programme, a slot in the original schedule specially for residents of East Germany. As well as providing news, it also reprised formats used against the Nazis, such as comedy skits, using some of the same wartime writing teams (Major 2013, 260–64). Besides espousing British values of tolerance and freedom of expression, its remit was to counter feelings of abandonment and to build up resistance to communist propaganda, but it stopped short of inciting regime-change. This marked it out from other western broadcasters at the time, especially American, which were far more "liberationist". Even in the critical year of 1953, when the GDR experienced an abortive uprising, "any attempt on our part to mobilise resistance, even if only passive", one controller warned German Service editors, "is both inconsistent and dangerous. Quite apart from anything else, we run the grave risk not only of jeopardising people's lives and liberty but also of involving the Corporation in political trials." (Oliver 2019, 576). The BBC appeared to be encouraging a culture of complaint, while enjoining GDR citizens to suffer in silence – a muddled, but archetypally British solution.

The western military presence in Cold War Germany was so great that garrisoned Anglo-American troops received their own radio stations, the American and British Forces Networks (AFN and BFN). One early BFN assignment was covering the Berlin Blockade of June 1948 to May 1949, as Heather Gumbert recounts in chapter 9. All land routes into the western sectors had been severed by the Soviets in reprisal for the western introduction of a new currency, the first step towards the formal division of Germany. BFN sent reporters Cliff Michelmore and Raymond Baxter, armed with two portable German tape recorders, on a Sunderland flying boat into the beleaguered city. Vox pops were conducted with Berliners expressing admiration for the Airlift.

"Can the British and Americans continue to bring enough food to feed my children?" asked one mother and widow (Grace 1996, 59–60). As capacity increased, two RAF Yorks flew part of the Berlin Symphony Orchestra out to Britain for a thank you tour. The Airlift, despite costing untold millions, was propaganda gold for the western Allies, and the BBC provided nightly news coverage, narrating tales of heroism in much the same way as it had done during the wartime bombing, and would later in 1961 and 1989 (Tusa 1989). It was also an opportunity to up the ante against the Soviets. When a transmission mast serving East Berlin, but situated in the French Sector, was found to be obstructing the new airport runway being built at Tegel, it was unceremoniously dynamited by French military government. Yet since the Russians had cut the power grid into the western sectors, electricity rationing made blockaded radio-listening random and sporadic, limited to a couple of hours a day (or night).

1948 was also the year that Whitehall went on the propaganda offensive. Inside the former German embassy at Carlton House Terrace, the FO's covert publicity arm emerged, the deliberately dull sounding "Information Research Department" (IRD). Under ex-BBC correspondent, but now diplomat, Ralph Murray – grandfather of comedian Al Murray – its job was to prime the global media with anti-communist stories. This required the expertise of SIS. Novelist Fay Weldon, who as a young woman worked as an IRD copywriter, remembered being told to face the wall as the spooks filed in (Lashmar and Oliver 1998, 67). The BBC cooperated, willingly. Ian Jacob, head of the East European Service and Director-General for much of the 1950s, had even allegedly turned down running SIS before joining the BBC in 1946. The FO's Russia Committee obligingly moved its weekly meeting to accommodate him (Defty 2004, 69–72). Part of IRD's remit in Berlin was to work with the BBC liaison officer, whose pass allowed unfettered access to East Berlin, whereas SIS was under a self-denying ordinance never to set foot there. In 1950–53 the BBC's man in Berlin was a young Charles Wheeler who had served in wartime naval intelligence under Ian Fleming, literary father of James Bond. On 16 June 1953 he was tipped off by his IRD contact to head immediately to East Berlin where something was afoot. In the Stalinallee he found building workers striking and demonstrating; by the next day a full-blown insurrection was underway. Along with the refugee crisis, extensively covered by the BBC, the rising was one of Cold War Berlin's formative moments. Although ultimately suppressed, 17 June was a seminal experience for the young reporter, who had walked alongside the marchers, clearly in sympathy, later admitting to becoming something of a "Cold Warrior". On a second stint as correspondent from 1962 to 1965, he was arrested by East Germany's secret police, the Stasi, after attending the funeral of one of the Wall's first victims, Peter Fechter. But he refused to be intimidated by his interrogators, relishing the opportunity "to tell a secret policeman that the regime he was serving was an international disgrace." His BBC protection worked; Wheeler was released without charge. "Witnessing it all in close-up in East Berlin", wrote his biographer, "Charles was transformed from writer of anti-GDR diatribes to on-the-ground foreign correspondent." (Wheeler 2023, 62, 128; Brant 1955).

At the end of his first Berlin posting Wheeler returned to London to work on the new current affairs television programme, *Panorama*, alongside veteran war reporter Richard Dimbleby. BBC news was entering the age of television with a recording studio at London's Lime Grove, and with new competition from Independent Television. *Panorama* was designed to blend actuality reporting with documentary features, becoming an enduring and much emulated format. At the beginning of November, 1959, "News from the Zoos" commenced the BBC's television reporting from Berlin (*Radio Times* 1959). In chapter 11 contributor Mark Fenemore explores how it presented the second Berlin Crisis of 1958–61, culminating in the building of the Berlin Wall in August 1961. The Wall was gruesomely photogenic. In his novel *Two Views* (*Zwei Ansichten*, 1965), Uwe Johnson's protagonist compulsively photographs the growing concrete barrier, irresistibly drawn to it like some Kubrickian monolith. He was not alone. "I was sitting on the biggest story in the world", recalled celebrated British press photographer, Don McCullin, of his first assignment to a Berlin which felt to him like a war zone. "I had an almost magnetic emotional sense of direction pulling me to extraordinary places." (McCullin 2010) On his German Rolleicord he snapped West Berlin bystanders peering through cracks in the breeze blocks or waving over the barbed wire. Visiting politicians and world leaders also came for photo opportunities at the Wall. In March 1965 British PM Harold Wilson was captured next to mayor Willy Brandt on one of the purpose-built viewing platforms, peering across a divided Potsdamer Platz covered in snow. Twelve years later, it was the Sex Pistols who were staring at the "new Belsen" ("Holidays in the Sun", 1977).

Cold War Berlin was becoming a theatre of the spectacle, the Brandenburg Gate a proscenium into an alternate reality (Freisinnier 2005; Sonnevend 2016). So concerned were the GDR authorities about its scopic power, that when John F. Kennedy made his famous "Ich bin ein Berliner" visit to West Berlin in June 1963, western views into the East were curtained off by red banners draped between its pillars (Daum 2008, 133). Less well known is Queen Elizabeth II's state visit two years later, presented in partnership with West German broadcasters, and live commentated by an ailing Richard Dimbleby (he died before the year was out). As the motorcade approached the

Wall at Potsdamer Platz, he explained to viewers: "You are now looking at the Iron Curtain almost close enough to stretch your hand out and touch it." (BBC1, 27 May 1965) Live broadcasting had its ups (unscripted moments when Berlin dignitaries at Schöneberg City Hall were drowned out by the rhythmic cries of "Eli-Za-Beth", much as the crowd had chanted "Ken-Ne-Dy" two years before); and its downs (when screens went blank for several minutes because of a technical fault). In the 1950s foreign broadcasts had still been shot on film and flown back to London; the satellite age did not begin until the 1960s; the digital age not until after the end of the Cold War. This was still an era when live television pictures had to be transmitted by cable; the images were grainy with poor contrast, but certainly belong on the BBC's archive website, a fabulous resource for researchers and students alike (https://www.bbc.co.uk/archive). In chapter 15 Kate Lacey investigates the *longue durée* of BBC reporting on the Wall, through its different anniversaries, as well as the rich archival possibilities emerging in this field. The BBC might have contributed further to Cold War soft diplomacy. Towards the end of 1965, its Symphony Orchestra was invited to perform in East Berlin. Suspecting an attempt by the GDR to enhance its respectability, the Foreign Office vetoed the suggestion (TNA 1965).

One young SIS recruit to visit the newly erected Wall in 1961 was David Cornwell, alias John le Carré. Berlin was famously the city of spies, but most public knowledge of such matters has been mediated through fiction, as well as BBC radio drama, for example *Orient Express* (1954) and *Pilgrim on the Island* (1960). There is now a veritable army of historical spy-thriller literature set in Berlin, following in the wake of the late lamented Philip Kerr's Bernie Gunther. What is striking about earlier thriller-writers is the number who had gained personal experience as spies or journalists, or both. Berlin seemed to bring a new realism to the genre, even to Ian Fleming's James Bond posted on a last mission to Berlin in "The Living Daylights" (*Sunday Times*, 4 February 1962). How many Berlin correspondents had a thriller manuscript in their bottom drawer? How many BBC Directors-General had a brother who happened to be Britain's most revered thriller-writer (Greene and Greene 1957)? There was a converse danger, of course, of a romanticised Cold War mystique inflecting journalists' reportage. Frederick Forsyth served as Reuters correspondent in East Berlin in 1963–64, before becoming a BBC correspondent in Africa, where, like Graham Greene, he was recruited by SIS. But Forsyth's Reuters superior, the later BBC correspondent David Sell, viewed his Berlin reporting with some alarm: "He views the world around him in rather unreal terms like a spectator at the cinema identifying himself with the larger-than-life characters and incidents depicted on the screen." (Read 1992, 371) Here, in chapter 14, Joseph Oldham takes a behind-the-scenes look at the adaptation of le Carré, the Cold War thriller-writer *par excellence*, in one of the BBC's defining dramas of the late 1970s, *Tinker, Taylor, Soldier, Spy*.

The BBC also became the target of real-world espionage in Berlin. One of the German Service's most popular radio programmes was the weekly "Letters without Signature" (*Briefe ohne Unterschrift*). It solicited letters from East Germans sent to cover addresses in West Berlin, excerpts from which were read out on air and commented on by the BBC's Austin Harrison, a dapper figure with a penchant for bow-ties and brylcreem, but somewhat mysterious to his colleagues. "Letters" had started with the open border when it was relatively easy for East Germans to post mail from West Berlin, and some even wrote messages at the BBC offices there. After the building of the Wall this became far more problematic, but it was still possible through various subterfuges. "Letters" became a major target of the GDR's Ministry of State Security (the Stasi), which monitored broadcasts and attempted to intercept letters (Schädlich 2017). The MfS was also convinced that Harrison was working for SIS on the side, trying to cultivate an East German dissident to become the next Alexander Solzhenitsyn. Unfortunately, the man in question was also working for the Stasi, but Harrison managed to evade arrest. Others were less fortunate, such as the 16-year-old schoolboy Karl-Heinz Borchardt, who was ultimately tracked down for writing to the BBC and imprisoned for two years ("London Calling" 2019).

An increasing number of letter-writers in the 1960s were younger listeners, entranced by Britain's soft-power superweapon: the Beatles. In 1961 BFN became British Forces Broadcasting Service (BFBS), its Berlin outpost eventually moving to Summit House in 1967 (Zöllner 1996). BFBS was able to recruit the legendary DJ John Peel, but also Alan Bangs, who DJed for BFBS Cologne from 1975 to 1989, and who also broke through to mainstream West German television, hosting WDR's (Westdeutscher Rundfunk) live *Rockpalast*, which introduced much British talent to German audiences (Bangs 1985). Although broadcast in English, such programmes were regularly eavesdropped by German youngsters, including as Will Studdert shows, from behind the Iron Curtain (see chapter 13). At the end of one home-recorded number by Wolf Biermann – East Germany's dissident singer-songwriter and public enemy number one – BFBS's station call-sign can distinctly be heard. Britain was able to syphon much cultural capital off the wave of sixties Beatlemania, which even surged over the Wall. In 1969, in one of Cold War Berlin's more surreal episodes, a West Berlin DJ wondered aloud on air what would happen if the Rolling Stones held a rooftop concert on top of the Axel Springer office block by the Berlin Wall, to coincide with the GDR's twentieth anniversary celebrations (Bundesbeauftragter 2014). As Chris Bowlby explores in chapter 12, hundreds of hopeful East German fans turned up, only to be met by the Volkspolizei. But policing the "airy curtains" of the ether was a perennial problem in many other Cold War contexts (Badenoch 2013).

The Cold War, and particularly the Wall, thus dominated BBC coverage of Berlin in the second half of the twentieth century, helping to fix an image of Germany struggling to escape from its recent past (Smith 1999). Occasionally, more complex versions of life in the city and its longer history were offered, for example, Michael Frayn's talk of 1975, focused on the imperial capital before 1914 (Frayn 1975), or more niched documentaries about life in Berlin, such as those on pre-war urban design (*Radio Times* 1982) or on the radical student movement of the late 1960s and 1970s (Mayne 1974). For the most part however, the BBC perpetuated the obsession with the Third Reich and the Cold War, often recycling its own greatest hits, with Corporation stalwarts such as Frank Gillard, Ludovic Kennedy, Charles Wheeler and Hugh Greene popping up in the 1970s and 1980s to reprise their memories and stories of Berlin (Gillard 1970; Kennedy 1977; Wheeler 1978; Greene 1981). Only with the fall of the Wall in 1989 and German reunification a year later, did alternative media narratives about the city emerge.

3 1989 and After

By the 1980s Berlin had become a lonely outpost of BBC overseas operations. The main BBC reporting for Germany came out of Bonn, the capital of the Federal Republic, and also from Frankfurt, the finance hub. In Berlin the BBC continued to operate from a small office above a shop in Savignyplatz, "Bale", which sold oriental goods. Apart from a secretary and a technician, the BBC correspondent, who usually doubled up as the BBC German Service representative, ran the office themselves, reliant on the telex service of the DPA news agency for breaking news (Bond 2024; Brayne 2022; Marsh 2024). Until 1990, Berlin correspondents remained part of the British military forces. Indeed, the Foreign and Commonwealth Office subsidised the BBC in Berlin (£8000 per annum in 1973), although that cost seems to have been borne by the German taxpayer, not the British, as part of the terms of the original occupation agreement of 1945 (TNA 1973; TNA 1986). This made the Berlin post attractive, as correspondents did not have to pay local tax and were given official army accommodation at Johannisburger Allee in the Grunewald. On the other hand, military status, in the shape of an orange ID card and military car number plates, could be a "millstone" (Brayne 2022; Marsh 2024), for crossing the city border as occupying forces personnel proved more of a challenge than it did for civilian journalists. When the BBC needed fuller coverage of a Berlin news story, it flew in TV and radio staff from London, for example, the Queen's visit to west Berlin in May 1987, to mark the 750th anniversary of the city, when various BBC shows, including the *Today* programme, broadcast live from Berlin (*Radio Times* 1987).

Two years later, when the Wall came down, the BBC again sent over its big hitters to cover the event – for example, Alastair Cooke, Brian Hanrahan and John Simpson – alongside its regular correspondents. Then, with each passing anniversary of 1989, further programmes and series have followed, with more stars: Clive James (in 1994), and later reflections too (Frei 2009; MacGregor 2014; Simpson 2019). The 1990s also marked a step-change in the BBC's presence in Berlin, particularly once the capital returned to the city in 1999. Alongside Savignyplatz, the BBC opened an office in Schadowstrasse, in the east of the city. Then, in July 1999, following the closure of the BBC German Service, TV and radio became combined in a new centre at Platz vor dem Neuen Tor in Mitte, opened by Interior Minister, Otto Schily. Correspondents from the time recall being in the new Reichstag most days, enjoying unprecedented access to politicians, and being able to take advantage of new technology (ISDN and then satellite) to broadcast live as part of the BBC World Service (Broomby 2024; Shubart 2024; Wyatt 2022).

As the Cold War wound down – British troops withdrew from Germany in 1994 – the BBC's coverage of the life and history of the city began to expand. Shedding its difficult past, Berlin has been re-presented as a 21st century metropolis. BBC programming now extended to the new architecture of the reconstructed and unified city (Bowlby 1997), as well as to focusing on its reputation for sexual liberation (Jobatey 1990) and high-tech start-ups (*Radio Times* 2012). As Beate Peter shows in chapter 16, the BBC also covered techno-music tourism, a vital new aspect of the city's culture. The BBC's Cold War gaze has also shifted slightly in the last quarter-century to include other periods of the city's history, for example Weimar, with new programmes about David Bowie and Iggy Pop's time in the city in the late 1970s (2024). At the same time, the lure of the old themes of Berlin's past lingers. Recent big BBC productions about the city include dramas set in the Third Reich ("Diary of a Metropolis" 2020); and ("KaDeWe" 2022), Cold War nostalgia ("Secret Life of the Wall" 2009) and espionage and escape ("The Tunnel" 2019). And on the front-line, Berlin remains at the centre of European news reporting, as indicated by the final contribution to this volume, a round-table discussion featuring BBC and other Berlin correspondents past and present. Almost one hundred years after the first Berlin broadcast, the BBC continues to inform, educate and entertain the world on the topic of this most remarkable city.

References

Anderton, Abby. 2019. *Rubble Music: Occupying the Ruins of Postwar Berlin, 1945–1950*. Bloomington, IN: Indiana UP.

Badenoch, Alexander, Andreas Fickers and Christian Henrich-Franke (eds). 2013. *Airy Curtains in the European Ether: Broadcasting and the Cold War*. Baden-Baden: Nomos.

Bangs, Alan. 1985. *Nightflights: Tagebuch eines DeeJay*. Düsseldorf: Econ.

Barwise, Patrick and Peter York. 2020. *The War Against the BBC: How an Unprecedented Combination of Hostile Forces is Destroying Britain's Greatest Cultural institution ... And why you Should Care*. London: Penguin.

Bauernfeind, Wolfgang. 2010. *Tonspuren: Das Haus des Rundfunks in Berlin*. Berlin: Links.

Bond, Martyn. 2024. Email to Miles Taylor. 17 February.

Bowlby. Chris. 1997. "Reinventing Berlin". BBC Radio 3. 30 November.

Brant, Stefan. 1955. *The East German Uprising: 17th June 1953*, translated and adapted by Charles Wheeler. London: Thames & Hudson.

Brayne, Mark. 2022. Email to Miles Taylor. 19 September.

Brinson, Charmian and Richard Dove (eds). 2003. *"Stimme der Wahrheit": German-Language Broadcasting by the BBC*. Amsterdam: Rodopi.

Broomby, Rob. 2024. Interview with Miles Taylor. 1 March.

Bundesbeauftragter für die Stasi-Unterlagen (ed.). 2014. *Gefängnis statt Rolling Stones: Ein Gerücht, die Stasi und die Folgen*. Berlin: BStU.

Cole, J.A. 1964. *Lord Haw-Haw – and William Joyce: The Full Story*. London: Faber.

Cullen, Stephen M. 2021. *Long Road to Berlin: Socialism, Stalinism and Nazism: Dorothy Eckersley's Journey to Wartime German Radio*. Warwick: Allotment Hut.

Daum, Andreas W. 2008. *Kennedy in Berlin*. Cambridge: Cambridge University Press.

Defty, Andrew. 2004. *Britain, America and Anti-Communist Propaganda 1945–53: The Information Research Department*. London: Routledge.

Doherty, M.A. 2000. *Nazi Wireless Propaganda: Lord Haw-Haw and British Public Opinion in the Second World War*. Edinburgh: Edinburgh University Press.

Dovifat, Emil. 1970. *Der NWDR in Berlin 1946–1954*. Berlin: Haude & Spener.

Frayn, Michael. 1975. "Imagine a City called Berlin". *The Listener*. 93, 2396. 6 March: 296–297.

Frei, Matt. 2009. *Berlin. Written and Presented by Matt Frei*. DVD. BBC/Open University.

Freissinier, Gilles. 2005. *La chute du mur de Berlin à la télévision française. De l'événement à l'histoire, 1961–2002*. Paris: Le Harmattan.

Galle, Petra. 2003. *RIAS Berlin und Berliner Rundfunk 1945–1949*. Münster: Lit-Verlag.

Gillard, Frank. 1970. "The Time of My Life". BBC Radio 4. 19 January.

Goody, Alex. 2020. "BBC Features, Radio Voices and the Propaganda of War 1939–1941". *Radio Modernisms: Features, Cultures and the BBC*. Eds. Aasiya Lodhi and Amanda Wrigley. London: Routledge. 36–53.

Grace, Alan. 1996. *This Is the British Forces Network: The Story of Forces Broadcasting in Germany*. Stroud: Sutton.

Greene, Hugh Carleton. 1945. "The Ugliest Capital in Europe". *The Listener*, 33, 842, 1 March: 229–30.

Greene, Hugh Carleton. 1981. "Night of the Humming Bird". BBC1. 30 June.

Greene, Graham and Hugh Greene. 1957. *The Spy's Bedside Book*. London: Rupert Hart-Davis.

Heinzerling, Larry and Randy Herschaft. 2024. *Newshawks in Berlin: The Associated Press and Nazi Germany*. New York: Columbia University Press.

Hensle, Michael P. 2003. *Rundfunkverbrechen: das Hören von "Feindsendern" im Nationalsozialismus*. Berlin: Metropol.

Hines, Mark. 2008. *The Story of Broadcasting House: Home of the BBC*. London/New York: Merrell.

Holmes, Colin. 2016. *Searching for Lord Haw-Haw: The Political Lives of William Joyce*. Abingdon: Routledge.

Hughes, Rhys W. 2013. "'Frau Wernicke' at the BBC: Wartime Satire and Propaganda". *Diasporas and Diplomacy: Cosmopolitan Contact Zones at the BBC World Service (1932–2012)*. Eds. Marie Gillespie and Alban Webb. London: Routledge.

Jackson, Carlton. 1979. *The Great Lili*. San Francisco, CA: Strawberry Hill.

Jobatey, Chemo. 1990. "B-Side Berlin". BBC Radio 3. 5 May.

Keene, Judith. 2008. *Treason on the Airwaves: Three Allied Broadcasters on Axis Radio during World War II*. Westport, CT: Praeger.

Kennedy. Ludovic. 1977. "The Writing on the Wall". BBC 1. 4 April.

Kowalke, Günther. 2016. *Das "Haus des Rundfunks" 1931 bis 1945*. Dessau: Funk-Verlag.

Lashmar, Paul & James Oliver. 1998. *Britain's Secret Propaganda War*. Stroud: Sutton.

Leibovitz, Liel and Matthew Miller. 2009. *Lili Marlene: The Soldiers' Song of World War II*. New York: Norton.

Lo Biundo, Ester. 2022. *London Calling Italy: BBC Broadcasts during the Second World War*. Manchester: Manchester University Press.

"London Calling". 2019. "Cold War Letters". BBC4, 8 November.

MacGregor, Neil. 2014. "The View from the Gate". BBC Radio 4. 29 September.

Major, Patrick. 2013. "Listening Behind the Curtain: BBC Broadcasting to East Germany and its Cold War Echo". *Cold War History* 13.2: 255–75.

Mansell, Gerard. 1982. *Let Truth Be Told: 50 Years of BBC External Broadcasting*. London: Weidenfeld & Nicolson.

McCullin, Don. 2010. *Shaped by War*. London: Jonathan Cape.

McDonough, Frank. 1992. "*The Times*, Norman Ebbutt and the Nazis, 1927–37", *Journal of Contemporary History*, 27.3: 407–24.

Marsh, Vivien. 2024. Interview with Miles Taylor. 15 March.

Mayne, Richard. 1974. "The German Student Left". BBC Radio 3. 27 January.

Milton, Richard. 2007. *Best of Enemies: Britain and Germany – 100 Years of Truth and Lies*. London: Icon.

Moorehead, Kristina. 2016. *Satire als Kriegswaffe: Strategien der britischen Rundfunkpropaganda im Zweiten Weltkrieg*. Marburg: Tectum.

Murphy, Sean. 2003. *Letting the Side Down: British Traitors of the Second World War*. Stroud: Sutton.

Naumann, Uwe. 1983. *Zwischen Tränen und Gelächter: Satirische Faschismuskritik 1933 bis 1945*. Cologne: Pahl-Rugenstein.

Newsome, Noel. 2019. *Giant at Bush House: At the Heart of the Radio War*. n. p. Real Press.

Nicholas, Sian. 1996. *The Echo of War: Home Front Propaganda and the Wartime BBC, 1939–45*. Manchester: Manchester University Press.

Oliver, Emily. 2019. "A Voice for East Germany: Developing the BBC German Service's East Zone Programme", *Historical Journal of Film, Radio and Television* 39.3: 568–83.

Oliver, Emily. 2020. "Tuning in to Germany: The BBC German Service and the British Occupation". *German in the World: The Transnational and Global Contexts of German Studies*. Eds. James R. Hodkinson and Benedict Schofield. Rochester, NY: Camden House.

Plock, Vike Martina. 2021. *The BBC German Service during the Second World War: Broadcasting to the Enemy*. Cham: Palgrave Macmillan.

Pomerantsev, Peter. *How to Win an Information War: The Propagandist Who Outwitted Hitler*. London: Faber. 2024.

Radio Times. 1929. 3 December.

Radio Times. 1932a. 14 November.

Radio Times. 1932b. 22 December.

Radio Times. 1959. 1 November.

Radio Times. 1982. "Berlin Siedlungen". BBC2. 6 May.

Radio Times. 1987. "Today". BBC Radio 4. 25 May.

Radio Times. 2012. "Start-Up City". BBC World Service. 17 November.

Raleigh, John McCutcheon. 1941. *Behind the Nazi Front*. London: Harrap.

Read, Donald. 1992. *The Power of News: The History of Reuters*. Oxford: Oxford University Press.

Ribeiro, Nelson and Stephanie Seul (eds). 2016. *Revisiting Transnational Broadcasting: The BBC's Foreign-Language Services during the Second World War*. London: Routledge.

Schädlich, Susanne. 2017. *Briefe ohne Unterschrift: Wie eine BBC-Sendung die DDR herausforderte*. Munich: Knaus.

Schlosser, Nicholas J. 2015. *Cold War on the Airwaves: The Radio Propaganda War against East Germany*. Urbana, Chicago and Springfield, IL: Illinois University Press.

Selwyn, Francis. 1987. *Hitler's Englishman: The Crime of Lord Haw-Haw*. London: Routledge & Kegan Paul.

Seul, Stephanie. 2015. "'Plain, Unvarnished News'?: The BBC German Service and Chamberlain's Propaganda Campaign Directed at Nazi Germany, 1939–1940". *Media History* 21.4: 378–96.

Sugarman, Martin. 2001. "Confounding the Enemy: Jewish RAF Special Operators in Radio Counter Measures with 101 Squadron, September 1943–May 1945". *Jewish Historical Studies* 37: 189–224.

Short, K. R. M. 1989. "A Note on BBC Television News and the Munich Crisis. 1938". *Historical Journal of Film, Radio & Television* 9.2:165–79.

Shubert, David. 2024. Interview with Miles Taylor. 1 March.

Simpson, John. 2019. "The Fall of the Berlin Wall". BBC4. 7 November.

Smith, Howard. 1999. 'Have they Changed at all? The Portrayal of Germany in BBC Television Programmes, 1946–55' in *Cold War Propaganda in the 1950s*. Ed. Gary D. Rawnsley Basingstoke, Macmillan: 145–64.

Socolow, Michael J. 2016. *Six Minutes in Berlin: Broadcast Spectacle and Rowing Gold at the Nazi Olympics*. Urbana, Illinois: University of Illinois Press.

Sonnevend, Julia. 2016. *Stories Without Borders: The Berlin Wall and the Making of a Global Media Event*. New York: Oxford University Press.

Taylor, Jennifer. 2006. "The Propagandists' Propagandist: Bruno Adler's 'Kurt und Willi' Dialogues as Expression of British Propaganda Objectives". *"Immortal Austria"?: Austrians in Exile in Britain*. Eds. Charmian Brinson, Richard Dove and Jennifer Taylor. Amsterdam: Rodopi.

TNA. 1965. A. H. Campbell. 'Invitation from East Germany to the BBC Symphony Orchestra'. 16 November. The National Archives, Kew. FO 371/183150.

TNA. 1973. C. M. James to Sir F Brimelow. 16 July. The National Archives, Kew. FO 26/1468.

TNA. 1986. P. R. M. Hinchcliffe to E. R. Bowman. 8 September. The National Archives, Kew. FO33/8695.

Tracey, Michael. 1983. *A Variety of Lives: A Biography of Sir Hugh Greene*. London: Bodley Head.

Tusa, Ann and John. 1989. *The Berlin Airlift*. London: Hodder & Stoughton.

Tworek, Heidi. 2019. *News from Germany: The Competition to Control World Communications, 1900–1945*. Cambridge, MA: Harvard University Press.

Vansittart, Sir Robert. 1941. *Black Record: Germans Past and Present*. London: Hamish Hamilton.

Wainewright, Will. 2017. *Reporting on Hitler: Rothay Reynolds and the British Press in Nazi Germany*. London: Biteback.

Weale, Adrian. 2001. *Patriot Traitors: Roger Casement, John Amery and the Real Meaning of Treason*. London: Viking.

Webb, Alban. 2014. *London Calling: Britain, the BBC World Service and the Cold War*. London: Bloomsbury.

Wheeler, Shirin. 2023. *Charles Wheeler: Witness to the Twentieth Century*. London: Manilla.

Wheeler, Charles. 1978. "A Tale of Three Cities. Part 1 Berlin, East and West". BBC2. 7 April.

Wyatt, Caroline. 2022. Email to Miles Taylor. 21 October.

Zöllner, Oliver. 1996. *BFBS: "Freund in der Fremde": British Forces Broadcasting Service (Germany) – der britische Militärrundfunk in Deutschland*. Göttingen: Cuvillier.

PART 1

Weimar and the Third Reich

∴

CHAPTER 2

'Star Correspondent': Vernon Bartlett and the Rise of the Nazis

Miles Taylor

Before the end of the Second World War the BBC only had one correspondent in Berlin. However, he was a radio star, whose broadcasts ultimately posed a problem for the BBC, as ever trying to hold the line between objective coverage and critical commentary. Vernon Bartlett (1894–1983) reported on Berlin between the beginning of 1929 and the end of 1933, when the BBC terminated his contract after a row about his journalistic independence. Already a Fleet Street veteran by his mid-30s, Bartlett was the only overseas correspondent for the corporation, covering not just Berlin but other European capitals such as Paris, Vienna and Warsaw. He witnessed the demise of the Weimar Republic, the Nazi seizure of power and the failure of disarmament talks. Most significantly, he was one of the few foreign journalists to secure an interview with Adolf Hitler in 1933. Bartlett belongs to the pre-history of the BBC correspondent, most studies of which focus on the war years and subsequent Cold War era (Nicholas 2005; Webb 2014; Johnston and Robertson 2019). Bartlett operated in a very different world to later generations of reporters, free of competition from other broadcasters and without the Foreign Office looking over his shoulder. He had not been trained by the corporation, he came to the job with an impressive CV and an ego to match, and was on personal terms with John Reith, the imposing Director-General of the BBC. For these reasons, Bartlett is also a case-study from its early years, of how the BBC deals with broadcasting personalities, whose fame can sometimes threaten to eclipse the reputation of their employer. In the annals of the BBC, "The Vernon Bartlett Affair" is told as a cautionary tale about the limits to editorial independence (Briggs 1965, 146; Haworth 1981; BBC 2024). In fact, the "affair" was more complex. For a start Bartlett did not resign because he was soft on Germany, as claimed by many. Rather, he returned to newspapers and a better salary. Moreover, treating the episode simply as another example of the difficult relations between the state and the national broadcaster misses the wider significance of how the BBC shaped public support for appeasement. Using the personnel files held by

Thanks to Simon Potter and Adrian Smith for their comments on an earlier draft of this chapter.

 | HTTPS://DOI.ORG/10.1515/9783111302508-002

the BBC Written Archives Centre at Caversham, as well as his own personal archive (in which he kept all his typewritten scripts), the story of Bartlett's Berlin years can be told from both sides, from the BBC's perspective and from his own.[1]

1 From Fleet Street to Savoy Hill

Bartlett was something of a catch for the BBC. An experienced journalist, with extensive expertise on contemporary Europe, he had an insider's knowledge of the workings of the League of Nations, the most powerful agency for international relations in the period. He started his career with the *Daily Mail* in 1917 after being invalided out of the First World War, then covered the Paris peace negotiations for Reuters in 1918, before joining *The Times* as one of its foreign correspondents in 1919. For *The Times* he covered the Kapp 'putsch' of March 1920, the German withdrawal from Danzig in the same year, and Benito Mussolini's march on Rome in October 1922. In 1923 Bartlett became bureau chief of the London office of the League of Nations, based in Northumberland Avenue, off Whitehall. Not only a seasoned newshound, Bartlett was also fluent in German and knew the old imperial capital. In the winter of 1913–14 he worked as an English language teacher in Köpenicker Strasse ("Berlin's East End") where some of his best friends, he later recalled, were Jews. The father of one of them offered to pay Bartlett's college fees in Berlin to be followed by the Sorbonne in Paris, an episode he later fictionalised as *Calf Love* (1929) and *No Man's Land* (1930), the latter also a war memoir. (Bartlett 1929a; Bartlett 1930; Bartlett 1937, 97; Miall 2004). At the time of his appointment by the BBC, Bartlett was also a well-known author. Cashing in on the revival of interest in the First World War, he successfully republished much of his journalism as collected essays and novellas, co-wrote the novel derived from R. C. Sherriff's West End hit, *Journey's End*, and polished off a couple of detective stories too. (Walters 2016)

By the later 1920s the BBC needed Berlin as part of its growing overseas network. Broadcasting technology in Germany had developed faster than in Britain. The main radio transmitter (the Funkturm) in Charlottenburg was one of the most powerful in Europe. Live relays could be transmitted from the concert halls of the city to England, via the local transmitter at Daventry. Situated in the heart of the continent, Berlin acted as a node for reporters east,

1 Apart from Miall (2004) there is no modern biography of Bartlett, although he wrote several volumes of autobiography.

south and west. In 1931, more than a year before the BBC moved from Savoy Hill into its new headquarters at Broadcasting House, the Haus des Rundfunks opened for business in the west of the city, the first purpose-built media centre in the world – "alarming on account of its very magnificence", Bartlett noted (Bartlett 1933a). From here Bartlett would not only report on Berlin, but also on other cities he visited such as Geneva, Rome and Warsaw. Berlin also lay at the heart of the burgeoning web of commercial air travel, both within Germany and across Europe. In particular, a daily service operated from Croydon airport via Amsterdam. "You can leave London in the morning, reach Amsterdam at lunch time and have your tea in Berlin", Bartlett commented in the summer of 1929, waxing lyrical over the Deutsche Luft Hansa airline set up three years previously (Bartlett 1929b; Dienel and Schiefelbusch 2000).

On the face of it, Bartlett, Berlin and the BBC were a perfect match. A well-known newsman and a public figure, who moved with ease around European capitals, who knew the diplomatic and press community in London (especially the Astor family), as well as senior members of Ramsay MacDonald's government such as Philip Snowden (the Chancellor of the Exchequer), Bartlett fitted the credentials for leading the BBC's foreign reporting.[2] Liberal in his politics, he seemed a safe pair of hands. Like many of his generation who had seen war service, Bartlett was, if not a pacifist, then avowedly anti-war. From his position at the League of Nations he tended in the late 1920s to follow former Prime Minister David Lloyd George's position: opposed to French insistence on heavy German reparations which would leave the country unable to rebuild (Bartlett 1929c; Rudman 2011). Bartlett supported appeasement long before the term developed a negative meaning. He described his semi-autobiographical account of the First World War as "propagandist", written from the point of view that "we shall never get rid of war until we bring the same spirit of comradeship and self-sacrifice into peace activities that we found during the war" (Bartlett 1930b). The BBC was a natural home for such views. In 1925 the Corporation established the International Broadcasting Union as part of its mission that "Nation shall speak peace unto nation", with talks, discussion groups and schools broadcasting designed to curb nationalistic propaganda. Already embedded in the League of Nations community, Bartlett was a natural choice to lead this strategy (League of Nations Secretariat 1930a; Potter, 2023). By 1927 he had broadcast frequently from Geneva for the BBC, and from the new year of 1928, he started a regular series, "The Way of the

2 A perusal of the Court Circular from *The Times* in the years 1928–32 finds Bartlett at receptions hosted by David Astor, Victor Gollancz, Ramsay MacDonald, Philip Snowden and the embassies of Austria, Estonia, Germany, Poland and Romania.

FIGURE 2.1
Vernon Bartlett (1894–1983) in 1929, shortly after he began broadcasting regularly for the BBC. (© Special Collections, University of Reading)

World". By the time he wound up at the end of March 1934, he had given more than 200 broadcasts, many of them from Berlin, including face-to-face interviews with the "Strong Men of Europe" as the BBC Yearbook of 1934 proudly noted. (BBC 1934, 60).

At first, the BBC hired Bartlett (see Figure 2.1) on a weekly rate, covering his talks and contributions to the *Listener*. Then, from the middle of 1929, they offered him an annual salary of £750 (around £40,000 in today's value), comparable, an internal memorandum noted, to the retainer paid by the *Sunday Times* to Desmond MacCarthy, sometime member of the Bloomsbury Group and former literary critic of the *New Statesman*. The BBC proposed maximising Bartlett's output. Not only broadcasts and articles for the *Listener*, but also schools talks and reporting from the League of Nations Assembly in Geneva. Additionally, the Corporation wanted to "bring him into the planning of national programmes ... as an expert adviser" (WAC 1929). Bartlett did not take up this offer, preferring the pro forma rate, which by October 1930, the BBC calculated was earning him £1000 per annum (c. £54,000 in today's value) (WAC 1930).

2 The New Germany

As part of a series, "The Way of the World", Bartlett made his first broadcast from Berlin at the beginning of 1929, with more to follow in the summer, when he toured across Germany. His initial talk, subsequently published in the *Listener*, set the tone for his commentary over the next five years (Bartlett 1929a; Bartlett 1929b). He admired the "new" Germany, its public transport, the well-lit cities, and the "Futurist" architecture – the *Listener* article was accompanied by a photograph of the Chilehaus in Hamburg (designed by Fritz Höger and completed in 1924). Above all, Bartlett praised "this extraordinary enthusiasm for everything that is new, this determination to forge ahead, which makes Germany today such a remarkable country", drawing the moral that the vanquished Germans had done better out of the war than the victorious Allies. Lest he appeared unfashionably "pro-German", Bartlett also pointed up the ongoing aftermath of Germany's defeat in the First World War. He looked up old friends in the city, only to find they had been driven out by inflation. Like France but unlike Britain, he claimed, Germany had chosen bankruptcy over the repayment of debts, removing the burden from the youth of the country, but neglecting the old and infirm.

Bartlett did not return to Berlin for another two years. Juggling his League of Nations work in London and Geneva with his BBC tasks meant a full diary. Moreover, without a regularised contract from the BBC, he sought lucrative work elsewhere, for example travelling to the USA in the spring of 1930 for lecturing engagements there (League of Nations Secretariat 1930b). When he did revisit Germany in the summer of 1931, he found a very different mood. Broadcasting from Berlin in mid-August, he described how people had lost "hope and courage", how the country was now engulfed in "a terribly bitter and dangerous struggle" between the young and the old, between those who fought in the war and those who didn't (Bartlett 1931a; Bartlett 1931b). Noting widespread unemployment, Bartlett commented that Germans had been led to believe that "the Versailles Treaty is the cause of all their hardships", owing to the heavy reparations still being paid, despite the Young Plan of 1929. Looking ahead, he anticipated Heinrich Brüning, the Chancellor, struggling to maintain power in the face of the threat from both Nazis and Communists, a theme he returned to in broadcasts made back in London later in the year (Bartlett 1931c; Bartlett 1931d).

The following year Bartlett finally secured proper employment terms with the BBC. In February 1932, he complained to the Corporation that despite his job being "roughly equivalent to that of a Star Correspondent of a national newspaper" he had no job security beyond each broadcast or article and had to cover his own expenses. And whereas a journalist could express his own opinions, a BBC man could not. At this point, Bartlett was not seeking a salary, appreciating that this would create "an awkward BBC precedent". However, he did desire a guaranteed annual income, around £960 per annum (c. £52,000 in today's value) (WAC 1932a). The BBC rejected the idea of a salary, as well as the analogy of print journalism. On the other hand, they accepted "the extraordinary range of [Bartlett's] popularity and welcomed the advent of 'microphone personalities'" that he typified. Bartlett appealed directly to Reith, but the Corporation proved reluctant to change its position (WAC 1932b; WAC 1932c). By the summer, however, there was a breakthrough. The BBC decided to create the position of head of the "Foreign Department". Bartlett and Philip Noel-Baker, the Labour politician, were both considered for the role. Bartlett interviewed on 2 August and was offered the job the same day. It came with an annual salary of £1,200 (c. £65,000 in today's values) plus per diem expenses. Moreover, the agreement seemed to promise Bartlett some of the journalistic independence he craved. Subject to the Corporation's agreement, he would be allowed to write articles and speak in public. As the BBC explained,

> [t]he post does not fall absolutely within the category of corporation staff appointments, particularly in that it involves duties, notably that of personal broadcasting, implying a certain independence of status and respectability. Owing to your long experience with the corporation, it is unnecessary to endeavour to define the position arising in this respect, and it would indeed be difficult to do so. (WAC 1932d)

Still, Bartlett wanted more. Appealing directly to Reith, he pointed out that his last income tax return was £2,400 (including £1000 salary from the League of Nations, which was tax-free). With two children being educated privately, he would suffer a substantial fall in income. He also held out for a personal secretary. The BBC upped their offer to £1350 per annum (c. £73,000 at today's values), but passed on the secretary (WAC 1932e; WAC 1932f). As the ink was drying on the negotiations, Bartlett used one of his weekly broadcasts to test the mettle of the Corporation further. "So many things must not be written or said because they might be unpopular" he declared on 8 September, adding "I fear that many newspapers hinder a man from knowing the whole truth instead of helping him to do so". As an example, Bartlett referred to the German desire for equality of armaments and moving beyond the harsh terms of the Versailles treaty, a position with which he sympathised (Bartlett 1932a). Considered as a statement of intent, this broadcast was an unequivocal assertion of his right to air his own views. The BBC knew what they were taking on.

It considered Bartlett a special case, if not quite a special correspondent. All seemed reasonably clear.[3] Bartlett now resigned from his post at the League of Nations Union. At the beginning of October, with the Reichstag elections pending, Bartlett set off on his first tour as the new (and only) foreign correspondent of the BBC, his itinerary taking in Paris, Berlin, Prague, Vienna, Budapest, Rome and Basle.

3 Nazi Berlin

Bartlett spent the best part of late 1932 and all of 1933 visiting the European continent, including three spells in Berlin. He witnessed Nazi meetings in the German capital in October 1932. He missed the burning of the Reichstag at the end of February 1933, but was back in Berlin the following month to see the Nazi consolidation of power (the Enabling Act) and he also saw the effects of the boycott of Jewish businesses on 1 April. During this second stay he interviewed Adolf Hitler. Bartlett then criss-crossed Europe through the summer and autumn of 1933, including trips around Germany – published as a light travelogue the following year (Bartlett 1934c) – and time in Geneva covering the disarmament conference, where he also interviewed Joseph Goebbels. In November, 1933, Bartlett returned to Berlin to cover the parliamentary elections. There were of course many foreign journalists in Berlin at this time, often running into one another at the Taverne club (Schnedermann 2018). Other reporters, such as Rothay Reynolds of the *Daily Mail*, Sefton Delmer of the *Daily Express* and Gareth Jones of the *Western Mail*, covered the Nazi machine. Reynolds interviewed Hitler as early as 1921, and both Delmer and Jones travelled with Hitler during 1932 and 1933 on his private aircraft (Wainewright, 2017; Bayer, 2008; Colley, 2008; Galbraith, 2022). For *The Times*, Norman Ebbutt proved a perceptive critic of Hitler, although not all of his pieces were published by the paper (McDonough 1992). However, only Bartlett reached a wider audience through radio.

Arriving in Berlin by train from Paris at the beginning of October, Bartlett noted differences from his previous visits immediately (Bartlett 1932b). The city seemed "less smart and prosperous", new commercial buildings had gone up, but not found any occupiers. Unemployment had hit the city hard, especially amongst the youth. He came across an "Adolf Hitler Haus", the new Nazi headquarters (Voßstraße 11) and attended a Nazi rally in Neukölln. Dur-

3 Later in the year Reith wrote privately to Bartlett: 'I have listened with much interest to your talks from the Continent': (Bartlett 1932c).

ing his first broadcast he played an excerpt from a recording of one of Hitler's recent speeches, as an example of "his immense and almost hypnotic influence over the masses". And he described the uniformed militias now appearing on the streets, which he likened to the Territorial Army and Officers' Training Corps back in Britain. Despite this voyeuristic fascination with the Nazis, Bartlett underestimated their strength. He claimed that the "Hitler movement" was losing support, that most of the youth attending rallies and donning paramilitary clothing were a reserve army of the unemployed. And he reckoned on the government of Franz von Papen remaining in office "for some time to come". By the time of his next visit to Berlin in March 1933 this optimism was gone.

Bartlett was back in London for the new year of 1933, delighted to return to the comfort of the studio at the BBC's headquarters in Broadcasting House. He confessed to his listeners that he sometimes felt constrained broadcasting from abroad, as he did not wish to offend the opinions of his hosts: "the BBC, I discovered, has a very great reputation, and there was an embarrassing amount of interest in what I was going to say to the British public" (Bartlett 1933a). The rising tide of nationalism prevented him saying exactly what he thought when he was overseas, although, as will become clear, such self-censorship did not limit his criticism of British policy. Still in London, Bartlett covered the burning of the Reichstag from afar (Bartlett 1933b; Bartlett 1933d). He doubted the explanation that the fire had been caused by either the Communists or the Social Democrats, as both parties were committed to parliamentary democracy. For the first time, he began to talk of a "brutal and bloody" civil war unfolding in Germany, and expressed his alarm at the Nazi arrests of opposition leaders and the suppression of the press. Bartlett turned to Hermann von Keyserling, the Estonian philosopher, for a critique of Nazi ideology, writing it off as a Prussian version of German identity which had little to do with the liberal attitudes of the south, or the Nordic temper of the north.[4] Nazism, he explained to a meeting of the Royal Institute of International Affairs on 14 February was a "perverted idealism", it might lead to civil conflict, but not another war in Europe (Bartlett 1933c, 6–7).

A few weeks later, back again in Berlin, Bartlett saw for himself the transformation of power (Bartlett 1933e; Bartlett 1933f). He attended the temporary Reichstag in the Kroll Opera House (opposite the burned-out building) and witnessed the deputies voting for all the new powers demanded by the Nazis. Bartlett drew the obvious conclusion, namely:

4 Von Keyserling's views on the Nazis were published in the *New York Times*, 17 April 1932, p. 3.

> when I spoke from Berlin before, I said how difficult it was to sum up the situation in Germany because the Germans themselves did not know what they wanted. They know now – or enough of them to run the country now. They want Hitler, brownshirts and the subordination of the interest of the private individual to those of the state.

Around this time, Bartlett also watched people buying photographic portraits of Hitler in Potsdamer Platz (Bartlett 1933g), which he likened to "religious devotion". For all his punchy observations about the cult of Hitler, Bartlett was more equivocal in describing the crackdown on the Nazis' opponents and their hostility towards Jews. In Berlin on 1 April, the day of the boycott of Jewish businesses, he commented that he had not seen anything unusual. Persecution was "not nearly so bad as many people in other countries believe", Bartlett explained. He went on to say that rumours were rife about mistreatment of the Jews, owing to information coming from exiles and due to the absence of independent reporting. He even claimed that the Nazis were taking measures to stop the persecutions. However, in the broadcast of 30 March, he also hinted at self-censorship: "I have grumbled before now about the difficulty of speaking about a foreign country, especially from that foreign country. I have never felt this difficulty so acutely as this evening".

Around 20 June, Bartlett interviewed Adolf Hitler "in a pleasant room overlooking the Wilhelmplatz" (Bartlett 1933f). Bartlett found Hitler a difficult subject, only managing to get in three of his own questions. "With his eyes fixed on anything in the room except me, he addressed me as though I were an audience of a thousand." Hitler, reported Bartlett, spoke mainly about relations with Austria, and also the new compulsory labour force, which he denied was a revival of militarism, rather a cure for youth unemployment, the state stepping in where private capitalism had failed. Bartlett accepted Hitler's statements at face value. "He is", he concluded, "an honest man who is passionately and unselfishly patriotic … he has built up a movement that is supported by most of the country's youth and many of its middle-aged." Bartlett urged his listeners to have patience with Hitler, reminding them that the Allies had let Hitler in by not giving enough support to the moderate German leadership of men such as Stresemann and Brüning. He ended his scoop with an endorsement of Hitler, "there is a lot of good in the Nazi movement and it's very much to our interest that we bring it out." On this occasion, broadcasting from Vienna and not Berlin, and therefore less concerned about his host's sensitivities, Bartlett might have been more critical of the Nazis. Why did he soft-soap Hitler in this way? Part of the explanation lies in Bartlett's conviction that his access to Hitler allowed him insights into the Nazi regime that other reporters did not have. In a broadcast at the end of July, Bartlett repeated his earlier claim that "there are far too many whose opinions of Germany are based almost entirely upon accounts of political exiles from that country." (Bartlett 1933h). He may also have wanted to keep favour with the Nazi leadership to secure further interviews.

In doing so, Bartlett once more tugged at the tether that bound him to the BBC. Instead of reprinting his broadcast of the interview with Hitler in the *Listener* – as he did with a similar interview with Benito Mussolini in June (Bartlett 1933i) – Bartlett sent the copy to the left-wing *Daily Herald*, which published it on 16 August with the title "Hitler shouted at me" and with Bartlett's byline as "the BBC's travelling expert on foreign affairs" (Bartlett 1933j; Smith 2000). Compared to the staid tones of the broadcast, the article raced along. Of Hitler he wrote, "Here was an ordinary looking man, with large brown eyes,[5] rather fuller cheeks than I had expected, and a moustache which is wider than it used to be, so that it is no longer possible to compare the chancellor with Charlie Chaplin." The article focused on Austria, with none of Bartlett's thoughts from the original broadcast on the nature of Nazism. The BBC took alarm on finding out about the piece in the *Daily Herald*. "[H]e [ie: Bartlett] is known as our 'Ambassador' and we are thus linked up with his expressed views", complained an internal memo, "Is it allowed in the contract?" A second memo raised the concern that Bartlett might be indiscreet: "For example, some of his remarks about Herr Hitler are not complimentary, and might result to [sic] a cold or even rude reception on his next visit to that country. It might also lead to the withholding of telephone or studio facilities." In the reply that followed, the Corporation concluded that there was nothing in the article that was incompatible with "the tone and attitude" of his broadcasts, and confirmed that Bartlett was free to contribute to newspapers, but should seek permission first (WAC 1933a; WAC 1933b). In other words, the BBC tolerated Bartlett's independence. The BBC also seemed to incline to be even more generous to Hitler than Bartlett, and wary of giving offence.

Both the BBC role and the Hitler interview enhanced Bartlett's status as an expert on Germany, and further publishing offers now came his way. In September he negotiated a contract with the left-wing house, Victor Gollancz, to publish an inside view of Nazi Germany. Gollancz had just published an English edition of *The Brown Book of the Reichstag Fire and Hitler Terror*, an account of what really happened back in Berlin in February and the reprisals that followed, co-written from exile in Paris by Willi Münzen-

5 Hitler's eyes were blue.

berg and other German Communists. Bartlett completed his volume, *Nazi Germany Explained*, at speed whilst covering the disarmament talks in Geneva, and it was published by the end of the year (Bartlett 1933k). Bartlett stated in the preface that the volume represented only his views, although much of the material came directly from his broadcast scripts and articles for the *Listener*. His argument was a familiar one to anyone who had listened to his radio coverage of the previous few years, but may have come as a surprise to the publisher. In three opening chapters Bartlett located the origins of the political despair that gave rise to Nazism in the harsh treatment inflicted on Germany by the Allies after 1918. He discussed Hitler's *Mein Kampf* at length (a feature missing from his broadcasts), likened Nazism to "religious revivalism" combined with economic autarky and collective national spirit, and repeated his claims that reports of anti-semitism inside Germany were fuelled mainly by exiles and refugees. Once again he stated his sympathy for German demands for rearmament, at the same time "emphatically" believing that Germany did not want war. On this occasion, Bartlett did request the permission of the BBC before proceeding with the commission, promising the Corporation that the book would be "very short" (actually it was almost 300 pages) and would not distract from his BBC work (WAC 1933c).

From Geneva in late September and early October, Bartlett's defence of Germany's claims for greater equity in armaments became more strident. He had a one-on-one meeting with Joseph Goebbels whilst covering the conference – "a pleasant little man with a friendly smile and a twinkle of humour in his eyes", although "intensely earnest and intensely uncompromising" on the principles of Nazism (Bartlett 1933l). When Goebbels and the rest of the German delegation left the conference and with it the League of Nations on 14 October, Bartlett could not hold himself back any longer. Broadcasting on the same day he prepared his listeners for what they were about to hear: "I know that I risk offending a lot of you by talking as I'm doing tonight. It would be easier to keep away from the microphone altogether" (Bartlett 1933m). In what followed Bartlett directly criticised John Simon, the Foreign Secretary in the National Government, and leader of the British delegation at Geneva, and called on the former Allied powers to "swallow our pride" and "understand and meet the German point of view". The broadcast brought an instant reaction, with newspapers back in Britain lining up to criticise or support Bartlett, and by association the BBC. In its editorial the *Daily Telegraph* led the attack on Bartlett's comments, which instead of elucidating the position of the government, leaned "heavily to the other side". Philip Snowden, the former Chancellor, wrote in to the paper the next day, calling its editorial "deplorable" (*Daily Telegraph*, 1933). For the opposite end of the political spectrum, the

Daily Herald led with "Foreign office alarm at broadcast. Chiefs want to muzzle Mr. Vernon Bartlett" (*Daily Herald*, 1933). There were private remonstrations too. Ramsay MacDonald, the Prime Minister, complained to Reith (Briggs 1965, 146), whilst J. L Garvin, editor of the *Observer*, told Bartlett he was "gravely wrong" and that "the BBC should never be used on critical occasions" (Bartlett 1933n).

However, nothing happened. Despite the furore in the press, the BBC did not respond to Bartlett's broadcast. They were having different problems with their star correspondent. As previously, his freelance activities were threatening to get in the way of his BBC schedule. In early November Bartlett was approached by the *News Chronicle* and invited to write a regular column.[6] Owned by the Cadbury family, the *News Chronicle* under the editorship of Aylmer Vallance had taken a more radical, anti-fascist direction earlier in the year, and was looking to recruit well-known names from the left of centre. Initially, the BBC said no to Bartlett combining both roles (WAC 1933d). Whilst these discussions were underway, Bartlett returned to Berlin to report on the Reichstag elections, and also on the referendum on the German withdrawal from the League of Nations (Bartlett 1933o, Bartlett 1933p). Visiting the polling booths, he noted how the elections were rigged: only Nazi candidates were allowed to stand. Still, Bartlett focused on describing the unfairness dealt out to Germany since the Armistice of 1918, and how it had created both a memory of "resentment and humiliation" and also a desire to avoid further war. From his hotel room he looked out on sheets of calico with slogans such as "Peace with honour and equality", "With Hitler against the World's Armaments Folly", and also quotations from recent speeches by Lloyd George. Bartlett placed his hopes in Germany returning to the talks at Geneva, as long as they were given assurances that they could increase their army from short service to long. Back in London in November, Bartlett returned to planning his future with the BBC. The Corporation now agreed to end his contract so that he could write for the *News Chronicle*. From January 1934, Bartlett would only contribute one broadcast commentary per week for the BBC for three months and be freed from his other obligations. Bartlett's disappointment over the reaction to his Geneva broadcast was mentioned by the BBC as a contributory factor in his decision, but so too were his finances (WAC 1933e). Bartlett took up his pen for the *News Chronicle*, his first article appearing on New Year's Day 1934.

All of this took place without any recrimination on either side about Bartlett's controversial broadcast from Geneva on 14 October. Only when Sir John Simon made a statement to Parliament about the Disarmament Conference

6 According to Miall (2004), Bartlett was also approached by the *Daily Herald*.

at the beginning of February, 1934, did an anti-appeasement MP, Brigadier-General Edward Spears, intervene to complain about Bartlett and his "sympathetic justification" of Germany's departure from the League, as well as his throwaway remarks in another broadcast about the inevitability of Austria capitulating to Germany – "We cannot get away from the fact that Austria is German" (Bartlett 1934a). In the House of Commons tempers flared as the Speaker denied that the government controlled the content of broadcasting policy (*Hansard* 1934). The BBC's position became potentially even more embarrassing ten days later, when Simon was a guest at an Aldwych Club lunch chaired by Sir John Reith. However, at the event Simon diplomatically praised the BBC, stating that "government direction of wireless would be a profound mistake" (*Daily Mirror* 1934). Its position clarified, the BBC then showed its trump card, confirming that Bartlett had already agreed to leave the Corporation at the end of March (*The Times* 1934). Inevitably, commentators suspected that Bartlett had been sacked. From Berlin it was claimed that Bartlett was "the victim of a long-standing systematic campaign of agitation against him by anti-Germans"[7] (*Berliner Tageblatt* 1934). However, it is clear that his amicable exit had been arranged two months previously. Bartlett continued to broadcast as planned until the Spring with no further fuss. Having said that, he felt poorly treated by the BBC, leaving as he did after six and a half years "without so much as a note of acknowledgement from a single official on the Staff." Reith pragmatically responded by arranging for a wireless set to be sent to him "as a reminder of our good will and gratitude" (Bartlett 1934b). Any rancour was soon forgotten. Bartlett returned to the BBC in 1936, with a series of schools talks. Then during the Second World War he joined the Brains Trust and also hosted programmes for the Forces network, interviewing women and men in arms. Poignantly, his last main broadcast came in 1954, when he covered the United Nations conference in Geneva.

4 Conclusion

For most of the rest of the twentieth century the BBC never again had a roving correspondent in Berlin quite like Bartlett. Direct reporting from Berlin soon dried up after 1933. Once Bartlett stepped down, the BBC turned to Cicely Hamilton, the veteran women's rights campaigner and European expert, for contributions. Although Hamilton had written extensively for *Time and Tide*

7 'Bartlett fällt als Opfer einer seit längerer Zeit gegen ihn von antideutscher Seite geführten systematischen Hetze.'

on the rise of Hitler, and authored a book about Germany, in which she was far more critical of the Nazis than Bartlett, she stuck to social commentary for the BBC, on topics such as family life, with her surveys covering all of Europe and not just Germany (Hamilton 1933; Hamilton 1934; Einhaus 2019). Then, in the summer of 1934, a young Richard Crossman gave a series based on his travels across Nazi Germany, one of which he broadcasted for the BBC from Berlin (Crossman 1934). Neither Hamilton not Crossman showed the inside knowledge and immediacy familiar to Bartlett's listeners. By the time of the Munich crisis of 1938, the BBC German service had been set up, and the government and the Corporation established a closer relationship, a foretaste of the broadcasting arrangements of the Second World War (Seul 2015).

As other essays in this volume describe, radio and television personalities did come to Berlin at critical moments such as the defeat of the Third Reich in 1945, the 1948 Airlift, the construction of the Wall in 1961 and its fall in 1989. However, from 1945, BBC-trained staff took on the role of Berlin correspondent, their background not so much Fleet Street as the armed forces, or, increasingly during the 1960s and 1970s, other news agencies such as Reuters. Bartlett had enjoyed and benefited from a uniquely "golden age of the wireless", as Asa Briggs memorably dubbed the 1930s. A friend and contemporary, Lord Conesford later described how "[f]rom 1928 to 1934 Mr Vernon Bartlett broadcast regularly, and thus had a virtual monopoly of addressing the British public on the subject [of foreign affairs]" (Hansard 1962). As a "microphone personality" he became a household name, his weekly broadcasts reached millions, giving him the kudos to stand successfully as an independent at the famous Bridgewater parliamentary by-election of 1938, when he came out as a strident critic of Neville Chamberlain's handling of Hitler. Yet, another way to locate Bartlett at the BBC is as an unacknowledged advocate of the first phase of appeasement, whose understandable sympathy for the plight of Germany after the First World War led him initially to dismiss the Nazis as a durable phenomenon, and then later to be taken in by Hitler's peace rhetoric. In particular, his pursuit of the sensational interview at the expense of more critical reporting diminished his testimony as a witness to the first year of the Third Reich. Ultimately, there was more than a touch of Evelyn Waugh's *Scoop* about the BBC's first ever "star correspondent".

References

Bartlett, Vernon. 1929a. *Calf Love*. London: Constable.

Bartlett, Vernon. 1929b. "A Holiday in Germany". 4 June. Ms 2788. Box 2/54. Vernon Bartlett Papers, University of Reading, UK.

Bartlett, Vernon. 1929c. *The Old Way and the New Way: Some Reflections on the Ninth Birthday of the League*. London: League of Nations Union.

Bartlett, Vernon. 1929d. "The Way of the World". 14 January. Ms 2788. Box 2/21.Vernon Bartlett Papers, University of Reading, UK.

Bartlett, Vernon. 1929e. "A Glimpse of the New Germany", *The Listener*. 1:2. (23 January): 61.

Bartlett, Vernon. 1930a. *No Man's Land*. London: George Allen & Unwin.

Bartlett, Vernon. 1930b. Bartlett to C. P. Scott. 5 February 1930. A/B17/2C. P. Scott correspondence, Manchester Guardian Archive, John Rylands University Library, Manchester, UK.

Bartlett, Vernon. 1931a. "The Way of the World". 14 August. Ms 2788. Box 3/20. Vernon Bartlett Papers, University of Reading, UK.

Bartlett, Vernon. 1931b. "Helping Germany to Help Itself". *The Listener*. 6:136. (19 August): 284.

Bartlett, Vernon. 1931c. "The Way of the World". 30 October. Ms 2788. Box 3/28. Vernon Bartlett Papers, University of Reading, UK.

Bartlett, Vernon. 1931d. "The Way of the World". 24 December. Ms 2788. Box 3/33. Vernon Bartlett Papers, University of Reading, UK.

Bartlett, Vernon. 1932a. "The Way of the World". 8 September. Ms 2788. Box 3/71. Vernon Bartlett Papers, University of Reading, UK.

Bartlett, Vernon. 1932b. "Berlin, 3 October 1932". Ms 2788. Box 3/78. Vernon Bartlett Papers, University of Reading, UK.

Bartlett, Vernon. 1932c. Sir John Reith to Bartlett, 29 November. British Library Add. Ms. 59,500: fol. 96.

Bartlett, Vernon. 1933a. "The Way of the World". 5 January. Ms 2788. Box 3/86.Vernon Bartlett Papers, University of Reading, UK.

Bartlett, Vernon. 1933b. "The World and Ourselves". 2 March. Ms 2788. Box 3/93. Vernon Bartlett Papers, University of Reading, UK.

Bartlett, Vernon. 1933c. "European Impressions". Record of a General Meeting held at Chatham House'. 14 February. RIIA 8/258. Chatham House Online Archive.

Bartlett, Vernon. 1933d. "Critical Days in Germany", *The Listener*. 9:217 (8 March): 367.

Bartlett, Vernon. 1933e. Untitled Typescript. 30 March. Ms 2788. Box 3/94. Vernon Bartlett Papers, University of Reading, UK.

Bartlett, Vernon. 1933f. "What I Have Seen in Nazi Germany". *The Listener*. 9:221 (5 April): 521–2.

Bartlett, Vernon. 1933g. "Broadcast from Vienna". 22 June. Ms 2788. Box 3/100. Vernon Bartlett Papers, University of Reading, UK.

Bartlett, Vernon. 1933h. "Dictators and Democracy". 27 July. Ms 2788. Box 3/106. Vernon Bartlett Papers, University of Reading, UK.

Bartlett, Vernon. 1933i. "My Talk with Mussolini". *The Listener*. 9.231. (14 June): 935–6.

Bartlett, Vernon. 1933j. "Hitler Shouted at Me." *Daily Herald*. 16 August.

Bartlett, Vernon. 1933k. *Nazi Germany Explained*. London, Victor Gollancz.

Bartlett, Vernon. 1933l. "Foreign Affairs". 28 September. Ms 2788. Box 3/110. Vernon Bartlett Papers, University of Reading, UK.

Bartlett, Vernon. 1933m. "Germany Leaves the League".14 October. Ms 2788. Box 3/115. Vernon Bartlett Papers, University of Reading, UK.

Bartlett, Vernon. 1933n. Letter from J. L. Garvin, 11 November. Ms 2788. Box 1/44. Vernon Bartlett Papers, University of Reading, UK.

Bartlett, Vernon. 1933o. "Armistice Day in Berlin". 11 November. Ms 2788. Box 3/123. Vernon Barlett Papers, University of Reading, UK.

Bartlett, Vernon. 1933p. "Today in Berlin". 13 November. Ms 2788. Box 3/124. Vernon Bartlett Papers, University of Reading, UK.

Bartlett, Vernon. 1934a. "Actions and Reactions in European Affairs". *The Listener*. 11. 264 (31 January). 25.

Bartlett, Vernon. 1934b. Sir John Reith to Bartlett. 15 June. Bartlett to Sir John Reith. 26 June. Ms 2788. Box 1/45-6. Vernon Bartlett Papers, University of Reading, UK.

Bartlett, Vernon. 1934c. *See Germany for Yourself*. London: Thomas Cook.

Bartlett, Vernon. 1937. *This is My Life*. London: Chatto and Windus.

Bayer, Karen. 2008. *How Dead is Hitler?: der britische Starreporter Sefton Delmer und die Deutschen*. Mainz: Zabern.

Berliner Tageblatt. 1934. 6 March.

Briggs, Asa. 1965. *The Golden Age of Wireless. The History of Broadcasting in the United Kingdom. Volume II*. London: Oxford University Press.

BBC. 1934. *The BBC Year-Book*. London: BBC.

BBC. 2024. "The Vernon Bartlett Affair – 1933" https://www.bbc.com/historyofthebbc/research/editorial-independence/vernon-bartlett Accessed 31 December 2024.

Colley, Margaret Siriol. 2008. *More than a Grain of Truth. The Biography of Gareth Jones*. Newark, Privately Printed.

Crossman, Richard. 1934. "Today in Germany". (2 July). Warwick University Digital Collections. https://cdm21047.contentdm.oclc.org/digital/collection/rcc/id/20/rec/3 (accessed 31 December 2024).

Daily Herald. 1933. 17 October.

Daily Mirror. 1934. 16 February.

Daily Telegraph. 1933. 19 October.

Dienel, Hans-Liudger and Martin Schiefelbusch. (2000). "German Commercial Air Transport until 1945". *Revue Belge de Philologie et Histoire*. 78: 945–67.

Einhaus, Ann-Marie 2019. "Wyndham Lewis, Cicely Hamilton, and Nazi Germany in *Time and Tide*". *Journal of Modern Periodical Studies*. 10.1–2: 76–97.

Galbraith, Kylie. 2022. *The British Press and Nazi Germany. Reporting from the Reich, 1933–9*. London: Bloomsbury Academic.

Hamilton, Cicely. 1933. *Modern Germanies as seen by an Englishwoman. With a Post-script on the Nazi Regime*. London: J. M. Dent.

Hamilton, Cicely. 1934. "Merits of the Well-Filled Cradle". *The Listener*. 11.273 (4 April): 29–30.

Hansard. 1934. House of Commons Debates, 285, 6 February: 1026–8.

Hansard. 1962. House of Lords Debates, 240. 9 May: 280.

Haworth. Bryan. 1981. "The British Broadcasting Corporation, Nazi Germany and the Foreign Office, 1933–1936". *Historical Journal of Film, Radio and Television* 1:1: 47–55.

Johnston, Gordon and Emma Robertson. 2019. *BBC World Service. Overseas Broadcasting, 1932–2018*. London: Palgrave.

League of Nations Secretariat. 1930a. Educational Broadcasting. Correspondence with the BBC. 5C/19607/12723. https://archives.ungeneva.org/educational-broadcasting-correspondence-with-the-british-broadcasting-corporation Accessed 31 December 2024.

League of Nations Secretariat. 1930b. Broadcasting and Lectures by Mr Vernon Bartlett. 13/19404/4000. https://archives.ungeneva.org/p43w-ky87-8qxx Accessed 31 December 2024.

McDonough, Frank. 1992. "*The Times*, Norman Ebbutt and the Nazis, 1927–3", *Journal of Contemporary History*, 27: 407–424.

Miall, Leonard. 2004. "Bartlett, (Charles) Vernon Oldfeld (1894–1983), journalist and broadcaster". *Oxford Dictionary of National Biography*. https://www.oxforddnb.com/view/10.1093/ref:odnb/9780198614128.001.0001/odnb-9780198614128-e-30795. (Accessed 31 December 2024).

Nicholas, Siân. 2005. "War Report (BBC 1944–5) and the Birth of the BBC War Correspondent". *War and the Media: Reportage and Propaganda, 1900–2003*. Eds. Mark Connelly and David Welch. London: I.B. Tauris. 139–61.

Potter, Simon. 2023. "Broadcasting in the Cause of Peace: Regulating International Radio Propaganda in Europe, 1921–1939". *International History Review* 45.6: 843–864.

Rudman, Stella. 2011. *Lloyd George and the Appeasement of Germany, 1919–1945*. Newcastle: Cambridge Scholars.

Schneidermann, Daniel. 2018. *La presse internationale face à Hitler*. Paris: Editions de Seuil: 94–131.

Seul, Stephanie. 2015. "'Plain, Unvarnished News'?: The BBC German Service and Chamberlain's Propaganda Campaign Directed at Nazi Germany, 1938–1940". *Media History* 21.4: 378–396.

Smith, Adrian. 2000. "The Fall and Fall of the Third *Daily Herald*, 1930–64". *Northcliffe's Legacy: Aspects of the British Popular Press, 1896–1996*. Eds. Peter Catterall and Colin Seymour-Ure. Basingstoke: Macmillan. 169–200.

The Times. 1934. 21 February.

Wainewright, Will. 2017. *Reporting on Hitler. Rohay Reynolds and the British Press in Nazi Germany*. London: Biteback.

Walters, Emily. 2016. "Between Entertainment and Elegy: The Unexpected Success of R. C. Sheriff's *Journey's End* (1928)". *Journal of British Studies*, 55.2: 344–73.

Webb, Alban. 2014. *London Calling: Britain, the BBC World Service and the Cold War*. London: Bloomsbury.

WAC. 1929. Internal Circulating Memo. "Mr Vernon Bartlett". 29 June. R Cont. 1. File 1a. Vernon Bartlett, 1929–32. BBC Written Archives Centre, Caversham, UK.

WAC. 1930. Internal Circulating Memo. "Mr Vernon Bartlett". 25 October. File 1a. BBC Written Archives Centre, Caversham, UK.

WAC. 1932a. Bartlett to Roger Eckersley, 15 January. R Cont. 1. File 1a. Vernon Bartlett, 1929–32. BBC Written Archives Centre, Caversham, UK.

WAC. 1932b. Internal Circulating Memo. "Mr Vernon Bartlett". 20 January. R Cont. 1. File 1a. Vernon Bartlett, 1929–32. BBC Written Archives Centre, Caversham, UK.

WAC. 1932c. Bartlett to Sir John Reith, 4 February. R Cont. 1. File 1a. Vernon Bartlett, 1929–32. BBC Written Archives Centre, Caversham, UK.

WAC. 1932d. Sir John Reith to Bartlett, 2 August. R Cont. 1. File 1a. Vernon Bartlett, 1929–32. BBC Written Archives Centre, Caversham, UK.

WAC. 1932e. Bartlett to Sir John Reith, 4 August. R Cont. 1. File 1a. Vernon Bartlett, 1929–32. BBC Written Archives Centre, Caversham, UK.

WAC. 1932f. Controller to Bartlett, 9 August. R Cont. 1. File 1a. Vernon Bartlett, 1929–32. BBC Written Archives Centre, Caversham, UK.

WAC. 1933a. Internal Circulating Memo. "V. Bartlett". 22 August. R Cont. 1. File 1b. Vernon Bartlett, 1932–34. Written Archives Centre, Caversham, UK.

WAC. 1933b. Internal Circulating Memo. "Mr Vernon Bartlett". 4 September. R Cont. 1. File 1b. Vernon Bartlett, 1932–34. BBC Written Archives Centre, Caversham, UK.

WAC. 1933c. Internal Circulating Memo. "Outside Work". 13 September. R Cont. 1. File 1b. Vernon Bartlett, 1932–34. BBC Written Archives Centre, Caversham, UK.

WAC. 1933d. BBC to G. A. Vallance, 9 November. R Cont. 1. File 1b. Vernon Bartlett, 1932–34. BBC Written Archives Centre, Caversham, UK.

WAC. 1933e. Internal Circulating Memo. "Vernon Bartlett". 8 December. R Cont. 1. File 1b. Vernon Bartlett, 1932–34. BBC Written Archives Centre, Caversham, UK.

CHAPTER 3

War in the Air: The BBC, Bomber Command and the Berlin Blitz, 1940–45

Patrick Major

> "As you know I am very critical of the B.B.C."
> Winston Churchill to Anthony Eden, 1 November 1954,
> on the BBC documentary series *War in the Air.* (TNA. 1954)

In September 1939 the BBC was put on an immediate war footing, becoming both the voice of state authority and empathetic sounding-board of the "people's war". But the Corporation was not a free agent. Its hybrid position meant that Broadcasting House never enjoyed Fleet Street's licence to criticise, as happened for instance in 1942 when Churchill endured negative press comment. Instead, BBC newsreaders informed the British home front in measured tones, while its external services engaged both friend and foe in the battle for world opinion. The BBC was broadcasting to multiple publics and had to calibrate output accordingly, walking a tightrope between overclaiming on the one hand, and under-reporting on the other. Regarding the now hugely controversial strategy of indiscriminate "area bombing" of enemy civilians, domestic broadcasting carefully managed the British public's knowledge of what was being done in its name. According to the historian of the Ministry of Information (MoI), which included various seconded BBC staff, "the Ministry did more than exercise discretion. It lied." (McLaine 1979, 159) Conversely, as Oliver has noted of messages to the enemy home front, the constant propaganda conundrum was "convincing ordinary Germans that Britain had their best interests at heart, when every day the country was taking direct action to kill more Germans." (Oliver 2020, 153–54).

Wartime necessarily imposed new journalistic restrictions. The BBC relied on the Air Ministry and Royal Air Force (RAF) for its bombing facts, which were almost impossible to verify independently. After the country had weathered the Battle of Britain in 1940, the only meaningful action in Europe for the next three years was the air war against the Axis. Britain had few victories to celebrate early on. Was the BBC guilty of exaggeration in the lean years to boost morale? From 1942 Bomber Command, under its publicity-hungry Commander-in-Chief, Arthur "Bomber" Harris, pressed home the new doctrine of

 | HTTPS://DOI.ORG/10.1515/9783111302508-003

area bombing, incendiarising German city centres and their occupants. The Reich capital itself was subjected to a brutal bombing campaign over the winter of 1943/44, costing Bomber Command crippling casualties too. (Berlin accounted for one-in-ten of total losses.) Did the BBC know the full facts behind area bombing? Did it tell the British public the complete picture and how did public opinion respond? The Corporation also pioneered new technologies to record sounds from the front, including one of the war's most famous transmissions, the live recording of a raid over Berlin on the night of 3/4 September 1943. These are all avenues to be explored.

Berlin – the "Big City" to RAF crews – was Bomber Command's ultimate target. It was simultaneously a political, industrial and morale objective. In the words of Air Minister Sir Archibald Sinclair: "Berlin is not only the home of Prussian Militarism and the capital of Nazi government, but it is also the greatest single centre of war industry in Germany." (WAC 1943l). The *Reichshauptstadt* was Germany's capital and nerve-centre of a continental empire, inviting attack on the Clausewitzian principle of decapitating the enemy. Any raid on Berlin guaranteed headlines. Industrially, Berlin earned pride of place in the Ministry of Economic Warfare's gazetteer of targets, the so-called "Bomber's Baedeker", its "key-point rating" almost equal to all the Ruhr towns combined (TNA 1942–45). As well as being a transport hub, it housed electrical and aeronautical giants such as Siemens, AEG, Daimler-Benz, Focke-Wulf, Heinkel and Dornier: "if I were allowed to choose only one target in Germany", explained Sinclair days later, "the target I would choose would be Berlin." (WAC 1943m). He did not, however, mention the two million workers – many ex-Communists and Social Democrats – whose packed tenement blocks represented Bomber Command's true firebombing target. The "Battle of Berlin" (November 1943 to March 1944) was to be a crucible to crack German home front morale and, in theory at least, end the war from the air (Willmy 2024, 412–71).

The idea of bombing enemy capitals was not new. In the First World War Germany had bombed London, both from Zeppelin airships and new, long-range bombers. It was Berlin's political status as enemy capital which first attracted Winston Churchill's attention. In July 1940 the recently appointed prime minister asked Bomber Command, the RAF's still fragile strategic offensive arm, to prepare a contingency plan against Berlin, "to return the compliment" should London be attacked. In late August 1940 the moment came when the Luftwaffe overshot targets in London's dockland, killing civilians in the East End. Bomber Command retaliated the next night with a minor raid, puncturing Berlin's supposed invulnerability. The BBC's 6 o'clock Home news reported that "[a]rmament factories in the Berlin area were bombed last night by the R.A.F." (WAC 1940). At this stage, crews probably *were* trying for precision targets, but their bombs fell hopelessly wide of the mark; only allotments were hit. Nevertheless, the MoI's Home Intelligence division reported "great satisfaction" among the British general public on the first news of reprisal raids on Berlin (TNA 1940a). In Cardiff there was reportedly "widespread criticism that our planes should bring back their bombs if unable to locate a definite target." Or in Manchester: "we should have no scruples about bombing civilians there." (TNA 1940b). As Britain reeled under the escalating Luftwaffe Blitz that autumn, newspaper editorials and readers' letters demanded retaliation, including bellicose headlines such as "Bomb Back, and Bomb Hard!" (Holman 2012, 394) At this stage, however, such calls were merely wishful thinking.

The problem of overclaiming had long been recognised. In January 1941 an Air Ministry conference assembled Whitehall's interested parties: RAF, MoI, Foreign Office, Ministry of Economic Warfare, Political Warfare, and the BBC. (Intriguingly, no press representatives attended; the BBC was evidently treated as an "insider".) One reporting constraint was secrecy: bulletins should not divulge information detrimental to the war effort. But, as one BBC attendee noted, "overshouting the odds" was equally likely to hurt Britain's credibility abroad, becoming a boomerang to be exploited by German counter-propaganda (WAC 1941a). The gathering agreed more self-restraint, especially over Berlin, where the large diplomatic community of neutrals could easily verify bombing results. (As the war progressed, their signal traffic, intercepted by Bletchley Park, became an important clandestine source on damage to Berlin, but the BBC was apparently not let into the Enigma secret.)

In the early war, the RAF simply lacked the capacity to mount heavy raids on a target almost 1,000 km away. Indeed, in late 1941 Bomber Command was suffering unsustainable losses. A particularly costly raid on Berlin in November, in appalling weather, lost 12.4% of the force in one night. The BBC went into heroic failure mode, with shades of Scott of the Antarctic, reporting temperatures of minus 37 °C in unpressurised cabins coated in frost. "It was agonizing even to touch the sextant and the pain bit into his fingers as though they were being scalded", reported one returning navigator. "I saw long icicles on the bottom of the pilot's oxygen mask", he continued; "he broke one off and threw it at me to show he was keeping cheerful enough" (WAC 1941c). Churchill was less amused. After an internal inquiry, he suspended strategic bombing over the winter of 1941/42 and sacked Bomber Command's C-in-C Richard Peirse. He was replaced by the controversial Arthur Harris who stood steadfastly – some would say fanatically – behind the new doctrine of area bombing. Yet, throughout 1942 he resisted Churchill's calls, while visiting Stalin for the first time in August for instance, to bomb Berlin for high-political reasons, to impress the Soviets with a "second front" in the air. Harris refused, preferring to wait for the build-up of a heavy bomber force including the four-engined Lancaster. Just one raid was mounted on Berlin in all 1942, when a solitary Mosquito fast fighter-bomber buzzed the city.

Yet a Mosquito's sting could cause huge irritation to the Nazi body politic. On 30 January 1943 an explicitly propagandistic hit-and-run raid was mounted in broad daylight, to disrupt German live radio broadcasting of the tenth anniversary celebrations of the NSDAP's coming-to-power in 1933. Six Mosquitoes roared over the German capital, with the first wave managing to interrupt Göring's 11am speech at the Aviation Ministry. It had to be postponed by an hour. "Just as the Reichsmarshal [sic] was about to speak", wrote Britain's Minister of Information, "there came a noise like the running down of a gramophone, followed by excited shouts about the unexpected difficulties delaying the Marshal. The noise of feet stampeding into shelters was then loudly covered up by fresh bursts from the battery of brass bands." (Harris 1943). A second wave tried the same during Goebbels' afternoon speech, with less success. The German live transmission had been picked up by BBC monitoring, however, and was re-broadcast to the Home and Forces programme four days later to air British *Schadenfreude*. SS internal security reports also noted the humiliation of Göring, who had famously claimed in 1940 that no enemy aircraft would ever reach Berlin, had become a talking-point in the Reich. (Boberach 1984–85, vol. xii, 4732).

1 Nation shall Speak Peace (and War) unto Nation: Dual Messaging to Friend and Foe

Arthur Harris was an intensely media-conscious Commander-in-Chief, constantly alert to the press coverage and broadcast time that Bomber Command was receiving compared with the Russian front, and from 1943 with American daylight bombing. Only a few months into the job, his nominal superior, the RAF's Vice-Chief of the Air Staff, lamented the unedifying spectacle of different arms of the service vying for publicity, and "in their efforts to attract the limelight they sometimes exaggerate and falsify facts. The worst offender is C.-in-C. Bomber Command." These commanders were supposedly surrounding themselves with public relations officers, "journalists or advertising agents disguised in uniform", feeding them a "continual diet of printed flattery", leading to "a prima donna-ish petulance whenever the customary tributes fail to appear or do not live up to expectations." (TNA 1942d). RAF now jokingly stood for "Royal Advertising Force".

Harris himself – or his words at least – were broadcast on the BBC German Service directly to the enemy populace at 8pm on 28 July 1942: "I will speak frankly to you about whether we bomb single military targets or whole cities. Obviously we prefer to hit factories, shipyards, and railways. It damages Hitler's war machine most", the Air Marshal explained. "But those people who work in these plants live close to them. Therefore, we hit your houses and you. We regret the necessity for this. ... Soon we shall be coming every night and every day, rain, blow or snow – we and the Americans", he warned. "We are going to scourge the Third Reich from end to end ... You have no chance." The address ended with a choice, however: "it is up to you to end the war and the bombing. You can overthrow the Nazis and make peace." (*The Times*, 29 July 1942, 2) In fact, this blunt message was not originally intended for broadcast, but for a leaflet drop over Germany (Kirchner 1991, 84–85). Yet Richard Crossman, German section head of the Political Warfare Executive (PWE), Britain's foreign propaganda arm, was so taken with Harris's text that it found its way onto the air without proper clearance. PWE noted that Nazi propaganda, often keen to jump on examples of supposed British atrocities, remained noticeably silent on this exceptionally "categorical description" of the "increasing extent of the attacks." (TNA 1942b). Berlin's news agency, DNB, did issue a communiqué, however, claiming the moral high ground: since the British "cannot win the war weapon for weapon", they had now "resorted to the illusion that they can decide it by fighting against women and children." DNB called Harris to future account, a man "who now speaks openly of murder" (*The Times* 1942, 3).

British propaganda was always in dialogue with the enemy, yet the speech also made waves when inadvertently broadcast on the BBC Home Service and reported in the press, since it came far closer to divulging the true aims of area bombing than the usual, euphemistic domestic reports on military targeting. Lord Addison in the House of Lords, alarmed that a forces' leader appeared to be making war aims policy on the hoof, complained that the speech "was so bombastic that anyone might have thought that Mussolini had made it. It was not a British habit to brag in advance", adding: "It was reminiscent of what Göring said about no bombs falling on the Reich, and was just as sensible." (*Hansard*, 1942). An internal PWE inquiry led to personal apologies to Harris, although anxieties about British public opinion appeared unfounded. A Home Intelligence special report recorded only limited interest, with opinion split between a "that's the stuff to give 'em" school and a more nuanced, educated group critical of "playing to the gallery" and "bombastic Vansittart stuff" [Britain's most fervent anti-German]. More pragmatic voices asked whether such transmissions could even be received in Germany: "If it is heard, what chance have the Germans of revolting?" Other pessimists wondered: "Will bombing really break morale … it didn't break ours." (TNA 1942c). They had a point.

15 months later, this mixed messaging exploded into a secret spat between Bomber Command and the Air Ministry, sparked by the deadly fire-bombing of Kassel in October 1943. The BBC had spoken of "a very heavy attack on the engineering and armament centre of Kassel, home of the Henschel Locomotive Works and the Fieseler aircraft assembly plant." (WAC 1943f). (In reality, the aiming-point had been the heart of the old town.) Vexed by this misrepresentation, and press reporting generally, Harris wrote to the Air Ministry demanding a fundamental rethink of RAF publicity policy. He objected to "the continued suggestion that Bomber Command is concerned, not with the obliteration of German cities and their inhabitants as such, but with the bombing of specific factory premises." (Henschel, in fact, manufactured the Tiger tank; Fieseler the Messerschmitt 109 fighter.) Harris worried that media half-truths were making his crews feel ashamed of their contribution. Moreover, American daylight bombing and Russian land advances were stealing the headlines.

> The aim of the Combined Bomber Offensive, and the part which Bomber Command is required by agreed British-U.S. strategy to play in it, should be unambiguously and publicly stated. That aim is the destruction of German cities, the killing of German workers and the disruption of civilised community life throughout Germany.
>
> It should be emphasised that the destruction of houses, public utilities, transport and lives; the creation of a refugee problem on an unprecedented scale; and the breakdown of morale both at home and at the battlefront by fear of extended and intensified bombing, are accepted and intended aims of our bombing policy. They are not by-products of attempts to hit factories. (TNA 1943b)

Whatever one may think of Harris, he was certainly honest. Too much so for the Air Ministry, which scrambled to keep a lid on the C-in-C. Here, it is worth quoting at length Director of Operations Richard Peck, senior RAF officer for media liaison and master of sophistry:

> The Air Ministry has certainly not, as yet, presented such an aim to the public. … The aim as described by the C.-in-C. appears to me to amount to one of delib-

> erate terror attack upon the civil population with factory damage as a by-product, in fact Warsaw, Rotterdam and Belgrade. ... Our original plans envisaged precision attack of military industrial targets on the lines now followed by the Americans. Tactical conditions forced us to attack these by night by area bombing. ... It is, of course, more effective to blow a whole town out, factories and all by fire, than to blow out only the factories but we have done it because forced to do so ... In other words, our aim has been the destruction of the war machine and has not been terror bombing. We know that the loss of civilian life is entailed – we make no secret of it, and the public knows it, but the public knows also that this has not been our assigned aim and we have avoided causing misgivings to any important body of opinion. ... especially in America attack on morale is thought ineffective as well as an unjustifiable aim. (TNA 1943c)

Kassel had been a "road to Berlin" target. Whereas in 1940–41 there had been some attempt to hit Berlin's power stations, Tempelhof airport or Siemensstadt in Spandau, by 1943 Bomber Command was conducting area bombing, pure and simple, where the aiming-point was often the Alexanderplatz. Nevertheless, BBC reporting continued to imply that the RAF was flying against military targets in industrial cities, where civilian casualties were, to borrow a modern term, "collateral damage". When Hamburg was hit in the devastating firestorm raids of July/August 1943, the BBC Home news, while reporting that fires could be seen from 200 miles away, explained to listeners that: "Hamburg, apart from its importance as a port, turns out more U-boats every year than any other town in the Reich." (WAC 1943d). It had launched the *Bismarck*. While true, Blohm & Voss's shipyards were decidedly *not* the RAF's target. Likewise, when the Battle of Berlin proper opened four months later in November 1943, BBC Home news still accentuated the military-industrial, reporting that "reconnaissance had shown that about 100 factories and industrial premises in Berlin had been damaged in the raids of August and September." (WAC 1943g). Even if this was not outright lying, it was selective sleight of hand, suppressing uncomfortable facts.

Yet the sheer weight of concentrated bombing on Berlin that winter forced a shift. Bomber Command's most devastating attack on the capital came on 22/23 November 1943, and the next night, in a series of rolling raids. German fire crews down below were almost overwhelmed; a large part of Tiergarten, occupied by the current Hansaviertel, was burnt out. Listeners were told, citing neutral Swedish sources, that the Propaganda and Foreign ministries had been hit in the government quarter, destroying Goebbels' and Ribbentrop's villas (WAC 1943h). Harris was adamant: "The battle of Berlin progresses. It will continue until the heart of Nazi Germany ceases to beat." (WAC 1943j). A

Ministry of Economic Warfare spokesperson was less sanguine: while claiming that "German spirits are low" and that industrial production had fallen generally, he realistically concluded that "there's not much evidence so far of actual defeatism, nor of any active opposition to, or sabotage of, the war effort." (WAC 1943i). The BBC was still seeking balance. Indeed, when Churchill passed on a Secret Intelligence Service assessment to Harris, its findings confirmed that area bombing was merely generating "fatalistic apathy": "But so long as the morale of the Gestapo and S.S. troops remains unaffected as it does at present, it is difficult to see how an even more serious decline in German civilian morale can bring about a rapid collapse as in 1918." (Harris 1944).

The BBC German Service also broadcast to German audiences, who could see with their own eyes the fearful results of Allied bombing. Goebbels as Propaganda Minister and plenipotentiary for air defence denounced Anglo-American bomber crews as "terror flyers" and "air gangsters". The MoI opted for pre-emptive denials. In a defensive pamphlet in 1944, *Aerial Bombing: The Facts*, it admitted growing "incidental damage" but not the "deliberate terror-bombing of civilians". And although the Battle of Berlin had involved "a series of paralysing raids", they were "designed not to terrify the civilian population, but simply and systematically to eliminate Berlin as the focal point of the German war effort." (McLaine 1979, 164–65) This was misleading, to say the least. Privately, Harris considered that area bombing should instil "fear of death". Aerial damage assessments also reveal area bombing's brutal logic. Allied Central Interpretation letter-coded damage to industry and transport ("A" for maximum, "E" for minimum), but ratings included public buildings, schools, churches and "hutted camps", many housing foreign forced labour. Meanwhile, the Ministry of Home Security's Research and Experiments Department (RE8) measured area attacks exclusively by building fabric destroyed and lives likely lost. These assessments included percentages from aerial reconnaissance of dwellings "demolished", "uninhabitable", "seriously damaged" and "readily repairable", as well as casualty estimates of killed and seriously injured. Thus, on the opening night of the Battle of Berlin on 18/19 November 1943, 9–18,000 were projected killed and a similar number seriously injured (wild overestimates, it transpired). RE8 reports included heat diagrams of cities attacked, with each square kilometre of built-up area shaded and assigned a value for levels of high-explosive and incendiary damage (TNA 1942–44). This was the technocratic face of area bombing, ministered to by scientists and statisticians. Indeed, media reporting often descended into battles of tonnages, keeping "score" on loads dropped, as if engaged in some macabre sporting competition (Knapp 2013, 45–51).

Rather than trying to justify bombing as a strategic attack on Germany's war economy, the default public rationale, especially towards the Germans themselves, was frequently moralistic. However, this was Old Testament morality of an eye for an eye, a tooth for a tooth. Churchill himself had set the tone in a speech in July 1941 and Harris followed: Nazi Germany had sown the wind, and the Allies were merely repaying in kind, with interest. The "whirlwind" of area bombing was therefore on the heads of the Germans. The BBC German Service delighted in repeating extracts of Hitler's September 1940 speech at the start of the London Blitz, when he had promised the British to "eradicate their cities." (Brinitzer 1969, 222) When German exiled Nobel laureate Thomas Mann broadcast shortly after the fire-bombing of his home town of Lübeck, he accepted the "principle of just retribution" for Coventry (Havers 2007, 182–83).

German Service comedy skits provided further opportunities to skewer German hypocrisy, by bringing up Warsaw, Rotterdam and Coventry (Moorehead 2016, 239–40). But the imagined conversations in the air-raid cellar of Frau Wernicke, evincing gobby *Berliner Schnauze*, reminded Reich listeners of the bombers' progress as well as unpicking the mechanisms of Goebbels' propaganda. The sketch "Frau Wernicke in the Air-Raid Shelter" of 16 October 1943 presented a *Hausfrau* aping the regime's die-hard slogans, while undermining them with the insane logic of a war on all fronts: "They can come from West and East and South – let 'em! There ain't enough points of the compass for us to lose the will to take one on the bonce for the Führer ... " (Adler 1990, 136 – all translations are mine.) The humour asks ostensibly rhetorical questions, to which there was propagandistically only one answer: of course Berlin can take it!; but which in the real world raised existential questions of personal survival: of course I don't want to die! The sketch-writers also mocked the Propaganda Minister's ill-advised accusation that German *Kultur* – its churches, monuments and art galleries – represented the real price of bombing, not human lives. In amongst the banter and transposed g's and s's of Frau Wernicke's *Berlinerisch* are deeper musings on the function of *Haltung* – analogous to "stiff upper lip" – which Goebbels held to be the moral bedrock underpinning the temporary slides of *Stimmung* or "mood". The function of comedy propaganda was to undermine the former, by chipping away at the more superficial moodiness of the populace, which carried a lesser penalty in terms of oppositional behaviour. Negotiating this fine line posed one of the biggest challenges of psychological warfare. If Harris was serious that Germans' only way out was insurrection, then this would involve some citizens putting their head above the parapet in one of the most feared police states of modern times.

2 Flying Correspondents: The BBC over Berlin

While Paulus's Sixth Army was collapsing at Stalingrad and Churchill and Roosevelt met at Casablanca to insist on "unconditional surrender", the Air Ministry opted to share the limelight by attacking Berlin for the first time in well over a year. Two back-to-back heavy raids, involving the new Lancaster bomber, were launched in January 1943. Berlin operations frequently coincided with high-level diplomatic encounters, as Harris sought to give his chief backer, Churchill, currency for his high-political "summitry" (Worrall 2019, 44). Later that year the Battle of Berlin proper coincided with the Teheran conference in November 1943, and in February 1945 Operation Thunderclap – initially aimed at Berlin, but fatefully morphing into the Dresden raid – coincided with Yalta. None of this was accidental; Berlin was first and foremost a political target, in Churchill's eyes at least.

The January raids still relied on visual navigation and the force lost its waypoints in the snows below, leading to scattered results. Bombing was an inherently visual business. Bomb-aimers needed to see the target, even if via radar. Results were chiefly gauged by aerial reconnaissance. Trophy images of burnt-out districts would be reproduced in Allied publications and leaflets dropped over Germany, but photographic cover often took days or weeks to arrive, in breaks in the weather, by which time readerships after "hot" news had often lost interest (TNA 19422). In 1943 the Americans were beginning to use movie technology to film raids. Hollywood's William Wyler shot *The Memphis Belle: A Story of a Flying Fortress* (1944), which combined visceral colour footage of a raid in May 1943 with the crew's frenetic intercom chatter. Bomber Command's nocturnal missions, shrouded in darkness, offered no such opportunities. Broadcasting was still a non-visual medium, working through sound.

Most RAF coverage had so far consisted of returning pilots being sent to Broadcasting House with an Air Ministry script. The results were often stilted and cliché-ridden: "Pilots constantly complain that it's not their own stuff", noted one BBC controller, "and that they'll get hell from the gang when they return to their station." (WAC 1942a). RAF censorship was killing stories. The BBC wanted to send reporters to bases and record livelier vox pops with air and ground crews, but was stonewalled by the Air Ministry's public relations gatekeeper, the eccentric Wing-Commander Eric Bentley Beauman. He had achieved minor celebrity between the wars as a Himalayan mountaineer and believer in "abominable snowmen" (*The Times* 1937, 13), but his name within Broadcasting House stood for micromanagement, high-handedness and foot-dragging. The last straw was the Air Ministry's demand in August 1942 to vet all BBC scripts on RAF matters, which was firmly rejected. Memoranda on rocky

RAF-BBC relations continued to fill BBC in-trays, requiring intervention at the highest level by one of the BBC Directors-General, Robert Foot, with Chief of the Air Staff, Sir Charles Portal. Despite invoking the Wykehamist old school-tie, things seemed little better three months later (WAC 1943b).

Embedding a reporter as a flying correspondent was one way around the Air Ministry. The Luftwaffe had already sent a radio *Kriegsberichterstatter* over Coventry in November 1940 on Operation "Moonlight Sonata". As the Blitz on Britain petered out, Bomber Command finally agreed to a British equivalent (TNA 1941). Three British press correspondents and the US broadcaster Ed Murrow of CBS, famed for his London Blitz broadcasts, were offered a trip to Berlin (WAC 1941b). Though this came to nothing, the BBC felt snubbed, once again outranked by Fleet Street. Only in 1942 did the Corporation begin to assert its unique selling-point of sound, training a new crop of frontline war correspondents (Hannon 2008, 176–78). John Snagge, BBC chief announcer and Presentation Director, urged more reporting of the air war from above. The "value of the recordings" should override "considerations of safety of personnel". Nor was it a job for the RAF: "The professional broadcaster knows what to look for" and "automatically sees things which are novel and strange to him but which to the professional person are perfectly normal." Fearing an American scoop, "it would show everybody that the Corporation is right on its toes and fulfilling its primary function of up-to-date radio". (WAC 1942).

What was needed was a high-profile target – such as Berlin – and a reporter daring enough to take to the air and accept the risk. Enter Richard Dimbleby, not yet thirty, one of the BBC's few true war correspondents, having just returned from North Africa with a reputation for intrepid and evocative front-line reporting. Despite later becoming the embodiment of the Corporation, he was viewed with mixed feelings by BBC management at the time. Dimbleby supposedly lacked detachment and was left kicking his heels at Broadcasting House. Assigning him to cover Bomber Command was not a plum posting, but he had flown with the RAF in the Middle East, and in December 1942 took his RAF medical in the hope of accompanying a live raid. The opportunity came soon enough on the night of 16/17 January 1943, when he flew to Berlin with Wing-Commander Guy Gibson, who was to go on to aviation immortality four months later leading the "Dam Busters". The reporter was filled with dread, and understandably so. The cumulative casualty rate among Bomber Command crews on their thirty-mission tours was almost fifty per cent. Although on this raid, with the element of surprise, only one Lancaster was shot down, if he had flown the following night, the odds of going "missing-in-action" were one-in-six. Flying correspondents had to sign a no-claims legal waiver.

On the outward leg Dimbleby suffered an oxygen-supply malfunction and passed out, but was revived. During evasive manoeuvres, to his embarrassment he vomited down the forward hatchway, narrowly missing the bombardier. Despite being unable to film using Gibson's ciné-camera, which jammed in the cold, the BBC man's gift was the ability to paint word pictures. As the aircraft neared the target, a burst of flak "lifted us in the air as if a giant hand had pushed up the belly of the machine." And then, "where a moment before there had been a dark patch of the city, a dazzling silver pattern spread itself. A rectangle of brilliant lights, hundreds of thousands winking and gleaming and lighting the outlines of the city around them." The reporter's language waxes lyrical, describing how "great incandescent flowerbeds spread themselves. It was a fascinating sight." (Dimbleby 1975, 169) Indeed, Dimbleby was not alone in ascribing beauty to the terrible destruction below. German ground observers were frequently transfixed by the sight of the "Christmas trees" of yellow, green and red indicator flares floating down towards them, until reminded that these were delineating a zone of death. Although the flying correspondent imagined the enormous 8,000lb blockbuster bomb unleashed by the Lancaster hurtling down towards "Hitler, Goering or Himmler or Goebbels ... cowering in a shelter", of the nearly 150 who died on the ground that night, Berlin's Hauptluftschutzstelle reported that 80 per cent were foreign forced workers and prisoners-of-war. (Landesarchiv Berlin 1943). And although Home Intelligence detected public pleasure over the broadcast, "a few people suggested that 'it would be better to carry bombs than war correspondents.'" (TNA 1943a).

After being brought back down to earth, a day later Dimbleby broadcast his account, reiterating his admiration for RAF crews who had to endure such dangers night after night. The script had been vetted by MoI's Air Ministry representative (TNA 1943a). Gibson's 106 Squadron sent a telegram simply saying "Nice work. We all read it and approved." (Dimbleby 1944, 51) This acceptance by "the boys" apparently meant more to him than BBC endorsement. Dimbleby flew on, including a daylight raid on Duisburg in November 1944 and a live recording of a low-level attack on Kleve in February 1945. In another he flew in a Mosquito Pathfinder, observing "skymarking" technique. After one operation, the reporter fell asleep at the wheel of his car and awoke in a ditch; on another occasion, while parked outside Broadcasting House, he returned to find his car stolen, along with all his flying kit. In total, Dimbleby flew around twenty RAF missions, not far off a full tour, becoming Broadcasting House's man in Bomber Command. But this embedded status was to test loyalties.

1943 witnessed further advances in recording technology to capture the sounds of live, airborne combat, not just an after-action report. Previous hopes of taking 500lbs of audio equipment into the air had foundered on sheer weight, but the Lancaster was more than equal. On 3/4 September 1943 BBC reporter Wynford Vaughan-Thomas also flew to Berlin, in "F" for Freddie with sound engineer Reg Pidsley (See Figure 3.1). The reporter had a specially adapted oxygen-mask with a built-in microphone, while Pidsley operated an acetate cutting-machine, pre-warming discs which still froze so rapidly at 19,000 feet that every three minutes a new one had to be laid on the turntable. Despite the technical challenge, this became one of the Second World War's most celebrated recordings. Vaughan-Thomas's oxygen-mask also malfunctioned, causing him to slur his words slightly, but his commentary remained lucid. Each crew member was introduced, including a Scottish flight-engineer, a Sussex farmer as tail-gunner and an Australian from Brisbane as navigator: a cross-section of nation and empire. Pidsley captured the long flight out, crossing the enemy coast. Like Dimbleby, Vaughan-Thomas conjured up word pictures as the aircraft reached a wall of searchlights at Berlin:

> Behind that wall there's a pool of fiercer light. It's glowing red and green and blue and over that pool there are myriads of flares hanging in the sky. That's the city itself. And there in the heart of the glow there goes a red flash – the biggest we've yet seen – that must be the first of the big four thousand-pound bombs going down. Flak coming up at us now. All you see is a quick red glow from the ground then up it comes on a level – a blinding flash. That one went then, and it was pretty near to me. Our aircraft rocked. ... we're running straight into the most gigantic display of soundless fireworks in the world. (WAC 1943e)

On its final bomb-run, the bomber was attacked by a night-fighter. The chatter of its mid-upper gun-turret replying is distinctly audible. The simultaneous release of the 4,000lb "Cookie" caused the Lancaster to lurch upwards – and Pidsley's recording-head to jump with it – perhaps saving the aircraft as the attacker's tracer rounds hurtled harmlessly beneath. It could not have been scripted more dramatically. After crew jubilation over purportedly shooting down the assailant, Vaughan-Thomas's parting vision, as the Lancaster banked away, was a "glimpse of that furious glowing carpet of light – that's all we can now see of Berlin", a "boiling cauldron".

Vaughan-Thomas and Pidsley were greeted in Broadcasting House as returning heroes. Excerpts of the recording made the main 4 September news. A "full" version, "Cutting, Skipper", was then aired on 28 September, but with a musical score and added narrated interludes. These explained how close "F" for Freddie had come to being shot down – 22 Lancasters were lost that night – and inserted dramatic dialogue of British civilians staring up at the departing bomber stream. Perhaps unsurprisingly, the item spared few imagi-

FIGURE 3.1 Wynford Vaughan-Thomas (1908–87) reporting in 1944. Wikimedia

nary thoughts for the Germans below; only the barked commands of a German flak crew. Yet what is most remarkable about the Lancaster crew responses, despite occasional lapses into banter ("it's a wizard prang"), is their coolness at moments of greatest danger: "O.K. steady. Right a little bit – right – steady." After likely cheating death by a split second, pilot Kenneth Letford simply says: "Now, not too much nattering, lads." It was epic British understatement.

The BBC conducted a listener survey, recording an approval rating of 92, matched by only one other feature on the Battle of Britain in 1940. Listeners were asked to describe their feelings, which were most commonly "admiration for the bomber crew and, not far short of it, admiration for the BBC men who took part in it." A great many described "the thrill which the broadcast gave them"; its realism "enabled them to identify themselves with those who had been over Berlin that night." And finally: "The matter of factness of the bomber crew also seems to have made a deep impression." But there were also minority views: "a few who took the occasion to deplore the necessity of bombing", and a very few who were "nauseated that BBC staff should take part in making a 'Roman holiday'" or for whom "the broadcast evoked a feeling of sympathy with the bombed." (WAC 1943e). Vaughan-Thomas's autobiography literarily embellished the raw account. Like Dimbleby, he gasped at the "most beautifully horrible sight" of coloured marker flares descending in the darkness, and the detonations of incendiary and high-explosive bombs were likened to "throwing jewellery down on black velvet" (Vaughan-Thomas 1980, 155).

Aestheticisation of violence comes close to anaesthetisation. An element of entertainment was creeping into BBC war reporting – the "thrill" which the listener survey had identified. The recording has recently even been turned into a virtual reality experience, *1943 Berlin Blitz* (BBC Media Applications Technologies Ltd, 2018), in which a digital reimagination has been superimposed onto the authentic sound. Users armed with a VR headset are placed in the cockpit in Vaughan-Thomas's point-of-view, free to look around at animated figures performing actions on audio cues. It is hard not to be swept along, as commentaries of YouTubers "flying" *Berlin Blitz* confirm. The programmers have succeeded in recreating the ghostly glow of the instrument panel on the flight-deck, and the shafts of light from searchlights, over the ruddy glow of a burning city. But is this immersive experience "history"? Despite the original sound, it is hard to avoid the visual affinities with video games, especially as the tail-gunner claims his night-fighter. The simulation, through distancing intertitles, does nevertheless remind viewers that "Industrial and civilian areas were hit. Civilians were killed", which is something.

Ed Murrow, America's hard-boiled radio reporter, finally secured a place on a subsequent RAF raid on Berlin on 2/3 December 1943. In "Orchestrated Hell" for CBS, he expressed the same awe at target pyrotechnics and crew professionalism, but signed off on a more downbeat note: "The job isn't pleasant; it's terribly tiring. Men die in the sky while others are roasted alive in cellars. Berlin last night wasn't a pretty sight" (cited in Persico 1988, 216). Such raids also revealed the perils of frontline reporting. On the same mission Nordahl Grieg, a Norwegian *Daily Mail* reporter and Norman Stockton, an Australian *Sydney Sun* correspondent, were shot down and killed (Cooper 2023, 201–15). Lowell Bennett, an American correspondent, bailed out but survived. He was treated to a tour of the shattered Ruhr by his Luftwaffe captors, and upon repatriation published the controversial memoir *Parachute to Berlin*, condemning area bombing (Bennett 1945). The only two wartime BBC correspondents killed on active duty both fell on bombing missions. Kent Stevenson was killed on an RAF raid on Germany's Wesseling oil refinery on 21/22 June 1944. And on 3 February 1945, luck finally ran out for Guy Byam, who had jumped with British paratroops on D-Day and at Arnhem, when his USAAF Flying Fortress, the "Rose of York", was hit during Berlin's heaviest raid of the war, crashing into the North Sea.

3 Air: The Forgotten Front?

Arthur Harris always feared being eclipsed by the Americans. After February 1944's "Big Week" raids, aimed at aircraft factories, in March the USAAF chose Berlin as a target which the Luftwaffe had to defend at all costs. The prospect of daylight raids on the Nazi capital captured the media imagination like few other stories. And daylight meant all-important pictures. The Americans were also more adept at handling war reporters. Bernard Moore, head of BBC Overseas News Broadcasts, explained the growing side-lining of Bomber Command to the Air Ministry: "Our experience, frankly, has been that the USAAF has shown a more ready appreciation of the value of this type of news", particularly after "the first daylight attacks on Germany and especially Berlin." The BBC hoped to redress the balance towards the RAF, but currently Bomber Command was at the bottom of the pecking order (TNA 1944b).

By spring 1944, night raids had evidently become yesterday's news. The RAF's heavy raids against Berlin ended just three days later, on 24/25 March. Certainly, a change in public attitudes towards the Berlin Blitz is detectable in Britain's Home Intelligence reports. In early December 1943 the tone was summarised as: "Berlin is regarded as 'a symbol of a great evil, and, therefore, to be wiped out'. Some sympathy is expressed for civilians, particularly children and conscripted foreign workers, but there is no desire to do other than continue." (TNA 1943d). Only a week later the raids were "looked on as a 'gruesome necessity' to make future land operations less costly; there is much speculation as to their effect on German morale. Though there is some sympathy for civilians, people generally are thought to display 'neither tenderness nor exultation' over the victims; any tendency to 'gloat' over their sufferings is disliked." (TNA 1943e). Yet five weeks later, after raids pressed even on Christmas Eve 1943, the mood appeared to be shifting: "Continued satisfaction, particularly with the Berlin raids – though some now take big raids for granted. Most people are pleased with the systematic destruction of Berlin, and want it kept up 'for practical and psychological reasons' … . A number, however, regard it regretfully 'as a job which just has to be done', while a few feel that the Allies are sinking to the level of the enemy and that the raids are terror raids." (TNA 1944a). And in the final week of the Battle of Berlin, British respondents even registered "surprise, tinged with admiration, that the Germans have stood it so long." (TNA 1944b). Berlin could take it.

Naturally the *vox populi* must be qualified. Whenever the Luftwaffe launched reprisal raids, as they did in a "little Blitz" in early 1944, or with flying bombs that summer, British public opinion hardened. A key influence was, unsurprisingly, the British press. Mark Connelly has demonstrated that the majority of newspaper messaging backed retaliatory bombing (Connelly 2002). Yet as Helen Frost has recently argued, media representation and public perception of bombing were two very different quantities, with less popular appetite for destruction than inferred by a more gung-ho tabloid press (Frost 2022, 80–81). On the BBC Home service after the notorious Coventry raid, Tom Harrisson of the Mass-Observation polling organisation denied hearing the calls for revenge among the bombed-out populace being reported by the press (Holman 2012, 394). Mass-Observation ran one of its special directives in December 1943, at the height of the Battle of Berlin, asking: "What do you feel about the recent bombing of Germany?" The results were mixed. Apparently 60 per cent gave full support; 20 per cent held attacks to be necessary, but had concerns about the fate of civilians; only 10 per cent found them unacceptable; and a further 10 per cent gave no clear response. Intriguingly, the BBC German Service then broadcast these very findings to German audiences on 18 February 1944, summarising: "Very few people like the idea of these heavy air raids, but very few want to end them. The majority are of the opinion that the bombing raids are an unpleasant necessity to shorten the war." (Brinitzer 1969, 222–23)

By 1945 Richard Dimbleby was becoming increasingly disenchanted with the sidelining of the RAF's effort, once the second front had moved on land after D-Day. On 6 January 1945 he complained to the BBC Controller of News that a piece he had written on Bomber Command's achievements in 1944, "its greatest year," had been passed over, and that he now had "the unenviable task of telling the Command that the BBC did not think the story of its efforts and sacrifices in 1944 worth 2¾ minutes in War Report." Dimbleby did not hold back: "In these circumstances we must surely not allow ourselves to believe that people are 'tired' of hearing about Bomber Command. I cannot imagine a more cynical or callous suggestion". (WAC 1945). Nevertheless, the Great British public probably *had* lost interest. The very nature of strategic bombing was gradual, attritional. BBC producers warned of its dwindling newsworthiness. Yet it was more than indifference. The mass deaths in the notorious Dresden raid of February 1945 appeared to waken a dormant pang of conscience in the British psyche. Churchill privately minuted that the "destruction of Dresden remains a serious query against the conduct of Allied bombing"; it was time to review "bombing of German cities simply for the sake of increasing the terror." (TNA 1945). The RAF was outraged at this hypocrisy. After all, Churchill had been the chief sponsor behind area bombing until detecting the beginnings of a public backlash. It was only in April 1945, after the flattening of Potsdam – virtually a suburb of Berlin, but already earmarked for the peace conference – that the doctrine was formally renounced, days before Germany's unconditional surrender.

The levels of destruction unleashed by Bomber Command were almost beyond rational comprehension. A colour film shot from a US spotter plane flying low over Berlin in July 1945, the month the Anglo-Americans occupied their sectors, recorded biblical ruination. Richard Dimbleby was among the first western reporters into the ghost city. Despite his partisanship for Bomber Command and the horrors he had witnessed at Bergen-Belsen, he immediately called for magnanimity in victory: "As we would say, in British Air Force slang, 'Berlin has had it'. As a clean, solid, efficient city, it has ceased to exist." Dimbleby witnessed Berliners cowed and submissive, in urgent need of humanitarian aid. But he was critical of the Russians, anticipating problems which were to beset the city in the next of its wars, the Cold War: "At the moment that trust is lacking. Somewhere between us and the Russians there's a barrier of suspicion and reserve. It's rather like trying to make friends with a fellow that you can't see on the other side of a high wall." (Miall 1966, 50–51) These were prophetic words, but not what Whitehall or the Corporation wished to hear at the time. This willingness to go off-message, and his big, maverick personality, left no obvious place for Dimbleby in the postwar BBC; in September 1945 he resigned. Arthur Harris retired the same month under a cloud: Bomber Command, which had suffered the worst casualties in British history, was even denied the honour of a campaign medal.

4 Conclusions

Integrity and telling truth to power are part of the BBC credo. Impartiality and semi-detachment from the state were recognised by wartime Whitehall as useful assets in contesting the ether. The BBC attempted a less jingoistic reporting than much of the British print media. But it submitted to governmental news management and was guilty of suggesting that Bomber Command was not chiefly targeting civilians, when the reverse was true. The BBC's disputes with the Air Ministry appear to have been mainly over presentational matters. It is hard to find evidence of any principled policy discussion of the overall rights and wrongs of area bombing, but there is one slender file on "Bombs and Bombing – Policy", which records two prevalent attitudes in Broadcasting House: "1. The so-called rational point of view – it is our business to explain that heavy bombing must be accepted, because it shortens the war. 2. The view that we must off-set pity by explaining the thing we are fighting against, e.g. by reminding listeners of the bombing of Rotterdam." The second might invite calls for revenge, but, so this moral economist calculated, a "possible compromise is to off-set smaller pity by larger pity. The war must be shortened, if necessary, by the most drastic methods, because Jews are being tortured and children are dying of hunger." A handwritten addendum simply suggested that "it was probably more important to avoid wrong handling of this subject than to think out any positive policy." (WAC 1943d). This was a rationale for doing nothing.

There is, of course, no conclusive evidence that area bombing did shorten the war; interrogated German leaders in 1945 had worried more about oil-refineries than city-centres. As the war progressed and Germany's fortunes worsened, Goebbels' propaganda became ever more unhinged. The BBC's propaganda value, despite sins of omission, still rested on a core of truth. The news never falsified numbers of RAF aircraft shot down, despite concealing how many sorties were flown (so that a loss ratio could never be calculated). The BBC was simply selective in the truths it told, practising "bias by elimination", as one insider called it (Eckersley 1941, 158). Goebbels, on the other hand, went on to ever greater lies. When casualty statistics came in from Dresden in spring 1945 in tens of thousands, he simply added a zero to magnify the horror (Taylor 2004, 370). "Lies have short legs", so the German saying goes. The truth caught up with the "Little Herr Doktor", as Frau Wernicke derisively called him. By the capitulation, the only Berliners still believing Goebbels' propaganda were either utterly fanatical or terminally indifferent.

The postwar BBC became a semi-militarised organisation, filling with demobbed forces' personnel. Hugh Greene himself had served in RAF intelligence in 1940, but in 1944 Wing-Commander Kenneth Horne teamed up with Squadron Leader Richard Murdoch, better known to BBC listeners from the pre-war comedy *Band Waggon*, in the anarchic hit *Much-Binding-in-the-Marsh*, set on a fictional RAF airbase-cum-airport (Johnston 2006, 57–97). Peacetime saw other senior soldiers and men from the ministry entering civvy street. General Ian Jacob, Churchill's military assistant secretary, became BBC European Service head in 1946 and Director-General in 1952 (Richardson 1991, 233–62). His deputy was Norman Bottomley, Arthur Harris's successor as head of RAF Bomber Command from 1945 to 1947. It is a quirk of town-planning that Harris's controversial statue in London's Strand is only a stone's throw from Bush House, keeping an eternal vigil on the building that had nightly broadcast "Hier ist England!". Opposite Bush House sits the former Air Ministry, all within sight of Nelson's Column. But the Air Marshal could never be accused of turning a blind eye to uncomfortable truths. At the height of the Battle of Berlin, he warned that a cover-up "will inevitably lead to deplorable controversies when the facts are fully and generally known" (TNA 1943F). While Harris got many things wrong, on this he was surely right.

Could British wartime society have stood more critical debate? Certainly. As shown above, the British public could read between the lines of BBC broadcasting – it was an open secret that area bombing killed German civilians. Yet, despite an abiding interest in the Second World War and Nazi atrocities, current public curiosity about the darker side of Britain's war effort seems at an all-time low. In 2023 BBC Radio 4's Today programme commemorated the eightieth anniversary of the Dam Busters, but there was no exploration of the concurrent fire-bombing raids, despite a state visit to Hamburg by the new King Charles III. Myths of national identity often cohere around moments of wartime defence, in the UK case the Battle of Britain. "London Can Take It!" ran the slogan. The air Battle of Berlin, by contrast, represented a phase of the war when Britain was dishing it out. Despite almost as many Berliners dying cumulatively as Dresdeners, Berlin's bombing does not figure prominently in British consciousness. This may be partly due to a repressed sense of shame, and partly to the Berlin Airlift, flown by many former bomber pilots, when an effort of common Cold War defiance produced a moment of postwar reconciliation. But it was also because the air Battle of Berlin rated as a defeat, or at best a draw. Britons were used to winning.

During Brexit, the (Dis)United Kingdom fractured across mythic fault-lines of identity politics, many harking back to 1939–45. Yet rarely is the jugular instinct that actually decides wars revealed in the Second World War's cultural remembrance. The hard-hitting docudrama *Bomber Harris* (BBC 1, 1989), starring John Thaw and nominated for a BAFTA, was one exception, exploring the killer *Realpolitik* behind Britain's wartime leaders. Older documentary series such as *War in the Air* (BBC TV, 1954–55), made with Air Ministry cooperation, while granting German civilians a defiant voice, still obfuscated the issue of area bombing. Other, more recent documentaries, such as *Bomber Boys* (BBC 1, 2012), while empathising with the suffering of Hamburg's survivors, suggest that the chief victims of the air war were the bomber crews themselves (MacKenzie 2019, 112–17, 143–51). But can one equate professional soldiers and volunteers with civilians, however much individuals may have been economically implicated in a criminal regime? Post-Elizabethan Britain seems finally able to confront historical blind-spots over slavery and wars of decolonisation, but are we ready to do the same for the hidden histories of the Second World War? Since the BBC helped script the national wartime narrative, it is a good place to begin deconstructing binary, heroic myths, towards a more complex history. Britain can take it!

References

Adler, Bruno. 1990. *Frau Wernicke: Kommentare einer „Volksjenossin"*. Ed. Uwe Naumann. Mannheim: Persona.

Bennett, Lowell. 1945. *Parachute to Berlin*. New York: Vanguard.

Boberach, Heinz. Ed. 1984–85. *Meldungen aus dem Reich: Die geheimen Lageberichte des Sicherheitsdienstes der SS 1938–1945*. 18 vols. Herrsching: Manfred Pawlak.

Brinitzer, Carl. 1969. *Hier spricht London: Von einem der dabei war*. Hamburg: Hoffmann & Campe.

Connelly, Mark. 2002. "The British People, the Press and the Strategic Air Campaign against Germany, 1939–45". *Contemporary British History* 16.2: 39–58.

Cooper, Anthony with Thorsten Perl. 2023. *Dispatch from Berlin, 1943: The Story of Five Journalists Who Risked Everything*. Sydney: New South.

Dimbleby, Jonathan. 1975. *Richard Dimbleby: A Biography*. London: Hodder & Stoughton.

Dimbleby, Richard. 1944. *The Waiting Year*. London: Hodder & Stoughton.

Eckersley, P.P. 1941. *The Power behind the Microphone*. London: Cape.

Frost, Helen Lorri. 2022. "The British Bombing Offensive: Media Representation and Public Perception, 1939–1945". (unpublished PhD thesis, University of Exeter).

Hannon, Brian P.D. 2008. "Creating the Correspondent: How the BBC Reached the Frontline in the Second World War". *Historical Journal of Film, Radio and Television* 2.2 (2008): 175–94.

Hansard, House of Lords Debates, 124 (4 August): 184.

Harris. 1943. Bracken to Harris, 2 February. Harris papers 87. Arthur Harris papers, RAF Museum, Hendon, London.

Harris. 1944. Morton to Harris, 21 January; Harris papers 65. Arthur Harris papers, RAF Museum, Hendon, London.

Havers, Richard. 2007. *Here Is the News: The BBC and the Second World War*. Stroud: Sutton.

Holman, Brett. 2012. "'Bomb Back, and Bomb Hard': Debating Reprisals during the Blitz". *Australian Journal of Politics and History*. 58.3. 394–407.

Johnston, Barry. 2006. *Round Mr Horne: The Life of Kenneth Horne*. London: Aurum.

Kirchner, Klaus. 1991. *Flugblattpropaganda im 2. Weltkrieg*, iv: *Flugblätter aus England G-1942*. Erlangen: D & C Verlag.

Knapp, Andrew. 2013. "The Allied Bombing Offensive in the British Media, 1942–45". *Liberal Democracies at War: Conflict and Representation*. Eds. Andrew Knapp and Hilary Footitt. London: Bloomsbury. 39–66.

Landesarchiv Berlin. 1943. Hauptluftschutzstelle. A Rep 05-007/55. Landesarchiv, Berlin Germany.

MacKenzie, S.P. 2019. *Bomber Boys on Screen: RAF Bomber Command in Film and Television Drama*. London: Bloomsbury.

McLaine, Ian. 1979. *Ministry of Morale: Home Front Morale and the Ministry of Information in World War II*. London: Allen & Unwin.

Miall, Leonard (ed.). 1966. *Richard Dimbleby, Broadcaster: By His Colleagues*. London: BBC.

Moorehead, Kristina. 2016. *Satire als Kriegswaffe: Strategien der britischen Rundfunkpropaganda im Zweiten Weltkrieg*. Marburg: Tectum.

Oliver, Emily. 2020. "Inventing a New Kind of German: The BBC German Service and the Bombing War". In *Allied Communication to the Public during the Second World War*. Eds. Simon Eliot and Marc Wiggam. London: Bloomsbury: 149–65.

Persico, Joseph E. 1988. *Edward R. Murrow: An American Original*. New York: McGraw-Hill.

Plock, Vike Martina. 2021. *The BBC German Service during the Second World War: Broadcasting to the Enemy*. London: Palgrave Macmillan.

Richardson, Charles. 1991. *From Churchill's Secret Circle to the BBC: The Biography of Lieutenant General Sir Ian Jacob*: London: Brassey's.

Taylor, Frederick. 2004. *Dresden: Tuesday 13 February 1945*. London: Bloomsbury.

TNA. 1940a. Home Intelligence 85. 26 August. INF 1/264. Ministry of Information. The National Archives (TNA), Kew, London, UK.

TNA. 1940b. Home Intelligence 86. 27 August. INF 1/264. Ministry of Information. The National Archives, Kew, London, UK.

TNA. 1941. Peirse to Peake. 25 April. AIR 2/5309. Air Ministry. The National Archives, Kew, London, UK.

TNA. 1942a. Freeman to ACAS(G). 6 April. AIR 20/2950. Air Ministry. The National Archives, Kew, London, UK.

TNA. 1942b. PWE/Propaganda Research. 2 August. FO 898/317. Foreign Office. The National Archives, Kew, London, UK.

TNA. 1942c. Home Intelligence Special Report. 7 August. INF 1/293. Ministry of Information. The National Archives, Kew, London, UK.

TNA. 1942d. Freeman to Portal, 16 September. AIR 20/2950. Air Ministry. The National Archives, Kew, London, UK.

TNA. 1942–44. "Area Attack Assessment" data sheets. HO 192/1642. Ministry of Home Security. Research and Experiments Department (RE8). The National Archives, Kew, London, UK.

TNA. 1942–45. "Damage Diagrams: German Cities [A-E] before and after Raids". AIR 14/3682. Air Ministry. The National Archives, Kew, London, UK.

TNA. 1943a. Bindon to Peck, 21 January. AIR 20/2950. Air Ministry. The National Archives, Kew, London, UK.

TNA. 1943b. Harris to Street. 25 October. AIR 2/7852. Air Ministry. The National Archives, Kew, London, UK.

TNA. 1943c. Peck to Bottomley. 3 November. AIR 2/7852. Air Ministry. The National Archives, Kew, London, UK.

TNA. 1943d. Home Intelligence 165. 2 December. INF 1/292. Ministry of Information. The National Archives, Kew, London, UK.

TNA. 1943e. Home Intelligence 166. 9 December. INF 1/292. Ministry of Information. The National Archives, Kew, London, UK.

TNA. 1943f. Harris to Air Council, 23 December. AIR 2/7852. Air Ministry. The National Archives, Kew, London, UK.

TNA. 1944a. Home Intelligence 171. 13 January. INF 1/292. Ministry of Information. The National Archives, Kew, London, UK.

TNA. 1944b. Moore to Peck. 21 March. AIR 20/4181. Air Ministry. The National Archives, Kew, London, UK.

TNA. 1944c. Home Intelligence 182. 30 March. INF 1/292. Ministry of Information. The National Archives, Kew, London, UK.

TNA. 1945. Churchill to Ismay, 28 March. AIR 8/427. Air Ministry. The National Archives, Kew, London, UK.

TNA. 1954. Winston Churchill to Anthony Eden. 1 November. FO 371/109343. Foreign Office. The National Archives, Kew, London, UK.

The Times. 1937. 17 July.

The Times. 1942. 31 July.

Vaughan-Thomas, Wynford. 1980. *Trust to Talk*. London: Hutchinson.

Willmy, Lukas. 2024. *Operation Donnerschlag: Imperiale Aufstandsbekämpfung aus der Luft und das „Morale Bombing" deutscher Städte durch die britische Royal Air Force 1945*. Göttingen: Wallstein.

Worrall, Richard. 2019. *Battle of Berlin 1943–44: Bomber Harris' Gamble to End the War*. Oxford and New York: Osprey.

WAC. 1940. 26 August, 18:00. Home News Bulletin 39. BBC Written Archives Centre, Caversham, UK.

WAC. 1941a. Ryan to C(H), 25 January. R34/856-1. BBC Written Archives Centre, Caversham, UK.

WAC. 1941b. Beauman memorandum. 4 May. R34/856-1. BBC Written Archives Centre, Caversham, UK.

WAC. 1941c. 8 November, 21:00. Home News Bulletin 65. BBC Written Archives Centre, Caversham, UK.

WAC. 1942a. Boyd to C(NC). 15 June; R34/856-1. BBC Written Archives Centre, Caversham, UK.

WAC. 1942. Snagge to C(NC). 22 June. R34/856-1. BBC Written Archives Centre, Caversham, UK.

WAC. 1943a. Foot to Portal. 5 February. R34/856-2. BBC Written Archives Centre, Caversham, UK.

WAC. 1943b. Foot to Peck. 10 May. R34/856-2. BBC Written Archives Centre, Caversham, UK.

WAC. 1943c. DT memorandum. 2 June. R34/261. BBC Written Archives Centre, Caversham, UK.

WAC. 1943d. 25 July, 21:00. Home News Bulletin 97. BBC Written Archives Centre, Caversham, UK.

WAC. 1943e. Listener Research report. 7 October. R46/8-1. BBC Written Archives Centre, Caversham, UK.

WAC. 1943f. 23 October, 13:00. Home News Bulletin 101. BBC Written Archives Centre, Caversham, UK.

WAC. 1943g. 19 November, 18:00. Home News Bulletin 103. BBC Written Archives Centre, Caversham, UK.

WAC. 1943h. 24 November, 13:00. Home News Bulletin 103. BBC Written Archives Centre, Caversham, UK.

WAC. 1943i. 24 November, 21:00. Home News Bulletin 103. BBC Written Archives Centre, Caversham, UK.

WAC. 1943j. 25 November, 21:00. Home News Bulletin 103. BBC Written Archives Centre, Caversham, UK.

WAC. 1943k. 25 November, 21:00. Home News Bulletin 103. BBC Written Archives Centre, Caversham, UK.

WAC. 1943l. 3 December, 18:00. Home News Bulletin 104. BBC Written Archives Centre, Caversham, UK.

WAC. 1943m. 3 December, Home News Bulletin 104. BBC Written Archives Centre, Caversham, UK.

WAC. 1945. Dimbleby to C(N), 6 January. L1/131/1. BBC Written Archives Centre, Caversham, UK.

CHAPTER 4

Music in the Shadow of War: National Identity, Broadcasting and the Changing Canon

Nicholas Kenyon

It was doubtless a coincidence that as we gathered for this Berlin and the BBC conference in the city, in the Philharmonie concert hall (which sits on the very edge of the old west Berlin but is now near the centre of today's cultural city) the world-famous Berliner Philharmoniker – as it now styles itself – played for the first time in its history the Symphony in F sharp written in 1947–52 by the Austrian composer Erich Wolfgang Korngold. Nothing surprising there you might think – a revival of an interesting rarity which might or might not establish itself in the repertory.

But in fact this was quite a statement, one of some relevance to the changing canon of classical music, especially as this distinguished orchestra was at that point in 2022 about to tour this symphony around the United States. This is an orchestra that formed its canonic repertory essentially around the nineteenth-century staples of Beethoven and Brahms. It used to be said that when Herbert von Karajan toured with the orchestra, the only question to be answered was in what order the four Brahms symphonies were to be played. Of course, the orchestra's repertory was and continued to be far wider than this, expanding outwards from this central core, but there was an important sense in which this orchestra's choices, and those of their conductors, defined the changing canon of mainstream classical music.

Erich Korngold (Carroll 2001) was an extreme example of a youthful prodigy, who had had his first piece performed by the Berlin Philharmonic when he was just fifteen, in 1912. This was the same year that Henry Wood introduced his music to the Proms in London, as far as we know the youngest composer ever featured there (rather to the irritation of some later prodigies). He was feted; Korngold became an extremely successful opera composer, widely performed in Germany. But with the coming of the National Socialist regime, he was silenced in the Philharmonic's repertory and in German music-making – a silence which continued and lasted for some seventy years. Why?

Korngold had been invited to work in America as a film composer, and his first project in 1934 was to arrange the music of another composer of Jewish descent, Felix Mendelssohn, in Max Reinhardt's magical film of *A Midsummer*

 | HTTPS://DOI.ORG/10.1515/9783111302508-004

Night's Dream. That score is a fascinating amalgam of past and present, in that Korngold arranges Mendelssohn's music but then adds to it, rescores it and makes it suitable for contemporary use in film. (It is reminiscent of what in a previous age Mozart added to Handel's Messiah to make it suitable for audiences of the time.) Korngold went on to develop what has been characterised as the genre of "symphonic film score", winning Academy Awards for *Anthony Adverse* and *The Adventures of Robin Hood*. In 1938 after the Anschluss in Austria, Korngold decided to stay and work in the United States.

Korngold's music was not heard at the Berlin Philharmonic for many years after the war and the end of the Nazi regime. He had fallen totally out of fashion in the post-war era, his film music causing snobbish disdain among many serious musicians, and the letters of rejection he had about this very symphony from prominent conductors were many. So here we have a somewhat toxic mixture of anti-Jewish prejudice, anti-film-music snobbism, and generally changing taste all combining to outlaw his music. By the time of his death at the age of 60 in 1957, he felt totally neglected – and that was true, until the later revival of his appealing Violin Concerto of 1937, which established itself in the repertory of many violin soloists. It turned a corner in the reception of his work, and stimulated a broader if gradual revival.

The Berlin Philharmonic's first performances of the symphony in 2022 are therefore surely a conscious act of restitution, and something of an act of homage by a German orchestra to its audiences in the United States who gave Korngold a home. In an equal signal of gradually shifting taste, the same symphony has recently been recorded in Britain with great success by the Sinfonia of London under conductor John Wilson, who not coincidentally has also revived much great film music (Korngold 2019).

This reclamation sadly didn't happen in Korngold's lifetime, but another example did. Berthold Goldschmidt (Matthews 1993) was an experienced conductor and composer who had worked in the 1920s on the premiere of Berg's opera *Wozzeck*, and wrote an opera which was due to be performed in Berlin in 1933 but which was cancelled. He left Berlin in 1935 and came to live in Belsize Park in North London. I think when he came to England he had hoped to be involved in the new opera company that was being formed at Glyndebourne, as he had worked with their conductor Carl Ebert in Darmstadt, and but that did not happen. There was stringent protectionism on the part of British musicians towards their jobs, and increasingly strong government edicts about providing work to immigrant aliens.

When Goldschmidt came to England his own music was not taken up by the BBC; but one ballet score was commissioned by Kurt Jooss's ballet company based at Dartington Hall in Devon, and income from the tours of that work, *Chronica,* sustained him. However, he did work for the BBC: towards the close of the war, Goldschmidt was employed by the BBC German Service. He collaborated with Martin Esslin on the provision of music for Germany, and was able to present to German listeners music that the Nazis had banned, for instance by Mahler and Mendelssohn, and performances by Jewish artists. After the war he was able to establish himself as a conductor: he worked with Glyndebourne, initially as chorus master, and then conducting Verdi's *Macbeth* with the company at the Edinburgh Festival in 1947. Goldschmidt became an advocate for Mahler, conducting the Philharmonia Orchestra in Mahler's Third Symphony for the composer's centenary in 1959, and was then involved in the completion of Mahler's Tenth Symphony by the BBC's Deryck Cooke. Goldschmidt conducted the BBC Proms premiere of that completion with the London Symphony Orchestra in 1964.

It was Simon Rattle, then conductor of the City of Birmingham Symphony Orchestra, who had the notion to bring one of Goldschmidt's pieces back to Berlin with his orchestra in 1987, and to bring the composer as well. The intendant of the Berlin Philharmonic, Elmar Weingarten, described movingly what happened: "Now for years nothing had been played by him in Berlin, and Simon made a little speech hinting at the importance of the situation which was really very touching. The *Ciaconna sinfonica* was played, and when the run-through was over Berthold Goldschmidt got up and said this one marvellous, unforgettable sentence – 'You Simon Rattle, and you the orchestra, are picking up a thread which I left here sixty years ago'" (Kenyon 2001, 24). We were all moved to tears. From then on Berthold's career in Germany started again. And indeed his music was then increasingly performed in the UK and broadcast by the BBC. Eventually the opera he wrote for the Festival of Britain in 1951, but which was never performed at the time, *Beatrice Cenci,* was heard. We performed his *Passacaglia* at the BBC Proms in 1996, shortly before his death in October that year.

The relations between Berlin and the BBC had a significant impact on the development of BBC music in its earliest formative years. The weightiness and seriousness of the German commitment to orchestral music had a real influence in Britain. It was undoubtedly the visit of the Berlin Philharmonic Orchestra to the UK in 1928 under Wilhelm Furtwängler which finally convinced us in Britain that something had to be done about our orchestral standards (Kenyon 1981). As was reported at the time, "its remarkable dexterity set the town aflame" and *The Times* critic recalled that "the British public was electrified when it heard their disciplined precision. This was apparently how an orchestra could and therefore ought to sound". That view reflected back on the BBC and criticism of its orchestral standards: *The Musical Times* wrote that "with all its assumed and conspicuous wealth, it has given and is giving us the worst orchestral performances ever heard in London" (Kenyon 1981, 14).

This situation, unacceptable to the relatively new BBC which took its standards very seriously, led directly to the plan to found the BBC Symphony Orchestra in 1930, based on full-time contracted players of the highest quality. BBC executives visited Berlin and "paid several visits to the headquarters of the Berlin Philharmonic, sat in on rehearsals, had discussions with the authorities about musicians' contracts, pay, hours worked and so on". They also went to Vienna and Budapest, and the BBC's Roger Eckersley added in his memoirs that "we did not have much excuse for going to Buda Pest but I did want to see some broadcasting studios which were more up to date than any others on the Continent" (Kenyon 1981, 15).

The subsequent success of the BBC's new orchestra from 1930 under their conductor Adrian Boult was immediate. And so it happened that in England it was the *broadcaster* which increasingly became the determiner of the repertory and the patron of composers. The fact that this turned out to be such a strongly-profiled repertory, as Annika Forkert discusses in her recent book, was due to a combination of Boult's remarkable open-mindedness, and the presence on the BBC's staff of the Schoenberg pupil Edward Clark (Forkert 2023, ch. 2). The commitment of the BBC to what could broadly be called adventurous musical modernism was criticised at the time, but it was also accepted as a logical part of the BBC's self-imposed top-down, always paternal role to inform and educate, if possibly not always in this case to entertain.

It was thanks to Clark that an extraordinary succession of BBC contemporary music concerts took place in the 1930s (Doctor 1999). The living composers supported by Clark and Boult who received performances (often UK premieres or first performances) in this series included Schoenberg, Webern and Manuel de Falla in 1931, Busoni and Bartók in 1932, Berg, Hindemith and Kodály in 1933, Stravinsky and Prokofiev in 1934. In his choice of important composing talent, Clark did not get it wrong. And it is notable that as the 1930s continued, composers no longer welcomed in Germany were performed, including the first UK performance under Webern of Berg's Violin Concerto, soon to become a classic of the repertory, as well as works by Weill and Hindemith.

Indeed, Hindemith who was also a viola player became something of a regular visitor to the BBC, and when King George V died in January 1936, at a moment when Hindemith was due to appear with the BBC Orchestra, the composer recalled "we debated for hours, but no suitable piece could be found, so we decided that I should write some funeral music myself ... a studio was cleared for me, copyists were gradually stoked up, and from 11 to 5 I did some fairly hefty mourning. I turned out a nice piece [called *Trauermusik*] ... It was very moving. Boult was, by English and his own personal standards, quite beside himself, and kept thanking me. I'm now going to specialise in deceased persons, maybe there will be more opportunities" (Kenyon 1981, 117). (This incident may be compared with the present BBC's more risk-averse response to the most recent death of the British monarch in 2022, which was to cancel the three remaining Proms concerts of the season.)

One of the issues raised by the BBC's support for advanced contemporary repertory was how far it should respond to the clamorous demands of the British musical profession to a better representation of national music on the air. The BBC's Music Advisory Committee, which represented entrenched national interests, was continually complaining about the absence of their own music, prompting the BBC executive Kenneth Wright to complain that "there is hardly one member of the committee who has any real sympathy with, true understanding of, or live interest in present-day musical developments" (Kenyon 1981, 93).

With what one senses was a feeling of dutiful weariness, the BBC promoted an entire Festival of British Music in 1934. This caused the composer Constant Lambert, whose own music was included in the series, to make the cutting remark that "if a work is a bad one it should not be considered representative of British music merely because the composer has been writing long enough to know better" (Kenyon 1981, 94). The series was designed to please the composers, not the audience, and rather few people came.

There was a point of principle here: the extent to which broadcasters, in creating a repertory for listeners, should in principle favour national music, whether or not they were operating under the shadow of war. In Germany the answer was usually in the affirmative because the country believed with some justification that it had produced the greatest quantity of great music of the past. The rise of radio in Germany, as in Britain, both took place in the 1920s; in Germany the rise of National Socialism coincided, and by the time the regime took over in 1933, the Minister of Propaganda, aware of the growing power of radio, seized control of the radio airwaves even before the press. However, Erik Levi suggests that the change in radio programming at this point was less radical than it might have been, because Joseph Goebbels did not want radio to lose its hold on people and personally instructed the broadcasters: "Do not think that you can serve the Nazi Government best by the sound of blaring marches evening after evening". There was however quite a shift to light music and entertainment music, while the serious music repertory was extended with coverage of the anti-semitic late-romantic composer Felix Draeseke, and a special performance of a long-forgotten and indeed justly neglected score *Fahnenschwur* by Wagner's son Siegfried in celebration of Hitler's birthday (Levi 1994, 131).

However as early as 1934, radio director Eugen Hadamovsky began an ambitious project to claim central monuments of European culture as specifically German and as Levi puts it "to fashion German musical heritage in terms of their own ideology" (Levi 1994, 132) The prime candidate for this role was the symphonic cycle of Beethoven whose nine symphonies were relayed from Berlin, Cologne, Frankfurt, Munich and Leipzig in two weeks in February 1934. As one radio magazine put it, "the Beethoven cycle is an incomparable achievement, and it elevates the entire German nation welding the radio into a reliable instrument for the Führer" (Levi 1994, 133). These broadcasts also fulfilled the role of demonstrating to the rest of Europe that the regime was sponsoring constructive cultural projects.

It is not our purpose here to revisit the much-discussed subject of Wilhelm Furtwängler's agonised interactions with the authorities over composers with Jewish origins and links, but it is worth reminding ourselves of the extent to which the Beethoven symphonies and the Ninth Symphony in particular became a crucial symbol of homage to the regime. This reached its apotheosis, as it were, in the infamous performance for Hitler's birthday in 1942 given on 19 April in the presence of Goebbels, which was filmed (newsreel versions are available on YouTube). Nazi banners drape the stage, the audience includes wounded soldiers, and at the end of the symphony Goebbels approaches the stage to shake hands with Furtwängler. (Does the conductor somehow move his handkerchief to wipe his hand? The film is not quite clear.)

The direct colonisation of Beethoven in the 1930s was followed by that of Wagner, in whom Hitler himself was even more interested, then Bach and then even Mozart – fourteen broadcasts of his music were said to be "a symbol of permanent greatness and the expression of the German spirit, proud, serene, strong, true and profound" (Levi 1994, 136). They even had an attempt at owning Handel, but the British were not going to let their adopted composer go so easily.

Furtwängler and the Berlin Philharmonic solidified the commitment to German music by choosing innocuous contemporary composers replacing the likes of Mahler, Schoenberg and Korngold. In the 1938 season, more than half the orchestra's repertoire consisted of music by six composers: Beethoven, Brahms, Bruckner, Haydn, Mozart and Richard Strauss. This is very striking: if you added Wagner to that then only 11 of the Philharmonic's 77 public concerts in Berlin did *not* contain their music. Much has rightly been written about the exclusion of Jewish and so-called decadent composers, but this list also deserves attention for what it shows about German identity.

The question that then arose was: to what extent were others prepared to let Beethoven, born in Bonn but a key part of Viennese musical tradition, be perceived as an exclusively German composer? As context for this it is instructive to look back and see what happened in England during the First World War. Before the BBC took over the Proms in 1927, the Proms were financially supported by a German financier, Edgar Speyer, who had become accepted as a member of the British establishment with a baronetcy and a seat on the Privy Council. He was immediately in a difficult position when war broke out, and as the 1914 Proms started there was intense caution: a Richard Strauss piece was dropped from the first night, and the traditional Wagner night the following Monday was hastily reprogrammed (Langley 2007).

But Proms conductor Henry Wood had always been committed to contemporary European repertory in the Proms season, and had premiered Debussy, Schoenberg, Mahler alongside much else. There was a rear-guard action, and the Proms manager Robert Newman wrote that "the directors hope, with the broad-minded co-operation of their audience—to carry through as nearly as possible the original scheme of the concerts. They take this opportunity of emphatically contradicting the statements that German music will be boycotted during the present season. The greatest examples of Music and Art are world possessions and unassailable even by the prejudices and passion of the hour" (Jacobs 1994, 149).

That position held, though new works by living Austro-German composers were still withdrawn. The composer Peter Warlock (the pen-name of Philip Heseltine) reported back to his friend Delius that "the programmes have been worse than usual and the audiences as a result proportionately larger" (Kenyon 2007, 260). Also indicative was the alternative route followed in 1916 by rival concerts at the Albert Hall under Thomas Beecham and others which banned all German music, even Bach and Beethoven. Those concerts failed with the public.

At this point, Beethoven was at the heart of a classical canon in the orchestral repertory that had emerged which was wholly Germanic in its outlines and its lineage. A historian of the musical canon, William Weber, has identified a performing canon which he says "involves the presentation of old works organised as repertoires and defined as sources of authenticity with regard to musical taste" (Weber 1999, 340). Meaning in simpler terms that there arose or was created a solid consensus as to which composers and what pieces are important.

The question of why performers choose to perform what they perform, has been the subject of very little reflection. For every performer who wants to expand the repertory, there are many, perhaps especially conductors, who want to perform what they know audiences want to hear. Is it the test of time that determines for example whether new work survives? That is a highly flexible and volatile concept shaped by the forces of history. In an analogous study of this in the context of literature, Barbara Herrnstein Smith says this test of time "is not an impersonal and impartial mechanism, for the cultural institutions though which it operates (schools, libraries, theatres, museums, publishing houses, editorial boards, prize-awarding commissions, state censors and so forth) are of course all managed by people and the texts that are selected and preserved by time will always tend to be those which fit their characteristic needs, interests, resources and purposes" (Smith 1983, 29; Cook and Everist 1999). And that is equally true of music and its institutions, and especially true in times of extreme nationalism, or under the shadow of war.

Those of us who programme concerts, festivals and radio broadcasts can all share the blame here. The point at issue is that the orchestral canon that emerged in the nineteenth century and arguably became over-ossified in the public mind was one based on the Germanic heritage with Beethoven in its centre: the succession of Haydn, Mozart, Beethoven, Brahms, Bruckner, Wagner, maybe adding Bach at the beginning and Richard Strauss at the end. That was, not at all coincidentally, what the Berlin Philharmonic foregrounded in the 30s.

But other music began to enter our repertory with ever greater regularity thanks usually to the passion of a few supporters and a few enlightened conductors, which had previously been regarded as eccentric (in the sense of outside the centre) for one reason or another: a good example is the music of Berlioz, with its French tradition of superbly coloured sound rather than dominating formal structure. (You can still come across Berlioz being patronised and written off because he didn't write in sonata form.) From outside the central tradition there are Rossini's operas and the Russian nationalists, Liszt's orchestral music too. Arnold Schoenberg tried to place himself as the author of a new reworked Germanic tradition, but it was rather the magpie-like, eclectic Igor Stravinsky who succeeded in forming so much of what we now think of as twentieth-century taste.

If we seek the critical change that blew this arguably stifling and dangerous consensus apart, it is now pretty obvious: it was *radio*, recordings, and the availability of a vast range of music through broadcasting and recording that had never occurred before. Because before, the only music was *live* music you heard in the concert hall, and maybe bought in piano duets to play at home.

Increasingly there was the availability of music of all times and ages as performers began to revive that repertory. Rather than a linear development, instead we now began to experience the simultaneity of all music. We were very slow to realise the implications of these developments, and they have of course been vastly accelerated in our generation by the easy availability of access through internet and search engines to the widest possible repertory, both classical and non-classical. But it highlights the vital importance of the BBC in Britain, and broadcasters in Germany, in forming public taste alongside the record companies.

In considering the part of the BBC in its centenary year in this radical cultural change, I have begun to look at how shifting ideas of national identity have changed our listening tastes, especially as created by the music of the more distant past. We have already noted how the BBC was committed to adventurous contemporary music as chronicled by Jenny Doctor (Doctor 1999). But it was also increasingly involved in the revival of earlier music, and the development of the 1930s was to bring to the airwaves the music of Henry Purcell, the choral music of the Elizabethan era, Tallis and Byrd, newly edited madrigals and instrumental music – and this is the context in which Toby Thacker's fascinating chapter on Ernst Hermann Meyer is so relevant. Meyer's intense and scholarly work on seventeenth-century instrumental music is a key link between Germany and the BBC (even though his attempts to have his *own* music broadcast by the BBC was no more successful than Berthold Goldschmidt's in this period). What Meyer and the BBC were doing together was to attempt to radically extend the canon in the direction of the past, just as Edward Clark was pushing it into the future.

The shifting and sometimes controversial picture can be seen clearly in arguments around the BBC's famous series *Foundations of Music*, which was inaugurated in 1927 and planned by the BBC's adviser Filson Young, a lively figure who also wrote about sport, and wrote the first book about the sinking of the Titanic. Filson Young's scheme for the *Foundations* series was highly traditional, and has been cited by Megan Prictor in her interesting chapter in the English/German essay collection *Music as a Bridge* (Prictor 2005), as demonstrating the continuing dominance of the Germanic canon on British music at this time, where she quotes the line that "Bach and Beethoven are Gods". But while those composers were indeed revered, the archives of the programme show that the repertory of the Foundations began to expand beyond its founder's conservative vision, and an outraged Filson Young complained to the BBC that the series had been "deluged by a flood of 16th-century plainsong [he actually meant polyphony] choral and harpsichord music – a kind of music which appeals to the very narrowest minority of cultivated musicians and to the general public hardly at all" (Kenyon 2022, 47).

Actually, taste was changing fast, and by the time we reach the landmark of the coronation of a new King in 1937, *The Times* critic was able to remark that "what distinguished the coronation of King George VI from those of George V and Edward VII was the prominence given to Tudor choral music, sung without orchestral accompaniment, a form which had undergone a major revival of interest following the English Musical Renaissance" (Kenyon 2022, 48). We do not want to linger here in the complex question of who or what the English Musical Renaissance actually was, but in the revival of music from Britain's distant past there was already a ready answer to the complaint – originally a German observation! – that we were the land without music (Schmidt 1914).

Britain remained committed to the central German repertory, and by the time of the Second World War, the judgement of author John Ramsden is that "there were few calls for the BBC to stop playing German music" (Ramsden 2006, 204–5; Kenyon 2007). Ironically, we created our own very powerful propaganda tool by taking the opening notes of Beethoven's Fifth Symphony, and creating the motto of V for Victory – an idea suggested in January 1941 by the Belgian Victor de Laveleye, who was the director of Belgian broadcasts in French on the BBC. Quite apart from its salience then, this V gesture has had an extremely long life from Churchill onwards – most recently in a series of video games praised as among the most playable series of war games available.

As a footnote, it was also the central repertory which formed a key part of one of the most distinctive British propaganda statements of the Second World War – Humphrey Jennings's stirring film *Listen to Britain*, made in the same year as the Furtwängler concert, 1942 (see Figure 4.1 overleaf). In this case it featured the music of Mozart and focussed on one of the pianist Myra Hess's famous concerts in the National Gallery, where she played a Mozart piano concerto to the delight of director Kenneth Clark and Queen Elizabeth (though they were apparently added later to the shot). With the empty picture frames as a reminder of the conflict, and a wounded solider, the healing power of music in the conflict is here boldly swept onwards into the external world of London, inspiring the hard industrial labour of working for victory. The sonorous introduction to the otherwise wordless film references "The BBC sending Truth on its journey around the world" (Jennings and McAllister 1942).

Everyone wants to claim great art. Only yards from where this conference on Berlin and the BBC took place, the conductor Leonard Bernstein colonised Beethoven's Ninth as the Berlin wall came down, and rewrote Schiller's text as a hymn to Freedom. Beethoven's Ninth remains an iconic work around the world, its message of universal brotherhood enabling it to stand for unity

FIGURE 4.1 Myra Hess (1890–1965), performing in concert at the National Gallery in London, originally broadcast by the BBC, and here featured in Humphrey Jennings' *Listen to Britain* (1942). (© Imperial War Museum)

across boundaries. Now fortunately the soft power of cultural exchange has replaced the desire for exclusive possession of musical repertoires. These exchanges can be heard every night on BBC radio through the enlightened programmes of countries in the European Broadcasting Union, enabling the concerts of participating countries and orchestras to be shared and heard by all. We can only hope that in the second century of the BBC's existence these cultural interactions between the BBC and Germany will prosper and flourish.

References

Brustle, Christa and Guido Heldt (eds). 2005. *Music as a Bridge: musikalische Beziehungen zwischen England und Deutschland 1920–1950*. Hildesheim, Zurich and New York: Olms.

Carroll, Brendan. 2001. "Erich Korngold". *The New Grove Dictionary of Music and Musicians*, 2nd edition. Ed. Stanley Sadie. London: Macmillan. 210.

Cook, Nicholas and Mark Everist. 1999. *Rethinking Music*. Oxford: Oxford University Press.

Doctor, Jennifer. 1999. *The BBC and Ultra-Modern Music, 1922–1936*. Cambridge: Cambridge University Press.

Everist, Mark. 1999. "Reception Theories, Canonic Discourses, and Musical Value". *Rethinking Music*. Eds. Nicholas Cook and Mark Everist. Oxford: Oxford University Press. 378–402.

Forkert, Annika. 2023. *Elisabeth Lutyens and Edward Clark: The Orchestration of Progress in British Twentieth-Century Music*. Cambridge: Cambridge University Press.

Jacobs, Arthur. 1994. *Henry J. Wood: Maker of the Proms*. London: Methuen.

Jennings, Humphrey and Stewart McAllister. 1942. "Listen to Britain". *Land of Promise: The British Documentary Movement 1930–1950*. London: BFI DVD. 756.

Kenyon, Nicholas. 1981. *The BBC Symphony Orchestra: the First Fifty Years*. London: BBC Publications.

Kenyon, Nicholas. 2001. *Simon Rattle: From Birmingham to Berlin*. London: Faber & Faber.

Kenyon, Nicholas. 2022. "Early Learning: Early Music at the BBC". *BBC Music Magazine* (December): 46–50.

Kenyon, Nicholas. 2007. "Planning the Proms Yesterday, Today, Tomorrow". *The Proms: a New History*. Eds. Jenny Doctor and David Wright. London: Thames and Hudson: 256–77.

Korngold, Erich Wolfgang. 2019. *Orchestral Works*. Vol. 4. London Sinfonia. Chandos.

Langley, Leanne. 2007. "Building an Orchestra, Creating an Audience". *The Proms: a New History*. Eds. Jenny Doctor and David Wright. London: Thames and Hudson: 32–73.

Levi, Erik. 1994. *Music in the Third Reich*. London: Macmillan.

Matthews, David. 1993. "Berthold Goldschmidt: a Biographical Sketch". *Tempo*, n. s.: 144: 2–6.

Prictor, Megan. 2005. "'Bach and Beethoven … are Gods'. The Role of the German Composer in English Music Appreciation, 1919–1939". *Music as a Bridge: musikalische Beziehungen zwischen England und Deutschland 1920–1950*. Eds. Christa Brustle and Guido Heidt. Hildesheim, Zurich and New York: Olms. 17–32.

Ramsden, John. 2006. *Don't Mention the War. The British and the Germans since 1890*. London: Little, Brown.

Schmidt, Oscar. 1914. *Das Land ohne Musik*, translated H. Herzl as *The Land without Music*. London: Jarrolds.

Smith, Barbara Herrnstein. 1983. "Contingencies of Value". *Critical Inquiry*. 10.1: 1–35.

Weber, William. 1999. "The History of Musical Canon". *Rethinking Music*. Eds. Nicholas Cook and Mark Everist. Oxford: Oxford University Press: 336–355.

CHAPTER 5

The Uses of Satire: Berlin and the BBC German Service during the Second World War

Vike Martina Plock

By the time the Second World War broke out, broadcasting had become a "means for world communication and exchange" (*BBC Handbook 1938*, 50). Technological advances in short-wave transmission put new radio publics around the world within the reach of European broadcasters vying for the attention of listeners faced with an increasingly globalised communications market. In January 1940, the BBC had become an important tool for wielding British soft power abroad, broadcasting daily news bulletins in thirteen foreign languages, including Afrikaans, Arabic, German, Polish, Romanian, Spanish and Turkish (*BBC Handbook 1940*, 15). In the early phase of the war, the Nazi state was equally, if not more effective in using transnational broadcasting as a means of political persuasion. In the summer of 1940, the *Reichs-Rundfunk Gesellschaft* (German Broadcasting Company) oversaw the production of broadcasts in thirty-one foreign languages (Bergmeier 1997, 22). Equally expansive were attempts by Nazi authorities to prevent the German population from listening in to programmes transmitted by the BBC and other so-called enemy stations. As Michael P. Hensle has demonstrated, fines as well as prison and death sentences were regularly imposed on so-called radio traitors (Hensle 2003, 72–97). However, while Hitler's totalitarian state aimed to isolate its citizens from the "disruptive" influence of British broadcasts (Birdsall 2012, 12), the number of Germans listening to BBC programmes throughout the war remained high. Contemporary sources estimate that between one and three million Germans regularly listened to BBC programmes during the first years of the war (Plock 2021, 238). These listeners clung to the British broadcaster's factual, ostensibly impartial news programmes that provided information withheld or distorted by Nazi media outlets.

Alongside news bulletins, the BBC experimented with satirical programmes to awaken and increase resistance against the Nazi system. As this chapter will show, Berlin inspired BBC writers and editors who tried to reach out to listeners in Nazi Germany. The temperament and the vernacular of the city's inhabitants had a reputation for plucky rebelliousness, an attitude that was meant to be roused in Germans tuning in to British broadcasts. Equally inspirational

© 2026 WALTER DE GRUYTER GMBH, BERLIN | HTTPS://DOI.ORG/10.1515/9783111302508-005

was a parodic art form that had become associated with the German capital during the years of the Weimar Republic. Outlawed or eroded of political content by the Nazi authorities, Berlin's lively cabaret scene of the 1920s was partially revived in the BBC's wartime German-language broadcasts. As was the case with the pro-democratic cabaret-revues of the Weimar years, these programmes aimed to exploit humour and laughter for subversive purposes. For some BBC German Service editors and script writers, Berlin had become an idealised abstraction for political disobedience that had found expression in parodic performances on cabaret stages in the German capital in the pre-Nazi era.

This time, however, geographical and ideological distance defined the relationship between performers and audiences. While Weimar cabaret stars could assume that spectators facing them in confined, often intimate performance spaces consisted of like-minded individuals, BBC editors were conscious that political satire programmes employed in the service of psychological persuasion had to contend with listeners potentially opposed to broadcasts targeting the Nazi regime. In this context, the frequent use of the stock Berliner was a useful ploy to sell Germans the idea that an Allied victory was inevitable and desirable. Easily recognisable and reassuringly familiar, the Berlin dialect and persona, it was believed at the BBC, could make listeners more receptive to the political messages disseminated in British radio programmes. These listeners could hardly ignore the fact that the voice of Britain was speaking to them in BBC broadcasts. News bulletins clearly reflected the British point of view of the war. But in satire programmes the situation became more complex. Here, the British broadcaster opted for a culturally hybrid transmission model, fusing British propaganda messages with linguistic, social and artistic codes drawn directly from German heritage contexts. Berlin as a place and concept was at the heart of this carefully designed BBC propaganda campaign.

1 Berlin Programmes and Vernacular Broadcasting

During the war, the BBC German Service generally avoided the use of place- and dialect-specific broadcasts (Plock 2021, 66–68). "Dialect Broadcasts," it was suggested, "would be out of the reach of the majority of listeners" (WAC 1941b). Airtime was precious and little could be gained in terms of propaganda delivery by commissioning and broadcasting regionally specialised programmes that were relevant for a small number of listeners. Because the use of dialect was such a contested issue, announcers on BBC German news programmes were instructed to aim for a neutral, linguistically inconspicuous delivery.

Unfortunately, this desire for neutrality in German-language news programmes took a decidedly anti-Semitic turn when incoming reports in 1940 suggested that target audiences had complained about the "Jewish voices of [...] BBC announcers." Declaring it "desirable, on principle, that Jews should not broadcast in German," the British Foreign Office and the BBC discriminated against individuals also targeted by the Nazi state (TNA 1940). There was room for sonic variety in the BBC's German-language broadcasts. But the right to use regional accents in news talks remained principally reserved for British personality speakers contributing programmes in German to the BBC's output for Nazi Germany. The principal example is Lindley Fraser, who became one of the most important British personality speakers for the BBC German Service during the war and who retained his Scottish accent when broadcasting to Nazi Germany (Plock 2021, 176–79). In cases like Fraser's, regionally specific accents detectable even if British broadcasters addressed listeners in German added authenticity to the delivery. They also assisted in the BBC's wider aim to pit British liberal democracy against Nazi totalitarianism. In Britain, these sonically varied broadcasts implied, diversity of voices and opinions is tolerated and actively encouraged.

In feature programmes relatability determined the creation of characters who spoke to German listeners on BBC airwaves. When the Jewish-Austrian refugee Robert Lucas designed a new satire programme for the BBC German Service in 1940, his character "Corporal Adolf Hirnschal" ["Hirnschal": "brain pan"] had to sound both authentic and generic. Speaking as the average German to other Germans, his idiom as well as his hometown had to remain untraceable (Lucas 1994, 254). In other feature programmes, geographical references remained similarly vague. The lead-in for one feature programme explained that it would take place "in the anteroom of a chamber of commerce in a north-west German city" ["im Vorraum des Wirtschaftsamtes in einem nordwestdeutschen Ort"] (WAC 1941c) [English translation mine]. Regionally specific dialect was conspicuously absent in the ensuing dialogue. In this and similar programmes, the BBC's propaganda campaign focused on using a widely recognisable architecture of everyday life to gain the attention and trust of listeners in Nazi Germany. Vernacular broadcasting and regional specificity might have reduced the relevance of these programmes.

Berlin was a notable exception in the BBC's inclusive approach to German-language broadcasting, featuring as the location chosen for two of the most popular satire programmes that the German Service produced during the Second World War. This happened even though the author of these programmes remained aware that the use of the Berlin dialect might be off-putting for listeners in other parts of Nazi Germany. "While it is an advantage that Frau

W. [his creation] does not speak the official news and paper language," he suggests, "it is on the other hand disadvantageous to the listeners of Southern German and Austrians to hear that Berlin dialect that they detest" (WAC 1940b). Despite the author's qualms, dialect was used freely and – as would be revealed after the war – effectively in these Berlin-focused satire programmes.

Launched in 1940, both of these satire programmes were written by the Jewish art historian Bruno Adler, who had been a Bauhaus lecturer before arriving in London as a refugee in 1936. Adler's first creation was "Frau Wernicke," a down-to-earth, intrepid housewife who spoke to German listeners about everyday concerns in a commonplace, everyday manner. Focusing on topics such as wartime shortages, air raids or casualty lists, "Frau Wernicke" expressed the fears and frustrations of German women living under Nazi rule. She continued to air her critical views about Hitler and the Nazi system until the programme was officially wrapped up on 29 January 1944 (Moorehead 2016, 380–88). "Kurt und Willi," Adler's other programme, focused on the concerns of a male radio public by reproducing conversations between teacher "Kurt Krüger" and his friend "Willi Schimanski," whose employment in Goebbels's Reich Ministry for Public Enlightenment and Propaganda allowed the character to explain and dismantle Nazi-fabricated propaganda lines. As Kristina Moorehead notes, "Kurt und Willi" programmes focused on "supposedly male-connotated topics such as military strategy, armament production, insurance policies and corruption within the Nazi leadership group" (Moorehead 2016, 158) [translation mine].

To create a sense of authenticity and immediacy, both Adler-penned programmes used Berlin locations as a backdrop for the characters' outspoken anti-Nazi commentaries. "Kurt" and "Willi" meet weekly for a glass of beer (or cognac) in their "usual café near the Potsdamer Platz" (WAC 1941d), while "Gertrud Wernicke" lives and operates in an East Berlin working-class neighbourhood on the Große Frankfurter Allee. Occasionally, however, "Frau Wernicke" also leaves her home to venture out into other parts of the big city. In a programme broadcast on 12 July 1941, for instance, she meets her sister Grete at the Potsdamer Platz. As the two women debate where to go, a prominent landmark of the interwar period becomes the focus of "Frau Wernicke's" comments which, eventually, culminate in a barely disguised satirical jibe at Hermann Göring:

> Where to? I don't mind, Grete. What? To Kempinski? No, no, what were you thinking, lassie, I won't enter until they've found a new name for that tavern. Did you know that you can win ten thousand coins if you find a good Aryan

> name? […] What do you think, for instance, of "Guesthouse Slim Pickens" under special direction of Reich Marshal Kitchen Master Blubberguts? [translation mine]
>
> [Wohin? Mir is det ejal, Jrete. Wat? Zu Kempinski? Nee, nee, wo denkste hin, Meechen, da setz ich keen Fuß rin, solange die nich nen neuen Namen jefunden ham for det Lokal. Du, weeßte, det de zehntausend Emmchen verdien' kannst, wenn de nen jut ar'schen Namen findest? […] Was meenste zum Beispiel zu »Jasthaus Schmalhans«, unter persönliche Leitung von Reichsmarschall Küchenmeister Fettwanst? (Adler 1990, 19)

The patriotically named *Haus Vaterland*, featuring as "Kempinski" in "Frau Wernicke's" remarks, was a symbol of interwar Germany's expanding culture industry, a site familiar to listeners in every corner of the German Reich as an entertainment hub containing an expansive number of nationally themed restaurants including a Turkish café and Japanese tea bar, a major cinema and a ballroom (Figure 5.1). Originally built before the First World War, its lease had been taken over in 1928 by the Kempinskis, a Jewish family of entrepreneurial restaurateurs who thoroughly modernised the building to make it a landmark destination for pleasure-seeking tourists from all around the world. Scathingly described by Siegfried Kracauer as a "pleasure barracks" "for visitors from the provinces," it had been designed, as Kracauer put it, to "calm a metropolitan population's hunger for glamour" (Kracauer 1998, 91).

German listeners tuning in to the BBC would have associated the *Vaterland* with the carefree, pleasure-driven years of the Weimar Republic. Its minimalistic architecture and its assembly of different country-specific eateries were representative of an open-minded internationalism and cultural modernity destroyed by the Nazi system. "Frau Wernicke's" humorous but correctly Aryan proposition for re-christening the venue criticises the narrow-minded fanaticism characterising Germany's hawkish new leaders. In this manner the metropolitan cityscape becomes much more than just the backdrop for Frau Wernicke's satirical attack on Germany's ruling powers. Berlin, the place of Weimar mass culture, emerges as another casualty of the Nazi administration. By the time "Frau Wernicke" enters its premises in July 1941, military marches dominate the atmosphere in the *Vaterland* while coffee and other beverages familiar to customers of the Weimar years have become unobtainable luxuries (Adler 1990, 20).

Grumpily discussing Hitler's war aims ["War for the most holy consumer goods – Oil and corn and so on. *We need* it, and if we don't have it, we must steal it / "Kriech for de heiligsten Vabrauchsjüter – Öl und Jetreide und so.

FIGURE 5.1 The Haus Vaterland, Potsdamer Platz, a restaurant mall, dating from the Weimar era, featured in the "Frau Wernicke" broadcasts on the BBC German Service during the Second World War. (© Alamy)

Wa *brauchen* det doch, und woher nehm' und nich stehlen." (Adler 1990, 21) [translation mine], "Frau Wernicke" moves on to deliver the programme's propaganda line. Because of Hitler's fanatical desire for resource extraction, the venue's consumerist inclusion of different nations and exotic cultural experiences presented as mindless entertainment to Weimar crowds has given way to a far more aggressive form of appropriation. It has led to war and literal incorporation of other nations. Foregrounding the experiences and opinions of the ordinary Berliner, the broadcast also invites listeners to consider the material consequences of Hitler's war by comparing past comforts with present-day austerity. They are told in no uncertain terms what they must already know or suspect instinctively. Despite Hitler's grandiose promises for prosperity, many of them had been better off in the pre-Nazi era.

Occasionally inserted references to Berlin landmarks in BBC German-language features confronted listeners in Nazi Germany with uncomfortable truths. Places such as the *Vaterland* were referenced because they had affective significance for people across the country who would understand "Frau Wernicke's" complaints about wartime shortages. Some of them, it was hoped at the BBC, might even agree with her remarks about the futility of Hitler's war. Discussing trivial issues such as consumer habits and the understandable desire for small indulgences, BBC features made the everyday concerns of ordinary people one of its most effective building blocks in designing propaganda campaigns directed at Nazi Germany. Berlin place names were included to increase authenticity but only if references were meaningful for a significant number of listeners. Additionally, the use of Berlin slang established an authentic-sounding character profile for "Frau Wernicke" that made her such a success as an outspoken opponent of the Hitler regime.

2 "Frau Wernicke's" Berliner Schnauze [Berlin Snout]

"Frau Wernicke's" character was grounded in a set of stereotypes associated with the born-and-bred Berliner. On BBC airwaves, the witty and irreverent character was presented to German housewives as Britain's "experiment in proto-feminist cultural warfare" (Williams 2013, 57). But in designing these programmes, Adler could also draw on a set of ready-made cultural associations relating to the Berlin dialect that would have made audiences in Germany particularly receptive to anti-Nazi propaganda delivered by someone assuming the persona of the metropolitan, defiant, working-class Berliner. Indeed, the BBC's German Planning Committee expressed hope that the character's class background would meet with widespread appeal among Germany's working-class listeners, noting that "'Frau Wernicke' might go down well with the workers one morning" (WAC 1940a).

By the time "Frau Wernicke" addressed listeners in her "plain and drastic Berlin dialect" (WAC 1940c), the so-called "Berliner Schnauze" had certainly gained a reputation for witticism and anti-authoritarianism. This was partly due to a longstanding tradition of popular media representations depicting "the average lower-class Berliner as half-educated yet cunning, self-assured, and slyly subversive of authority" (Jelavich 1993, 31). On the popular nineteenth-century stage in Germany, this persona was frequently represented by a "roster of characters" including "cabdrivers, hawkers," or "shoemakers' apprentices" (Jelavich 1993, 31). The Berlin journalist Adolph Glasbrenner had popularised the image of the rebellious, urban, lower-class Berliner in the journal *Berliner Don Quixote* (1832) and in a string of humorous pamphlets such as *Berlin wie es ist – und trinkt* [*Berlin as it is – and drinks*], using "traditional local humour and dialect" to "discuss current issues and events" (Townsend 1987, 34).

Walter Benjamin claimed that this culturally mediated persona had real-life equivalents in the German capital's residents and language varieties. In one of his radio talks for children, broadcast by Radio Berlin in 1929, he aligned cultural representations of the Berliner and their dialect with the practices, attitudes and experiences of the city's inhabitants: "Berlinisch is a language that comes from work. It developed not from writers or scholars, but rather from the locker room and the card table, on the bus and at the pawn shop, at sporting arenas and in factories," he suggested. "Berlinisch," he continued, "is a language of people who have no time, who often must communicate by using only the slightest hint, glance or half-word. It's not for people who meet socially from time to time. It's only for those who see one another regularly, daily, under very precise and fixed conditions" (Benjamin 2014, 6). Because the Berlin dialect already had a reputation for being an intimate register used by individuals well-known to each other, it could be productively exploited by the BBC. It was used strategically to increase solidarity between German listeners and a character such as "Frau Wernicke," designed to communicate British propaganda lines. Moreover, Benjamin also confirmed that the Berlin dialect was an expression of cultural modernity. It was inclusive and culturally hybrid, drawing its energy from "people from all walks of life" who "live piled together, and at a tremendous pace. Berlinisch, today," he concluded, "is one of the most beautiful and most precise expressions of this frenzied pace of life" (Benjamin 2014, 6). Fast-paced, constantly updated and expressive of the multiculturality associated with a city made up of immigrants and crowds of working-class inhabitants, the Berlin dialect represented a mindset that fitted British propaganda ideals of German citizens and that was meant to be revived by BBC German Service programmes: confident, daring, and independent-thinking.

Among the many satire programmes transmitted by the BBC German Service during the Second World War, the "Frau Wernicke" broadcasts were the ones most obviously working in and projecting this long-standing tradition associating Berlin's dialect and residents with wit and assertiveness. Delivered in monologue format, many of the short programmes were set in the character's sitting room to replicate the atmosphere of cosy domesticity that had been evoked in radio programmes designed for women since the advent of broadcasting in the 1920s (Andrews 2012). Paired with friends, neighbours and an occasional Nazi functionary, "Frau Wernicke" chatters away, using satire to make sure her views and opinions can find an outlet. One programme, for example, unpacks Nazi obituary rhetoric by having her discuss wartime death notices with a friend:

> Just look at this newspaper – it makes you miserable to read it! [...] Of course, there's plenty to laugh at in the front part, but the back pages with all those black edges, goodness me, they're no pleasure. "With proud grief?" – There you ask me too much. I'd just like to know myself what that means. Usually a body is proud if he's done something – but proud because something's been taken away from him – no, that's beyond me! I only know that Louise Spindler isn't at all proud that her Heinz has been torn to pieces by shells. And the Kütemeiers over the road are not proud either that their two boys got drowned last year somewhere in the North Sea. (WAC 1941e).

Grief and anger are the emotions lurking behind this matter-of-fact analysis of wartime obituary clichés. Transmitted only weeks after Nazi Germany had launched "Operation Barbarossa," the broadcast was well-timed to express and increase German women's worst fears about potential new casualties in the East.

As is the case with many "Frau Wernicke" broadcasts, a concrete event or the description of an activity eventually lead to outspoken criticism of Nazi policy-making. In this case, "Frau Wernicke" expatiates on the ruthlessness with which German soldiers are turned into cannon fodder by the warmongering Nazis.

> Well, you see, that's how we Germans are made. A German is born to kill in a war, or be killed! Then they give them leave so that they can go home and produce a new generation, as long as they can. And then when the new generation is old enough they have another war and the boys are sent to the front, are sent home on leave to produce the next generation – and so it goes on. Our life

> is nothing but one long war – with certain intervals, which unfortunately we must have, otherwise we can't prepare properly for the next war. (WAC 1941e)

A caustic note is introduced when "Frau Wernicke" equates Hitler's hawkishness with the harmless pastimes pursued by other men:

> The Führer's got his mind set on the Russians. It's quite a passion with him. Everyone has one to his own tastes. My old man, Gustav, he's got a crush on Skat, and the other likes to play a bit at Napoleon. One likes to drink white beer with a dash, and the other has a thirst for blood … . (WAC 1941e)

Referring to the war as Hitler's hobbyhorse makes fun of Germany's hyped-up *Führer*. But it also emphasises the Nazi leader's lack of concern for human suffering. A carefully placed comment on Napoleon's failed Russian campaign further hints that Hitler's war in the East will be futile. Countless soldiers, "Frau Wernicke" implicitly suggests, are about to be sacrificed. German newspapers will have to print many more obituary notices.

Intrepid and feisty, "Frau Wernicke" is not afraid to speak her mind even if confronted with Nazi authority figures. One programme, dated 17 May 1941, sees her in conversation with a local *Blockwart* [block warden] and *Kreisleiter* [district leader]. They seek her company to ascertain how ordinary citizens in Germany reacted to the news about Rudolf Heß's recent flight to Scotland. On the face of it, "Frau Wernicke" toes the line by trying to refute rumours about Heß's motives for leaving the country. But her actual aim is to feed speculations about Hitler's dwindling power and persuasiveness:

> But Herr Pahl, why get so artificially worked up about this – let the people say that something is rotten at the top, […] and that he is the first rat to leave the ship by Messerschmitt and that he will disclose all he knows of the secrets of the headquarters to the English … *who* says this? I don't say that anyone says this, I'm just rehearsing the arguments, you see, because it could be *that* someone will say this …. [translation mine]

> [Aber Herr Pahl, wat rejen Se sich den so künstlich uff – lassen Se de Leute doch reden, det da oben wat faul is, […] und det er de erste Ratte is, die det Schiff per Messerschmitt verläßt, und det er allet, wat er weeß von de Jeheimnisse an Führerhöfen, den Engländern petzen wird … *wer* det sacht? Ick saje ja nich, det et eena sacht, ick setzte bloß den Fall, vastehn Se, denn et könnte doch sein, *det* et eena sacht ….] (Adler, 1990, 17)

If his deputy is hastily leaving the country on an unauthorised flight to Britain, Hitler's grip on Nazi politicians, the programme implies, is clearly waning. If those closest to him are taking drastic action because morale is low within Hitler's entourage, what, "Frau Wernicke" asks, were ordinary people in Nazi Germany supposed to be thinking – and doing?

A BBC broadcast transmitted on 20 September 1941 might have provided ideas. Here, "Frau Wernicke" called on German citizens to find ways to boycott the regime. In August 1941, only a few months after Heß's flight, the BBC had rolled out a "Go Slow" campaign, urging workers in Germany to hold up production by taking long breaks and by taking their time at work. A month later, "Frau Wernicke" directly alludes to the "Go Slow" campaign in a conversation with a grief-stricken neighbour who has decided to adopt the new working routine after the death of his soldier-son:

> So – that is sensational! You are no longer playing along? Taking your time while working, you say. 'Go slowly ahead' is the new slogan […]. [translation mine]

> [Sooo – det is ja hochintressant! Nich mehr mitspielen tun Se! Zeit lassen Se sich bei'n Arbeeten, sajen Se. »Nur imma langsam voran!« is de neue Parole.] (Adler, 1990, 32)

As a taste for disobedience was an innate trait of the Berliner, "Frau Wernicke" broadcasts were ideal places to launch this British propaganda campaign. Because they were delivered by someone speaking with an easily recognisable "Berliner Schnauze," such appeals for resistance were persuasive because they were so decidedly in character.

3 Interwar Berlin Cabaret and German Features at the BBC

In his 1929 broadcast, Walter Benjamin had noted the spontaneity and down-to-earth quality of the Berlin dialect. It was the language of the streets, not one used by scholars and the educated. And yet, it had been the art historian Bruno Adler, who had never lived in Berlin, who had been tasked by the BBC to pen the "Frau Wernicke" broadcasts. To sound authentic, Adler's scripted talks had to be translated into the lingo of a fast-talking, outspoken Berlin housewife. It was lucky for the BBC that they were able to find a person ideally suited to perform "Frau Wernicke" on air: the Jewish actress Annemarie Hase, who had left Germany in 1936 and who now lived in exile in London and was looking for work. Born Annita Maria Hirsch in 1900, she had been trained in the Max-Reinhardt Schauspielschule in Berlin before making a name for herself as a regular presence in the city's interwar cabaret scene. This professional association with the political satire tradition made Hase the perfect choice for impersonating the BBC's rebellious German housewife. But the choice of Hase as "Frau Wernicke" performer also reveals continuities between Berlin's cabaret scene of the Weimar years and the BBC German Service inaugurated over a decade later. The political energy associated with Berlin's cabaret stages was harnessed for propaganda purposes when the BBC began broadcasting German-language features in 1940.

Hase, it needs to be said at this juncture, was not the only former Berlin cabaret star who occasionally found work at the BBC. Some musical numbers that were broadcast to Germany as the BBC's output became more refined were written by the Russian-born composer Mischa Spoliansky (1899–1985), whose name, like Hase's, had become associated with Berlin's cabaret scene during the Weimar years. During the 1920s, he had been one of the most significant composers of cabaret and revue songs, working in famed Berlin venues such as Max Reinhardt's Schall *und Rauch* [*Sound and Smoke*] alongside Friedrich Holländer, Kurt Tucholsky, Joachim Ringelnatz, Walter Mehring and other cabaret celebrities. One of his most famous compositions was "Das Lila Lied" ["The Lavender Song"], celebrating queer identities and experiences. It was dedicated to Magnus Hirschfeld, whose Institut für Sexualwissenschaft [Institute for Sexual Sciences] was founded in Berlin in 1919 to advocate liberal approaches to sex education and to the scientific study of sex in all its variations. Pro-republican and antimilitarist cabaret revues emerging on Weimar stages after 1926 were Spoliansky's particular focus. Famous among his works is the music for the 1928 revue *Es liegt in der Luft* [*It's in the Air*], co-produced with the cabaret author Marcellus Schiffer. It featured Marlene Dietrich before she landed her breakthrough role in *The Blue Angel* (1930).

Although Spoliansky had acquired German citizenship by the time the Nazis rose to power, his Jewish background and association with Berlin's cabaret scene made emigration inevitable. By 1933, he was in London and began a second career as a composer of film scores, many of which were included in Alexander Korda movies. He also began to work for the BBC, composing music for satirical songs that were broadcast to Nazi Germany. His staff files in the BBC Written Archives Centre identify him as the creator of the following, frequently played songs: "Die Moritat vom Volkswagen" ["Ballad of Volkswagen"], "Wir fahren immer hin und her" ["We're On the Move"], "Das Lied vom Stacheldraht" ["The Song of the Barbed Wire"], "Lied für die deutschen Soldaten" ["Song for the German Soldiers"] and "Fliegerlied" ["Aviator Song"] (WAC

1942; WAC 1941a). Another Spoliansky BBC composition, "The Girl I Left Behind Me," set lyrics by Bertolt Brecht to music. The song was performed by Lucie Mannheim, another Jewish artist of the Weimar period who had found refuge in Britain and who began a second career in the British film industry.

Those of Spoliansky's musical compositions that have survived show that he had the skills that were required to produce British propaganda materials. "We're On the Move", for example, is a perpetuum mobile piece. The fast-paced, repetitive but jolly tune mirrors the image of a ceaselessly moving train, acting as a personification of the German war apparatus that carries German soldiers across the continent from one front line to another. Comic potential emerges because the catchy, jaunty tune is ill-suited to express longing and dissatisfaction. The music and lyrics, arresting forward motion and progress through repetition, resemble the song's dominant image of a perpetually moving train. Rhyming couplets contain the soldiers' lament in the same way as the train contains their bodies and moves them around in a cyclical fashion. While memorable and jovial, Spoliansky's melody allows for little sonic development, offering practically no variation on a simple tune. The repeat chorus emphatically conveys the frustrated existence of German soldiers in transit, far from home.

Once again, once again in the everlasting train,
where the smells and the noise nearly drive a man insane,
and the wheels shriek "trouble, war and sorrow"
No one knows where we shall be tomorrow.
Maybe East, maybe North, maybe South or maybe West –
never home where we think after all it should be best—
Somewhere strange this blinkering train will lead us,
where they hate and never understand us.

CHORUS:
We're on the move from morn till night,
our wives for ever lost to sight:
poor exiles we from hearth and home
condemned in foreign lands to roam.

Shoved about like a dog and no comfort far or near:
restless nights, foreign food, not a drop of German beer,
treated ev'rywhere as robber-bandit.
What a life! How is a man to stand it.
Fatherland, fatherland, up and call us back again.

"Not a hope, not a hope," growls the everlasting train,
"you are doomed to wandering existence."
And it carries us into the distance.

Repeat CHORUS.

[Wieder mal, wieder mal, in der ollen Eisenbahn,
und es riecht so nach Krieg und nach ekelhaftem Tran,
und die Bahn, sie schaukelt zum Verrecken,
und wer weiss denn, wo wir morgen stecken.
Alles fremd, alles feind, und man hört kein deutsches Wort,
ja warum und wozu mussten wir aus Deutschland fort
nach dem Osten, Norden oder Westen,
denn zu Hause hat man's noch am Besten.

CHORUS: Wir sind von Hof und Herd verbannt
und rollen nur von Land zu Land.
Wir fahren immer hin und her,
wir haben keine Heimat mehr.

Keine Rast, keine Ruh, und ein Leben wie ein Tier,
und es schmeckt niemals gut, und es gibt kein deutsches Bier.
Hol's der Teufel! Schinderei und Plage,
und das ewige Geschiebe und Gejage,
Heimatland, Heimatland, raff Dich auf und hol' uns 'ran.
"Hoffnungslos, hoffnungslos", knurrt die olle Eisenbahn.
Und wir kämen heim nur gar zu gerne,
doch sie trägt uns weiter in die Ferne.

Repeat CHORUS] (Spoliansky, "We are on the Move" (WAC 1941–42))

This and similar satirical songs broadcast by the BBC German Service during the war aimed to capture the rebellious spirit of political cabaret revues that had flourished on Berlin stages during the second part of the Weimar years. As Peter Jelavich explains, as part of the regime's organised propaganda apparatus, the Nazis temporarily authorised "positive cabaret" meant to "attack people who disturbed the homogenous mindset" (Jelavich 1993, 245) but they had prohibited all other forms of political satire. Both its recovery in BBC programmes for German listeners and its prohibition by the Nazis are easy to comprehend. Satire uses humour to highlight discrepancies between ideal conceptions and political reality, providing immediate and focused commentary on topical issues and very often poking fun at those in positions of power and authority. While scripted, cabaret gives the impression of immediacy and spontaneity. This aspect of cabaret, Jelavich notes, “made it an art form that was continually up-to-date” (6). In Nazi Germany, cabaret’s ability to express political criticism was noted with concern. Joseph Goebbels, Germany’s *Reichsminister* for Public Enlightenment and Propaganda, tried to intervene in debates about the place of cabaret within National Socialism by indicting artists and producers, by aiming to define Nazi humour and by threatening to close venues that repeatedly provoked the wrath of party officials (Goebbels 1998, 163, 244, 245). On 3 February 1939, he recorded in his diary his ambitions to “eradicate” political jokes “root and branch” (247). While Goebbels never succeeded in banning political references and jokes from staged performances, cabaret in the Nazi period lost its acerbic wit and political subversiveness. When war broke out in 1939, it had become reduced to “the type of noncritical vaudeville that had been so prominent in the 1890s” (Jelavich 1993, 249). But the political humour associated with Berlin’s cabaret shows of the interwar period had obvious propaganda potential for the BBC. When used effectively, it could expose Nazi officials as liars. It could also challenge the most frequently repeated Nazi propaganda lines focusing on Germany’s military superiority and the inevitability of the country’s victory.

After the war, countless Germans confirmed that fines and prison sentences had not prevented them from regularly tuning in to the BBC’s German-language broadcasts. Satire programmes, exploiting political humour to challenge Nazi authority, had been especially popular (Plock 2021, 237–40). And yet, it is unclear how much these broadcasts contributed to the destruction of the Nazi system. They were vehicles for delivering anti-fascist critique but their ability to turn followers and terrified citizens into resistance fighters was surely minimal. The nature of the Nazi totalitarian system meant that resistance and uprisings were sparse (Ramet 2020, 15–86). The generic form chosen by the BBC to encourage acts of opposition and sabotage in Germany might also have been at fault. Jelavich explains the “pitfalls of cabaret: it could be a safety valve, where the spectators would ‘let off steam’ through laughter, but then proceed to live as they always had” (34). Satirical programmes broadcast by the BBC might have had a similar effect on listeners in that they “sustain[ed] the status quo inadvertently, insofar as [they] diffused tensions that otherwise might have been stored up longer and eventually released in much more forceful forms” (Jelavich 1993, 34).

In 1931, Walter Benjamin had already noted satire’s ineptitude when used by left-wing intellectuals claiming to work in support of political reform.

Accusing contemporary satirists of turning negativist aesthetics into commercially viable, reputation-building exhibits, he unmasked political satire as a self-serving, promotional gesture that confirmed the socio-economic status quo. "And indeed," he wrote about the work of contemporary authors and satirists Erich Kästner, Walter Mehring and Kurt Tucholsky, "for the past fifteen years this left-wing intelligentsia has been continually the agent of intellectual booms, from Activism, via Expressionism, to the New Objectivity. Its political significance, however, was exhausted by the transposition of revolutionary reflexes (insofar as they arose in the bourgeoisie) into objects of distraction, of amusement, which can be supplied for consumption" (Benjamin 2001, 424). Adler's "Frau Wernicke" programmes and Spoliansky's tunes and the lyrics they accompanied might have expressed the fatigue, frustration and the anxieties of German women and of the soldiers serving in Hitler's army. It is an entirely different question if these broadcasts ever elicited more than silent approval.

But it is worth keeping in mind that the BBC's aim in designing German-language programmes during the war was future-orientated, looking beyond Germany's unconditional surrender and towards the post-war period. Designed to assist in bringing about an Allied victory, they were also meant to familiarise German listeners with British culture, therefore working in support of creating a post-war climate of international understanding and collaboration between the two countries currently at war with one another. As Marie Gillespie and Alban Webb explain, after the Second World War, "BBC programmes were a passport for listeners to life in Britain and, to the everyday lives of its people, and became the window through which much of the rest of the world came to know Britain as a society and as a diplomatic agent in international relations" (Gillespie and Webb 2013, 6). In 1959, Hugh Carleton Greene, who had been Head of the BBC German Service during the Second World War, pointed out that intercultural communication had been a significant driver in planning broadcasts for listeners in Nazi Germany. He claimed that it was our "task to build an invisible bridge between Germany and Britain" (WAC 1959, 10). A pre-war BBC report had already noted that "appropriate reference should be made in the [news] bulletins to items showing friendly relationships and collaboration between Great Britain and Germany" (WAC 1939). "We have a magnificent chance to sell England," one BBC German Service broadcaster also noted in 1944 (WAC 1944).

During the war years, the BBC consciously worked on the creation of a loyal German radio public receptive to British cultural diplomacy. At the time, the British broadcaster developed its reputation as a trustworthy and objective news provider in countries where headlines were dominated by totalitarian propaganda lines. Alongside regular news bulletins, the BBC German Service's feature programme was similarly instrumental in gaining listeners' trust. Importing satire from Berlin's interwar cabaret stages provided the BBC with opportunities to sound reassuringly familiar to listeners in Germany who might have cared little for Britain but who were nostalgically looking back to the politically liberal and culturally expansive experiments of the interwar period. In the 1920s, Berlin's political cabaret had gained a reputation as a fast-paced modern art form, representing the class stratifications and cultural diversity of the capital's population. During the Second World War, it continued its existence—not in Germany but in BBC German-language broadcasts —assisting the British broadcaster in presenting itself as the supporter of "cosmopolitan contact zones" (Gillespie and Webb 2013, 7) where articulations of critical viewpoints outlawed and persecuted across mainland Europe continued to thrive.

References

Adler, Bruno. 1990. *Frau Wernicke: Kommentare einer 'Volksjenossin'.* Ed. Uwe Naumann. Mannheim: Persona.

Andrews, Maggie. 2012. *Domesticating the Airwaves: Broadcasting, Domesticity, and Femininity.* London: Continuum.

BBC Handbook 1938. London: British Broadcasting Corporation.

BBC Handbook 1940. London: British Broadcasting Corporation.

Benjamin, Walter. 2001. *Writings.* Ed. Michael W. Jennings. Cambridge, MA: Harvard University Press.

Benjamin, Walter. 2014. *Radio Benjamin.* Ed. Lecia Rosenthal. London: Verso.

Bergmeier, Horst J. P. 1997. *Hitler's Airwaves: The Inside Story of Nazi Radio Broadcasting and Propaganda Swing.* New Haven: Yale University Press.

Birdsall, Carolyn. 2012. *Nazi Soundscapes: Sound, Technology and Urban Space in Germany, 1933–1945.* Amsterdam: Amsterdam University Press.

Gillespie, Marie and Alban Webb (eds). 2013. *Diasporas and Diplomacy: Cosmopolitan Contact Zones at the BBC World Service, 1932–2012.* London and New York: Routledge.

Goebbels, Joseph. 1998. *Die Tagebücher von Joseph Goebbels: Teil 1: Aufzeichnungen 1923–191, Band 6: August 1938–Juni 1939.* Munich: K. G. Saur.

Hensle, Michael P. 2003. *Rundfunkverbrechen: Das Hören von „Feindsendern" im Nationalsozialismus."* Berlin: Metropol.

Jelavich, Peter. 1993. *Berlin Cabaret.* Cambridge, MA: Harvard University Press.

Kracauer, Siegfried. 1998. *The Salaried Masses.* London: Verso.

Lucas, Robert. 1994. *Die Briefe des Gefreiten Hirnschal: BBC, Radio, Satiren, 1940–1945.* Vienna: Verlag für Gesellschaftskritik.

Moorehead, Kristina. 2016. *Satire als Kriegswaffe: Strategien der britischen Rundfunkpropaganda im Zweiten Weltkrieg.* Marburg: Tectum.

Plock, Vike Martina. 2021. *The BBC German Service during the Second World War: Broadcasting to the Enemy.* Cham: Palgrave Macmillan.

Ramet, Sabrina P. 2020. *Non-Conformity, Dissent, Opposition, and Resistance in Germany, 1933–1990: The Freedom to Conform.* Cham: Palgrave Macmillan.

TNA. 1940. Planning and Broadcasting Committee Minutes. 31 January – 27 February 1939. FO 898/7. The National Archives, Kew, UK.

Townsend, Mary Lee. 1987. "The Politics of Humour: Adolph Glassbrenner and the Rediscovery of the German *Vormärz.*" *Central European History* 20.1: 29–57.

Williams, Rhys W. 2013. "'Frau Wernicke' at the BBC: Wartime Satire and Propaganda." *Diasporas and Diplomacy: Cosmopolitan Contact Zones at the BBC World Service, 1932–2012.* Eds. Marie Gillespie and Alban Webb. London and New York: Routledge. 57–69.

WAC. 1939. European News Service, January-February 1939. E9/12/2. BBC Written Archives Centre, Caversham, UK.

WAC. 1940a. German Planning Committee Minutes. 19 July. E2/344. BBC Written Archives Centre, Caversham, UK.

WAC. 1940b. Bruno Adler to Christina Gibson. 20 August, Bruno Adler Talks File 1: 1940–1962. BBC Written Archives Centre, Caversham, UK.

WAC. 1940c. Bruno Adler to Christina Gibson. 28 August. Bruno Adler Talks File 1: 1940–1962. BBC Written Archives Centre, Caversham, UK.

WAC. 1941a. Mischa Spoliansky. Copyright File, 1940–1962. 13 January. BBC Written Archives Centre, Caversham, UK.

WAC. 1941b. German Planning Committee Minutes. 8 March. E2/344. BBC Written Archives Centre, Caversham, UK.

WAC. 1941c. Bruno Adler. "Im Warteraum" [In the Waiting Room]. 6 July. German Scripts: Features (July 1941). BBC Written Archives Centre, Caversham, UK.

WAC. 1941d. Bruno Adler. "Kurt and Willi on Hitler's Responsibility". 6 August. German Scripts: Features (August 1941). BBC Written Archives Centre, Caversham, UK.

WAC. 1941e. Bruno Adler. "Frau Wernicke on Obituaries". 9 August. German Scripts: Features (August 1941). BBC Written Archives Centre, Caversham, UK.

WAC. 1941–42. "German Soldiers' Song: Wir fahren immer hin und her." Tangye Lean's Office, German Radio: File 1, 1941–42. BBC Written Archives Centre. Caversham, UK.

WAC. 1942. Mischa Spoliansky. Artist File 1, 1940–1962. 9 December. BBC Written Archives Centre, Caversham, UK.

WAC. 1944. Patrick Gordon Walker to Hugh Carleton Greene. 30 October. EI/742. BBC Written Archives Centre, Caversham, UK.

WAC. 1959. "Hier ist der Londoner Rundfunk: Rückblick und Ausblick nach 21 Jahren." 20 September. D356-6. BBC Written Archives Centre, Caversham, UK.

CHAPTER 6

Turning Hearers into Listeners: Music on the BBC German Service during the Second World War

Emily Oliver

"Hier ist England. Hier ist England. Hier ist England." If as a German listener you had been turning the dial on your *Volksempfänger* during the Second World War and you had come across this announcement, you might have done one of two things: listen intently to the subsequent broadcast, or quickly change the frequency for fear of being caught listening to an enemy broadcaster. From 1938 onwards, the BBC began broadcasting in German, in order to offer German listeners an alternative to Nazi-controlled media and thus win their hearts and minds for the British cause – a service which increased in importance over the course of the Second World War. The German Service was always intended primarily as a talk radio service, and the issue of whether and how music should be used within its programming remained controversial throughout the war.

Research on the BBC German Service during the Second World War has tended to focus on the different personalities behind the programming, on news reporting, comedy, features, and other spoken-word content (Brinson and Dove 2003; Moorehead 2016; Oliver 2019; Plock 2021; Seul 2015). However, very little of this work examines the use of music on the German Service, with the notable exception of Thacker's (2003) chapter on "Liberating German Musical Life", which outlines in broad strokes the music policies followed by the BBC German Service during the Second World War, but focuses mainly on the immediate post-war period. Meanwhile, there is ample evidence that the Third Reich liberally used music as a propaganda tool in its own broadcasts throughout the Second World War (Bergmeier and Lötz 1997; Dolaplis 2019; Morley 2021; Studdert 2017). While there has been significant work on the role of music in Nazi broadcasting, very little of this work puts German music propaganda efforts in conversation with their British counterparts. As this chapter highlights, it is particularly the Anglo-German cross-fertilisation of different songs and ideas during this time which constituted propaganda opportunities for the BBC to exploit.

In addition to its focus on the spoken word, there were a number of practical issues preventing the widespread use of music on the BBC German Service.

 | HTTPS://DOI.ORG/10.1515/9783111302508-006

One concern was the Nazis' consistent attempts at jamming broadcasts from London by transmitting interference noises on the same frequency, which could utterly destroy any aesthetic pleasure in music broadcasts. Another problem was that clandestine listeners were putting themselves in danger of detection. For instance, in 1940 the German Service decided against using a jingle in its programming, since "a musical slogan would materially help the Gestapo detect black [i.e. illegal] listeners" (WAC 1940b). The closest the German Service came to a call sign was aligning itself with the BBC's other European Services by using the first four notes of Beethoven's Fifth Symphony played on a drum, since the dot-dot-dot-dash pattern spelled out the letter "V" for victory in Morse code (BBC 2024). Looking beyond these four notes, there is evidence that music was used regularly in German Service broadcasts, and it is worth examining to what extent this aligned with the Service's overall mission and propaganda aims.

The BBC German Service's key objectives, as set out by its director Hugh Carleton Greene in 1940, were "1) to convince the audience that we are likely to win; 2) to make them want us to win" (WAC 1940b). He elaborated the double-edged nature of this mission a little more in 1943, stating that the German Service consistently aimed

> to break down the will to fight of the German people by convincing them that defeat is certain, but that defeat at the hands of the Allies would not have intolerable consequences for the ordinary citizen. In short [...] to provide a judicious blend of "despair" and "hope" propaganda. (WAC 1943b)

The stylistic implications of this were a calm, measured delivery by all speakers and a matter-of-fact tone in the commentaries to contrast with the hectoring sounds of Nazi programmes (Mansell 1982, 163–64; Cannon 1988, 10).

With its mix of "despair" and "hope" propaganda, the German Service attempted to address a broad audience of ordinary Germans, whilst judiciously differentiating between warmongering Nazis and the supposedly peaceful German population (Seul 2015, 385). As Greene stated in his report on the European Services' output, "we have always made a distinction between the German war machine and the German people" (WAC 1943b). The key element at the heart of all programming was truthful, accurate and up-to-date news. Other types of programmes included talks, satirical features, and discussions. Music, like all of these other formats, was to act as "a vehicle for propaganda" and "bait for the news" (WAC 1940). Therefore, any music used in programming had an ancillary function, but nevertheless an important one, and in contrast to many of the other formats, it was ideally suited to turning accidental hearers into intent listeners.

Whereas hearing refers to the continuous, physiological act of perceiving sound waves through the ears, listening is the conscious, temporary process of interpreting these sound signals and making sense of them. Music is particularly interesting in this context, since it is so difficult to define in semiotic terms. To what extent can it be said to signify? Andrew Crisell maintains that "while music may *allow* us to use our imagination it does not 'refer to' anything in the way that speech does and so does not *require* us to use it" (Crisell 1994, 14). It is perfectly possible for us to hear music and think about something else entirely. Crisell admits that:

> [m]usic with lyrics seems to present less of a difficulty since we could say that the significance or meaning of the music is expressed in the words; but it might equally be argued that the music means one thing and the lyrics mean another and that they are quite capable of counterpointing as well as complementing each other. (Crisell 1994, 48)

This chapter outlines four different ways in which the BBC German Service employed music, which vary according to the level of careful attention they demand from a listener, and also in the extent to which music and lyrics overlap with, complement, or contradict each other's meanings. It evaluates to what extent each of these modes fulfilled the propaganda aims set out for the German Service by Hugh Greene.

1 Music Banned by the Third Reich

In 1941, the BBC introduced a thirty-minute slot every weekday for music interspersed with news flashes, called "Aus der freien Welt" ["From the Free World"]. The BBC's European Music Supervisor saw two aims in music for propaganda purposes:

> firstly to give so notable a projection of British music that our programmes will be listened to on their own rights, and secondly to demonstrate [...] that it is from England alone that the forbidden national or non-Aryan music can be heard, and that it is England which provides not only this artistic and cultural freedom, but also the practical military and political liberation which is connoted by the music we freely play. (WAC 1943d)

Accordingly, "Aus der freien Welt" included British music, but also composers, performers, and music styles which the Nazis had banned (WAC 1941b). How exactly the programme's musical content might connote "military and political liberation", however, remained somewhat obscure.

The inclusion of a dedicated music programme may well have been a response to competition from German radio at the time, particularly from the *Deutschlandsender*. A BBC Monitoring report concluded that "[m]usic takes up by far the greater part of German broadcasting time", and that the "highest proportion of broadcasting time is devoted to 'entertainment music'" (WAC 1941g). There was also a concern at the BBC that "England has been represented by Germans to Germany for many generations as 'Das Land ohne Musik' ['the country without music']" (WAC 1943d), a perception which the inclusion of British composers and performers in "Aus der freien Welt" sought to counter. Douglas Ritchie, at the time Assistant Director of European Broadcasts, was in favour of including "besides such men as Elgar, Walton, Ireland, Holst, Vaughan Williams and Benjamin Britten, some of the good lighter composers like Eric Coates" (WAC 1943a). Instead of explicitly contrasting these composers with German output, Ritchie envisaged that "the one characteristic common to all should be [...] a quality of brightness, cheerfulness and 'bigness' so that listeners are given a feeling of elation and confidence" (WAC 1943a). While the propaganda aims of broadcasting British composers necessarily remained somewhat vague, it is interesting to note that some at the BBC apparently favoured the approach of using music to instil confidence in their German listeners, which ran counter to Greene's notion of "break[ing] down the will to fight of the German people by convincing them that defeat is certain" (WAC 1943b).

Another type of music the BBC could offer, which was known to be popular among younger Germans and the armed forces, yet banned in the Third Reich, was jazz. However, jazz remained a controversial genre even within the BBC, meeting with considerable snobbery (Thacker 2003, 82–83). Only a few months after the programme's introduction, a report on the German Service's output asked:

> Is the title "Aus der Freienwelt" [*sic*] altogether appropriate, seeing that the chief content is jazz? [...] The Germans have a fair degree of musical culture and why do we "Aus der Freienwelt" suggest that we are fighting this war for the re-introduction of jazz into Germany? (WAC 1941e, 12)

This particular listener did not hold back with his dislike of jazz, noting for Tuesday, 6 May 1941:

> The programme ends with a couple wailing to each other "You say the sweetest things, baby" (Who would risk his neck to listen to this American *Blödsinn* [nonsense]? Or do the Germans rub their hands in triumph and say: "Thank God Hitler has got rid of that?") This programme must be most discouraging to any Germans of a serious kind who place their hope in England. (WAC 1941e, 10)

Apparently, to some at the BBC, the only thing worse than losing the propaganda war to Hitler's Germany was the thought of being associated with American culture. Nevertheless, this comment points to a serious concern regarding the transmission of jazz to German listeners: since it did not require high levels of listener attention to be intelligible, it was also easily recognisable as an enemy broadcast. As listening to the BBC was punishable by imprisonment or even death, there was a serious argument to be made against using precious airtime purely for aesthetic enjoyment of music styles which did not in themselves convey propaganda messages or impart information.

Reporting on the European Services' music offerings in July 1944, Douglas Ritchie justified his department's consistent aim of inspiring German listeners, instead of breaking down their will to fight:

> The policy of the musical programmes in the European Service – for which I have responsibility – has been […] to give music which is of an inspiring character. This involves music of all kinds, from symphony to swing, but there is no attempt merely to entertain without reference to the aims outlined. Thus, theatre organ music, crooning, the lower types of "popular" music and poor performance of anything at all are rigorously excluded. (WAC 1944c).

There is a hint of defensiveness in Ritchie's comments, perhaps suggesting that some of his colleagues continued to question the propaganda value of broadcasting British and banned music, particularly jazz. While the inclusion of music by British and banned artists was a laudable goal in itself (and also provided much needed performance opportunities for individual artists), there is little evidence to suggest that the BBC's music section ever really figured out how these genres could be employed to further the German Service's overall propaganda aims. Broadcasting jazz might make German listeners more aware of their government's rigid control of cultural output, and demonstrating that British music could be impressive might eventually convince listeners that Britain could win the war, but it was equally possible for either of these genres simply to function as a welcome distraction for listeners going about their daily business without questioning the policies of the Third Reich.

2 Reclaiming Traditional German Culture

As late as 1942, the BBC's Assistant Controller for European Services remained convinced that "[t]here is very little that we can do through the medium of music to make known our ideals of civilisation" (WAC 1942a). However, several radio features which integrated German songs prove that the German Service did find a way of using music to do just that. One example is a feature by British actor Marius Goring, who worked as the German Service's Head of Features throughout the war.[1] The script revolves around the German song "Freiheit, die ich meine", whose words were written by Max von Schenckendorf in 1815 and set to music by Karl August Groos in 1818. The song was considered part of German *Volksliedgut* and, despite its origins in the liberal student movements of the early nineteenth century, by 1932 it had been co-opted by the Nazis, appearing in the *Nationalsozialistisches Volksliederbuch*, and a year later in the *SA-Liederbuch* (Fischer 2008).

Goring begins by describing the song as "ein altes deutsches Lied" ["an old German song"], recalling the first time he heard it in 1931 as a student at Ludwig-Maximilians-Universität in Munich, which he praises for its commitment to freedom of thought at that time (WAC 1943g).[2] The script goes on to chronicle the rise of Nazism among Goring's fellow students, before introducing a key news item: the execution of Hans and Sophie Scholl, and Christoph Probst, for high treason against the Third Reich. Goring characterises his fellow students of 1931 as "eine untergehende Generation, [...] die von den Nazi Lehren vollkommen vergiftet wird" ["a doomed generation, which is being entirely poisoned by Nazi teachings"], but expresses the hope that this new generation of students from Munich University has "ein anderes Weltbild" ["a different world view"] (WAC 1943g). He quotes Hans Scholl's statement to the judge who sentenced him, "ich bin Deutscher und es wird nicht mehr lange dauern, dann werden Sie da stehen, wo ich heute stehe" ["I am German, and it will not be long before you will find yourself standing where I stand today"], followed immediately by a verse from the song:

Wo sich Männer finden,	[Where men can be found]
Die führ [*sic*] Ehr und Recht,	[Who for honour and justice]

1 On air Goring always appeared under the pseudonym Charles Richardson, presumably wishing to avoid any confusion between his surname and *Reichsmarschall* Goering.

2 All translations are my own unless otherwise indicated.

Mutig sich verbinden,	[Join together bravely]
Weilt ein frei Geschlecht.	[There dwells a free people]
(WAC 1943g)	

Through this juxtaposition, Goring is reclaiming the original meaning of the song, and reminding his listeners of a former, better Germany before the days of Hitler. Instead of broadcasting foreign or forbidden types of music as propaganda, this emotive appeal to a shared sense of free "Germanness" uses a folk song with which listeners will be familiar, recontextualising it to show that the members of the White Rose resistance group died for their commitment to values which pre-dated the rise of Nazism and should be shared by all Germans. Through its slow, calm melody, the song creates an intimate listening experience, inviting contemplation. We can perhaps see here an example of that "blend of 'despair' and 'hope' propaganda" the German Service sought to achieve.

At Christmas that same year, the BBC returned to the strategy of reminding its listeners of traditional German folk songs, but this time focusing exclusively on the lyrics. Martin Esslin (under his given name Julius Pereszlenyi) wrote a script for broadcast on 25 December 1943, in which he deployed well-known poems to encourage listeners to recall their shared longing for peace. The speaker suggests an affinity with Germany by reminiscing about spending a German Christmas with a friend from his student days, and speculating as to what this friend must be thinking during the fifth wartime Christmas. He asks:

> was ist das Bleibende, der wahre Geist eines Volkes, sein ewiger Bestandteil, überliefert aus der Vergangenheit, aber unvergänglich und darum in die Zukunft weisend, jener Geist, der die Stimme eines ganzen Volkes sein kann, die Stimme seiner Seele, seines Gewissens? (WAC 1943j)
>
> [what is the enduring thing, a people's true spirit, its eternal essence, handed down from the past, but unending, and thereby pointing towards the future; that spirit which can be the voice of a whole people, the voice of its soul, of its conscience?]

His answer is to quote in full Matthias Claudius's "Kriegslied", written in 1778 during the war of Bavarian succession, which ends with the lines "'Sist leider Krieg und ich begehre / Nicht schuld daran zu sein" ["'Tis pity it is war, and I desire / Not to be responsible for it"] (WAC 1943j). After repeating these lines, the speaker speculates that his German friend must be asking himself what Germans can expect of the future during the fifth wartime Christmas.

The script then moves on to the desire for peace, quoting in full a song from the well-known nineteenth-century folklore collection *Des Knaben Wunderhorn* (von Arnim and Brentano 1808). The words of the song from the Seven Years War are an extended plea for the dove of peace ("Süße, liebe Friedenstaube") to settle in German lands. The speaker uses the last two lines "Gib der Welt den Frieden wieder, / Und nimm ihn dann auch für dich" ["Give the world peace again / And then claim it for yourself"] to launch an impassioned plea for peace on behalf of his German friend, claiming that in these words resounds "die wahre, ewige Stimme seines Volkes und seine tiefe Sehnsucht nach Frieden" ["the true, eternal voice of his people and their deep longing for peace"] (WAC 1943j). Having reminded his German listeners of their true shared nature, the speaker suggests that this nature is what unites Germans, not just with the English, but with all people across the whole world:

> Aber ich glaube auch sagen zu können, dass über die Kluft, die der Krieg zwischen Ihnen dort drüben in Deutschland und uns hier in England gerissen hat, [...] hinweg die Worte jenes alten Liedes der Friedenssehnsucht aller Menschen in der Welt Ausdruck verleihen, aller Menschen in allen Ländern, in allen Lagern, an diesem Weihnachtsabend. Im fünften Kriegsjahr sehnen sich die Völker – alle Völker – nach Frieden. (WAC 1943j)
>
> [But I think I can also say that across the chasm, which this war has wrought between you over there in Germany and us here in England, the words of this old song give voice to all people's longing for peace in the world, the longing of all people in all countries, in all camps, on this Christmas Eve. In the fifth year of war, people, all people, long for peace.]

This deployment of traditional German folklore was much more aligned with the BBC's goals as set out by Hugh Greene, since it drew on a shared German history and culture to suggest that Germans were, at heart, peace-loving, and that this peace could be achieved by hastening the end of the war, and thus reclaiming their affinity with the English and all other peace-loving nations of the world.

3 Original Songs as Anti-Nazi Propaganda

In addition to broadcasting traditional German music and banned artists, the BBC also commissioned its own songs in German. One example of this is "Das Lied vom Stacheldraht" (1941), an attempt at overt and very direct musical propaganda. It is one of several original songs written for the BBC by Russian-born pianist and composer Mischa Spoliansky (WAC 1941a). Before emigrating to London, Spoliansky had worked in the Berlin cabaret scene, most notably for Max Reinhardt's Schall *und Rauch*, setting lyrics by Kurt Tucholsky and Joachim Ringelnatz to music, and giving the young Marlene Dietrich her stage breakthrough in a number of revues.

Consisting of five verses and a four-line coda, the song "Stacheldraht" is an aggressive personification of the Nazi regime as a terrifying beast only capable of producing barbed wire to force the rest of Europe under its yoke. Since the lyrics do not survive in any script, they are given in full here, transcribed from an audio recording:

Wir produzieren früh und spat	[Day and night we produce]
Stacheldraht, Stacheldraht.	[Barbed wire, barbed wire]
Wir binden deutschen Stacheldraht	[We tie German barbed wire]
Von Staat zu Staat, von Staat zu Staat.	[From state to state, from state to state]
Jetzt hat Europa den Salat	[Now Europe is in a mess]
Aus Stacheldraht, aus Stacheldraht.	[Made of barbed wire, of barbed wire]
Europa ist ein Stachelstaat;	[Europe is a barbed state]
Damit macht es sehr wenig Staat.	[You can't get far with that]
Wohin wir säen unsre Saat,	[Wherever we sow our seed]
Wächst Stacheldraht, wächst Stacheldraht.	[There grows barbed wire, barbed wire]
Mit unsrer Lügendrachensaat,	[With our lying dragon's seed]
Zeugt Stacheldraht in Ewigkeit.	[Barbed wire procreates eternally]
Wir haben weder Fraß noch Kleid	[We have neither fodder nor clothes]
Und außerdem sehr wenig Zeit.	[And moreover very little time]
Wir fressen nichts als Stacheldraht,	[We eat nothing but barbed wire]
Nur echten deutschen Stacheldraht.	[Only real German barbed wire]
Die Welt ist nur ein Schützengraben,	[The world is but a trench]
Drin wimmeln braun die deutschen Schaben,	[In which the brown German vermin crawls]
Wie rostzerfress'ner Stacheldraht,	[Like rust-eaten barbed wire]
Weil wir nichts Besseres zu beißen haben,	[Because we have nothing better to eat]
Nichts Besseres zu bieten haben.	[Nothing better to offer]
So produziert der Nazi-Staat,	[Thus, the Nazi state produces]

So produziert der Nazi-Staat,	[Thus, the Nazi state produces]
Nur Stacheldraht, nur Stacheldraht.	[Only barbed wire, only barbed wire]
Wie zackig kommt das deutsche Wort	[How jagged comes the German word]
Mit Stacheln spitz, es lautet: „Mord!"	[With pointed barbs, the word is "murder!"]
Fliegen Fetzen durch die Luft	[Shreds fly through the air]
Von Worten, Bomben, Mensch und Staat,	[Of words, bombs, people, and states]
Die Welt verdreckt im Stacheldraht,	[The world turns filthy in barbed wire]
Im Stacheldraht aus deutschem Stahl.	[In barbed wire from German steel]
Es bleibt den Menschen keine Wahl,	[The people have no choice]
Europa windet sich in Qual.	[Europe twists in agony]
Nur Deutsche winden Stacheldraht,	[Only Germans twist barbed wire]
Von früh bis spät nur Stacheldraht,	[From dawn till dusk only barbed wire]
Nur Stacheldraht, nur Stacheldraht.	[Only barbed wire, only barbed wire]
... Nur Stacheldraht!	[... Only barbed wire!]
Das ist der Deutschen deutscheste Erfindung,	[That is the Germans' most German invention]
Der Völker blutigste Verbindung.	[The bloodiest link between peoples]
Verbunden durch den Stacheldraht,	[Linked by the barbed wire]
Türmt sich der Nazi-Leichenstaat.[3]	[The Nazi corpse state rises up]
(Deutsches Rundfunkarchiv 1998)	

Sung by Austrian actor Peter Illing (pseudonym of Peter Ihle), the song's breathless lyrics include frequent repetitions of "Stacheldraht" and corresponding rhyme words ("Europa ist ein Stachelstaat"), as they exploit the hard consonant combinations of the German language to create a crescendo at the end of every verse. The song repeatedly characterises barbed wire as a specifically German invention, made from German steel. Moreover, the lyrics cast all Germans as vermin crawling through the world's trenches like barbed wire corroded by rust. Although the song names the Nazi state as culprit three times, this is easily superseded by the seven instances of the word "deutsch", either as a noun or an adjective. Indicting all Germans, rather than specifically those who supported the Nazis, ran counter to the strategy of distinguishing

3 An excerpt from the song also features in the radio documentary "Beating Hitler with Humour" (BBC 2019).

between ordinary Germans and the Nazi war machine, and thereby risked offending all German listeners equally.

With orchestration reminiscent of several Brecht/Weill songs, "Stacheldraht" creates the impression of a musical harangue: its lasting effect is haunting, but the song itself is exhausting to listen to. This may also have limited its popularity: it would presumably only appeal to those already interested in avant-garde music, and those already convinced of the Nazi regime's evil character. Here, the propaganda scales are tipped very much towards despair rather than hope, since the lyrics only emphasise the terrifying nature of the present situation without suggesting a better alternative.

Other Spoliansky songs for the BBC were less confrontational, instead urging Germans to pause and consider where the regime's actions had led them. Recorded in 1941, the "Nachtwächterlied" ["Night Watchman's Song"] was used in a number of New Year's Eve broadcasts (WAC 1943k). It is based on a traditional German song, probably of early modern origin, in which a night watchman calls out every hour from one to twelve, connecting each stroke of the bell with a religious message, e.g. "Hört, Ihr Herrn, und lasst euch sagen, / Uns're Glock' hat zehn geschlagen! / Zehn Gebote setzt Gott ein; / Gib, dass wir gehorsam sein!" ["Listen, gentlemen, and let it be said / The bell has tolled ten / Ten commandments God employs / That we might be obedient"] (Erk 1856, 406).[4] In the BBC's version, however, the clock only ever strikes twelve.

Hört, ihr Leut', und lasst euch sagen:	[Listen, people, and let it be said]
Die Glocke hat schon zwölf geschlagen.	[The bell has already tolled twelve]
Zwölf schlägt die Glock'	[Twelve tolls the bell]
Vergesst das Feuer nicht und Licht,	[Do not forget the fire or the light]
Vergesset auch die Wahrheit nicht.	[Do not forget the truth either]
Zwölf schlägt die Glock'	[Twelve tolls the bell]
Hört, ihr Leut', und lasst euch sagen:	[Listen, people, and let it be said]
Die letzte Stund' im Jahr hat g'schlagen	[The last hour of the year has tolled]
Zwölf schlägt die Glock'	[Twelve tolls the bell]
Sich zu besinnen wird's nun Zeit,	[It is now time to realise]
Dass nur durch Hitler all' dies Leid	[That only Hitler is the cause of all this suffering]
Zwölf schlägt die Glock'	[Twelve tolls the bell]

4 For an overview of verses, see: Zachcial 2000.

Hört, ihr Mütter, lasst euch sagen:	[Listen, mothers, let it be said]
Hört eure toten Söhne klagen.	[Hear your dead sons lament]
Zwölf schlägt die Glock‘	[Twelve tolls the bell]
Umsonst waren Hunger, Tod und Seuch‘	[In vain were hunger, death, and disease]
Vergehen wird das Dritte Reich.	[The Third Reich will perish]
Zwölf schlägt die Glock‘	[Twelve tolls the bell]
Hört, ihr Männer, lasst euch sagen:	[Listen, men, let it be said]
Lasst eure Kinder nicht einst fragen	[Don't let your children one day ask]
Zwölf schlägt die Glock‘	[Twelve tolls the bell]
Konntet ihr selbst euch nicht befrei'n?	[Couldn't you liberate yourselves?]
Wie soll's mit Deutschlands Ehre sein?	[What shall become of Germany's honour?]
Zwölf schlägt die Glock‘	[Twelve tolls the bell]
Hört ihr Leut‘ und lasst euch sagen:	[Listen, people, and let it be said]
Die letzte Stund‘ des Kriegs mag schlagen	[The war's last hour may be tolling]
Zwölf schlägt die Glock‘	[Twelve tolls the bell]
Doch erst muss Hitler aus der Welt;	[But first Hitler must leave this Earth]
Nichts kann ersteh'n, bevor er fällt.	[Nothing can arise before he falls]
Zwölf schlägt die Glock‘	[Twelve tolls the bell]
(Deutsches Rundfunkarchiv 1998)	

This song combines a reminder of German folklore and traditions with topical references to the current situation. Although Spoliansky's version uses the first two lines of the original, and starts with a traditional reminder to put out lights and fires, the following verses very specifically reference the Third Reich and the horrors of the ongoing war. Verses 3 and 4 go beyond the traditional address to all people, specifically appealing to mothers and men, emphasising the high human cost of the war ("eure toten Söhne"), and urging Germans to consider how future generations will judge their actions ("Lasst eure Kinder nicht einst fragen"). Occurring a total of ten times, the song's key line "zwölf schlägt die Glock‘" emphasises the notion that time is running out on Hitler's regime, and that it is high time for the German people to redress the crimes perpetrated by their leaders.

The song was used to ring in the year 1944 on the German Service: with the English New Year's programme finishing at midnight on the first stroke of Big Ben, the first two verses of the "Night Watchman's Song" set in immediately after the twelfth stroke (WAC 1943k). After repeating the phrase "zwölf schlägt die Glock'", the speaker reminds his listeners of Hitler's broken promises from previous years: "Das Nachtwächterlied, das Sie eben hörten, brachten wir zum ersten Mal im Londoner Sender vor genau 2 Jahren, in der Sylvesternacht [*sic*] 1941, in den letzten Minuten des Jahres, für das Hitler dem deutschen Volk den Endsieg versprochen hatte" ["Radio London first broadcast the "Night Watchman's Song", which you have just heard, exactly two years ago on New Year's Eve, during the last few minutes of the year for which Hitler had promised the German people the final victory"] (WAC 1943k, 1). The remainder of the script contains news bulletins followed by a "New Year's concert" of other songs which had previously been broadcast in other German Service programmes, before the New Year's broadcast concludes with the last three verses of the Night Watchman's Song.

Other notable songs Spoliansky wrote for the BBC include a setting of Bertolt Brecht's poem "Und was bekam des Soldaten Weib" (1942), which chronicles the progress of the war through different luxury gifts a soldier sends home to his wife from European capitals, until the final object she receives is a widow's veil from Russia (Brecht 1993, 71–72; Grosch 2006). Scripts and correspondence also reference a number of Spoliansky songs for which no lyrics or recordings survive, including "Die Moritat vom Volkswagen" (WAC 1941b), "Wir wollen heim ins Reich" – sometimes referred to as "Deutsches Soldatenlied" (WAC 1941a), "Lappenlied" or "Lappenkrank" (WAC 1941d), and "Deutsches Fliegerlied" (WAC 1941f). A further song was called "Zwischen den Zeilen", for which only the lyrics by Austrian librettist Paul Knepler survive.

Von Siegen wird stets nur berichtet,	[They only report victories]
Verluste des Feindes erdichtet	[And make up the enemy's losses]
Wenn Hiebe sie kriegen	[When they get a thrashing]
Das wird verschwiegen,	[That is omitted]
Gefälscht wird ganz ohne Scham	[They falsify shamelessly]
Wie's ihnen passt in den Kram,	[Just as it suits their purposes]
Wer glaubt noch den Lügen den plumpen,	[Who still believes these brazen lies]
Wer traut heute noch diesen Lumpen	[Who still believes these hoodlums]
Man hat es gelernt schon bisweilen,	[One has learnt meanwhile]
Zu lesen zwischen den Zeilen.	[To read between the lines]

(WAC 1943f)

In contrast to the examples above, this song is much more specific in its attack on the Third Reich. Instead of pointing out its general evils, the lyrics put forward a strategy for dealing with misinformation in a closed media system by urging German listeners to doubt what they are reading in the press, and instead read between the lines to discover what the regime is trying to cover up.

The final example of an original Spoliansky song for the German Service also appears to have been one of its most successful ones. Marius Goring described "Wir fahren immer hin und her" ("We keep going back and forth", 1941) as "a very great success", which had been used "on numerous occasions" (WAC 1942b). In fact, having made repeated use of the song, the BBC considered it worthwhile recording an entirely re-orchestrated version in late 1942, which according to Goring "has already proved most successful, has been reproduced already three times and will be reproduced several times in the near future" (WAC 1942b). It also featured in the 1944 New Year's broadcast, when it was introduced through an anecdote, presumably to authenticate its origins within the German army itself:

> im Herbst 1940 malte ein deutscher Soldat, der in Polen und Frankreich gekämpft hatte, an die Wand des Viehwagens auf dem er wieder einmal vom Westen nach dem Osten verschickt worden war, die Worte:
> "Wir fahren immer hin und her,
> Wir haben keine Heimat mehr."
> Und aus diesen Worten entstand das Lied (WAC 1943k, 1)
> [in the autumn of 1940, a German soldier who had fought in Poland and France daubed the following words on the wall of a cattle wagon in which he was once again being sent from West to East:
> "We keep going back and forth,
> We have no homeland anymore."
> And from these words the song was created].

Whether true or not, the anecdote might seem plausible to listeners, with the lines written by the anonymous soldier forming the basis of the chorus.

The song's chorus is hummed and whistled in the introduction, and also exists in a recording with a swing band (this may have been the re-orchestration mentioned by Goring).[5] The markedly upbeat tune contrasts with the melancholic lyrics, which speak of war-weariness, rootlessness, and a desire to return home (Dümling 1988).[6]

5 A brief excerpt of the swing version, followed by the BBC's New Year's broadcast, is available at (BBC 2021).

6 For the lyric, see also Vike Plock's chapter in this volume.

The catchy chorus is repeated twice at the end, and stays in the listener's memory long after first listening to it. Meanwhile, the whistled introduction in particular gives this song a gently subversive quality akin to the British "Colonel Bogey March": it is possible to imagine soldiers whistling and humming it while marching, carrying out everyday tasks, or riding a train. This memorable quality would make it a more effective form of propaganda than spoken-word broadcasts. Once heard, the song could rapidly spread among a population by word of mouth, with its lyrics constantly reminding Germans that the war was rendering them homeless.

The uneven distribution of surviving archival evidence makes it difficult to judge the propaganda success of these original compositions. One aspect of note is Mischa Spoliansky's obvious talent for producing tunes in very diverse music styles, and the prolific nature of his output for the BBC. If frequency of broadcast is a measure of success, "Wir fahren immer hin und her" would clearly be the most successful of his compositions, followed by the "Night Watchman's Song", which was used in at least three New Year's Eve broadcasts. Since these two songs differ so radically from each other, there does not seem to be an identifiable formula for producing a good anti-Nazi propaganda song. However, perhaps the juxtaposition of jolly tune and melancholic lyrics in "Wir fahren immer hin und her" can be seen as the musical embodiment of Greene's mix of "despair" and "hope" propaganda. Its catchy tune also points to another important strategy the BBC employed to pursue its propaganda aims through music: hijacking an already popular melody and rewriting the lyrics.

4 Parodies of German Hits

Familiarity with songs was an important factor when it came to integrating music into features scripts, so that the song would support the message of the spoken words, and could be spread rapidly among those parts of the population who did not (yet) listen to the BBC German Service. In his study of popular songs during the Third Reich, Eckhard John maintains "dass populäre Lieder längerfristig oftmals eine Eigendynamik entwickeln, die sich politischen oder ideologischen Steuerungsmechanismen partiell auch entzieht" ["that in the long run, popular songs often take on a life of their own, which manages partly to dodge political and ideological control mechanisms"] (John 2006, 165). The German Service attempted to harness this potential by commissioning several parodies of songs which were already popular, yet in some ways also controversial, within the Third Reich.

In April 1943 the BBC broadcast its own version of the most famous German popular song at the time, "Lili Marleen". Originally written as a poem by First World War soldier Hans Leip in 1915, the words focus on a soldier's love and longing for Lili Marleen, with whom he used to meet regularly by a street lamp outside his barracks. The tune was composed in 1938 by Norbert Schultze, who produced a number of hits and propaganda songs for the Nazi regime, including the infamous "Bomben auf Engelland" (1939). First recorded by German singer Lale Andersen in 1939 (see Figure 6.1), "Lili Marleen" was not successful at all initially, but became increasingly popular from the summer of 1941 onwards through its frequent use on Radio Belgrade (Protte 2004, 365). Following the Third Reich's invasion of Yugoslavia, the *Wehrmacht* soldiers in charge of the newly-created forces' radio station in Belgrade broadcast the song every night just before 10 pm at the end of a programme of personal greetings between soldiers and loved ones (John 2006, 169). Due to the station's enormous broadcasting range, which included Britain and continental Europe, North Africa, Turkey, Iran, and parts of the Soviet Union, "Lili Marleen" soon became internationally famous among Allied troops as well (Protte 2004, 368).

Although Lale Andersen's career received a considerable boost through "Lili Marleen", by 1942 she had fallen out of favour with the regime, as her correspondence with Jewish exiles in Switzerland had been discovered. In September 1942, she was excluded from the *Reichskulturkammer*, and Goebbels simultaneously issued a ban on broadcasting any Lale Andersen records – with the exception of "Lili Marleen" (John 2006, 175). A year later, Andersen was temporarily banned from performing, on the grounds of political unreliability (John 2006, 175). It was at this point that the BBC German Service intervened in an uncharacteristically bold manner to draw attention to the singer's plight, whilst also furthering its own propaganda aims.

"Lili Marleen" opens a German Service broadcast on 3 April 1943, with actress Lucie Mannheim (who by this point was married to Marius Goring) singing the first verse in its original German form. The speaker then asks listeners: "Ist es Ihnen aufgefallen, dass Sie dieses Lied schon lange nicht gehört haben? Warum nicht? Vielleicht deshalb, weil Lilli Marlen [sic] im Konzentrationslager ist" ["Have you noticed that you have not heard this song for a long time? Why not? Perhaps because Lili Marleen is in a concentration camp"] (WAC 1943e). Having planted this idea in the listener's head, the broadcast presents three deeply satirical verses of the song, before the speaker comes in again to state that "Lala Andersen [*sic*], die Lili Marleen kreiert hat, ist im K.Z. Ja, so ist es eben in Hitlers Deutschland. Wer ein unbedachtes Wort sagt oder ein Buch liest, das dem Regime nicht ganz genehm ist, der wandert ins K.Z." ["Lala Andersen, who created Lili Marleen, is in a concentration

FIGURE 6.1
Lale Andersen (1905–72) first recorded the song "Lili Marleen", and it became popular amongst German troops, before becoming parodied by the BBC German Service, as part of its war-time counter-propaganda. (© Alamy)

camp. That's just how it is in Hitler's Germany. Whoever says something without thinking, or reads a book the regime doesn't approve of, winds up in a concentration camp"] (WAC 1943e). It is unclear where the German service got the inaccurate news that Lale Andersen had been interned in a concentration camp. The broadcast gives no further details on why Andersen had allegedly been arrested, which suggests that no further information was available to the BBC. The news of Andersen's supposed internment is a rare example of the German Service broadcasting an unconfirmed rumour, but it may have helped to spare Andersen from more serious consequences, as the regime took note that her plight was being reported abroad. Although banned from the German airwaves, Andersen was asked in May 1943 to perform on German broadcasts to America and Africa in order to counter rumours that she had been killed by the Nazis (Protte 2004, 375).

The BBC's parody of "Lili Marleen" itself does not reference Lale Andersen's plight at all, but instead emphasises the terrible turn the war has taken. The speaker claims that "die Worte dieses Liedes sind heute nicht mehr aktuell. Wie würden sie lauten, wenn Lili Marleen ihren [*sic*] Soldaten heute ein [*sic*] Brief schriebe?" ["the words of this song are no longer topical. What would they be if Lili Marleen wrote her soldier a letter today?"] (WAC 1943e). As the song progresses, the lyrics depart further and further from the story of two lovers meeting under a street lamp, instead emphasising the woman's loneliness, then underlining the singer's certainty that her lover will die in the war, and finally focusing on Hitler's ruthless exploitation of his own people:

Was ich still hier leide	[What I suffer quietly here]
Weiß nur der Mond und ich –	[Only the moon and I know]
Einst schien er auf uns beide –	[Once it shone on us both]
Nun scheint er nur auf mich.	[Now it only shines on me]
Mein Herz tut mir so bitter weh,	[My heart hurts so terribly]
Wenn ich an der Laterne steh,	[When I stand by the lamppost]
Mit meinem eigenen Schatten	[With my own shadow]
Wie einst Lili Marleen.	[As once, Lili Marleen]
Vielleicht fällst du in Russland	[Perhaps you'll die in Russia]
Vielleicht in Afrika!	[Perhaps in Africa]
Doch irgendwo da fällst Du	[But somewhere you'll definitely die]
So will's der Führer ja!	[That is the Führer's will]
Und wenn wir doch uns wiederseh'n,	[And if we should see each other again]
O, möge die Laterne steh'n	[Oh, may the lamppost stand]
In einem anderen Deutschland	[In a different Germany]
Wie einst Lili Marleen	[As once, Lili Marleen]
Der Führer ist ein Schinder	[The Führer is a knacker]
Das seh'n wir hier genau	[We see that clearly here]
Zu Waisen macht er Kinder,	[He makes orphans out of children]
Zur Witwe jede Frau.	[And a widow out of every woman]
Und der an allem schuld ist, den	[And the one whose fault this is]
Will ich an der Laterne seh'n,	[It's him I want to see at the lamppost]
Hängt ihn an die Laterne!	[Hang him from the lamppost]
Von der Lili Marleen	[Of Lili Marleen]

(WAC 1943e)

Here, the image of longing to see someone under a street light is cleverly subverted to include Hitler himself, followed by the outspoken appeal to lynch Hitler on a lamppost: "Hängt ihn an die Laterne". Moreover, the BBC's version is the only one (in either German or English) to speak at least partly from the woman's point of view. All other versions speak *to* "Lili Marleen" from the soldier's point of view, instead of speaking *as* "Lili Marleen" (despite the most popular versions being sung by female artists). Using a popular song as its starting point, this parody perhaps targets the widest possible audience by appealing to both women on the home front and men fighting in the war, before culminating in a shared fantasy of revenge on Hitler for causing ordinary Germans their wartime suffering.

A similar example of this strategic employment of music is the BBC's version of the 1942 hit song "Es geht alles vorüber", composed by Fred Raymond (John 2006, 166). Although the original lyrics by Max Wallner and Kurt Feltz also centre on two lovers separated by war, they focus much more on the idea of *Durchhalten*, i.e. of getting through the boredom and perils of war in order to be reunited:

Auf Posten in einsamer Nacht,	[At his post during a lonely night]
Da steht ein Soldat und hält Wacht,	[Stands a soldier and keeps watch]
Träumt von Hanne und dem Glück,	[Dreams of Hanne and of the bliss]
Das zu Hause blieb zurück.	[Which he left at home]
Die Wolken am Himmel, sie zieh'n	[The clouds in the sky all go]
Ja alle zur Heimat dahin,	[Towards home]
Und sein Herz, das denkt ganz still für sich:	[And his heart thinks quietly to itself]
Dahin ziehe einmal auch ich.	[I will also go there someday.]
Es geht alles vorüber, es geht alles vorbei.	[Everything passes; everything goes by]
Auf jeden Dezember folgt wieder ein Mai.	[Every December is followed by May]
Es geht alles vorüber, es geht alles vorbei.	[Everything passes; everything goes by]
Doch zwei die sich lieben, die bleiben sich treu.	[But two people who love each other stay faithful]
(John 2006, 163–64)	

This song also owed its enormous wartime popularity to Radio Belgrade, where it was played daily from May 1942 onwards to open the greetings programme which ended with "Lili Marleen" (John 2006, 170).

Coupled with a jolly waltz tune, the expression of a private desire to get through the war and leave it far behind lends itself to the BBC's gleeful imagining of a world after the war, from which the Nazis have been banished:

Doch wenn erst der Krieg einmal aus,	[But when the war finally ends]
Dann kehrt auch der Landser nach Haus,	[The soldier also comes home]
Und am Abend brennt das Licht,	[And in the evenings the light stays on]
Denn Nazis, die gibt es dann nicht.	[For there are no more Nazis]

Nicht Kraft durch Furcht wie bisher,	[Not strength through fear as it used to be]
Und Goebbels, der lügt auch nicht mehr.	[And Goebbels doesn't lie anymore either]
Und verschwunden wohin ich auch seh'	[And disappeared no matter where I look is]
Die ganze NSDAP.	[The entire NSDAP]
("Composite Programme" 1943)	

The comic effect is heightened by the *rallentando* on the last line before the chorus, drawing out the letters N-S-D-A-P as a kind of punch line, before launching back into the gleeful refrain ("Es geht alles vorüber ... ").

The song was used repeatedly on the German Service, featuring in at least six scripts between April 1943 and November 1944 (WAC 1943e; WAC 1943h; WAC 1943i; WAC 1944a; WAC 1944b; WAC 1944d). Updated versions were easy to come by, since it was relatively simple to create new variations of the chorus, as long as they rhymed with the word "vorbei". Here are just a few examples:

Dann ist es mit Hitler und den Bonzen vorbei,	[Then it will be over with Hitler and the bigwigs]
Von all dem Gesindel wird Deutschland dann frei.	[Germany will finally be free from all of those scumbags]
(WAC 1943e)	

To widen the circle of guilt, other Nazi officials besides Hitler could be included by name: "Mit Göring und Goebbels, mit Sauckel und Ley" (WAC 1943e), or the chorus could be used to chronicle the progress of the war: "Stalingrad im Dezember und Tunis im Mai" (WAC 1943h). As a song which lends itself to parody, "Es geht alles vorüber" was a gift to the BBC's propaganda purposes, since all that was required was to extend the general wish that the war might be over to the idea that it should be over because the Nazis had lost.

Smuggling transgressively comical lyrics into German listeners' minds under the cover of a popular song proved to be a successful tactic, as witnessed by the repeated use of the song in a variety of different scripts. It creates a private joke for the individual listener, while also offering possibly the only opportunity for something to "go viral" in the 1940s: transported through the song, the lyrics have a much better chance of being remembered and passed on to others. Moreover, if the clandestine listener was not detected at the very moment of listening, this transgression left no trace (as would be the case with written or pictorial communication).

Presumably this type of broadcast appealed to the broadest possible category of listeners, since it used musical material which was already popular within Germany. In this sense, it constituted a compromise between broadcasting popular styles purely for musical enjoyment, and broadcasting original compositions, in which the lyrics could be more direct, but the song was unlikely to become a hit. While audiences might derive pleasure simply from hearing the tune, carefully listening to the lyrics might foster the hope that everything would indeed soon be "vorbei", until, as the BBC's version would have it: "Auf jeden Dezember folgt ein friedlicher Mai" ["Every December is followed by a peaceful May"] (WAC 1943e).

References

Arnim, Achim von, and Brentano, Clemens, comp. 1808. *Des Knaben Wunderhorn: alte deutsche Lieder.* Heidelberg: Mohr und Zimmer.

Bergmeier, Horst J.P. and Rainer E. Lötz. 1997. *Hitler's Airwaves: The Inside Story of Nazi Radio Broadcasting and Propaganda Swing.* New Haven: Yale University Press.

Brecht, Bertolt. 1993. *Große kommentierte Berliner und Frankfurter Ausgabe*, vol. 15 *Gedichte und Gedichtfragmente 1940–1956.* Ed. Werner Hecht et al. Berlin: Suhrkamp.

Brinson, Charmian and Richard Dove (eds). 2003. *"Stimme der Wahrheit": German-Language Broadcasting by the BBC.* Amsterdam: Rodopi.

BBC. 2019. "Beating Hitler with Humour". Prod. Ashley Byrne, Iain Mackness, and Kristina Moorehead. Radio 4, 31 August. https://www.bbc.co.uk/programmes/m00082zr.

BBC. 2021. Mischa Spoliansky. "Wir fahren immer hin und her". BBC Radio Edit. https://www.youtube.com/watch?v=orj_lByytmQ. Accessed 29 December 2023.

BBC. 2024. "BBC Programming: The War that Made the BBC's Reputation". https://www.bbc.com/historyofthebbc/research/bbc-at-war/overseas-programming/ Accessed: 1 January 2024.

Cannon, Gunda (ed.). 1988. *„Hier ist England – Live aus London": Das deutsche Programm der British Broadcasting Corporation 1938–1988.* London: BBC External Services.

Crisell, Andrew. 1994. *Understanding Radio.* 2nd ed. London: Routledge.

Deutsches Rundfunkarchiv. 1998. *„Hier ist England": Historische Aufnahmen des Deutschen Dienstes der BBC.* (CD)

Dolaplis, Dimitrios. 2019. *Musik als Propagandainstrument im Nationalsozialismus: Politische und soziale Funktionen von Soldatenliedern im NS-Regime*. Baden-Baden: Tectum.

Dümling Albrecht (ed.). 1988. *Entartete Musik: eine Tondokumentation zur Düsseldorfer Ausstellung von 1938*. Berlin, POOL Musikproduktion. (CD).

Erk, Ludwig. 1856. *Deutscher Liederhort. Auswahl der vorzuglichern deutschen Volkslieder aus der Vorzeit und der Gegenwart mit ihren eigenthümlichen Melodien*. Berlin: Eslin.

Fischer, Michael. 2008. „Freiheit die ich meine". *Historisch-kritisches Liederlexikon: populäre und traditionelle Lieder*. Eds. Eckhard John and Tobias Widmaier. https://www.liederlexikon.de/lieder/freiheit_die_ich_meine/?searchterm=Freiheit%20die%20ich%20meine Accessed 1 January 2024.

Grosch, Nils. 2005/2006. „Vom Weib des Nazisoldaten': Musik, Propaganda und Aufführungen eines Brecht-Songs". *Lied und populäre Kultur / Song and Popular Culture* 50–51: 137–61.

John, Eckhard. 2005/2006. „Es geht alles vorüber, es geht alles vorbei: Geschichte eines 'Durchhalteschlagers'" *Lied und Populäre Kultur / Song and Popular Culture*. 50–51: 163–222.

Mansell, Gerard. 1982. *Let Truth Be Told: 50 Years of BBC External Broadcasting*. London: Weidenfeld and Nicolson.

Moorehead, Kristina. 2016. *Satire als Kriegswaffe: Strategien der britischen Rundfunkpropaganda im Zweiten Weltkrieg*. Baden-Baden: Tectum.

Morley, Nathan. 2021. *Radio Hitler: Nazi Airwaves in the Second World War*. Stroud: Amberley Publishing.

Oliver, Emily. 2019. "Inventing a New Kind of German: The BBC German Service and the Bombing War". *Allied Communication to the Public during the Second World War: National and Transnational Networks*. Eds. Simon Eliot and Marc Wiggam. London: Bloomsbury: 149–66.

Plock, Vike Martina. 2021. *The BBC German Service during the Second World War: Broadcasting to the Enemy*. London: Palgrave MacMillan.

Protte, Katja. 2004. „Mythos 'Lili Marleen': Ein Lied im Zeitalter der Weltkriege". *Militärgeschichtliche Zeitschrift* 63: 355–400.

Seul, Stefanie. 2015. "'Plain, Unvarnished News?' The BBC German Service and Chamberlain's Propaganda Campaign Directed at Nazi Germany, 1938–1940". *Media History* 21: 378–396.

Studdert, Will. 2017. *Jazz War, The: Radio, Nazism and the Struggle for the Airwaves in World War II*. London: I.B. Tauris.

Thacker, Toby. 2003. "'Liberating German Musical Life': The BBC German Service and Planning for Music Control in Occupied Germany 1944–1949". *"Stimme der Wahr-*

heit": German-Language Broadcasting by the BBC. Eds. Charmian Brinson and Richard Dove. Amsterdam: Rodopi: 77–92.

WAC. 1940a "Music in Broadcasts to Germany". Memo from European Programme Organiser to C.H. 20 August. E1/758/1. BBC Written Archives Centre, Caversham, UK.

WAC. 1940b. Hugh Carleton Greene. "Layout of BBC Broadcasts in German". 3 September. E1/758/1. BBC Written Archives Centre, Caversham, UK.

WAC 1941a. "Mr. Spoliansky's Commission". Memo from Walter Rilla to Miss Peacock, 13 January. RCONT 1, Mischa Spoliansky: Copyright, File I: 1940–1962. BBC Written Archives Centre, Caversham, UK.

WAC. 1941b. "Weekly Bulletin". 13 February. E1/758/1. BBC Written Archives Centre, Caversham, UK.

WAC. 1941c. "'Lied vom Stacheldraht' – M. Spoliansky". Memo from Miss E.M. Peacock to Miss Waters. 20 February. RCONT 1, Mischa Spoliansky: Copyright, File I: 1940–1962. BBC Written Archives Centre, Caversham, UK.

WAC. 1941d. "Copyright – Mons. Spoliansky". Memo from European Programme Executive to Programme Copyright, 10 March. RCONT 1, Mischa Spoliansky: Copyright, File I: 1940–1962. BBC Written Archives Centre, Caversham, UK.

WAC. 1941e. "Output Listening Scheme: Report on Bulletins and Programmes in German, 5th–10th May 1941". E1/758/1. BBC Written Archives Centre, Caversham, UK.

WAC. 1941f. "Deutsches Fliegerlied". Memo from Overseas Music Director to Programme Copyright, 31 May. RCONT 1, Mischa Spoliansky: Copyright, File I: 1940–1962. BBC Written Archives Centre, Caversham, UK.

WAC. 1941g. Rollo Myers. "The Place of Music in German Broadcasting". 15 September. E1/758/1. BBC Written Archives Centre, Caversham, UK.

WAC. 1942a. "European Music Schedule". Memo from Harman Grisewood to Arthur Bliss. 16 March. R27/94/1. BBC Written Archives Centre, Caversham, UK.

WAC. 1942b. "German Song: 'Wir fahren immer hin und her'". Memo from Marius Goring to Arthur Wynn, 9 December. RCONT 1, Mischa Spoliansky: Artists, File I: 1941–1962. BBC Written Archives Centre, Caversham, UK.

WAC. 1943a. Douglas Ernest Ritchie. "Music Programmes". Memo to Eur MS, (undated, probably 1943). R27/94/1. BBC Written Archives Centre, Caversham, UK.

WAC. 1943b. Hugh Carleton Greene. "Extract from Output Report of B.B.C. European Services dated January 10th–16th 1943". E1/758/2. BBC Written Archives Centre, Caversham, UK.

WAC. 1943c. Steuart Wilson. "Memorandum on European Music", January. R27/94/1. BBC Written Archives Centre, Caversham, UK.

WAC. 1943d. "New Schedule". Memo from Leonard Isaacs to Harman Grisewood, 3 February. R27/94/1. BBC Written Archives Centre, Caversham, UK.

WAC. 1943e. “Composite Programme”. 3 April. German Scripts: Features (April 1943). BBC Written Archives Centre, Caversham, UK.

WAC. 1943f. Robert Ehrenzweig and Julius Pereszlenyi. “Zwischen den Zeilen”. 10 April. German Scripts: Features (April 1943). BBC Written Archives Centre, Caversham, UK.

WAC. 1943fg. Marius Goring. “Freiheit die ich meine”. 25 April. German Scripts: Features (April 1943). BBC Written Archives Centre, Caversham, UK.

WAC. 1943h. Julius Pereszlenyi. “Alles vorüber?”, 29 May. German Scripts: Features (May 1943). BBC Written Archives Centre, Caversham, UK.

WAC. 1943i. Robert Ehrenzweig. “Auf jeden Dezember”. 29 May. German Scripts: Features (May 1943). BBC Written Archives Centre, Caversham, UK.

WAC. 1943j. Julius Pereszlenyi. “Christmas 1943”. 25 December. German Scripts: Features (December 1943). BBC Written Archives Centre, Caversham, UK.

WAC. 1943k. Marius Goring and Julius Pereszlenyi. “New Year’s Night”, 31 December. German Scripts: Features (December 1943). BBC Written Archives Centre, Caversham, UK.

WAC. 1944a. Julius Pereszlenyi and Marius Goring. “Everything Passes”, 3 January. German Scripts: Features (January 1944). BBC Written Archives Centre, Caversham, UK.

WAC. 1944b. “Es geht alles vorüber”, 3 June. German Scripts: Features (June 1944). BBC Written Archives Centre, Caversham, UK.

WAC. 1944c. Douglas Ernest Ritchie. “Policy of European Music Programmes”. Memo to Eur MS, 29 July. R27/94/1. BBC Written Archives Centre, Caversham, UK.

WAC. 1944d. Robert Ehrenzweig. “Everything Comes Back”. 16 November. German Scripts: Features (November 1944). BBC Written Archives Centre, Caversham, UK.

Zachcial, Michael (ed.). 2000. „Hört, ihr Herrn, und lasst euch sagen“. *Volksliederarchiv*, Bremen: Müller-Lüdenscheidt-Verlag. https://www.volksliederarchiv.de/hoert-ihr-herrn-und-lasst-euch-sagen/ Accessed 29 December 2023.

PART 2

The Cold War

∵

CHAPTER 7

Frau Wernicke, the Remigrant: Annemarie Hase in Postwar Berlin

Sheer Ganor

"Do you remember Frau Wernicke?" The author at the *Neues Deutschland* paper rhetorically inquired and immediately responded: "But of course. She was the cheeky Berlinerin who during the Nazi years unabashedly spoke the truth with a Berlin dialect through the BBC broadcasts, and whose harsh but warm voice we secretly heard from the speaker. Now she stands before us in person" (*Neues Deutschland*, 1948). The woman figuratively standing before the readers of this 1948 report was Annemarie Hase, a cabaret and theatre performer who recently returned to her hometown of Berlin from England, where she had found refuge in 1936 after fleeing antisemitic persecution in Germany. Though she had been away from her home country for more than a decade, Hase was able to maintain a curious connection to German society in absentia. During the Second World War, she was the voice behind the fictional Frau Wernicke, one of the most successful characters created for the German-language propaganda broadcasts produced by the BBC. From studios in London, she spoke to German listeners who broke their government's prohibition and tuned into the enemy's broadcasting. She spoke to them, in the words of the author who described her voice in 1948, harshly but warmly, aiming to expose them to the criminal nature of the Nazi regime and to persuade them of the futility of Germany's war. Now here she was in person again, hoping to rebuild her life and her career in the divided and war-torn city.

Annemarie Hase's decision to return to Berlin in the aftermath of the German capitulation appears intuitive and counterintuitive at the same time. On the one hand, as she herself told several reporters who interviewed her soon after her arrival, Berlin was her home town, the place where she was born and where she spent a happy childhood. Having lived her entire life in Berlin before the Nazi regime forced her to leave, her desire to return to the one place she called home was understandable. On the other hand, Hase's return contrasted with the vast majority of refugees who fled Central Europe following racial persecution. Scholars estimate that less than 5% of German Jews who were able to leave during the Nazi period chose to return to the country after the war. (Borneman and Peck 1995, 4; Krauss 2001, 9) The traumatic

 | HTTPS://DOI.ORG/10.1515/9783111302508-007

experiences of discrimination, violence, rejection and loss made it difficult for most to imagine rebuilding their lives in Germany ever again. Even among those who reconstituted connections with old German friends, who travelled to Germany often and who preserved a lifelong connection to the country, fully transplanting their lives back there seemed undesirable, if not impossible. To be sure, there were exceptions. Though it is difficult to assess in figures, anecdotally it appears that performing artists, writers and other professionals who already had an established career in 1933, and whose work required a German-speaking audience, did return at higher rates than other German-Jewish refugees (Feinberg 2013; Krauss 2001, 90–1). Hase was thus perhaps not typical in her rapid return to Berlin, but she was also not alone.

What distinguishes her experience of remigration is that, unlike other Jewish artists who were forcibly cut off from their home audience in Germany, when she performed as Frau Wernicke, she had ongoing (though vicarious, distant and one-sided) access to German audiences. In fact, through the clandestine broadcasts of the BBC, Hase was probably able to reach a broader German audience than she had during the height of her performance career on various cabaret stages of the Weimar Republic. But as Wernicke, Hase had to remain anonymous in order not to jeopardise the impact of her propaganda. When Hase returned to Berlin in 1947, her arrival revealed to most of Wernicke's German fans the person behind the voice. For the German public, therefore, Hase's postwar return was seen as more than the homecoming of another exiled artist, or the unlikely appearance of a Jewish refugee. It was the return of Frau Wernicke herself, the popular character that they forged a bond with without putting too much thought into the how and why she came into existence.

In the following chapter, I examine Annemarie Hase's return to Berlin and the responses that followed from the German media and public. By analysing the coverage of her comeback to Germany and her career path in the postwar decades, I show that the reception to this dual encounter – the return of Hase, the exiled artist, on one hand, and the arrival of Wernicke, a fictional embodiment of the "good German", on the other – was rooted in a false and dishonest sense of identification. Frau Wernicke's value as a tool of psychological warfare was her appeal to ordinary Germans as one of their own. When Hase spoke to German listeners as Wernicke, she reflected to them their own experiences of life in the National Socialist state and under the conditions of total war. When Hase reemerged in Berlin in 1947, she was greeted back as "our Wernicke", while her own life, her story of persecution, marginalisation and displacement, was left out of focus.

1 From the Stage into Exile

An "original Berliner", as one reviewer described her (AdK 1962a), Hase was born in the German capital in 1900 with the name Annita Hirsch. Her father owned a soap manufacturing business and the family enjoyed a stable middle class life until the father's death by suicide in 1913. Already at a young age she had dreamt of becoming an actor and at the age of eighteen, she was admitted into Max Reinhardt's acting school, where instructors quickly spotted her potential as a comedian (Anon. 1999, 17–19). Hase was well-placed to benefit from the surge of opportunities in theatre and performing arts that took place during the Weimar Republic. She had her first big break in 1921, performing at the Wilde Bühne cabaret, and soon became a regular on the stages of popular political cabarets in Berlin, performing songs written by Kurt Tucholsky, Erich Kästner, Friedrich Holländer and others. Hase also performed in theatre productions across Germany, playing small roles in classical Shakespeare plays and original pieces by Bertolt Brecht. But her main success was in cabaret and variety shows, where she made a name for herself as a chansonnière and comedy artist.

Hase's relationship to Jewishness was not straightforward. She was born into a Jewish family but was baptised at birth, though it appears that the family had preserved connections to a secular Jewish culture. At the time, it was not uncommon for German Jews who either converted or who had their children baptised for practical reasons to remain a part of a Jewish social milieu (Endelman 2015; Fetheringill Zwicker and Ulysses Rose 2020, 708–9; Spector 2006). Though she did not speak about her attitudes towards Jewishness in public, it is possible to glean some insights from her performances and her career path. Her open resistance to antisemitism was evident in her recording of the 1931 satirical song, "The Jews are to blame for everything" ["An allem sind die Juden schuld"], one of the only original recordings remaining from her pre-1933 career. When all Jewish artists were forbidden from performing to German audiences, she joined the Jewish Cultural Association [Jüdischer Kulturbund] that provided employment to artists like herself and organised a variety of cultural events for Jewish audiences (Rovit 2012). While living in England, she was invited to perform for the Jewish Liberal Club, a German-Jewish refugee organisation (Tergit 1943). And in the postwar years, she was cast in "Jewish roles," and gave several performances at Jewish community institutions (Feinberg 2018, 82; Frühauf 2021, 188). Hase may not have had a religious affiliation to Judaism or a regular presence in Jewish communal life, but she never severed her connections to Jewishness either. In fact, her relationship to Jewishness fits well within a subculture of secular, assimilated German Jews born around the fin-de-siècle period who chose a flexible mode of belonging that rejected neat categorisation. In any case, to audiences in Weimar-era Germany she would have been identifiable as a Jew – baptism or not. And to the Nazi regime as well.

The anti-Jewish agenda affected Annemarie Hase almost immediately following the establishment of the Nazi dictatorship in 1933. Cabaret performers like herself were attacked, vilified and accused of corrupting the German spirit. Under the antisemitic legislation that banned Jews from German cultural life and tried to expunge them from the public sphere, she was, as mentioned, prohibited from performing to non-Jewish audiences. Following the legislation of the Nuremberg Laws in September 1935, she was also forbidden from using her stage name Hase and was required to perform under her birthname Hirsch (Anon. 1999, 42). The cultural activities of the Jewish Kulturbund helped stave off the financial effects of these restrictions, but with the dispossession, degradation and discrimination aimed at Jews continuously intensifying, Hase decided to leave the country. In November 1936, she emigrated to Britain, joining her brother who had already escaped and settled there.

As a refugee in London, Annemarie Hase was safe from the threat of Nazi violence but exposed to the difficulties of life in displacement. She took on a series of odd jobs to sustain herself under precarious conditions. But she did not stay away from the stage and found opportunities to perform alongside other refugees in theatre productions of refugee clubs and antifascist cultural organisations, such as the "Free German Cultural League" [Freie Deutsche Kulturbund] (Brinson and Dove 2008; Larsen 1957; Naumann 1983, 169–227). The group staged shows in both German and English, and many of their performances conveyed a vocal and decisive message against Nazism, tyranny and racism (figure 7.1). Occasionally, the shows caught the attention of the British press. One review of the play *Four and Twenty Black Sheep* from 1939 reported that "Frau Annamarie Hase, formerly so celebrated, provides one of the most moving performances with her fairy story, which she tells to two children. This is a brilliant evocation of the feelings of the refugee; sad and comic truths are mixed in a manner which should stir the most placid nature" (*New Statesman* 1939). Another review of the play *Mr. Gulliver Goes to School* concluded in 1943: "London has no exact parallel to this type of production [...] Humour at the refugees' theatre is often wry; these players can laugh at themselves and at their lives in exile – the revue is essentially a family affair – but it is never long before they turn from shooting folly as it flies to strike at the Nazi regime or to salute the spirit of Russia – and of Britain" (AdK 1943a).

The reviewer's note about the lack of an "exact parallel" in London to the kind of artistic production of the "refugees' theatre" alluded to the unique circumstances that led Annemarie Hase to the BBC, and to the creation of the satirical propaganda programmes in general. The German-speaking refugee performers brought with them into displacement their unique cultural content, which in peacetime may have been considered an intriguing source of entertainment, but under the conditions of total war became invaluable for developing psychological warfare aimed at German listeners. And so, when the BBC German Service producers considered a character that would appeal especially to women and to the average working-class listener, to deliver cheeky, eye-to-eye, honest portrayals of everyday life in the Third Reich, and to scare German listeners into defeatism using their own sense of humour as a weapon against them, they needed an insider who could develop and sell that character reliably and with empathy. Paradoxically, the best suitable people living in London at the time were those who were deemed by German society to be undesired outsiders, and who thus found their way to England as refugees. People like Annemarie Hase.

Hase's account of how she became Frau Wernicke is typically playful. In the early summer of 1940, she recalled, she was woken up by a phone call. The voice on the other end identified itself as "Mrs. Gibson from the BBC," referring to Christina Gibson, who was in charge of German-language propaganda broadcasting targeting female listeners. When Gibson invited Hase to record a broadcast on that call, Hase, assuming she was being pranked, responded: "Cut the nonsense, kids, and don't wake me in the middle of the night." When she was convinced that the invitation was in earnest, she hurried to Broadcasting House and was given a script to learn and then record. The Wernicke pilot aired a few days afterwards, and Hase was then offered the role of Gertrude Wernicke on a weekly basis (Naumann 1990, 163–4). The Wernicke scripts were written by Bruno Adler, another Jewish refugee employed at the German Service. Adler's biting satire and Hase's comedic talents fused together perfectly to form the character of the grumpy but kind-hearted Berliner who was not afraid of getting into trouble with the Nazis.

Frau Wernicke was a subversive protagonist who openly protested against what she saw as the exploitation of the German population by Nazi "party bosses" and their cadre of opportunistic profiteers. Her broadcasts put into words resentments and criticisms against the regime as they came into play in various day-to-day situations. She pointed out how the regime's policies were hurting the German people with food shortages, financial ruin and endless loss of life. When she talked to her friend, Luise, about an old rag she discovered after discarding it, Wernicke noted: "We used to throw this kind of stuff away and now it's the finest of the finest, huh? Yea, you're right about

FIGURE 7.1 Annemarie Hase (1900–71) the cabaret and theatre performer who voiced the character of "Frau Wernicke" on the BBC German Service 1940–44. (© Persona Verlag)

that. What used to be a piece of trash previously, before the great years, is considered a great thing now, in the trash years." (Naumann 1990, 10).

Wernicke's biting remarks against the regime even got her into serious trouble, and, as part of the series, she was sent to a concentration camp and released upon condition that she help disseminate Nazi indoctrination in her neighbourhood. But she stuck to her guns and continued to voice her opposition, which resounded even more bitterly as she sarcastically recited the Nazi propaganda she was tasked with spreading. When she faux-chastised a group of neighbours for their lacklustre enthusiasm for the war, she proclaimed: "Peace is maybe good enough for the degenerate Platucrats [sic], or whatever those wimps are called. Our ideal, my dear Volksgenossen, is that nothing on this earth is as beautiful as war. Life is hardly worth living if you're not allowed to die for the Führer and the Third Reich!" (Naumann 1990, 23–4; Moorhead 2016, 114–35; Plock 2021, 122–6)

A key advantage of Wernicke's propaganda was that she spoke to the audience as one of their own. Her social status as a blue-collar worker and her streetwise demeanour marked her as someone who addressed German listeners as an equal. Through her, British intelligence authorities were able to design a relatable and agreeable package for their messaging. The character's positionality was also important for communicating the British approach towards the broader German population. Like all broadcasts on the BBC German Service, Frau Wernicke also reiterated the distinction between Nazi leadership and ideologues, who bore direct responsibility for the regime's criminal acts, and those in German society who were presumably forced to play along and carry the burden. For example, when Wernicke was asked by one of her fictional interlocutors if she was not afraid of the enemy's revenge against Germany, she responded: "Come now, they won't do anything to us. We're not a part of Hitler's Bloody Hands Inc." (Naumann 1990, 83). The British government, this messaging signalled to listeners behind enemy lines, did not hold the entire German nation accountable for the regime's actions: if they had done nothing wrong, why should they be concerned themselves?

If Wernicke was persuasive, it was to a great extent thanks to Bruno Adler's poignant and humorous writing and to Annemarie Hase's precise delivery. Hase was, in many ways, perfect for the role. The Berlin dialect that was so essential to the character was like a native language for her (Williams 2013, 65–6). And while Bruno Adler was remarkably fluent in it, considering his Austro-Hungarian background, Hase did on occasion interject with suggestions that made Wernicke's speech more authentic in the local jargon (Williams 2013, 67). In addition to her masterful command of the dialect, Hase had years of experience performing political satire in front of German audiences. The role of a saucy and observant underdog was one that she was well familiar with from multiple shows from her pre-1933 career.

Though measuring Wernicke's success as a propagandist is difficult, the character clearly resonated with listeners. Reportedly, it was even a favourite of Joseph Goebbels himself (Ebermayer et al. 1953, 215). The full extent of Wernicke's popularity was only revealed after 1945, but the BBC was able to gather evidence of it while the war was still raging. When Hase asked for a raise for her role, BBC editor Leonard Miall supported her request and wrote to their superiors that Frau Wernicke "is one of the very best of the regular features of our German Service and evidence from inside Germany shows us that her propaganda value is enormous. Hence Miss Hase is, for us, an extremely valuable person." (Williams 2013, 58). Letters from listeners writing from neutral countries confirmed this. One writer from Switzerland who professed her love of Wernicke signed her letter with a "true and good Berlinerin". (WAC 1944). A professor of meteorology in Windhoek, South West Africa [today Namibia], even inquired whether Wernicke was not, by any chance, the daughter of the school-caretaker at the Humboldt Gymnasium in Berlin (AdK 1943b). These letters testify that listeners were easily able to imagine Wernicke – vocalised through Hase – as a real Berlin persona, and some even wove her into their own emotional landscape of the city.

Frau Wernicke's broadcasts also garnered media attention inside Britain. One paper exclaimed: "She is the voice of true Germany, calling Hitler's bluffs, and warning her fellow-countrymen of the fate they will suffer if they do not get rid of their Nazi overlords before it is too late." (AdK 1943b). Another emphasised the originality and authenticity of her broadcasts: "It is not just English material translated and spoken stiffly, but real, live, racy German." (AdK n.d.). One paper reported in 1941: "In Germany she's known as Frau Wernicke, the shrill-voiced, truculent, irrepressibly fearless Berlin housewife who Speaks Her Mind. At the B.B.C. [...] she's known as a gifted German ex-actress whose real name must remain a secret. To Dr. Goebbels she's a major headache, because Frau Wernicke's monologues are rapidly becoming the rage among German listeners." (AdK 1941). The fact that the voice behind Frau Wernicke had to be kept a secret appeared in other reports as well. It seems that the BBC feared that revealing her true identity as a Jewish refugee would compromise Wernicke's appeal with German listeners who thought of her as a fellow German, and not just that – a true working-class *Berliner Schnauze*.

This policy was not unique to Hase. The refugees who took part in the German Service's broadcasts, and who were tremendously important to its success, remained nameless and anonymous during their years working for the BBC (Ganor 2020). Their skills as effective propagandists would have too easily revealed their identities as former fellow citizens who were no longer welcome in their own countries. In Hase's case, her background and personal history as a native Berliner, her talent as an actor and her vast experience of entertaining German audiences gave her just the right pitch that the character of Frau Wernicke needed. But it was precisely that combination that required the concealment of her identity. It is difficult to assess the damage that disclosing it would have inflicted on the show's reception. There was a time when German audiences cheered on Annemarie Hase's performances and granted her affection, but those days were gone. And even if not all German covert listeners were ardent followers of Hitler, that still did not mean that they would be willing to accept a Jewish refugee as a voice against the regime. In any case, that was not a gamble that the BBC was willing to take. Wernicke was Wernicke, and Annemarie Hase was to remain anonymous.

Frau Wernicke's series aired from the summer of 1940 and until the end of January 1944, with a brief hiatus between December 1940 and March 1941 (Naumann 1990, 172–3; Williams 2013, 64–5). It is not entirely clear why the BBC decided to take the show off the air while the war was still ongoing, especially considering that it was considered one of the top hits of the German Service satires, and that other successful shows continued to run until 1945. Hase was bitterly disappointed by the decision to discontinue the series. She wrote to Christina Gibson: "I can't deny that your decision to take the Wernicke-Programme off the air was a great disappointment to me, not so much in economical as in ideological respect. I have always looked at my work at the B.B.C. [...] as a contribution – if only a small one – to the allied cause and a means of conveying genuine true and democratic spirit to some of my fellow countrymen." (Moorehead 2016, 247) Wernicke's role was clearly not like any other role in Hase's acting portfolio. It gave her a sense of mission and invited her to play a not insignificant role in world-historical events. Importantly, it allowed her to continue speaking to her "fellow countrymen", even if she seemed to acknowledge that only some would truly listen to her message.

2 A Double Homecoming

After Wernicke went off the air, Hase continued to perform with groups of German-speaking artists in London. It seems that her hopes were set on returning to Berlin as soon as it became possible. Already in 1943, on the occasion of Frau Wernicke's three-year anniversary, an English newspaper stated that the unnamed voice of the character "hopes very strongly that this will be her last anniversary in exile and that soon she will be able to drop her mask and appear in the open ... before her friends in liberated Europe." (AdK 1943b). Hase was, in fact, among the first refugees to return to Germany in the immediate postwar years, arriving in the spring of 1947. At the time, the devastation of the war years was still highly visible and palpable in Berlin, while the shifting of the city towards the Cold War order was simultaneously under way.

Hase's motivations to come back to a city roiled in such a state are not immediately obvious, but they were probably varied and complex. Her career in Britain was insecure, especially without her only stable source of income – playing the role of Frau Wernicke. Even if the series had lasted a little longer, it was entirely tied to the conditions of war. She never managed to secure a professional footing as an English-speaking actor during her life in Britain, and roles for German-speaking cabaret performers seemed unlikely in the postwar era. Returning to Germany held the promise of being able to re-establish her Weimar-era success. Hase was not alone in this hope. Some of her colleagues and friends from the theatre world were also making their way back to Germany from their places of exile (especially non-Jewish refugees, who were more likely to consider returning). Many more, however, chose to stay in their countries of displacement. What kind of communities and social networks could she hope to find upon her return? Her family members who were fortunate to escape Germany in time, also chose to continue their lives scattered in Britain, the United States and in Africa (AdK 1970).

With the onset of the Cold War, ideology may have also played a role in Hase's decision to return. Though she settled in the Western part of Berlin, many of her early performances after returning were in the Soviet Zone of occupation. Once the two German states were formed in 1949, Hase worked almost exclusively in the German Democratic Republic while continuing living in the Western part of the divided city. Between 1949 and 1956, she was a member of Bertolt Brecht's Berliner Ensemble Theatre, and she also had small roles in various film productions of DEFA, the state-owned East German film studios. In 1950 Hase even resurrected the character of Frau Wernicke in support of the GDR, and briefly broadcast East German propaganda on the wavelength of the *Deutschlandsender*, the broadcasting service aimed at West German listeners, to the chagrin of some members in her "community of fate" of displaced German Jews (*Aufbau* 1950).

As with her attitudes towards Jewishness, Hase's interviews and her archival collection do not reveal much about her political affiliation, but this show of support for the nascent East German state provides a strong indication for her identification with, at the very least, the ideals of socialism. And yet, when the Berlin Wall was erected in 1961, Hase did not leave her residence in the Western part of the city to fully join the fold of the Eastern Bloc. Instead, she opted to remain in the West, where she continued to pursue her waning acting career, and where she passed away in February of 1970 (Feinberg 2018, 72; Frühauf 2021, 188).

Hase's liminal existence in both East and West Berlin – for as long as it was possible for her to live in one and work for the other – complicates our understanding of the motivations of the Jewish returnees to Germany. Among those who were politically drawn to the prospect of participating in the creation of a Socialist society, the antifascist commitments of the GDR were a conveniently straightforward explanation for why, despite everything that had transpired under Nazism, they chose to once again live on German soil. This ideological reasoning was not available for those who settled in the West, and in their reflections on their choice to return, circumstantial life events feature more prominently than politics, diminishing the importance of an active choice in the matter (Bollenbeck 2005, 22–3; Borneman and Peck 1995; Walther, 2020). Between her affiliation with East German cultural production and her continuous residence in the West, Hase's case shows that the spectrum of motivations was more fluid and dynamic than it sometimes appears.

If politics and career strategy shaped Hase's decision to move back to Germany to some degree, she found it important to stress another reason too. When asked by one journalist, who wrote of her return in April 1947, why she decided to come back, she responded: "[E]lsewhere might be nicer but, after all, here at the Kaiserallee is where I played marbles as a kid" (AdK 1947a). She repeated this explanation, in different variations, in at least one other newspaper interview as well as in some of her live performances (AdK 1949a; AdK 1965). Hase clearly wanted to reiterate her deep emotional connection not only to Germany but to the city of Berlin, her childhood home. That a reason even needed to be put into words signals that her decision to return was not self-evident, even to the German public. Or perhaps when journalists posed the question, they were hoping to hear a confirmation that a new era in Germany was beginning, one in which even someone like Annemarie Hase can feel at home again.

Reading the media coverage of Hase's return today, we can detect traces of curiosity about her choice to re-emerge on the scene. But the dominant tone of the press coverage, while celebratory, was not one of surprise. The media almost always treated Hase's return as a natural development, an occurrence that on the one hand was newsworthy enough to merit coverage but, on the other hand, made intuitive sense. This rendition took two forms. In the first, Hase's return was portrayed not simply as a remigration of an exiled former citizen, but also the homecoming of Frau Wernicke herself, the character that many Germans grew so fond of during the war years. Hase, in a way, incorporated both realities. Her personal story included flight, life in a foreign country and working for the former enemy. Wernicke's stories, as told through the German Service broadcasts, were about waiting in air raid shelters, dealing with food shortages, counting the war dead – events and experiences familiar to the average German living through the war years. Hase may have come back from exile, but Frau Wernicke – was she ever really away?

This sentiment was evident in one of the very first reports of Hase's return, which appeared in *Die Neue Zeitung* in 1947. In this piece, Wernicke's broadcasts were portrayed as a link between Hase and her home audience that remained unbroken despite the artificial distance placed between them: "The warm, dark jeer of her voice, with its abrupt grotesque screeching, was easy to identify when it resounded on the BBC German broadcasts through the muted radio. Word came out quickly, who Frau Wernicke was: Annemarie Hase – an untransplantable person ["eine Unverpflanzbare"]." Whether Hase's voice was truly so identifiable as the article suggests is debatable, though it is not unlikely that theatre enthusiasts and regulars of Berlin's cabaret scene would have indeed recognised her over the airwaves. Regardless, the article clearly sought to situate Hase via Wernicke as an insider who, under undisclosed circumstances, was temporarily transplanted elsewhere, but who could never truly find her place outside of Berlin, where she emerged again. Hase is jovially quoted in the article, saying: "I'm of good spirits and I'm glad that my Frau Wernicke broadcasts kept my memory alive," again stressing a sense of ongoing intimacy (AdK 1947a). The occasion noted in the article was described almost as a reunion, though a reunion with whom seemed less clear. Was it Hase who maintained a connection to Germany thanks to her role as Wernicke, or was it Wernicke who made German audiences think of Hase as one of their own? And was Wernicke's impact so powerful as to blur the reality of the rejection, persecution and dehumanisation that Hase had endured only so recently, rendering her – a so-called "untransplantable" – a refugee living in displacement?

In "Frau Wernicke in Köpenick," the 1948 article cited at the beginning of this chapter, we again encounter a sense of an ambiguous reunion. After declaring that the memorable Frau Wernicke "stands before us in person," the author continued to introduce her: "Her name is Annemarie Hase, famous already in the heyday of the Trude Hesterberg Cabaret, a chansonnière with class." In 1948 Wernicke was fresh enough in the German public's mind, but Hase was depicted simultaneously as a well-known personality and as a stranger that needed to be reintroduced (*Neues Deutschland* 1948). Similarly, when the short-lived revival of Wernicke's broadcasts in the service of the GDR was announced in 1950, the advertisement for the show read: "Frau Wernicke – Annemarie Hase. Two names, but one concept." The advertisement invited readers to revisit the recent past: "Who doesn't recall those days during the Nazi time, when secretly, behind locked doors, one adjusted the radio to listen to Frau Wernicke, spoken by Annemarie Hase at the BBC on the English wavelength. Frau Wernicke, who, as a woman from the people of common sense ["Volke mit gesundem Menschenverstand"], denounced the conditions of the time and gave us hope for a better future." Now, the ad continued, Wernicke is once again tasked with being the voice of the *Volk*, with the West German government in Bonn providing a new target for her sharp criticisms (AdK 1950).

If announcements and reports like these suggested that Germans were excited to reunite with Wernicke aka Hase, others hinted at a more complicated reality. In 1949, in an interview with the East German *Nachtexpress*, Hase revealed a more ambivalent impression. “She came back from England two years ago,” wrote the interviewer, “and Berlin warmly welcomed its Frau Wernicke. A lot of water has flowed down the Spree since, and the warmth, Annemarie Hase notes with a soft smile, has dwindled somewhat too.” Difficulty finding work and the economic precarity that came with it were the main source of frustration, according to the piece, but they were exacerbated by a general lack of empathy, even antagonism, that she experienced as a *Remigrant* in her country. Hase explained: “Of course people were very kind to me after my return. But occasionally I would hear: ‘You don’t get a say. You weren’t even here.’” (AdK 1949b). If simplistic media representations stressed the affinity of Frau Wernicke with the German *Volk* and celebrated her as the voice of the German war experience, the lived reality of Annemarie Hase made it clear that a serious gulf still existed between her and the German public.

Hase’s experience was not unique. Returnees to Germany following the end of the war frequently sensed alienation from the receiving society. They were told that they, the refugees, had it easy in exile compared to the horrors that Germans had to endure during the war years, and many were treated with suspicion and resentment. In the case of Jewish returnees, these animosities were often tinged with antisemitism (Bergmann 2008; Herweg 2017). Though her celebrity status likely protected her from the more insidious iterations of these sentiments, Hase clearly was also made to learn the unofficial axiom that returnees needed to know their place in the post-Nazi Germanys. And they especially needed to refrain from burdening German society with questions of collective responsibility and the necessity of remediation.

It is in this context that we see the second layer of the public response to Hase’s return, rendering it a simultaneously noteworthy yet natural event. Most of the coverage of Hase’s comeback and of her renewed career in postwar Germany avoided mentioning the circumstances that forced her into exile. The vehement racism that targeted her as a Jew and altered her life course remained vague, obscured or even absent, and with it the broader implications of the Nazis’ genocidal violence. This silence was characteristic of the general mindset widespread in the early postwar period, in which Germans, while accepting their status as vanquished, nevertheless perceived themselves among the primary victims of the Nazi regime, having endured dictatorship, total war, defeat and occupation (Grossmann, 2007, 15–46; Hoffmann 2015). In this climate, recognition of the extent of Nazi brutalities, let alone remorse and empathy towards its victims, was scant. In the absence of an honest confrontation with the conditions that made flight necessary for someone like Annemarie Hase, the event of her (and others') return could be depicted as a matter of course.

This sentiment is captured in one article that was printed briefly after her arrival in Germany. "The zigzag lines of her destiny and her career could fill a thrilling novel," read the piece. "In the scenes that played between her previous successes at the Holländer Revues of those days and her work as Frau Wernicke at the BBC in London, it was fate that took the role of director, forcing many actors to play such parts that they would rather only perform on stage." Representing Hase's displacement as "zigzag lines", and the antisemitic persecution that she suffered as "fate" was typical of the tendency to obscure the lived realities of victims of Nazism in German public discourse. While it alludes – though barely – to coercion, without spelling it out, the piece aimed for a playful and happy portrayal, summed up in its title: "The Homecoming of an Optimist." (AdK 1947b).

Hase's displacement was often misrepresented in the German coverage, obscured by hints and euphemisms. It was sometimes described with the designation "emigration," which was commonly used to refer to the forced migration of individuals targeted by the Nazis (Neues Deutschland 1948; Remané 1951). A brief report in *Der Spiegel*, announcing that Hase would soon begin broadcasting at radio *Berliner Rundfunk*, framed it as a casual crossing of borders: "Before she went to London in 1936, she was active on Berlin stages and in cabarets." (*Der Spiegel* 1947) Another paper referred to her "ten years of absence." (AdK 1949a). Later in the postwar decades, when Hase put on solo cabaret shows and made recordings in which she performed songs and skits from different stages of her career, reviews often omitted any mention of her history in displacement. (AdK 1957a; AdK 1957b; AdK 1957c). This absence was even more glaring in reviews that did include a biographical sketch of Hase's life before 1933 and then quickly jumped to the present, as if nothing worth noting had happened in between (AdK 1962c; AdK 1962d; *Neue Zeit* 1965).

The German public did not need a detailed explanation of what Hase's "absence" or "emigration" had meant, or why she needed to leave. But the unspoken agreement that dominated the public sphere at the time was that it would be preferable not to be explicitly reminded of it. Hase had seen firsthand the consequences of breaking this code of silence. One of the very first movie roles she landed after her return was in the film *Morituri* (1948), a drama about the fate of concentration camp prisoners who, after escaping, join a secret forest encampment of partisans and runaways and stage resistance actions against the Nazis. Hase played the very small role of Mother Simon, a Jewish woman who was hiding with her family in the encampment and who was gravely ill. The film, produced by Polish-Jewish survivor Artur Brauner, was one of the very first to portray the horrific magnitude of Nazi violence, with dramatised scenes taking place inside a camp, and with a deliberate focus not on the fate of Germans during wartime, but on multiple victim groups, including Jews, Polish citizens and POWs of various nationalities. The film's reception made clear that such wound-picking was unwelcome, certainly in 1948. *Morituri* was not only a financial flop, it even stirred open resentment. Brauner recalled being told that "'this kind of thing' doesn't make money," struggling to find cinemas willing to screen it. After the film did make its way to cinemas across the Western zones (the Soviets refused to screen it altogether), the director, Eugen York, received threatening letters that accused him of being anti-German. One cinema reportedly cancelled all screenings after the angered audience destroyed some of the seats during the first showing (Riess 1958, 172; Bach 2014).

Morituri was released only one year after Hase's return to Germany and only three since the German capitulation. The reverberations of the war and the Nazi dictatorship were still palpable at the time. But the sentiments constraining honest reflections about Germany's embrace of fascism lingered, and they continued to impact the public life of returnees like Hase. An illuminating demonstration of this is found in the comparison between two pieces that reviewed a solo programme in celebration of the 40th anniversary of Hase's performance career. Both pieces were written by the same author, Hans Sellenthin, and they were published within a mere eight days of each other. And though they bore similarities – Sellenthin even repeated some wordings in both – they nevertheless read very differently.

The first article was published in the paper affiliated with the Jewish community, the *Berliner Allgemeine Wochenzeitung der Juden in Deutschland.* It opened with a review of Hase's biography and her success as a comedian on Weimar-era stages, which Sellenthin described as a particular Jewish kind of humour. Moving on to the Nazi period, Sellenthin let Hase interject in her own words: "'And then Hitler came,' she tells me dryly." He continued with his biographical review: "In 1936 she went to England, where she belonged to the group of Jewish migrants who did not lose their courage and who defended themselves with the weapons of wit and word [...] She became Frau Wernicke at the BBC's German Service, and with a Berliner's energy and cheekiness was able to teach those brown gentlemen a lesson." (AdK 1962d). Sellenthin's second article appeared in the *Berliner Stimme,* a publication affiliated with the Social Democratic Party in West Germany. Though the subject was Hase's performance, the title read "Frau Wernicke Celebrates Triumph," showing the lasting impact of the character, whose final broadcast aired more than 15 years prior. Here, not only was Hase's background as a Jewish performer entirely omitted, but there was also no mention of the personal impact she endured under Nazism or of her life as a refugee in Britain. The Nazi regime is mentioned only in the context of Hase's role as Wernicke: "Everyone present [at the performance] fondly remembered that, during the war, Annemarie Hase was the brash Frau Wernicke at the BBC London, who taught Hitler a lesson in the broadcasts to Germany." (AdK 1962a). While the second piece tried to emphasise a shared war experience in which "everyone" could tap into the memory of Wernicke's biting monologues, the stark differences between the two articles show just how tenuous this effort was. Hase's life was narrated in two different registers for two different audiences. For one, she was presented as a Jewish victim of Nazism who fought back. For the other, she was first and foremost Frau Wernicke.

3 Continuity of Omissions

The overarching tone in the reporting of Hase's return to Germany and the coverage of her postwar career there were characteristic of the discourse of omission that dominated the German public sphere (in both Germanys) during the early postwar decades. Her arrival at the end of the war was one thread among many that signalled the beginning of recovery and the possibility for restoration of order, and it was thus greeted with enthusiasm. But Hase's presence in post-Nazi Germany also posed a threatening reminder of injuries that the German public hoped to look away from. The German media overwhelmingly tried to depict Annemarie Hase in a way that the postwar public could best handle: as "one of us," a true Berliner who spoke on behalf of an entire nation when she took on the role of Frau Wernicke to condemn Nazism. This triumphant version of her story required ignoring crucial facets of it: that she became the target of racial hatred, that her art was portrayed as an intentional degradation of the German people, that she was robbed of her place on the stage and in society, and that she was forced to flee her home country that betrayed her.

One newspaper article that went against this trend asked readers in 1948 to consider that "[w]e know what we went through during those days. But we still know little about the experiences of the others – the political refugees, the victims of a murderous system" one of whom, the piece continued, was Annemarie Hase, "who under the pseudonym Frau Wernicke became an emblem of the BBC for all strict anti-Nazis". (AdK 1948). This demand that German readers consider the example of Hase to reflect on the experience of victims of

Nazism in exile is meaningful. But even this piece omitted any mention of the specificities of Jewish persecution under Nazism, which, for Hase, was the main reason for flight.

Contemporary commentators from Hannah Arendt to Klaus Mann were quick to diagnose this mindset in postwar German society, which refused empathy and solidarity with victims of Nazism and delayed conversations of collective responsibility (Arendt 1950; Mann 1994, 464–79). Scholars have followed in their path, examining multiple manifestations of this phenomenon and how it was shaped by Cold War politics, by the economic boom of the 1950s or by lingering bigotry and fascist loyalties. The case of Annemarie Hase's return to Germany and the public engagement with her life story in the early postwar period offer a powerful demonstration of these dynamics. But her experience as the anonymised voice of anti-Nazi propaganda adds a unique angle to this history.

For years during the Second World War Hase passionately recorded broadcasts that encouraged Germans to defy Nazi tyranny. Across enemy lines, German audiences listened to her, in the role of Frau Wernicke, communicate the messaging of British psychological warfare. Wernicke was created to drive a wedge between Germans and Nazis, and in order to do so effectively, she had to manifest the distinction. She personified the spirit of home-grown opposition and invited listeners to identify with her audacious outspokenness, even if they were not particularly outspoken themselves. She knew in detail the great sacrifices and losses that they endured under Nazism. She also reassured them that the British understood the predicament of everyday Germans who unwillingly became entangled in the Nazis' web and would treat them fairly. Meanwhile, Hase's identity, her fate as a victim of antisemitism and Nazi brutalities, and the circumstances of her exile in England were intentionally kept hidden.

It is worth considering how the BBC's policy of blurring the identities and the experiences of refugee employees like Hase contributed to an atmosphere in which postwar Germans could smoothly reclaim an affinity with her, embrace her Frau Wernicke as an emblem of their life during wartime and resist efforts to openly and honestly confront the extent of the damage that National Socialism has wrought on its victims. The BBC had good reasons to feel compelled to adopt this strategy, but it appears that its implications for people like Annemarie Hase were of little concern. Reflecting on his work with German-Jewish refugees at the German Service, their British colleague, Edward Tangye Lean, saw it as "their personal tragedy that they can find no direct expression for their anger at what has been done to them". Nevertheless, he noted: "The facts the BBC gives are merely facts, and the views mostly English. If the voice which speaks them would like to say more, it must temporarily forget." The reception of Annemarie Hase's return to postwar Germany, extending to her life there in the 1950s and 1960s, shows that this pressure to forget was not so temporary after all (Lean 1943, 44–5).

References

AdK. n.d. "B.B.C. Has its Lady Haw-Haw". Unattributed Excerpt from Hase's Scrapbook. HASE 85. Annemarie-Hase-Archiv, Akademie der Künste (AdK), Berlin, Germany.

AdK. 1941. "Frau Buggins speaks her mind. And all Germany listens". *Daily Express*. 17 September. HASE 85. Annemarie-Hase-Archiv, Akademie der Künste, Berlin, Germany.

AdK. 1943a. "Exiles Laugh at Their Woes". *The Observer*, 1 January. HASE 85. Annemarie-Hase-Archiv, Akademie der Künste, Berlin, Germany.

AdK. 1943b. "Hampstead Woman is Goebbels' Headache. 'Frau Wernicke' Celebrates Her Third Birthday". *Hampstead and St. John's Wood News and Golders Green Gazette*, 17 June. HASE 85. Annemarie-Hase-Archiv, Akademie der Künste, Berlin, Germany.

AdK. 1947a. "Frau Wernicke vom Wedding". *Die Neue Zeitung*, 1 April. HASE 85. Annemarie-Hase-Archiv, Akademie der Künste, Berlin, Germany.

AdK. 1947b. "Heimkehr der Optimistin". *Telegraf*, 4 April. HASE 85. Annemarie-Hase-Archiv, Akademie der Künste, Berlin, Germany.

AdK. 1948. "Von der 'Berolina zur 'Frau Wernicke'– 25 Jahre Kabarett'". *Telegraf*, 1 May. HASE 85. Annemarie-Hase-Archiv, Akademie der Künste, Berlin, Germany.

AdK. 1949a, *Nachtexpress*, 22 February. HASE 86. Annemarie-Hase-Archiv, Akademie der Künste, Berlin, Germany.

AdK. 1949b. H.H. "Zwei Jahre Wieder in Berlin. Nachdenkliches Gespräch mit einer Heimgekehrten". *Nachtexpress*, 10 June. HASE 86. Annemarie-Hase-Archiv, Akademie der Künste, Berlin, Germany.

AdK. 1950. "Frau Wernicke – Annemarie Hase". Pub. Unknown. HASE 86. Annemarie-Hase-Archiv, Akademie der Künste, Berlin, Germany.

AdK. 1957a. "Das war sehr gut". *BZ am Abend*, 10 April. HASE 85. Annemarie-Hase-Archiv, Akademie der Künste, Berlin, Germany.; D.L., "das war gut, Annemarie Hase!" *National Zeitung*, May 5, 1957. All in HASE 85.

AdK. 1957b. Hans-Dieter Tok. "Ein heiter besinnlicher Abend". *Volkzeitung Leipzig*, 3 April. HASE 85. Annemarie-Hase-Archiv, Akademie der Künste, Berlin, Germany.

AdK. 1957c. "Das war gut, Annemarie Hase!". Hase 85. Annemarie-Hase-Archiv, Akademie der Künste, Berlin, Germany.

AdK. 1962a. H. G. Sellenthin. "'Frau Wernicke' feiert Triumphe". *Berliner Stimme.* 20 January 20. HASE 87. Annemarie-Hase-Archiv, Akademie der Künste, Berlin, Germany.

AdK. 1962b. H. G. Sellenthin. "Porträt einer sentimentalen Komikerin. Annemarie Hase feiert ihr 40 jähriges Bühnejubiläum". *Berliner Allgemeine Wochenzeitung der Juden in Deutschland,* 12 January. HASE 87. Annemarie-Hase-Archiv, Akademie der Künste, Berlin, Germany.

AdK. 1962c. *Telegraf,* 7 January. HASE 85. Annemarie-Hase-Archiv, Akademie der Künste, Berlin, Germany.

AdK. 1962d. "Kabarett hält jung: Wiedersehen mit der Chansonette Annemarie Hase". *Berliner Morgenpost,* 11 January. HASE 85, Annemarie-Hase-Archiv, Akademie der Künste, Berlin, Germany.

ADK. 1965. Hase to Lowinsky. September. ELOW 27. Erich-Lowinsky-Archiv, Akademie der Künste, Berlin, Germany.

AdK. 1970. Hase to Lowinsky, 22 June. ELOW 27. Erich-Lowinsky-Archiv, Akademie der Künste, Berlin, Germany.

Anon. 1999. *Das Zersägen einer lebenden Dame.* Neckargemünd: Edition Mnemosyne.

Aufbau (New York). 5 May: 6.

Arendt, Hannah. 1950. "The Aftermath of Nazi Rule: Report from Germany". *Commentary,* October. https://www.commentary.org/articles/hannah-arendt/the-aftermath-of-nazi-rulereport-from-germany/. Accessed 1 July 2023.

Bach, Ulrich. 2014. "Review of Lang ist der Weg directed by Herbert B. Fredersdorf and Marek Goldstein, and Morituri directed by Eugen York". *Film & History* 44.1: 22–24.

Bergmann, Werner. 2008. "'Wir haben Sie nicht gerufen': Reaktionen auf Jüdische Remigranten in der Bevölkerung und Öffentlichkeit der frühen Bundesrepublik". *'Auch in Deutschland waren wir nicht wirklich zuhause': Jüdische Remigration nach 1945.* Eds. Irmela von der Lühe, Axel Schildt and Stefanie Schüler Springorum. Göttingen: Wallstein: 19–39.

Bollenbeck, Georg. 2005. "Restaurationsdiskurse und die Remigranten. Zur kulturellen Lage im westlichen Nachkriegsdeutschland". *Fremdes Heimatland: Remigration und literarisches Leben nach 1945.* Eds. Irmela von der Lühe and Claus-Dieter Krohn. Göttingen: Wallstein. 17–38.

Borneman, John, and Jeffrey M. Peck. 1995. *Sojourners: The Return of German Jews and the Question of Identity.* Lincoln, NE and London: University of Nebraska Press.

Brinson, Charmaine, and Richard Dove. 2008. "The Continuation of Politics by Other Means: The Freie Deutsche Kulturbund in London, 1939–1946". *'I Didn't Want to Float; I Wanted to Belong to Something'. Refugee Organizations in Britain, 1933–1945.* Eds. Anthony Grenville and Andrea Reiter. Leiden: Brill: 1–25.

Der Spiegel. 1947. "Annemarie Hase". 18 April.

Ebermayer, Erich, Hans-Otto Meissner and Louis Hagen. 1953. *Evil Genius: The Story of Joseph Goebbels*, London: Wingate.

Endelman, Todd M. 2015. *Leaving the Jewish Fold: Conversion and Radical Assimilation in Modern Jewish History*. Princeton: Princeton University Press.

Feinberg, Anat. 2018. *Wieder im Rampenlicht: Jüdische Rückkehrer in deutschen Theatern nach 1945*. Göttingen: Wallstein.

Fetheringill Zwicker, Lisa and Jason Ulysses Rose. 2020. "Marriage or Profession? Marriage and Profession? Marriage Patterns Among Highly Successful Women of Jewish Descent and Other Women in Nineteenth- and Twentieth-Century German-Speaking Central Europe". *Central European History* 53,4: 703–740.

Frühauf, Tina. 2021. *Transcending Dystopia: Music, Mobility, and the Jewish Community in Germany, 1945–1989*. New York: Oxford University Press.

Ganor, Shere. 2020. "Forbidden Words, Banished Voices: Jewish Refugees at the Service of BBC Propaganda to Wartime Germany". *Journal of Contemporary History* 55.1: 97–119.

Grossmann, Atina, *Jews, Germans, and Allies: Close Encounters in Occupied Germany*, Princeton: Princeton University Press, 2007.

Herweg, Nikola. 2017. "Bilderbuchheimkehrer, Persilscheine und Schweige-gebot. Voraussetzungen und Bedingungen der Remigration in die Bundesrepublik Deutschland". *Bilderbuch-Heimkehr? Remigration im Kontext*. Eds. Katharina Prager and Wolfgang Straub Wuppertal: Arco: 63–77

Hoffmann, Stefan-Ludwig. 2015. "Germans into Allies: Writing a Diary in 1945". *Seeking Peace in the Wake of War. Europe, 1943–1947*. Eds. Stefan-Ludwig Hoffmann, Sandrine Kott, Peter Romijn and Olivier Wieviorka. Amsterdam: Amsterdam University Press: 63–90

Krauss, Marita. 2001. *Heimkehr in ein fremdes Land: Geschichte der Remigration nach 1945*. Munich: Beck.

Larsen, Egon. 1957. "Deutsches Theater in London 1939–1945. Ein unbekanntes Kapitel Kulturgeschichte". *Deutsche Rundschau*. 83: 378–383.

Lean, Edward Tangye. 1943. *Voices in the Darkness. The Story of the European Radio War*. London: Secker and Warburg.

Mann, Klaus, Uwe Naumann and Michael Töteberg. 1994. *Auf verlorenem Posten: Aufsätze, Reden, Kritiken 1942–1949*. 1994. Reinbek bei Hamburg: Rowohlt.

Moorehead, Kristina. 2016. *Satire als Kriegswaffe. Strategien der britischen Rundfunkpropaganda im Zweiten Weltkrieg*. Marburg: Tectum.

Naumann, Uwe. 1983. *Zwischen Tränen und Gelächter, Satirische Faschismuskritik*. Cologne: Pahl-Rugenstein.

Naumann, Uwe with Bruno Adler. 1990. *Frau Wernicke: Kommentare einer "Volksjenossin"*. Mannheim: Persona.

Neue Zeit. 1965. "Lottchens Beichte und Berliner Couplets". 10 September.

Neues Deutschland. 1948. "Frau Wernicke in Köpenick". 29 October: 5.

New Statesman. 1939. Review of "Four and Twenty Black Sheep". 22 September.

Plock, Vike. 2021. *The BBC German Service during the Second World War* London: Palgrave Macmillan.

Remané, L. 1951. "Los, Annemarie, mach mal! Ein Querschnitt durch 25 Jahre Kabarett/ Annemarie Hase sang und sprach". *Berliner Zeitung* 20 June.

Riess, Curt. 1958. *Das gibts nur Einmal: Das Buch des deutschen Films nach 1945*. Hamburg: Henri Nannen.

Rovit, Rebecca. 2012. *The Jewish Kulturbund Theatre Company in Nazi Berlin.* Iowa City: University of Iowa Press.

Spector, Scott. 2006. "Forget Assimilation: Introducing Subjectivity to German-Jewish History". *Jewish History* 20.3/4: 349–61.

Tergit, Gabriele. 1943. "Annemarie Hase-Abend in London". *Aufbau*, 13 August.

Walther, Alexander. 2020. "Jewish Life in the German Democratic Republic". *Rebuilding Jewish Life in Germany.* Eds. Jay Howard Geller and Michael Meng. New Brunswick. Rutgers University Press: 101–17.

Williams, Rhys W. 2013. "'Frau Wernicke' at the BBC. Wartime Satire and Propaganda". *Diasporas and Diplomacy: Cosmopolitan contact zones at the BBC World Service (1932–2012)*. Eds. Marie Gillespie and Alban Webb. London and New York. Routledge: 57–79.

WAC 1944. "Comments from Berlin". E1/755. BBC Written Archives Centre, Caversham, UK.

CHAPTER 8

An Unlikely Partnership: Ernst Hermann Meyer, the GDR's Foremost Musician, and the BBC

Toby Thacker

Between June 1948 and his death in October 1988, only months before the collapse of the Workers' and Peasants' State, Ernst Hermann Meyer was the GDR's foremost musician. He worked at once as a composer, musicologist, theorist, historian, teacher, and ideologue. As a composer he wrote in 1950 the *Mansfelder Oratorium*, a large scale choral work celebrating 600 years of copper mining in the Erzgebirge, which served as the exemplar of the socialist realism demanded of the GDR's other composers (zur Weihen 1999, 61; Golan 2015, 34–57). The oratorio was performed repeatedly around the GDR, and featured on school curricula there. Meyer followed this with a stream of vocal and instrumental works, including cantatas, songs, an opera, and with film scores for DEFA (Deutsche Film-Aktiengesellschaft) productions. He occupied the chair of musicology at the Humboldt University in East Berlin, publishing in 1952 the foundational theoretical text *Musik im Zeitgeschehen* (Meyer 1952), and other books exploring the relationship between individual composers and their time. Meyer was appointed to the *Akademie der Künste* in 1950, where he chaired the *Sektion Musik*. He was the first editor of the GDR's leading music journal *Musik und Gesellschaft*, and the founder of the *Verband der Komponisten und Musikwissenschaftler der DDR*. He used this position to make public the expectation that all music in the GDR should conform to the doctrines laid down in the notorious "Zhdanov decree" issued in the Soviet Union in 1948: it should honour the classical inheritance, draw on national traditions, foreground melody, and avoid any taint of formalism or cosmopolitanism, which Meyer called "manifestations of degeneration" (Meyer 1951). In the labyrinthine structures of the GDR's party and mass organisations there was no body dealing with music which he did not dominate. Meyer was a tireless organiser, chairing numerous committees and conferences, and providing the ideological and academic grounding for the public celebration of composers such as Bach in 1950, Beethoven in 1952, Schubert in 1953, and Handel at annual festivals in Halle from 1953 to 1988.

Through this whole period, Meyer enjoyed the complete trust of the leadership of the Sozialistische Einheitspartei Deutschlands (SED). He was rewarded

 | HTTPS://DOI.ORG/10.1515/9783111302508-008

for his loyal service with honours, prizes, decorations, and material comforts. He was awarded the GDR's National Prize in 1950, 1952 and 1975, and was elected as a member of the SED Central Committee in 1971, a position he held unto his death. Meyer was trusted to represent the GDR abroad, travelling frequently to the Soviet Union and other East European states to liaise with Communist musicians and composers. In 1965 he was sent to speak in English at the East-West Music Festival in Bombay. In 1964 he was entrusted, together with the ideologue Kurt Hager, with the responsibility of laying a wreath at the grave of Karl Marx in Highgate Cemetery. In 1970 he was commissioned by the Central Committee of the SED and the Communist Party of Great Britain to present in London a lecture on the GDR's understanding of Beethoven's historical significance on the 200th anniversary of the great composer's birth (Thacker 2005, 212–13). Books were published celebrating Meyer's life and work (Niemann 1975; Brennecke and Hansen 1979). It is no exaggeration to state that on any question relating to music in the GDR, the party leadership sought and accepted his judgement. It may then come as a surprise to learn that Meyer had previously worked for fifteen years with the BBC in London, and that this had served as a starting point for his entry into the British academic world.

Meyer had in fact first contacted the BBC in August 1931, probably after meeting Edward Clark, then Chief Programme Builder in the Music Department of the BBC, in Berlin. Meyer had joined the Communist Party in 1930, and was as a young postgraduate involved with a radical group of composers, taking instruction from Hanns Eisler and Max Butting. Among the numerous experimental strands of music being pioneered in Berlin was the idea of music especially suited to and composed for the new medium of radio (Brennecke and Hansen 1979, 86–103). Meyer wrote to the BBC to see if there was interest there in "radio music", and while he was briefly in England to attend a musicological conference, he called at the BBC offices to promote this idea (WAC 1931). Evidently the BBC was not interested, and nothing came of this. On his return to Berlin, Meyer continued to explore his main area of scholarly interest, the instrumental music of the fifteenth and sixteenth centuries, particularly that originating in north-western Europe. He was also active in politics, writing for the Communist newspaper *Die Rote Fahne*, and directing workers' choirs. When the Nazis came to power in January 1933, Meyer knew that as a Jew and a Communist, he was in terrible danger. For some months he hid by cycling around Germany, before getting to France for a musicological conference. He was then invited to Cambridge for another conference by the musicologist Edward Dent, and managed to travel to England in July 1933. The next few months were very difficult for Meyer, living hand to mouth from a succession of low paid, temporary jobs, and struggling to find his way in a foreign land. He worked as a language tutor, as a copy typist, and a swimming teacher. Most galling, he had to earn money writing out voice parts for a "third rate publisher of hits" (Brennecke and Hansen 1979, 136; Niemann 1975, 12–13). He explored the possibility of emigrating to the USA, but nothing came of this. Meyer was effectively rescued by his contacts at the BBC. It was Edward Clark, supported by Dent, who secured acceptance of the idea of getting Meyer to research and present a week-long set of broadcasts of sixteenth-century instrumental music, in itself a notable extension of the then standard musical repertoire of the BBC. Nicholas Kenyon has explored the evolution of the BBC's relationship with "early music", and it is clear from his research that this was not an entirely new departure for the corporation, but nonetheless, it was an ambitious and slightly risky venture (Kenyon 2022, 1).[1]

It must then have been an enormous relief for Meyer to receive, in December 1933, a letter from Clark, inviting him to research and direct a series of six broadcasts as part of the "Foundations of Music" series, and offering him a fee of 15 guineas for his services (WAC 1933). Musicians such as Rudolph, Carl, Nathalie, and Millicent Dolmetsch, and the harpsichordist Ernest Lush were engaged to perform the pieces which Meyer then selected. The broadcasts presented music from a wide span of European countries, including some hitherto unknown works which Meyer had discovered in the British Library (WAC 1934a). In the BBC's internal review of the series, two strands of commentary emerged, both of which were to be echoed as Meyer's broadcasting career developed. Audience reaction to the music presented, and to the accompanying scholarly commentary was very positive. The programmes were favourably reviewed in the *Guardian* and in *The Musical Times*. The standard of the playing was high, but the BBC's reviewer felt that "Dr Meyer was not sufficiently at home in the practical side of the performance of this music" (WAC 1934b). Nonetheless, senior figures at the BBC clearly felt that this was an avenue to be explored further, and Meyer was rewarded in June 1935 with a commission to present a longer broadcast on "Music of Purcell's Day" (WAC 1935). Again the broadcast was well received, but it was decided to minimise Meyer's future work as a performer. Nonetheless, as Meyer later said, "From then on, things went gradually forward" (Brennecke and Hansen, 1979, 137). He was engaged by Radio Netherlands, broadcasting from Hilversum, to present an early music programme, and the work with the BBC undoubtedly helped Meyer to build contacts in the British musical world, particularly with others involved in early music, such as the Casa d'Arte Music Circle. It spurred him to develop his

1 For a problematisation of the term "early music", see Haskell 1988.

FIGURE 8.1 Ernst Meyer (1905–88), the composer and musicologist who worked at the BBC between 1933 and 1948, in exile in London, 1938. (© Breitkopf & Härtel KG)

research, focused increasingly on early instrumental English music. He was appointed to a fellowship at Bedford College in 1939, and found a niche composing music to accompany documentary films with the General Post Office Film Unit, working alongside figures such as Benjamin Britten and Len Lye.

Meyer (see Figure 8.1) saw himself first and foremost as a composer, and naturally, having gained an entrée to the BBC, he tried on several occasions to get his compositions broadcast. The procedure in the 1930s, before the development of magnetic tape recording, was for a composer to send in manuscript music to the BBC, which was then circulated to a panel of three reviewers for adjudication. Meyer's music was on each occasion turned down as unsuitable for broadcasting, something which undoubtedly rankled with him. He later referred to these panels as a “firing squad” which “turned down everything” (WAC 1949). The difficulties of Meyer’s exile were compounded by the increasingly grim news he received from Germany. His father was killed after the Kristallnacht pogrom in November 1938, and he learned at first hand from other refugees of their suffering at the hands of the Nazis. Although Meyer’s brother Klaus and sister Susanne managed to escape and join him in England, his mother and his younger brother Ulrich were both subsequently murdered in Auschwitz. It is hardly surprising that Meyer, despite a brief period of arrest as a suspected alien at the beginning of the war, was happy to contribute to the Allied war effort. During the war years he wrote scores for many short documentary films, with titles such as *Atlantic Convoy* and *Mobilise your Scrap*. After 1940 he worked on educational films with Halas and Batchelor Cartoon Films. In a similar vein he wrote the music to accompany the BBC broadcast *Pass the Ammunition* in 1943. He agreed in October 1945 to provide a script in German on early English music for a programme on the BBC German Service.

Meyer’s greatest success still came with broadcasts of early music which he researched and presented, rather than performed. A letter from Val Drewry, then in charge of chamber music at the BBC, to Meyer in December 1944 reads: “Let me thank you once more for making it possible for us to broadcast such a magnificent programme as last night’s. From all quarters I have heard nothing but appreciation for the excellent music.” Drewry added that he hoped Meyer would agree to provide more programmes in the future (WAC 1944). The creation of a BBC station dedicated to classical music after 1945 gave Meyer further scope, and he was commissioned, together with Arnold Goldsbrough and Norbert Brianin, to direct a series on music of the sixteenth and seventeenth centuries entitled “New Life for Old Music” for the Third Programme in July 1947. This made it clear that the Third Programme was intending to be, in the words of Nicholas Kenyon, “a vital advocate” for early music (Kenyon 2022, 2).

Meyer had been appointed to a Guest Fellowship at King’s College, Cambridge in 1945, and his position as a leading figure in English musicology was secured with the publication of his *Early English Chamber Music* in 1946 (Meyer 1946). It was then hardly surprising that when the BBC planned a new “History of European Music in Sound” series for the Third Programme in 1947, employing specialist researchers and performers (“the best available in Europe”), Meyer was approached to provide four programmes of early music, for a fee of 100 guineas (WAC 1947). This was an extraordinarily ambitious series, originally intended to cover the fifteenth to the nineteenth centuries in 104 programmes broadcast over two years, accompanied by the publication of an educational booklet and gramophone recordings of the music selected for broadcasting.

Meyer was though by this time in a difficult situation. He had to come to terms with the appalling news of the murder of his close relatives by the Nazis, and, after that, to decide whether to stay in England, where he now had an established professional reputation and many friends, or whether to return to occupied Germany and to immerse himself in the increasingly confrontational cultural and political scene there. He appears to have suffered a breakdown of some sort in 1946, and spent time briefly recovering at a sanatorium in Switzerland (Niemann 1975, 87). Meyer was nonetheless identified by the newly formed Socialist Unity Party in the Soviet Zone of Germany as a potential asset. Its Administration for People's Education assessed him in October 1947 as "an exceedingly valuable comrade, who could play a leading role in the musical life of a new democratic Germany" (SAPMO 1947a). Along with other Communist émigrés such as Hanns Eisler, Meyer was encouraged by the SED to return to Berlin, and enticed with the prospect of cultural, political, and material opportunities. In June 1948 Meyer was offered, and accepted, the newly created chair of Music Sociology at the Humboldt University. He arrived in blockaded Berlin in September 1948, and threw himself, with characteristic energy, into the musical and political life of the Soviet Zone.

This prompts the question of how far authorities at the BBC were aware of Meyer's scarcely concealed Communist sympathies, and whether any such awareness provoked questions about the suitability of employing him, particularly in the early years of the Cold War. In the surviving documents held by the BBC there is nothing whatsoever which might shed any light on these questions. The BBC obviously considered very carefully Meyer's academic and artistic credentials, but appears not to have been concerned with his politics. As plans for the "History of European Music in Sound" series advanced, the corporation wrote to Meyer in Berlin to confirm his engagement and made arrangements for his travel to London to take part. A permit allowing him to stay in Britain for a month was secured from the Ministry of Labour, and in August 1949 the BBC wrote to the Entry and Exit Permit Section of the British military administration in Berlin, stating: "Dr. Meyer urgently needed by B.B.C. London for programmes. Please assist to travel at earliest date possible." Ironically, the SED had already written to Harry Pollitt, the leader of the Communist Party of Great Britain, to ask if he had any objection to Meyer's returning to England (SAPMO 1947b, SAPMO 1949). Meyer had already indicated in a long and friendly letter to Basil Lam at the BBC that he was keen to come back to help with the four programmes he had devised (WAC 1949). One wonders whether Meyer was aware that so many different people were concerned about his travel plans.

After this, Meyer's engagement with the BBC, not surprisingly, declined in the increasingly hostile atmosphere of the early Cold War. Meyer quickly emerged as the leader of the newly established German Democratic Republic's musical life, and led the campaign for socialist realism there. The institutions he dominated, at the Humboldt University, at the Academy of Arts, and the Association of Composers and Musicologists all rehearsed and propagated the party line of hostility to the capitalist world and the warmongering lackeys of American imperialism (Thacker 2007, 111–17). The BBC's German Service had now taken on an important role in broadcasting into the Soviet Zone of Germany, and was considered by the SED as a hostile propaganda instrument, used not least, as a vehicle for introducing degenerate and poisonous dance and boogie-woogie music into the young Republic.[2] It is all the more intriguing then to see that as late as 1957 Meyer, when he was in London, was still proposing to the BBC that they should broadcast some of his latest compositions, and providing tapes of recordings to help their consideration. Harry Croft-Jackson, the Music Programme Organiser, doubtless confirmed Meyer's dismal view of the "firing-squad" at the BBC by turning down four of these compositions, but did reply that the BBC would consider broadcasting nine piano miniatures *From a Little Girl's Diary* if "a suitable opportunity" occurred (WAC 1957). It is not clear whether this idea ever came to fruition.

In conclusion, we should ask whether Meyer's involvement with the BBC had any larger impact, and this provokes three further questions: First, did Meyer's programmes influence the reception and performance of early music in Britain? Second, did his engagement with this whole area influence the reception and performance of early music in the GDR? And finally, how did Meyer's work with the BBC influence his own career, particularly in the GDR after 1948? The first question can be answered with a clear affirmative. Meyer's first programmes for the BBC did not start the early musical revival in Britain, but they had a significant impact in introducing parts of this repertoire to a larger national audience. The programmes he directed after 1945 gave a further impetus after the Second World War, and the whole movement has blossomed. The "early music revival" has not been a straightforward linear progression, but understandings of the canon of "classical music" have now been entirely revised to include ever more composers who lived and worked before Bach and Handel. Meyer's programmes also had a significant impact on performance practice, introducing instruments such as the harpsichord, lute

2 On the role of the BBC German Service more broadly, see Brinson and Dove 2003.

and viol to new audiences, and spurring interest in their manufacture and use. Nicholas Kenyon, in a recent Radio Three series, noted how the performance style of groups used by Meyer in his programmes, such as the Boyd Neel Orchestra, encouraged a complete revision of the way that works of the eighteenth century were played. The tendency towards more lean and spare ensembles which Meyer's programmes introduced has been continued, and was, in Kenyon's words, "a vital part of the Third Programme's legacy" (Kenyon 2022, 2). In Britain today, any remotely ambitious performance of music by Bach, Handel, Purcell, or Monteverdi would use instruments such as the harpsichord and lute, and only a small group of strings. Counter-tenor or male alto singers are again popular. Ensembles such as the Monteverdi Choir, His Majesty's Sagbutts and Cornetts, and Fretwork, are much in demand, and are extending the work undertaken by the BBC in the 1930s and 1940s. The quest for authenticity is now revising the performance of works by Mozart, Beethoven, and their contemporaries.

Perhaps surprisingly given Meyer's influential position there, "early music" was less important in the cultural life of the GDR. A recently published survey of classical music in the GDR with contributions from international scholars does not mention early music, but stresses instead the GDR's state sponsorship of what it called "the classical inheritance", that is to say the music of the eighteenth and nineteenth centuries, and its tangled relationship with musical modernism (Frackman and Powell, 2015). It is fascinating to observe then that the most significant promotion of "early music" in the GDR came through its so-called "Handel Renaissance", centred around annual festivals held in Halle after 1955, and that it involved British musicians whom Meyer had come into contact with at the BBC. Meyer was the Chairman of the Händel Gesellschaft established in 1955, and he provided the academic underpinning for a revised historical understanding of the composer which, although acknowledging the pioneering work of the Handel revival in Göttingen in the 1920s, claimed him now as a progressive humanist whose legacy was only correctly understood and cultivated in the GDR. Meyer was of course well placed to give this revision some academic heft, and to integrate within it Handel's life in England and his engagement with English culture (Thacker 2006, 17–42). He also, through his work with the BBC, was in touch with leading performers in England, and through the Cold War years, engaged many of them to sing and play in the GDR. Thus in 1959, Thurston Dart and Ernest Stride accompanied the Deal and Walmer Handel Choir in a performance of *L'Allegro ed il Penseroso* in Halle. Alfred Deller, whose counter-tenor singing had been a central feature of Meyer's post-war programmes for the Third Programme, performed a set of English madrigals with his sextet at the same festival. The Deller Consort sang again in 1970 and 1976 in Halle. In 1965, Peter Williams played music by Byrd, Purcell, and Handel in Halle, and in 1981 a group of six singers from the Consort of Musicke performed there (Thacker 2005, 211–24).

What of Meyer himself? Did his sustained engagement with the quintessentially liberal institution of the BBC change him or his politics? Perhaps sadly, it appears not. Meyer had joined the German Communist Party in 1930, and he never thereafter deviated from the party line. Although in his English language writing and broadcasting Meyer wore his Marxist commitment lightly, he kept up his party work while in exile, and once he had returned to Berlin in 1948 he made his Stalinist position absolutely clear. At subsequent critical points in the history of the GDR, when others faltered, took up critical stances, or even defected, Meyer always remained *linientreu*. In February 1953, shortly before the death of the Soviet dictator, Meyer published an article in *Musik und Gesellschaft* with the improbable title "The lessons of Stalin's new work for music" in which he reaffirmed the state's commitment to the principles of socialist realism as outlined in Zhdanov's "historic decree" of 1948 (Meyer 1953).

After the demonstrations and disturbances of 17 June 1953, Meyer's journal *Musik und Gesellschaft* argued that the public dissatisfaction with the Ulbricht government had been fostered by American dance music and boogie-woogie. Almost ludicrously, it proclaimed that the demonstrations had been led by "Texas boys" and "riot heroes", accompanying this with a picture of seemingly bored young men with slicked-back hair and cowboy boots. After convening a meeting at the Academy of Arts in Berlin to discuss the disturbances, Meyer published a letter in the Party's daily newspaper *Neues Deutschland* on 19 July, in which he blamed the "provocations" on "fascist bandits". They should, he wrote, be ruthlessly pursued and "exterminated" (Thacker 2007, 164). In 1956, when Soviet troops and tanks intervened to crush the nascent Hungarian revolution, many Communists in Britain felt they had to reconsider their commitment to the Party, but Meyer in Berlin did not. He gathered the GDR's leading musicians at his flat to debate how they might best support Hungarian musicians who were loyal to the Soviets. Meyer was of course centrally involved in all controversies about types of music, and individual pieces of music in the GDR, and he invariably supported the Party line. In the debate in 1951 about whether or not Paul Dessau's setting of Brecht's *Das Verhör des Lukullus* should be performed in public, it was Meyer who declared that Dessau's music contained "all the elements of formalism" (zur Weihen 1999, 122). Where others, such as his friend and colleague from exile in Britain Georg Knepler, reconsidered their attachment to Stalinist dogma in later decades, Meyer never publicly did. In the 1960s, Meyer led the criticism of the songwriter and poet Wolf Biermann from the Academy of the Arts. It is striking how when Biermann spoke about this in 2009, he identified the "Ernst Hermann Meyer people" as his chief opponents in what became a long-running debate about whether or not he should be allowed to sing and perform in public in the GDR (Biermann 2009). Although the GDR very slowly became more tolerant of developments in twentieth-century modernist music, Meyer never relinquished his hostility to the music of Schönberg and his followers.

To be fair to Meyer, we should note finally that in his later years, he spoke fondly of his work at the BBC, and was fulsome in his praise for many of the individual artists he had collaborated with there. He appears nonetheless to have identified the BBC as an institution with the broader complex of the British state, and therefore as an enemy of the Soviet Union and the GDR. We shall leave the last word to him. He said in 1979: "I hate English monopoly capitalism, but I love English culture, and I like the English people, the 'average English person'" (Brennecke and Hansen 1979, 190).

References

Biermann, Wolf. 2009. "Wolf Biermann: Interview with James Miller". https://www.pwf.cz/archivy/texts/interviews/wolf-biermann-interview-with-james-miller_1807.html Accessed 3 January 2024.

Brennecke, Dietrich and Matthias Hansen (eds). 1979. *Ernst Hermann Meyer. Kontraste. Konflikte.* Berlin: Verlag Neue Musik.

Brinson, Charmian and Richard Dove (eds). 2003. "Stimme der Wahrheit'. German-Language Broadcasting by the BBC". *Yearbook of the Research Centre for German and Austrian Exile Studies* 5: 27–42.

Frackman, Kyle and Larson Powell (eds). 2015. *Classical Music in the German Democratic Republic.* New York: Camden House.

Gur, Golan. 2015. "Classicism as Anti-Fascist Heritage: Realism and Myth in Ernst Hermann Meyer's *Mansfelder Oratorium* (1950)". *Classical Music in the German Democratic Republic.* Eds. Kyle Frackman and Larson Powell. New York: Camden House: 35–57

Haskell, Harry. 1988. *The Early Music Revival: A History.* London: Thames and Hudson.

Kenyon, Nicholas. 2022. "Renewing the Past: The BBC and Early Music.1930s, Creating a National Music". BBC Radio 3, 1 November. https://www.bbc.co.uk/programmes/m001dfww, Accessed 7 December 2023.

Meyer, Ernst Hermann. 1946. *Early English Chamber Music.* London: Lawrence & Wishart.

Meyer, Ernst Hermann. 1951. „Geleitwort. Was will diese Zeitschrift?". *Musik und Gesellschaft*, 1:1.

Meyer, Ernst Hermann. 1952. *Musik im Zeitgeschehen*. Berlin: B. Henschel.

Meyer, Ernst Hermann. 1953. „Lehren aus dem XIX. Parteitag der KPdSU". *Musik und Gesellschaft* 2: 48–49.

Niemann, Konrad. 1975. *Ernst Hermann Meyer. Für Sie Porträtiert*. Leipzig: VEB Deutscher Verlag für Musik.

SAPMO 1947a. DY 30/IV 2/11/v.5054. Betr. Dr. Ernst Meyer, Stiftung Archiv der Parteien-und Massenorganisationen der DDR, Bundesarchiv, Berlin, Germany.

SAPMO. 1947b. Pollitt, Harry. 'To Whom it May Concern', 22 July 1947. DY 30/IV 2/11/v.5054. Dr. Ernst Meyer, Stiftung Archiv der Parteien-und Massenorganisationen der DDR, Bundesarchiv, Berlin, Germany.

SAPMO. 1949. Joos to Daub, 7 November. DY 30/IV 2/11/v.5054. Dr. Ernst Meyer, Stiftung Archiv der Parteien-und Massenorganisationen der DDR, Bundesarchiv, Berlin, Germany.

Thacker, Toby. 2005. "Something Different from the Hampstead Perspective': An Outline of Selected Musical Transactions between the British Left and the GDR". *The Other Germany. Perceptions and Influences in British-East German Relations, 1945–1990*. Eds. Stefan and Norman LaPorte. Augsburg: Wißner Verlag: 211–24.

Thacker, Toby. 2006. "'Renovating Bach and Handel': New Musical Biographies in the German Democratic Republic". *Musical Biography: Towards New Paradigms*. Ed. Jolanta Pekacz. Aldershot: Ashgate. 17–42.

Thacker, Toby. 2007. *Music after Hitler, 1945–1955*. Aldershot: Ashgate.

Thacker, Toby. 2015. "The 'Handel Renaissance' in the German Democratic Republic. Why Did the British Take Part? ". *Händel-Jahrbuch* 61: 311–24.

zur Weihen, Daniel. 1999. *Komponieren in der DDR. Institutionen, Organisationen und die erste Komponistengeneration bis 1961*. Cologne, Weimar, and Vienna: Böhlau Verlag.

WAC. 1931. Meyer to Clarke, 17 August; and Meyer to Clarke, n.d. BBC/R/RCONT/RCONT1/25488. BBC Written Archives Centre, Caversham. UK.

WAC. 1933. BBC to Dr. Ernst Meyer, 16 December. BBC/R/RCONT/RCONT1/25488. BBC Written Archives Centre, Caversham. UK.

WAC. 1934a. "Foundations of Music". January-June. BBC/R/OM/R27/106/1. BBC Written Archives Centre, Caversham. UK.

WAC. 1934b. "Reports on Artists". 6 March. BBC/R/RCONT/RCONT1/25488. BBC Written Archives Centre, Caversham. UK.

WAC. 1935. BBC to Meyer, 6 August, BBC/R/RCONT/RCONT1/25488. BBC Written Archives Centre, Caversham. UK.

WAC. 1944. Drewry to Meyer, 15 December. BBC/R/RCONT/RCONT1/25488. BBC Written Archives Centre, Caversham. UK.

WAC. 1947. Abraham to Meyer, 2 July. "History in Sound of European Music, 1947–1950, A: Correspondence". 2 July. BBC/R/OM/R27/132/1. BBC Written Archives Centre, Caversham. UK.

WAC. 1949. Meyer to Lam, 25 June. "History in Sound of European Music, 1947–1950, A: Correspondence, 1949". BBC/R/OM/R27/132/1. BBC Written Archives Centre, Caversham. UK.

WAC. 1957. Croft-Jackson to Meyer, 9 September. BBC/R/RCONT/RCONT1/25487. BBC Written Archives Centre, Caversham. UK.

CHAPTER 9

Constructing Imperial Liberalism on Television: The BBC and the Berlin Blockade

Heather Gumbert

In March 1949 British Prime Minister Clement Attlee flew to Berlin for a whirlwind three-day visit. The *New York Times* reported it as a "compliment and expression of thanks to the British and American air and ground crews" involved in the Airlift, underway since the previous summer, and assured readers "there is nothing political in it" (*New York Times* 1949, 19). BBC Television provided pictures, illustrating Airlift-era Berlin with scenes of devastation and renewal that would have been familiar to cinemagoers from Pathé newsreels over the past few years. The programme visited former centres of power in Berlin, including the bombed-out Government Quarter, the once resplendent now shabby shopping street Kurfürstendamm, and the denuded Tiergarten park. The cityscape is reduced to rubble, and Berliners scavenge for firewood and food. But important signs of life also exist: newspapers are available, cinemas are open, and stores sell "dearly priced" goods to the consumer.

It does not take hindsight to interpret such a visit at this highly fraught historical moment or the accompanying footage as "political". Having defeated the German military machine, occupation authorities now confronted the difficulties of winning the peace. Disagreements over occupation policies had opened a rift among the Allies. More broadly, the nature and magnitude of the war's destruction spurred narratives of Europe as a civilisation in crisis for which "renewal" had become one of the most important political missions of the postwar period (Betts 2020). At the same time, the mass media – radio, film and television – became central to occupation and reconstruction. Harnessed by elites to bolster economic growth and create citizen-consumers, the media did not simply inform, educate and entertain, but rather were central to creating the postwar world, reshaping structures of communication, circuits of information, and the exercise of power. The mass media tuned audience attention and opened new windows on the world, while also circumscribing wider understanding of underreported events and issues. It reshaped the space of the nation, projecting the so-called British way of life, and delineating the boundaries of us (understood as a reconstituted Commonwealth in the postwar

 | HTTPS://DOI.ORG/10.1515/9783111302508-009

period) and them (which variously included Germans, Soviets, and Americans, among others).

At the same time, observers and cultural critics produced and began to codify ways of thinking about the media and their effects. These were based in large part on the experience of the American media, the BBC, and Nazi media, which scholars perceived as fundamentally different models of communication. Contemporary discourses about the media were deeply political, less empirical than ideological, and enlisted to demarcate the boundaries between liberal and communist, "free" and "authoritarian". Indeed, the models of communication that emerged in the early postwar period were as rigid as the early social scientific understanding of the differences between capitalism and communism and similarly based on normative models of development. In sum, contemporary discourses did not simply (or perhaps even faithfully) reflect the period, but rather were crucial constituents of Cold War conflict. The media were not neutral tools of information and edification; instead they were instrumentalised, invented to serve particular ends; they did not simply reflect geopolitical conflict, but were themselves constitutive of it.

In this chapter I revisit the period of the Berlin Airlift and early postwar television to suggest ways in which we might better understand the operation, significance, and legacy of the BBC. I want to make three interrelated arguments. First, I suggest that the public service mission widely understood to be the bedrock of the BBC itself needs to be historicised. As social and economic conditions changed in Britain, as new media and publics emerged, conceptions of media in the public service similarly shifted. The disordered world of 1945 challenged established certainties, giving the media new purpose. BBC reporting spoke to the contemporary concerns of the British people and, more importantly, worked to re-situate British power and authority in a world diminished due to the loss of empire, economic strength, and moral authority. It participated in the projection of a particular set of values: what we might call imperial liberalism. In her intellectual history of imperial liberalism political theorist Jennifer Pitts has demonstrated that esteemed nineteenth-century liberal thinkers (de Tocqueville and Mill, for example) rejected the anti-colonialism of the previous generation (Smith and Bentham), and instead argued for liberal ideas at home and (even outright) despotism abroad (Pitts 2006, 3). By the early twentieth century, argues media scholar Lee Grieveson, liberalism had become protectionist and anti-communist, an economic and political ideology that instrumentalised culture to maintain the power of British elites in the context of economic instability and imperial decline (Grieveson 2017). Illiberalism, then, was baked into the liberal practice of power in

Britain and its empire. Television joined that battle, promising topical treatments of current events, at home and abroad. Berlin emerged as the centre of the burgeoning Cold War as early as 1946, a role that was consolidated by the end of the Berlin Blockade and Airlift in 1949, and the BBC was there to report on it. I use the history of the BBC's reporting of the Berlin Blockade to challenge the liberal assumptions that underpin much of British media history, which often fails to situate the media in its historical context (Hampton 2001; Hilmes 2012, 312).

Second, I want to make a methodological argument about the implications of audio-visual media for historical understanding of the past. British media had made its reputation in the forge of wartime reporting, which set the mandate and even mode of address for the postwar media (Webb 2006, 118). BBC Television, first broadcast in 1936 and best known for its outside broadcast of the coronation of King George VI, had, however, been on hiatus since 1939. Returned to the air in 1946, postwar television joined an existing media universe with (partially-)established institutions, regulations, conventions, professional norms, and representational lexicons. Television's reporting from Berlin drew upon and expanded a language long-tested in cinema and newsreels, constructing a visual imaginary that reinforced the certitudes of imperial liberalism and the British place in the new postwar world (Pronay 1976; Hoffman 2016; Brodroghkozy 2018; Steinle 2007; Hiley and McKernan 2001). This reporting contributed to, but was also highly dependent on an international market in "content" – film clips, programmes, and eventually whole series – without which the expansion of television broadcast across space (Europe and the world) and time (the broadcast day, which expanded from three hours a day in the 1930s to twenty-four hours a day several decades later) would not have been possible. Such content was created in a historically specific context, defined by what was logistically and technologically possible, and also that which was rhetorically and narratively desirable, but it was traded and disseminated in a variety of contexts, not limited to British televisions in the late 1940s. Thus BBC Television (and newsreel companies before it) generated a particular vision of contemporary events, which it then circulated in the global market.

Finally, this history is significant because the specific stories told at this moment in the Cold War have been similarly trenchant, if not entirely unexamined. BBC reporting of the Blockade and Airlift constructed a heroic Anglo-American story of freedom arrayed against tyranny that not only circumscribed the ways in which contemporaries could confront the diplomatic crisis unfolding in Berlin, but also tended to inform post-Blockade rhetoric and decision-making. The media – British, German, American, Soviet – did not simply report, but rather co-created the emerging Cold War, shaping not just occupation-era Berlin, but interpretations of and responses to all subsequent crises. Most important, the stories they told have found new life in the triumphalist rhetoric that accompanied the fall of communism and persist to shape political debate and even the practice of democracy today.

1 Understanding the Role of the Media in the Modern World

This work builds on a literature that is rethinking the historical role of the media in the creation of the modern world. Early concepts of communication and the elaboration of communications as an academic discipline emerged in the highly politicised moment of the early Cold War and are deeply entangled in its history (Rajagopal 2014). The work of prominent postwar American communications scholars such as Daniel Lerner, Harold Lasswell, William Paley, and Wilbur Schramm was rooted in the ideas and methods of Second World War psychological warfare operations and used to help explain (and fight) the communist world (Simpson 1996, 29, 115). This group produced some of the most important and long-lived "theoretical" texts on communication in the 1950s (Curran and Sparks 2000, 3, 36). For example, in 1956 Fred Siebert, Theodore Petersen and Wilbur Schramm published *Four Theories of the Press*, outlining a particular vision of the history and development of the world's communication systems. The work owed (and contributed) much to modernisation theory: media had once been the exclusive preserve of the elite (royalty) and served only the ends of maintaining power; by the twentieth century it had in its best instances come to serve as a check on government (Siebert 1956, 3; Nordenstreng 2014). In their view, the media operated differently in different political regimes: it functioned as a sort of fourth estate in the United States, but in authoritarian regimes and especially the communist world the media continued to serve its political masters, shackling ideas and the freedom of expression (Siebert 1956, 121–22). Their work enshrined a normative vision of the media that arrayed (commercial) press freedom against the repression of state direction. This vision persisted through the decades even as comparative research undermined the simplistic understanding of state directed media. Already in 1967, media scholar Burton Paulu noted that European broadcasting could not be dismissed as simply state directed, but instead was a system comprising a complex mix of state direction and commercial broadcasting, guided by a commitment to public service (Paulu 1967, 237). More recently scholars of socialist media have demonstrated that the boundaries between liberal democratic and socialist media cannot be so clearly drawn. Anikó Imre and Sabine Mihelj, for example, have demonstrated remarkable continuities among media within and beyond the Soviet sphere. As in the West, authorities perceived television as an instrument of social transformation, a vehicle for raising the level of education, cultural and political literacy, and taste among undereducated populations (Imre 2016; Mihelj 2011, 2014). Moreover, scholars of the global information economy have persistently and perpetually warned of the deep structural inequalities created by the twentieth century communication order (Frau-Meigs et al. 2012). Yet early scholarship, such as Siebert's, still shapes current understanding. For British media scholar Colin Sparks the conception of communication of the immediate postwar period, although "false ... [still structures] the thinking even of those who wish to be extremely critical [of it] ... [and] has tended to obscure any real analysis of the ways in which the media actually do function with regard to social power" (Sparks 2000, 36–37).

Much of the subsequent scholarship that took up the intellectual framework of *Four Theories of the Press* noted the specifics of other societies that did not match up with the wider vision. But it did so without challenging the fundamental concept. And along the way, the prejudices, assumptions, and anecdotal evidence mobilised in service of that intellectual vision survived and solidified as knowledge about television, its history, and its operation in specific contexts. Indeed, the historical reality of television and the memory of that history began to diverge. For example, commentators in the 1960s wrote widely about the imperialist nature of the early spread of television. The cultural imperialist school rediscovered that history in the 1970s, but the actual history of American and European media companies' entanglements in national media systems of South America and Africa was otherwise forgotten in popular memory (Dizard 1965; Green 1972).

Modernisation theory and the communications scholarship it informed envisioned television as a forum for political exchange and pointed journalism, and that is also how popular memory remembers it. Indeed, such writings enshrined the very idea of what comprised valid, valued, appropriate, or even interesting, programming and the social, political, and cultural uses of the medium. American political scientist Wilson Dizard asserted that interesting programming followed (western) kings and queens, high political events such as diplomatic visits of the leaders of the Great Powers), or so-called world events, defined as international sporting events or space achievements, for example (Dizard 1965). Writing in 1972 author Timothy Green concurred, noting that Soviet television did not live up to the norms established by western television. Soviet television demonstrated a "lack of occasion" or eventlessness, he argued. The Soviets did not report space achievements live, (which has been interpreted by later commentators as evading public scrutiny), and preferred to broadcast political speeches or economic achievements to "human interest" stories such as a plane crash (Green 1972, 161–62). That is, in not replicating the norms of the British television programme, the Soviets were not doing television correctly or competently, a fact attributable to the authoritarian nature of their society. By the late 1970s critics could already historicise such normative assumptions and show that the agenda of world events served the ideological and economic interests of the West (Nordenstreng 2014).

The vision of television as a pillar of freedom in Western societies was also built on a nostalgic view of the role of the medium as a forum of debate and a check on government. American media scholar Thomas Doherty argues that this is a reputation of the medium's own making, highlighting its own (sometimes dubious) achievements. In his study of American television in the McCarthy era, Doherty argues that television made its name in the crucible of Joseph McCarthy's anticommunist crusade, although print journalism did most of the work to undermine him. Television found its voice, learned it could stand up to those in power, and "slew the dragon" of McCarthyism in a particularly public way (Doherty 2003, 178).

Nevertheless, the liberal view of the media is particularly entrenched and thriving in British media history. In 2002 eminent media scholar James Curran identified three competing historiographical traditions of British media history: liberal, feminist, and populist (Curran 2002, 135–54). The "oldest and best established" interpretation was the liberal view that British media history is the story of expanding democracy facilitated by the media. Per Curran, liberal scholars argued that the media was unfettered by government control by the mid-nineteenth century; that it empowered Britons to hold the government accountable; and that it aided the expansion of the political community into new areas of the country (not just London) and social strata, thereby "facilitating public debate" (Curran 2009). This view was so dominant that just seven years later Curran could identify four additional historiographical narratives of British media that similarly hewed to the narrative of "social progress and linearity" (Bailey 2010, 233).

Yet these narratives gloss over repressive structures of the expanding media market. As described by media scholar Mark Hampton, the debate that emerged over British media institutions (the press) in the mid-nineteenth century was characterised by a "general consensus around liberalism" that "helped produce a complacency about existing British institutions" (Hampton 2001, 215). But already in the nineteenth century "commercialisation" had become a spectre haunting the British public sphere. It became a "trope, an imagined nemesis that figured in elite attempts to understand the press in the era of the 'new journalism'" (Hampton 2001, 219). It was classist in its fear of the unedified working class and lost faith in the possibility of "rational persuasion". Commercialisation of the press late in the century challenged conceptions of its "educational" mission (as a forum for discussion and consensus, as well as a "commitment" to convince readers of the "common good") and gave rise to an understanding of the press instead as a medium of representation (Hampton 2001, 213–15). Multiple publics responding to new, less political, and more "commonplace" (quotidian) content began to emerge, but, uninformed about important matters of politics and public opinion, it was assumed that they would not be "equal participants in political power relations." That is, working-class publics were "increasingly included in a public conversation, but effectively excluded from conversations about the government and public affairs" (Hampton 2001, 227, Sparks 1991).

This very brief sketch suggests the kinds of thinking that similarly shaped the public service mission of BBC radio and later television: providing (unequal) access to information, events, and issues, while also attempting to raise the level of taste among a new, larger national audience (Cardiff and Scannell 2013, 158). Indeed, David Cardiff and Paddy Scannell have argued that the BBC's public service mission "eroded from the very moment the corporation came into being, and by the end of the Second World War, the emergence of a three-pronged programme had sufficiently compartmentalised the audience that "'the nation as community' was lost" (Cardiff et al. 2013, 170). Moreover, Asa Briggs has noted that the BBC was not a forum of debate or hard-hitting journalism in the 1950s and 1960s (Briggs 1979, 615).

The neoliberal turn has also begun to destabilise the historical ground on which the liberal version of events rests, untethering political and economic progress in the modern project. Scholars such as David Harvey, Quinn Slobodian, Wendy Brown, and Stephanie Lee Mudge have demonstrated that neoliberals favoured a "constrained democracy" and were skeptical of the nation-state (Harvey 2005; Brown 2015; Slobodian 2018; Mudge 2008). To protect the economy, they focused on the political structures that could limit or expand the independence and freedom of capital. They sought to remove governance of the world economy from the purview of national, democratic governments and place it instead under the control of supranational organisations. The market could not survive on its own – it was not good at self-regulation – instead, it would be overseen by a transnational elite of economic decision -makers. One of the fruits of recent scholarship on neoliberalism is its displacement of the postwar period, locating the roots of this movement more expansively in the early twentieth century and the continental European world. For example, Quinn Slobodian's account of the Central European school of neoliberalism argues for its intellectual roots in the destruction of the Habsburg Empire, the "confrontation with mass democracy", and what neoliberals perceived as the unfortunate "politicization of the economic" "governed by Keynesian delusions and misguided fantasies of global economic equality" (Slobodian 2018, 14, 17).

The neoliberal turn has refocused our attention on the political economy of the media, and media scholars are exploring the transnational, transmedial, and transdisciplinary to resituate the twentieth-century media in the broader structures of the modern world. Cinema scholar Lee Grieveson, for example, has reframed the story of media as a crucial constituent of the liberal political and economic world of the twentieth century – not a product of the liberal world, but a system deliberately built for the "expansion of a *militantly neo*liberal world system that has been ... brutally violent, unequal, and destructive" – challenging time-worn ideas about media independence and objectivity (Grieveson 2017, 1). Grieveson explores the early history of radio and (mostly) cinema in the United States and Britain and argues that elites – states, corporations, and investment banks – utilised these technologies to shape popular opinion and attitudes by integrating them into an "expansive liberal praxis" determined to create the ideal conditions for twentieth-century corporate capitalism and a consumer economy (Grieveson 2017, 1–3). Government policies framed the economic and political usefulness of the media. US authorities were convinced that film would be a "powerful influence on behalf of American goods" that would help expand their "Market Empire" across Europe and beyond. By contrast, the British used it to define and shore up an imperial market (Grieveson 2017, 6; de Grazia 2006). Alliances among government authorities, corporations (General Electric and AT&T in the United States; in the UK this role was undertaken by the Federation of British Industries (1916–65)), and investment bankers developed the institutions and infrastructure. In Britain, the real and perceived success of imported American narratives of abundance shook authorities, causing the government, under pressure from British industry, to embark on a programme of economic protectionism. They used tariffs to reinforce the boundaries of the imperial marketplace, regulation to limit the power of American images and advertising, and the domestic film industry to project state power, disseminate a vision of the so-called British way of life, and discourage consumption of American goods in favour of those produced in the Commonwealth (Grieveson 2017, 7). In both cases, he argues, "corporate and capital control over media, subsumed under the imperatives to generate capital, marked a radical diminution of the possibilities of media culture and produced a media system that is patently antithetical to the communicative requirements of democratic society" (Grieveson 2017, 4).

In Britain, the interdependence of government, capital and media was exemplified by institutions such as BBC External Services and the Empire Marketing Board (later reorganised into the Crown Film Unit of the Ministry for Information) (Webb 2006). The latter included members of the BBC and innovated the documentary form in the service of liberal empire under the leadership of John Grierson. We can begin to see the visual vocabulary of imperial liberalism in the film material collected by Grierson. Grierson was excited to exploit "'the visually dramatic material in which the Empire is so rich'" by which he meant not the vibrant diversity of peoples, cultures and traditions, but rather the structures and infrastructures of modern life – bridges, dams, factories, canals, and the like, all of which had been built by the imperial state. These are not too far removed from the pageants of socialist success broadcast in the postwar period, which is unsurprising, given television's role in projecting the modernising state's preoccupation with the technologies of industrialism. Audiences quickly became accustomed to "elaborate and expensive fictions of abundance" argues Grieveson (Grieveson 2017, 170).

Television, too, contributed to the imperial liberal vision of the future, structurally and narratively. British television followed a well-established pattern of mobilising private capital to develop the technology – early on this was carried out by Baird and Marconi-EMI – and infrastructure of communications (electricity, transportation, the facilities and apparatus of transmission, as well as production facilities). Private concerns (including receiver manufacturers, newspaper magnates, and others, among them a number of former BBC employees) also populated the independent contractors that later served the Independent Television Authority (ITA), such as Associated Broadcasting and Associated Re-Diffusion. A government commission convened in 1943 to explore the future of television argued that it was fundamental to postwar economic recovery and recommended its reintroduction as quickly as possible at war's end (Briggs 1979, 175–87). Television development would provide work for decommissioned military engineers, as would the manufacture of receivers and construction of facilities to be located both in Britain and across the Empire (in places such as Canada or Africa) (Goldie 1977, 35). In other words, in a lean period of (persistent) postwar rationing, measures of television's impact, its success, and its public service mission turned on Britain's ability to maintain its status as a pioneer of television technology, and television's ability to shore up the economic foundation of the postwar state.

2 Projecting the Cold War on Television

The wartime experience similarly shaped the postwar public service mission. Wartime cinema and radio had made their reputation for reaching mass audiences at home and abroad, comprising the only "free" voice in occupied Europe. BBC authorities understood their programme as "'projecting the essential merits of our own way of life" – while avoiding attacks on other people's ways of life (Briggs 1979, 511). This mandate persisted into the post-war period, but sharpened as the Cold War accelerated. The events of 1948 including the Berlin Blockade and the Czech coup drove a renewed sense of the national interest among British media and politicians, as well as their conviction, first developed during the war, that the nation should speak with one (authoritative and objective) voice (Webb 2006, 118). The Government re-committed the BBC to providing External Services and disseminating British views abroad (Jacob 1959, 4). The mandate to project a unified vision of Britain and the so-called British way of life gave way to a decidedly more aggressive campaign to directly challenge the Soviets (Steinle 2007, Webb 2006, Webb 2014).

It is important to remember that early postwar television was a fundamentally different beast from that with which we are familiar even from ten years later. Lauded for its ability to project actual events *as they happened*, in the early 1950s the technology was still confined to the indoors. Television was little known and enjoyed little regard. It emerged in a media universe that made its achievements seem Lilliputian, both in terms of the picture postcard sized images emanating from receivers and its perceived cultural significance. Cinema audiences apprised themselves of current events through contemporary newsreels in the millions; much smaller television audiences watched tiny figures talk to one another in the studio. By 1958 only about half of British television broadcasts contained real-life items, of which outside broadcast material comprised about a third. Indeed, the defining feature of – and enduring dilemma faced by – broadcasting has been the problem of content. There was never enough of it, especially as the television schedule (and channel universe) expanded across the twentieth century.

Our expectations of media reporting also have been defined by a set of ideal principles, including balance, fairness, objectivity, and access, that have not been easy to achieve – or even desirable – historically. For example, the global capacity to capture images of the present was still finite in the 1930s and 1940s, limited to still photography, newsreels and film. In the interwar period just a handful of newsreel companies could provide footage of far-flung current events only because they split expansive territories among them, then pooled the film for sale (Hulbert 2002). Film historian Tony Aldgate has shown that, although newsreels "consciously invoked the neutral ideology of the contemporary news media", in fact they provided material that echoed the Government's agenda without context or analysis (Aldgate 2013, 146). Newsreel companies reported events after the fact, often developing a set of points to illustrate, then finding visual material that matched well enough (Hiley and McKernan 2001, 194–95). In 1952 a UN report noted that newsreel companies "distribute films on a large scale, and control exhibition circuits". The material they presented was limited in scope, and sports and celebrities tended to dominate international news (Baechlin and Müller-Strauss 1952, 33). The authors found it troubling that newsreels presented a "convincing ... likeness of reality" and were the sole source of information for many audiences, playing an outsized role in forming opinion (Baechlin and Müller-Strauss 1952, 38–40). The television broadcast schedule put additional pressure on media producers and blurred the lines among media: in 1958 the Newsreel Association sanctioned British Movietone for providing material to its greatest competitor – the BBC – (Hulbert 2002, 265). The demand for content was insatiable and often (even benignly) indifferent to the ideal principles of the liberal media.

The market for content also played a greater part in shaping the evolution of BBC television than has been widely appreciated. In her study of the transnational network of exchange between the BBC and American networks, Michelle Hilmes argues that, by 1952 BBC officials had already recognised the possibilities of the global market for television, and they began to privilege the production of programmes for export as a means of funding the wider BBC schedule. This meant producing fewer live single plays that appealed to elite British audiences in favour of more – and more "British" – filmed serials for distribution in a global market. Film was superior to kinescopes: programmes could be recorded outside the studio and shipped internationally; more broadly film enabled the economies of scale of "package production". This shaped both the economics of BBC production and introduced new aesthetic principles "centred on familiarity, repetition, and the everyday, ... narrative structure and visual representation" (Hilmes 2012, 218). It also shaped the representation of "Britishness," privileging representations of the "streets of London, the English countryside, the old market towns, the country houses, the cathedral and university towns" that were appealing markers of Britishness (from a certain class perspective) and "would be an immense attraction for the American viewer" (Greene 1953, 219; Hilmes 2012, 198). That is, the BBC was highly attuned to the conditions of the global market, which could not only finance further production but also underpinned the vision they served that audience.

What was the BBC doing in Berlin? The BBC reported on conditions in defeated Germany to its domestic and global audience; collaborated (briefly) with the Americans to produce the *Welt im Film* series of mandatory re-education films; and developed its German service (radio), first broadcast in 1938. The diplomatic crisis in Berlin destabilised the Allied relationship, but also that between the British and Germans more generally. The war had turned the tables on British attitudes to the Germans and Soviets. Nazism, not the so-called good Germans that still populated Germany, comprised the enemy, until the experience of the Blitz hardened British attitudes against Germans (Chapman 2001, 221). Media scholar Howard Smith has shown that BBC television mediated a narrative shift from German collective guilt to that of an aggressive state that victimised its own citizenry (Smith 1999, 145). But wartime fears faded in the escalating confrontation with the Soviet Union, a potentially more threatening enemy. Long-standing anti-Russian and anti-Communist beliefs resurfaced, and BBC reporting suggested similarities between – if not yet exactly equating – the Nazi regime and the Soviet Union (Knowles 2017, 184–5). In the emerging Cold War, not punishment and re-education, but economic recovery, reconstruction, and even rearmament seemed necessary for the protection of the UK and Western Europe (Knowles 2017, 183).

Thus, the diplomatic crisis in Berlin offered a prime opportunity for the BBC to engage in – and begin to make its reputation on – the imperial liberal project I described above. Television proper could hardly do so before it had developed the infrastructure of Cold War topicality, beginning in 1949. That year the service acquired new cameras for improved outside broadcasts as well as zoom lenses (Jacob 1962, 20).[1] In 1950 the BBC broadcast the first television transmission from the Continent, transmitting pictures from Calais, France (Jacob 1959, 4). By 1952 the BBC was experimenting with the magnet tape (video) technology VERA (superseded by AMPEX, which became the industry standard in 1958). At the same time, the BBC experimented with producing its own newsreel, that is, filmed content broadcast on its network. Smith argues that this content offered a "unique contribution to the public debate", treating specific issues in greater depth and breadth than in the cinema (Smith 1999, 145). Yet, BBC programmes were no less political or more objective than cinematic newsreels, presenting what Smith defined as "obtrusively personal views in a media widely regarded as balanced and impartial" (Smith 1999, 150).

The BBC tackled the so-called German Question in a number of reports between 1946 and 1958. Some were one-off productions, while others contrib-

1 For an example, see https://www.bbc.co.uk/programmes/m000j1j7.

uted to serial programmes such as *Foreign Correspondent*, *Viewfinder*, or *Special Inquiry*. They variously utilised original footage, voiceover commentary, studio interviews, and studio reenactments of events, and involved a number of BBC staff well-known to television studies today including Grace Wyndham Goldie, Norman Collins, Charles de Jaeger, Philip Dorte, and Chester Wilmot. These programmes demonstrate how quickly BBC reporting shifted from the language and interpretive framework of postwar to Cold War (Smith 1999). Earlier programming described the difficult conditions of wartime destruction and postwar recovery in Germany (noting on 9 July 1948, for example, that "whilst we are helping them to rebuild a peace potential, we are steadily destroying their war potential") then evolved into raising the alarm against totalitarianism ("the possible alliance between totalitarian regimes (Russia and a newly Nazified Germany) is the greatest danger to Europe" broadcast 28 October 1949). Smith notes that there are few programmes for which pre-production treatments, film and sound exist; where images are available, he does not dwell on them, noting in short that one programme presented "well shot but rather disconnected descriptive sequences" while another offered "brief scenes of defeat, followed by brief scenes of reconstruction" (Smith 1999, 146, 148, 158). The aural aspects of this body of work indeed suggest the narrative of shifting relationships among (former) enemy and allies. The images, while often "disconnected", support that narrative. But those images have an afterlife beyond the programmes in which they first appeared. Images persist in our cultural memory, even more so as they are traded and re-circulated in intertwined networks of information. Untethered from context they became the building blocks of a wider visual imaginary of the Cold War, as well as important constituents of British imperial liberalism.

3 Reporting the Berlin Blockade

Here I would like to focus on two films to demonstrate the operation of the visual narrative of imperial liberalism that was fundamental to the British self-image and the representation of their administration of Berlin as seen on the BBC. The first is the late-Blockade programme "Mr. Attlee Visits Berlin" (11 March 1949) (BBC 1949a). I will compare that briefly with a more triumphalist vision of postwar imperial liberalism broadcast in the first programme after the end of the Blockade, catalogued as "News Special: The Blockade Ends" (15 May 1949) (BBC 1949b). There are two points to be made here. First, the imagery of imperial liberalism pervades the representation of the occupation. Capital, consumption, and the literal machinery of modern life is central to the resurrection of Berlin, from planes (and airports), to generating stations, automobile traffic, and the canal locks of the Berliner Tor. Second, the depiction of the Soviet Union and the areas under their control emphasise lifelessness, lack of industry or "legitimate consumerism," and implied fear. (BBC 1949a).

"Mr Attlee Visits Berlin" purports to follow Prime Minister Attlee on his trip to Berlin, but in fact it takes most of its time illustrating the boundaries – territorial but also conceptual – of the geopolitical divisions in the former capital. Attlee appears only in the first few minutes of the film; thereafter the film visits infamous former National Socialist sites, shows us examples of recovery and renewal, and visits sector boundaries to illustrate the bounds of Soviet and British influence in the city. The film is composed of primarily of exterior shots of various sites in the city including Kurfürstendamm, Potsdamer Platz, and sector borders. Footage illustrated and commented on German defeat through images of the bombed-out sites of the former state: the Reichstag, former Propaganda Minister Goebbels' house, the Reich Chancellery, and the Führer bunker. Unlike the defunct institutions of the former German state, German public life continued (visually asserted by the shift from inanimate to animate – from static shots of buildings to pictures of (primarily) women working). Nondescript Berlin sites were reduced to rubble, but streets and sidewalks were clear and shops, cinemas, newspapers, public notice boards, and other institutions of public life could be found intact. The film made no comment on the widespread destruction of German residential neighbourhoods, even when they appeared on screen. Instead, a brief set of interior shots represented the resurrection of German home and family life. In a tight shot framing a cramped and spartan kitchen, a housewife cooks *Eintopf*, irons clothing, darns socks and serves tea by the light of a single bare bulb. Defeated Germans confront difficult conditions: food and household goods are scarce, and Berliners scavenge for firewood and food. Street vendors offer only "odds and ends, but nothing substantial, nothing to help with the rations." Such images suggested that the aggressive German state had been soundly defeated, and the British occupation made possible the return of a semblance of normal life.

But the point of the film was not so much to detail the conditions under which Germans lived, as it was to illustrate the British role in reconstructing the infrastructure of normal modern life. Cheerfully industrious "rubble women" reclaim debris, destined to build runways at the British airport in Berlin-Gatow. One sequence focuses on the operation of a British generating station that provides the electrical power (even if rationed) that drives modern industrial society. The film highlights the significance of the generating station through a low angle shot in which the building fills the screen, appearing dramatic and imposing. That sequence is visually juxtaposed with the cramped interior of the German apartment described above. Newspapers are abundant, and commerce is underway. "Legitimate shopping" (visually framed here as women's work) is possible in the western sectors, at least, even if out of reach of many Germans. The British have returned industry to Berlin, as illustrated by the hard work of the rubble women and the availability of electrical power, news and information, commerce and consumer goods.

Moreover, the film differentiates between the activities of British and Soviet authorities in the reconstruction of Berlin. While the British lay the foundation of postwar freedom and prosperity, the Soviets help themselves, building extravagant monuments to their war dead, spreading communist ideology, fostering the illegitimate black market, and generally suppressing freedom in their sector. The film shows us the newly built, imposing, and pristine Soviet memorial to their own dead. It looms large on screen, framed with nothing on the horizon to compete with it, then is juxtaposed with the once monumental and impressive (now battered and diminished) Reichstag (the former enemy replaced by a new more powerful one). A large central statue of a Soviet soldier appears to dwarf the smaller, more classically designed statues of Prussian royalty found elsewhere on the Siegesallee. Similarly, shots of the Rundfunkhaus (Broadcasting House) and transmission towers suggest the power of the Soviets to spread (dis)information and propaganda. The film suggests that electricity in the eastern sector is only to be found in the Soviet Cultural House, which attracts young Germans and captures them for the study of Soviet ideology. While life abounds in the western sector – illustrated by industriousness, pedestrian and automobile traffic, and the representation of a German home – the eastern sector is barren, devoid of people or industry, save the lone Soviet soldier striding confidently across his domain. The only centre of activity is at the black market at Potsdamer Platz, where shadowy figures – depicted primarily as men, crowded close together – conduct their business. The newsreel voiceover underscores the point: "That there is any life at all in the Western sectors is a result of the Airlift" (BBC 1949a).

On the one hand, this narrative is striking in its caution, especially given what is today known about the period of the Airlift. In contrast to historical memory of the period there is no imagery of starvation here, commerce is alive and well if "dear", and sector borders are open and unpatrolled. This aligns with the contemporary British Foreign Office mandate against challenging the Soviets too directly (Webb 2006; Webb 2014). On the other hand, we can see how the BBC was engaged in mediating a certain set of ideas about the Soviet Union. Literary scholar Svetlana Koroleva has examined the "British myth of Russia," identifying a set of fairly stable tropes that emerged over the centuries to become layered upon one another, which found new life at the end of the Second World War. By the nineteenth century, for example, the British perception of Russia had shifted from that of a "pseudo-Christian primitive country" to a "'powerful, despotic, aggressor state" and "'potential enemy'" (Koroleva 2022, 318.) The collapse of the British Empire was the linchpin of an emerging narrative that posed Russia as a "new" threat to the British – an even more powerful and far-reaching enemy characterised now by its "inhumanity" and exercise of "absolute power" (Koroleva 2022, 284). The BBC participated in the construction of this myth, even if in this film the contrast between the British and Soviets is primarily one of ideology, not yet outright cruelty.

A special report on the end of the Berlin Blockade aired in May projected an early triumphalist vision of postwar liberal capitalism. The report used some of the same film material as the earlier film, but focused more on the consumer advantages to be found in the West, framed within the return of western trains and goods to Berlin (BBC 1949b). The implicit bleakness of the Soviet zone two months earlier became explicit in this film. Both reports, however, positioned Germans living in the western zones as agents who could exercise freedom of choice and consumers who aspired to the (not yet achievable in the 1950s) habits and practices of the emerging middle class, mass consumerist society (Gumbert 2017).

These are just two programmes, but they are part of a much larger infrastructure of storytelling that defined our visual imaginary of liberalism (imperial or otherwise) and authoritarianism, interpretations that often belied the historical facts of the event, even becoming so influential that they – even now – forestall historical reckoning with the past.

Film clips have become visual shorthand mobilised to explain key moments in the Cold War. BBC television newsreels, for example, helped create and spread the popular myth of a heroic Airlift that saved a city from want and fear. The heroic narrative of the Airlift asserts that the western Allies were the saviours of would-be victims of Soviet greed. The success of the Airlift, measured in the zero sum terms of the Truman Doctrine, burnished the Allies' reputations among the Germans whom they had so recently defeated. At the same time, Airlift footage illustrating the tons of transported goods alongside dramatic pictures of planes flying (and crashing) in peacetime, was an exercise in advertising liberal capitalist modernity. Moreover, images from these and other films, as well as the narrative they helped create and disseminate, can be found in historical documentaries from the BBC-CNN co-produced *Cold War* series to homegrown retrospectives such as *The Berlin Airlift*, uncredited, uploaded to YouTube by vintage plane aficionado "London Aircraft" (London Aircraft 2022).

Historian Carolyn Eisenberg has argued that the popular memory of the West as saviour in the Airlift has proven particularly resistant to revisionism and shaped American reception of postwar foreign policy (Eisenberg 2004). The heroic narrative obscured the factors underlying the Blockade: the unilateral western decision to create the Bizone, implement the currency reform in the western zones, and ultimately found a west German state. Eisenberg and others have shown, too, that the provision of the city was not in question during the Blockade (Eisenberg 2004; Stivers 1997). These decisions precluded a diplomatic resolution to German division in which all the Allies would have been forced to compromise. Instead, the Airlift reframed the confrontation as a matter of Soviet greed rather than western antipathy to compromise. For Eisenberg, western unwillingness to compromise in turn necessitated the development of overwhelming military power, a nuclear arsenal, and, she suggests, "the creation of a permanent national security state organized around military solutions" (Eisenberg 2004, 200).

One recent publication illustrates the afterlife of this narrative and its contemporary implications. In a recent book exploring the existentialist movement, British author and curator Sarah Bakewell dismisses the contemporaneous Berlin Blockade in a few short sentences, and asserts that "[The Soviets] set out to starve Berlin into submission, just as the Germans had starved Leningrad during the war" (Bakewell 2016). Not only does this statement misrepresent the Blockade, it also promotes a false equivalence rooted in a conservative historiographical trope that equates the Nazi regime with the Soviet Union. Since the 1980s that trope has been used to normalise the genocidal Nazi regime; in the twenty-first century it has been taken up by extreme right-wing populist movements to demand expanded victim status in the new Europe (Ghodsee 2014).

4 Conclusion

The hundredth anniversary of the BBC has been an opportune moment to reconsider the history, significance, and legacy of one of the most high-profile media institutions of the twentieth century. It is particularly welcome to explore a moment in the history of early postwar television, given that so much of media studies work has been focused on the late twentieth century.

The "presentism" of media research has had the paradoxical effect of casting a veil of certainty over the past, which undermines our ability to adequately interpret the origins of the present.

The first point to make is methodological and has to do with how historians work with images. The market for content shaped our historical memory of the period and will continue to do so as images are recirculated in the twenty-first century. The global capacity to capture images of the present was finite in the 1940s, limited to still photography, newsreels and film. Contemporary newsreel companies, the Anglo-American *Welt im Film* collaborative, and BBC Television created an international market in Cold War B-Roll: the circulation of a finite group of texts that helped create a fairly stable visual imaginary of the Cold War. Moreover, the creation of these images was not neutral or "objective," but partisan, broadcasting the imperial liberal worldview as I suggested above. The resulting footage framed events in the service of particular stories, and even had the effect of limiting potential counter-narratives. That is, a finite group of images, framed and reframed – cut for broadcast and re-cut for use at home and abroad in documentaries, educational films, or even feature films – mostly abstracted from their original context define our vision of the Cold War.

The complexity of visual evidence has long been recognised. In a 1967 review in the film journal *Sight and Sound* British film critic Penelope Houston warned that "Newsreels are a heavily edited form of source material that speak with the authority not of impartiality but of national public relations." She imagined a difficult future for historians: "TV News treatment is ruthlessly professional in shaping material, inserting stock shot, cutting film to commentary .... Historians may find it harder than they expect to track down basic film material that hasn't been severely processed, or chopped about for day to day journalistic purposes" (Houston 2002, 299). Though the reality effect of film suggests its usefulness as one kind of evidence – what happened – in fact it is not. Instead, it allows us to ask much more involved and complex questions about how and why such images were variously captured, edited, traded, projected, disseminated, and received.

My second point is historiographical. In the liberal narrative of progress over the last two centuries, the extremism of the interwar period has appeared exceptional, followed by a golden age of peace, expanded prosperity, democracy, education, and invention fostered and even driven by the media in the postwar period. But from the perspective of the twenty-first century, it is the postwar period that appears increasingly exceptional: the fruits of the golden age do not appear to have survived the end of the Cold War – or at least no longer appear to serve humanity. The roots of our current crises – rising inequality, climate crisis, and disinformation and distrust in public institutions, for example, demand renewed examination of the structures that have framed our understanding of the world in which we live; structures that were often produced and codified during the postwar information boom.

Finally, this chapter has taken a fresh look at BBC television at a formative moment in the history of the medium and the corporation. Television emerged anew – no longer a mechanical medium but an electronic one – at war's end. Circumstances – the collapsing British Empire and waning British influence in the world – and events – the Berlin Blockade and Airlift – forged its purpose. It was so successful in defining its own story that the BBC has come to be seen as the paragon of liberal democratic media and the measure against which all other media have been judged. Yet here I have argued that it participated in projecting imperial liberalism: recreating the British power anew in the context of collapsing territorial empire. The BBC served a particular vision of the world; even if it sometimes spoke truth to power, those moments perhaps were rather more the exception than the rule. The history I have related here is but a microcosm of the challenge facing the area formerly known as the so-called free world, which has yet to come to terms with the illiberal nature of its own Cold War. Without such a reckoning, we will continue to operate as if the ends justify the means.

References

Aldgate, Tony. 2013. "The Newsreels, Public Order and the Projection of Britain." *Impacts and Influences: Media Impacts in the Twentieth Century*. Ed. James Curran, et al. London: Routledge. 145–56.

Baechlin, Peter and Maurice Müller-Strauss. 1952. *Newsreels Across the World*. Paris: UNESCO.

Bailey, Michael (ed.). 2010. "Roundtable: Narrating Media History." *Media History* 16.2: 233–51.

Bakewell, Sarah. 2016. *At the Existentialist Café*. New York: Other Press.

BBC. 1949a. "Mr. Attlee Visits Berlin." 11 March 1949.

BBC. 1949b. "Newsreel Special: The Blockade Ends." 15 May 1949.

Betts, Paul. 2020. *Ruin and Renewal: Civilizing Europe After World War II*. New York: Basic Books.

Briggs, Asa. 1979. *Sound and Vision*. Volume IV. *The History of Broadcasting in the United Kingdom*. Oxford: Oxford University Press.

Bodroghkozy, Aniko. 2018. "Historicizing Television News in the 1960s". *Rediscovering US Newsfilm: Cinema, Television, and the Archive.* Eds. Mark Garrett Cooper, et al. London: Routledge. 87–97.

Brown, Wendy. 2015. *Undoing the Demos: Neoliberalism's Stealth Revolution.* New York: Zone Books.

Brownell, Kathryn Cramer. 2023. "24/7 Politics: Cable Television and the Fragmenting of America from Watergate to Fox News", Washington History Seminar, 20 November. https://www.youtube.com/watch?v=1NMFgwox1vs Accessed 1 October 2025.

Cardiff, David and Paddy Scannell. 2013. "Broadcasting and National Unity." *Impacts and Influences: Media Impacts in the Twentieth Century.* Eds. James Curran et al. London: Routledge. 157–73.

Chapman, James. 2001. *The British at War: Cinema, State and Propaganda, 1939–1945.* London: I.B. Tauris.

Curran, James and Myung-Jin Park. 2002. "Beyond Globalization Theory." *De-Westernizing Media Studies.* Eds. James Curran and Myung-Jin Park. London: Routledge. 1–15.

Curran, James. 2002. "Media and the Making of British Society, c.1700–2000." *Media History* 8.2: 135–54.

Curran, James. 2009. "Narratives of Media History Revisited." *Narrating Media History.* Ed. Michael Bailey. London: Routledge. 1–21.

De Grazia, Victoria. 2006. *Irresistible Empire: America's Advance through Twentieth-Century Europe.* Cambridge, MA: Belknap Press.

Dizard, Wilson P. 1965. *TV: A World* View. Syracuse, NY: Syracuse University Press.

Doherty, Thomas. 2003. *Cold War, Cool Medium.* New York: Columbia University Press.

Eisenberg, Carolyn. 2004. "The Myth of the Berlin Blockade and the Early Cold War". *Cold War Triumphalism: The Misuse of History after the Fall of Communism.* Ed. Ellen Schrecker. New York, NY: The New Press. 174–200.

Frau-Meigs, Divina, Jeremie Nicey, Michael Palmer, Julia Pohle, and Patricio Tupper (eds.). 2012. *From NWICO to WSIS: 30 Years of Communication Geopolitics: Actors and Flows, Structures and Divides.* Bristol: Intellect Books.

Ghodsee, Kristin. 2014. "A Tale of 'Two Totalitarianisms': The Crisis of Capitalism and the Historical Memory of Communism." *History of the Present* 4.2: 115–42.

Goldie, Grace Wyndham. 1977. *Facing the Nation: Television & Politics, 1936–76.* London: The Bodley Head.

Green, Timothy. 1972. *The Universal Eye.* New York: Stein and Day.

Greene, Hugh Carleton. 1953. "Television Transcription: The Economic Possibilities." *BBC Quarterly* 7: 216–21.

Grieveson, Lee. 2017. *Cinema and the Wealth of Nations: Media, Capital, and the Liberal World System.* Berkeley: University of California Press.

Gumbert, Heather. 2017. "Early Narratives of the Network City." Unpublished paper, Gateway to Cinema and Media Studies, SCMS Regional Conference. London, UK, 17 June 2017.

Hampton, Mark. "'Understanding Media': Theories of the Press in Britain, 1850–1914." *Media, Culture & Society* 23.2: 213–31.

Harvey, David. 2005. *A Brief History of Neoliberalism*. Oxford: Oxford University Press.

Hiley, Nicholas and Luke McKernan. 2001. "Reconstructing the New: British Newsreel Documentation and the British Universities Newsreel Project". *Film History* 13: 194–95.

Hilmes, Michele. 2012. *Network Nations: A Transnational History of British and American Broadcasting*. Hoboken: Taylor & Francis.

Hoffmann, Hilde. 2016. "The Visual Memory of the Cold War." *Constructions of Cultural Identities in Newsreel Cinema and Television after 1945*. Eds. Kornelia Imesch, et al. Bielefeld: Transcript Verlag. 81–100.

Houston, Penelope. 2002. "The Nature of the Evidence." *Yesterday's News: The British Cinema Newsreel Reader*. Eds. Luke McKernan and Nicholas Hiley. London: British Universities Film & Video Council: 290–99.

Hulbert, Jeff. 2002. "The Newsreel Association in Britain and Ireland." *Yesterday's News: The British Cinema Newsreel Reader*. Eds. Luke McKernan and Nicholas Hiley. London: British Universities Film & Video Council. 257–67.

Imre, Anikó. 2016. *TV Socialism*. Durham NC: Duke University Press.

Jacob, Ian. 1962. "Television in the Public Service." *EBU Review* 71: 20.

Jacob, Ian. 1959. "Television in the Public Service," *EBU Review* 54: 4.

Koroleva, Svetlana. 2022. *The British Myth of Russia*. Cambridge: Cambridge Scholars Publishing.

Knowles, Christopher. 2017. *Winning the Peace: The British in Occupied Germany, 1945–1948*. London: Bloomsbury Academic.

London Aircraft. "Berlin Airlift Documentary including archive film and interviews," YouTube, https://www.youtube.com/watch?v=bYWzvbJe9iY. Last accessed 27 October 2022.

Mihelj, Sabine. 2014. "Understanding Socialist Television: Concepts, Objects, Methods". *VIEW Journal* 3: 7–16.

Mihelj, Sabine. 2011. *Media Nations: Communicating Belonging and Exclusion in the Modern World*. Houndmills: Palgrave Macmillan.

Mudge, Stephanie Lee. 2008. "Neo-Liberalism's Three Faces". Working Paper, EUI MWP, https://cadmus.eui.eu/handle/1814/9108. Accessed 27 October 2022.

New York Times. 1949. "Attlee to Visit Berlin". *The New York Times*. 2 March.

Nordenstreng, Kaarle. 2014. "Free Flow Doctrine in Global Media Policy." *The Handbook of Global Media and Communication Policy*. Eds. Robin Mansell and Marc Raboy. London: John Wiley & Sons.

Paulu, Burton. 1967. *Broadcasting on the European Continent.* Minneapolis: University of Minnesota Press.

Pitts, Jennifer. 2006. *A Turn to Empire : The Rise of Imperial Liberalism in Britain and France.* Princeton: Princeton University Press.

Pronay, Nicholas. 1976. "The Newsreels: the Illusion of Actuality". *The Historian and Film.* Ed. Paul Smith. Cambridge: Cambridge University Press. 95–120.

Rajagopal, Arvind. 2014. "Communication as a Cold War Concept: A View from the Global South." Lecture given at Virginia Tech, 18 April.

Rajagopal, Arvind. 2001. *Politics after Television: Religious Nationalism and the Reshaping of the Indian Public.* Cambridge: Cambridge University Press.

Siebert, Fred et al. 1956. *Four Theories of the Press.* Urbana: University of Illinois Press.

Simpson, Christopher. 1996. *Science of Coercion: Communication Research and Psychological Warfare, 1945–1960.* Oxford: Oxford University Press.

Slobodian, Quinn. 2018. *Globalists: The End of Empire and the Birth of Neoliberalism.* Cambridge, MA: Harvard University Press.

Smith, Howard. 1999. "Have They Changed at All? The Portrayal of Germany in BBC Television Programmes, 1946–55." *Cold-War Propaganda in the 1950s.* Ed. Gary Rawnsley. New York: St. Martin's Press. 145–64.

Sparks, Colin. 2000. "Media Theory after the Fall of Communism." *De-Westernizing Media Studies.* Eds. James Curran and Myung-Jin Park. London: Routledge. 39–42.

Sparks, Colin. 1991. "'Goodbye Hildy Johnson: the Vanishing Serious Press." *Communication and Citizenship: Journalism and the Public Sphere.* Eds. Peter Dahlgren and C. Sparks. London: Routledge. 58–74.

Steinle, Matthias. 2007. "Visualizing the Enemy: Representations of the 'Other Germany' in Documentaries Produced by the FRG and GDR in the 1950s." *Framing the 'Fifties: Cinema in a Divided Germany.* Eds. John Davidson and Sabine Hake. New York: Berghahn Books. 120–36.

Stivers, William. 1997. "The Incomplete Blockade: Soviet Zone Supply of West Berlin, 1948–49". *Diplomatic History* 21: 569–602.

Webb, Alban. 2006. "Auntie Goes to War Again: The BBC External Services, the Foreign Office and the Early Cold War". *Media History* 12.2: 117–32

Webb, Alban. 2014. *London Calling: The BBC, the World Service, and the Cold War.* London: Bloomsbury Publishing.

CHAPTER 10

The BBC as a Role Model for Cold War Germany

Frank Bösch

The great importance of the BBC German Service during the Second World War is well known and has been widely analysed. In contrast, the role of the German BBC Service beyond 1945 has not been much researched and is less familiar. The majority of East and West Germans who grew up in the 1970s and 1980s are unaware that a German BBC programme existed after 1945, because foreign broadcasters like RIAS, BFBS, AFN or Radio Luxembourg were much more popular during this time. However, the BBC German Service was highly influential in both parts of Germany in the first two post-war decades. I argue in this chapter that the BBC German Service was important in three connected spheres: first, it shaped the structure and culture of West German radio and broadcasting; second, it produced an influential programme, especially for East Germany until the 1960s; and third, it presented politics and culture in an authoritative and entertaining way. As this chapter shows, this concept followed on from the BBC German Service programme in the Second World War.

In contrast to the rich literature on the BBC German Service during the war, there is almost no research on it after the war (Brinson and Dove 2003; Cannon 1988); the little research that exists merely points out the importance of the BBC in general for building up the public broadcasting model in West Germany (see Rüden and Wagner 2005; Wagner 2005). While the few existing publications on the BBC German Service after 1945 are based on the BBC Written Archives Centre at Caversham (Major 2013) or on the Stasi files on those who wrote letters to the BBC (Schädlich 2017), this chapter analyses the sources of the Deutsches Rundfunkarchiv (DRA) in Potsdam-Babelsberg.

1 The BBC as a Model for West German Broadcasting

The BBC was a role model for German broadcasting. Immediately after 1945, the BBC played an important role in the foundation of German radio, especially in the British occupation zone. The BBC influenced German broadcasting in four chief areas: (1) the position of radio and later of television in the

 | HTTPS://DOI.ORG/10.1515/9783111302508-010

German legal system, (2) its organisational structure and control, (3) its programme mandate and the programme itself, and finally (4) the norms and self-perception of the journalists (Marchal 2004, 311).

As is well known, the Allies rebuilt the German media from the ground up after 1945. All German media were closed and reorganised under Allied control – including licensing publishers, hiring staff, and practising a certain degree of censorship. The media were part of the Allied re-education programme, which even included music on the radio.

The BBC played a significant role in this setting. Some British government officials had argued in 1945 that the BBC's German Service should replace German broadcasters temporarily. However, they decided to create a new German radio station based on the centralised BBC model. British officials tried to launch one single radio station for all four German zones, but the Soviets rejected this idea (Wagner 2005, 20–4). In Hamburg, a single central main radio station was created for the whole British occupation zone, differing greatly from the federal German radio landscape in the Weimar Republic. A crucial meeting in London on 20 November 1945 defined the "Respective functions of B.B.C. Service and Nordwestdeutscher Rundfunk" (NWDR): "The function of Nordwestdeutscher Rundfunk is to provide for the British Zone a 'Home Service' in the line of the B.B.C. Home Service. The German Service [...] speaks with a British voice." (Wagner 2005, 21). This agreement laid down the BBC as a model, but also specifics for a NWDR programme in the future. For instance, the meeting's participants pointed out: "Excessive attention by Nordwestdeutscher Rundfunk to the political and historical re-education of the Germans will destroy its credibility" (Schwarzkopf 2007, 10). So, from early on the British were aware that too much re-education content might be counterproductive.

While US officials were in favour of their pluralistic private radio system, the Soviets and many Germans supported a governmentally controlled radio regime similar to the one before 1933. As a compromise, the BBC model of a public broadcasting monopoly succeeded with an organisation independently financed and organised by the regional *Länder* governments, but controlled by major parties and groups. In contrast to a system of various private broadcasters, the public monopoly model was seen as the best way to unite, inform and educate Germany's fragmented post-war society (Dussel 2022, 219–24). As before 1933, the Germans saw the American model as a chaotic, uncontrollable catalyst for disintegration.

Besides the overriding BBC model, NWDR's structure, practice and programme content were strongly influenced by members of the BBC's German Service. About 100 German repatriates who returned after 1945 worked in German radio stations (Wagner 2003, 140). They were a minority, but often held important positions. Several Germans who had worked for the BBC during the war years started a new career at different German radio stations after 1945. For example, Eberhard Schütz worked as a programme director for NWDR, then for RIAS in the 1950s, and finally for SFB (Sender Freies Berlin) from 1966 to 1971; Walter D. Schultz soon took on leading positions at NWDR, Edward Rothe at NWDR and later WDR (Westdeutscher Rundfunk), and Fritz Eberhard worked as Artistic Director of Süddeutscher Rundfunk (Sösemann 2001, 63). Karl-Eduard von Schnitzler, later a major TV commentator in the GDR, came from the BBC and was employed at NWDR until he was fired in 1947 (Holzweißig 2018). Others had worked as prisoners-of-war in Ascot for the BBC German Service and returned after the war to work at NWDR. Carl-Heinz Lüders, who joined NWDR too, was among them. In the 1950s Lüders went on to become one of the most influential government officials in media politics. Unlike his colleagues in the ministries, he tried much harder to integrate different positions and parties (Palm 2023, 120–35).

Other repatriates from Britain who joined NWDR had worked for other British radio stations. Alexander Maaß came from Radio Calais. British military officers who had previously broadcast on British radio joined German radio stations up until 1946. The priest and BBC presenter Horace Saunders-Jacobs, for instance, was in charge of broadcasting for NWDR in Cologne from 1945 and started to broadcast church services as practised in Britain, despite criticism from German clergy (Wagner 2005, 28). Other former German members of the BBC German Service changed to West German print media, such as Willy Eichler. Therefore, the wartime BBC German Service had educated and created a network of broadcasters who built up the German media after 1945, transferring concepts from the BBC German Service to German radio and other media.

The most important and well-known British BBC journalist in this context was of course Hugh Carleton Greene (see Figure 10.1), head of the BBC German Service during the war who then in 1945 became "Chief Controller" of the largest German broadcaster, Nordwestdeutscher Rundfunk. Greene implemented a liberal staffing policy and did not just promote former emigrants and BBC journalists; even former communists and some Nazi supporters got jobs. In 1947, he went as far as firing many former NSDAP members who had made false declarations on their denazification questionnaires, which led to strong public criticism. In this way Greene tried to set limits for the continued employment of former Nazis, cross-checking applicants against the Berlin Document Center's NSDAP member index.

FIGURE 10.1 Hugh Greene (1910–87), controller of broadcasting in the British-occupied zone of Gemany after 1945 (and later Director General of the BBC), at the NWDR Staff Training School in 1948. (© Hans-Bredow-Institut)

Following the British model, Greene only allowed regional programmes with different stations or "Funkhäuser" within a centralist NWDR, unlike the American zone's different independent radio stations in each federal state. Between 1946 and 1954, NWDR also maintained a Funkhaus in Berlin at Heidelberger Platz 3. Due to the centralised BBC concept, Greene and his British colleagues also tried to prevent a separate German radio station in Berlin (Schäfers 2005, 355). However, the remit of the Funkhaus was special, conceived as a bridge between East and West and as a regional broadcaster for Berlin. Yet this proved beyond the means of this small outpost of NWDR. In 1954, when the studio was transferred to Sender Freies Berlin, only 250 people worked there. This indicates that the British model was influential in Berlin too, but due to centralist thinking it had much smaller support than American support for RIAS. On top of that, the overlap with the BBC German Service was simply too strong.

Greene fought hard to keep NWDR as independent from governmental and party influence as the BBC was in Britain. He initiated a small board of directors with only four politicians and nine other public figures. However, Greene lost this battle against the Germans in 1948 when he returned to Britain; NWDR ended up with a board dominated by politicians. Besides shaping the structure, Greene and his BBC colleagues also transmitted a certain pro-democratic spirit from Britain (Tracey 1983, 116; Kutsch 1991, 116–9). Many German editors remembered the liberal atmosphere in these years. The former BBC members taught them how to discuss matters openly and critically both in public and within the radio station. For instance, journalists at the early NWDR, such as Peter von Zahn, felt quite free to criticise the British forces.[1]

Greene also established, following the London model, an NWDR Staff Training School to educate young journalists which proved crucial in supporting open political discussions. One major lesson was the separation of news and views, another the validation of facts with a second source. These courses were taught by repatriates such as Alexander Maaß, victims of the dictatorship, and even former Wehrmacht soldiers (Schwarzkopf 2007). This cooperation with former BBC members influenced the self-perception and habitus of many German colleagues who described this attitude with words such as *Bescheidenheit* (humility) or *Dienst am Hörer* (serving the listener). The German stations of NWDR adopted the main principles of the BBC: objectivity, different positions, and a combination of news, education, and entertainment. As Toby Thacker has pointed out, even the music was based on BBC concepts. Composers whose works had been proscribed or who came from foreign countries were aired, while popular songs and composers from the Nazi period were banned (Thacker 2003).

In the following years, Greene and his colleagues organised an exchange with the BBC that many journalists remember as an important experience. Famous German journalists – such as Gerd Ruge, Hans-Joachim Friedrichs, and Peter von Zahn – spent months in the British studios of the BBC (Marchal 2004, 313). Some started transnational careers. Franz Wördemann, for example, became an editor at the BBC in London in 1950. In 1953 he switched to Bonn as a BBC correspondent and in 1957 he became WDR editor and chief editor at WDR radio in Cologne. Rudolf Walter Leonhardt, who had been working for the BBC since 1953, moved on to become chief editor of *Die Zeit*'s magazine supplement. Another example is the former BBC journalist Fritz Eberhard, who was reputed to be a very liberal boss at Süddeutscher Rundfunk and supported young journalists with new ideas (Sösemann 2001, 251). For some colleagues, such a BBC background was legendary.

Yet others mistrusted those repatriates as relics of the Allied occupation and started to tease and discredit them, as the media historian Hans-Ulrich Wagner has pointed out. They were attacked as communists who used to spread anti-German propaganda and were now broadcasting socialist opinions (Wagner 2003, 149; Wagner 2015). Many Christian Democrats even

1 See Greene's speech in 1947 answering the critique of different parties (Greene 1947).

lamented a Marxist spirit that ostensibly stemmed from the influence of the British Labour party on this liberal organisation and its programming. German radio directors such as the right-wing Social Democrat Adolf Grimme were attacked as socialist relics of the British occupation. In the 1950s, the West German government did not accept criticism of its policies and considered independent BBC-style journalism as dangerous ideological infiltration. However, several attempts by the government to control the media with stricter laws failed due to media protest.

Like the BBC, the early German radio stations tried to educate their listeners; at the same time, they had to make compromises to satisfy the desire for lighter entertainment. The BBC also influenced the German radio programmes and formats. For instance, the BBC introduced the journalistic format of "features", which were rarely known in Germany. This combination of reportage, personal thoughts, and dialogues with music built on former experiments at the BBC (Marchal 2004, 314). The cultural late-night programme after ten o'clock, which was developed in 1947, adapted elements of the BBC's Third Programme founded one year before. Famous intellectuals such as Adorno, Gehlen, König and Schelsky appeared on the show in the 1950s. By contrast with the BBC's Third Programme, however, the German evening schedule focused more on the intellectual self-understanding of Germany (Boll 2004, 58).

There were many close cooperative ventures between the BBC and German broadcasters, such as joint programmes or the exchange of news reports. For instance, the Hessische Rundfunk had a joint programme with the BBC between 1947 and 1968 called "Quiz London-Frankfurt" which, of course, contained questions concerning high culture, but was very popular. Between 1956 and 1985, the BBC German Service, together with RIAS, aired a monthly political discussion between three British and German journalists and intellectuals („Darüber lässt sich streiten"/"That's debatable"). Reports of the BBC German Service about important events in Britain, like the coronation of Queen Elizabeth in 1953 or the visit of West German President Theodor Heuss to London in 1957, were also picked up by German radio stations.

Personal exchange continued in the following decades. As Christian Potschka has shown, Greene, in his position as BBC Director-General in the 1960s, had a close rapport with WDR director Klaus von Bismarck (Potschka 2012, 71–8). They swapped speeches and information, for instance about organisational structure, and both broadcasters continued to exchange radio programmes and staff, during election broadcasts for example. Bismarck also used cooperation with the BBC to further his goal of increasing programme content exchange with socialist Eastern Europe; here the BBC already had more experience. Klaus von Bismarck also adapted the famous BBC Reith Lectures from 1948; the German equivalent was named the Von Bismarck Lectures (Potschka 2012, 71–8). In the 1960s, the BBC also served as a role model in listener research. The BBC was a pioneer in conducting audience research. Such empirical evaluation of media users began very late in the Federal Republic: WDR only introduced audience research in 1963, also under pressure from its new competitor, Radio Luxembourg, and against the objections of many editors (Rumpf 2007, 57).

When television became available, the BBC considerably influenced its rise in West Germany. Once again, Hamburg was the driving force, and the Intendant Adolf Grimme recommended that television follow the BBC's example once again (Hickethier and Hoff 1998, 66–72). However, when German TV developed in the early 1950s, British influence was much weaker than during the foundation of radio. Consequently, more former employees from Nazi television's founding generation joined. In the late 1950s, the BBC became a model for critical political television. Rüdiger Proske, head of NDR TV's politics desk, transferred the BBC format *Panorama* wholesale to German television, even using the same name (Lampe 2000, 16). Since the 1960s, the transfer of TV series increased, for example *Maigret* (in 1959/1960–63) or the controversial *Till Death Us Do Part,* which was adapted as *Ein Herz und eine Seele* in a German version (Hodenberg 2015). However, many other series were transferred or translated from the BBC's competitor, ITV, such as *The Avengers* or *Coronation Street.*

In the second half of the 1950s, the new competition between the BBC and ITV was seen as a model by conservative Germans, who demanded a second channel financed by advertising. However, Chancellor Adenauer favoured a programme in cooperation with the big publishing houses, which would be more under government control. This plan failed due to the protest of the federal German states (Hickethier and Hoff 1998, 141). Instead, a new second channel emerged, called ZDF, which was a combination of an independent BBC model and the German model of a party-controlled channel.

Besides, the German and World Service BBC was a model for the two stations that broadcast beyond West German borders: Deutsche Welle and Deutschlandfunk, which became additional competitors for the BBC. Deutsche Welle started to broadcast in different European languages in 1953 and then launched Arabic, Asian and African language services in the 1960s, as a soft power instrument of West German foreign policy. The West German embassies in these states often compared the quality of Deutsche Welle with the BBC World Service. After the first Persian broadcasts to Iran, for example, the commentators were said to be "still somewhat lacking in practice" in comparison with the BBC's soft power. Listeners also compared the programme content of Deutsche Welle with the BBC in their letters (Hagedorn 2016, 219, 304).

Like the BBC's foreign broadcasting, Deutsche Welle was financed by the government (the Ministry of the Interior) and therefore was less independent. However, unlike at the BBC, Germany's political parties and churches exercised much more influence on the leading staff (Hagedorn 2016, 183). Like Deutsche Welle, the BBC German Service criticised human rights violation in socialist countries; however, even former members of Radio Moscow conceded that the BBC remained much more objective than others (Ostrogorski 2003, 202). In comparison to the BBC, Deutsche Welle seemed to broadcast more reports about Germany that propagated the achievements of the West and criticised the situation in the East. This changed in the late 1960s. During the Greek dictatorship from 1967 to 1974, Deutsche Welle's highly critical Greek service became the most popular platform of the Greek opposition. West German diplomats were very upset, because the Greek government complained constantly. The German foreign office tried to put an end to this critical reportage by intervening with Deutsche Welle and recommending the more neutral programming of the BBC as a model (Bösch 2024, 190–98). In general, conservatives saw the BBC in the 1970s as more neutral than the seemingly "red broadcasting" of some German stations (Bösch 2012, 191–210).

Last but not least, we should not forget the BBC's influence on Deutschlandfunk, which started in 1962 as a West German radio station aimed at East Germany. Like the BBC, it focused on news, information, and culture. The GDR service was the main rationale for Deutschlandfunk, but its schedule also addressed a West German audience. Consequently, Deutschlandfunk became another competitor of the BBC and was partly responsible for the decline of London's German Service from the 1960s on.

2 The German Service of the BBC

Germany was a key target for the Cold War broadcasting of the BBC's foreign language service. In 1948, the German Service had the largest staff in the developing BBC World Service, with about 120 people (Major 2013, 258, 260; Brinson and Dove 2003, xii). The BBC had the advantage that it was known to many wartime listeners and considered an objective, informative, and entertaining voice. There was continuity in the form of some familiar exiled wartime radio announcers, represented for example by Lindley Fraser, director of the German Service from 1947 (Fraser 1959). Likewise, the German émigré Carl Brinitzer, a leading presenter and translator during the war, remained at the BBC

German Service as programme director until the 1960s (Brinitzer 1969). Robert Ehrenzweig and Bruno Adler, who created characters like "Frau Wernicke" or "Kurt und Willi", also continued their work in London.

With its language-learning broadcasts, which started in 1945, the BBC became a language school for the German nation. The programme "Lernt Englisch im Londoner Rundfunk" became so popular in Germany, because its presenter, the exiled German actor Carl Heinz Jaffe, had an entertaining style, which differed from German schools. The young publisher Axel Springer started to print accompanying booklets in 1947, which had a circulation of 100,000. Likewise, imitating the cooperation between the BBC and the *Listener*, Springer printed transcripts of selected lectures and articles from NWDR (Arnim 2012, 33, 37). Unlike the BBC, however, NWDR was not allowed to publish its own radio magazine. Again, Springer printed the radio schedule in a magazine, not unlike the *Radio Times*, which was an important pillar for his nascent media empire. The BBC's English courses remained one of the most prominent and popular programmes. When the German Service celebrated its twenty-fifth anniversary in 1963, it asked why the station was still necessary. The top answer: English language courses!

The BBC German Service faced a double challenge. On the one hand, it had to transform itself from a wartime broadcaster to a peacetime station that supported democratic practices in allied West Germany. On the other hand, the BBC wanted to broadcast for the people of the GDR – a new hostile state and communist enemy. This dual role for West and East was a major problem. From 1949, the BBC aired its East Zone Programme, which avoided the word "GDR" and was still called the slightly less disparaging "East German Programme" from the 1960s on. It was broadcast between the regular German programmes and started at 8:15 p.m. for about 45 minutes and was repeated the next morning at 5:30–6:00 a.m. and 6:45–7:15 a.m. (DRA 1964). The programme was announced with the line: "Und nun unser Programm für die Ostzone" ("and now our programme for the Eastern zone"). However, BBC broadcasts for East and West were inter-related, and their reception shifted. For instance, the programme "Funkbriefkasten" (Radio Mail Bag), which started on 4 July 1945, was one of the most popular programmes in post-war Germany. An important segment was to respond to letters from the German audience in order to foster a political discussion and report individual problems (Major 2013, 258; Oliver 2020, 243–44). Germans in Britain also valued this BBC programme in the post-war years as the most important source for informing themselves about the thoughts of ordinary Germans, as a correspondence between the historians Friedrich Meinecke and Gustav Mayer suggests (Ritter 2006, 467).

This programme for all occupation zones was transformed into the East German programme “Letters without Signature” after 1949. Once again, listeners who decided to submit a letter were taking a certain risk, and as Susanne Schädlich has shown, some of those who dared to write to the studio were arrested or harassed by the East German secret police, the Stasi (Schädlich 2017). The fault-finding letters read out in the programme allowed a critical, often polemical tone, which contrasted with the more neutral style of the BBC, enabling an anti-communist dialogue. Such letters also created a surrogate for a free public sphere in East Germany, which was largely absent. The listeners saw themselves as a community that longed for the help of the Western allies against the lies of the Sozialistische Einheitspartei Deutschlands (SED). The letters represented a human need to communicate about experiences and feelings, to receive encouragement, and to influence matters publicly.

“Letters without Signature” encouraged protest against the East German communist party, the SED, although the BBC reminded writers to be careful. In 1958, for instance, one aired letter called for ballot papers in the GDR’s single-list elections to be invalidated and the election results checked (DRA 1958). GDR citizens wrote many letters to elites and politicians in the West to tell them about their concerns, too (Becker and Bösch 2024). They also sent such letters to GDR authorities and radio broadcasters to demand more music and entertainment on eastern stations and less politics (Classen 2013, 97). The specific reason for sending mail to the BBC was the hope that their views would be shared in public with others.

The West German government emulated this BBC programme, although in an authoritarian style. The Bundespresseamt, the government press office, produced a radio feature called “Antwort aus Bonn” (Answers from Bonn), which posed fictional questions to facilitate a presentation of government politics. In the 1960s, the Bundespresseamt produced more than 1,000 broadcasts, most of them about the GDR (Hodenberg 2006, 175–6).

The BBC’s wartime German Service became a model for the service for the GDR. 1950s programming reprised elements of anti-Nazi broadcasts and redeployed them against the SED. Satirical elements such as “Hitler vs. Hitler”, “Der verwunderte Zeitungsleser” (The Baffled Newspaper Reader) or the dialogues of “Kurt und Willi” were turned into the satirical dialogue of “Die zwei Genossen” (The Two Comrades). Bruno Adler modelled this on his own wartime programme (Brinson and Dove 2003, xiii). Once again, it used witty Berlin dialect and humorous irony to skewer official ideology. For instance, “The Two Comrades” joked using circular logic in 1963 that elections were superfluous nonsense, "because everyone is already one hundred per cent convinced, as the elections clearly prove" (DRA 1963). They praised the Berlin Wall as "Baukunst" ("high architecture"), which "protects us from the attack of the 'Ultras' in the front city" (DRA 1968), but wondered why the guns of the East German soldiers pointed to the East (DRA 1961). In the GDR, the former BBC member Karl-Eduard von Schnitzler adapted the BBC wartime programme "Hitler vs. Hitler". As Kristin Rebien has argued, von Schnitzler now used the technique of deconstructing Hitler's speeches for his own television programme "Der schwarze Kanal" (The Black Channel), which overlaid footage from West German TV with his critical commentaries (Rebien 2003, 165).

The consensus that the GDR was a totalitarian state supported the continuity of BBC German Service broadcasting (Major 2013, 129). Charles Wheeler, a BBC correspondent in Berlin between 1949 and 1953, remembered that he saw himself as a "Kalte[r] Krieger" ("Cold Warrior"). Broadcasting to East Germany "was political – as political as the German Service during the Nazi-period", because the GDR "was also a dictatorship. There were concentration camps" (DRA 1988). While West German journalists could not cross the borders at this time, the BBC staff in West Berlin was very privileged and had close contacts to many East Germans. As they were financed by the British Foreign Office, they enjoyed the status of the British Military Government. This enabled free access to East Germany across the East Berlin border. They had more chances to speak with SED officials or with people on the street or at the Leipzig Trade Fair. Austin Harrison, head of the BBC German Service, did just that on a regular basis. These talks were not recorded, because this might endanger East Germans (DRA 1998). In this way, the BBC staff of the 1960s anticipated the work of the West German correspondents in East Berlin one decade later, when they were accredited there following de facto mutual recognition under *Ostpolitik* in 1973. Before the Berlin Wall was built, East Germans came frequently to the BBC office in West Berlin, which changed its address several times and was finally located on Savignyplatz. After 1961, only East German pensioners or a few deported dissidents were able to visit the BBC in West Berlin. As Peter B. Johnson remembered, some East German contacts even turned into friendships (Johnson 2003, 208–12). East German intellectuals such as Regine Hildebrandt had regular contacts with BBC correspondents, because one of them also sang in East Berlin's Domkantorei choir and visited her apartment near Alexanderplatz (DRA 1998b). However, we need further research to find out whether these contacts led to specific investigative news. Less adventurous former BBC journalists in West Berlin remember instead spending their days ploughing through the rather boring East German press.

The post-war BBC German Service did not have the luxury of a Nobel Prize-winning speaker such as Thomas Mann, as it had before 1945. The most famous intellectual on air was probably the Austrian-born poet Erich Fried. The former communist had fled to London after the Nazis killed his father. Between 1952 and 1968, Fried made political commentaries on the BBC German Service against the SED dictatorship and its oligarchy. Wolf Biermann, one of the most prominent intellectuals in the GDR, later remembered Fried's programme as the "heart and soul" ("Kopf und Herz") of the BBC German Service. According to Biermann, "Every morning, millions of people in the Eastern Bloc got up early enough to quickly listen to this one particular programme, which Erich Fried himself read out in his slightly Viennese dialect. He provided information about events all over the world", with "wordplay" and "truths" (Biermann 2017, 152). Fried, too, reprised the satirical style of the BBC's wartime broadcasting. The programme "Frau Kleinova" resembled, for instance, Bruno Adler's "Frau Wernicke" from before 1945 (Lawrie 2003). Fried eventually left the BBC because he was fed up with Cold War rhetoric, not so much the BBC's but the language surrounding the Vietnam War in general. In contrast to wartime broadcasting, refugees from East Germany rarely hosted programmes. More often, former East Germans became critical journalists at West German media, such as Carola Stern or Gerhard Löwenthal, who went to RIAS, then to SFB and ZDF.

Due to the BBC German Service's wartime fame, its programmes had many listeners in the postwar decade. Between a quarter and a third of GDR refugees to West Germany in the late 1950s, who were asked for their radio choices, claimed that they had listened to the BBC German service. This was half the number of RIAS listeners. (RIAS was of course a much bigger station, with a broader programme schedule of 20 hours a day and an audience in the whole GDR.) Still, it received up to 400 letters a day and 1,800 telephone calls (Hixson 1997, 74). Broadcast signal jamming did not impact the BBC as much as RIAS (Classen 2013). Due to its focus on information, the BBC audience was considered more educated than that of RIAS and SFB (Major 2013, 257). Also in the other socialist countries, US-supported stations like Radio Free Europe had a bigger audience, but the BBC targeted the educated class, the famous German *Bildungsbürgertum* (Puddington 2003, 95; Starkmann 2003, 192).

3 Audiences and the Transformation of the German Service

The BBC German Service in East and West Germany seems not to have been an overall success story, because from the 1960s ever more East Germans preferred the all-day schedule of RIAS or of West German broadcasters such as Sender Freies Berlin (SFB). Especially for young Germans, the BBC was certainly not the most appealing British radio station. More influential for them was probably the army station BFN (British Forces Network) or BFBS (British Forces Broadcasting Service), which brought Western rock music to Germany. The English language did not put them off, but made the station seem easygoing, not unlike the American Forces Network (AFN) and, from 1957, Radio Luxembourg (Rumpf 2007; Siegfried 2017). In other words, Radio Luxembourg's foreign-language stations can be seen as a joint challenge for the BBC and the German stations, all of which were in danger of losing young listeners in particular (Hilgert 2015, 332). In the 1950s, therefore, German stations hired the British BFN editor Christopher Howland, who was to win over young people with popular music (Hilgert 2015, 333).

This led to a certain reform of the BBC German Service from the mid-1960s, which offered more music for the younger generation. Peter Sahla hosted new formats like "Hit 66!" in 1966 (title changed with every year) and "Platten à la carte". Guntram Kremer presented "Friendly Fan Club" and Heidi Grundmann "Eine kleine Beatmusik", usually with songs from the Beatles and Rolling Stones (Baumann 2014). Later on, Jochen Grussendorf presented "London Heartbreak". As swinging London became the centre of modern music, BBC London tried to transform its staid image. East German listeners could request songs, which were then recorded by the audience with tape recorders. As contemporary witnesses recalled, the BBC also played lesser-known songs (Korbik 2017). British radio star presenter John Peel later became the lead music DJ of the BBC German Service, but also hosted programmes at rival stations such as BFBS or Radio Bremen (Peel and Ravenscroft 2006, 458, 529). However, many East German teenagers in the 1970/80s did not even know that a German BBC station existed. Despite these new music programmes for younger listeners, the BBC German Service continued to be a broadcaster for educated West Germans, probably of their parents' generation.

When English became more common in schools, British culture became more popular. The British monarchy, its nobility, castles and gardens fascinated many Germans, as well as its everyday culture of pubs and tea. Consequently, the programme "Tips für Touristen" (Tips for Tourists) became one of the most popular programmes beginning in 1974. About 3,000 Germans wrote to its host, Irene von Mühlendahl (Blatz 2003, 225). If we look at the letters to the BBC German Service in general, 80% of them in the 1980s came from West Germany, mostly from Berlin. So what started as broadcasting to a GDR audience was transforming into output for a West German cultural elite. In addition, German Service features in the 1980s dealt with British history. They reported about celebrated British politicians, authors and scientists, and about the history of famous British newspapers and of British football.

Even from the perspective of British foreign policy, the German Service remained necessary. In 1961, the Foreign Office recommended cancelling 19 "language services" that it considered dispensable, including all Western European offerings except the German Service (Johnston and Robertson 2019, 195). Similarly, the "Duncan Report" of 1969, which called for the dropping of many foreign language transmissions, emphasised that the German Service, like the Arabic or the Russian, was a strategically crucial language broadcaster (Johnston and Robertson 2019, 201).

However, the BBC changed its German programming after the establishment of détente and Willy Brandt's *Ostpolitik*. In April 1972, the whole schedule was still very much focussed on the "Programm für Ostdeutschland" ("Programm for East Germany"), as it was called (DRA 1972). One year later, the evening schedule just had the new neutral title "Erste Abendsendung 20.00–21.00" and "Zweite Abendsendung" (first/second evening programme). News, reports about British culture and music for the young dominated transmissions now. "The Baffled Newspaper Reader", which ridiculed GDR news, was cancelled in 1972, as was "Letters without Signature" two years later. Only the more intellectual broadcast "Aus der kommunistischen Welt" on Wednesdays and Fridays still recalled the former Cold War programme, but the latter was cancelled, too.

Broadcasts aimed at the GDR remained critical, but became more balanced. For instance, a special 1974 feature on twenty-five years of the GDR started: "The GDR is one of the leading industrial states in the world and has a modern efficient social system." Even if this was followed by the usual critique of lack of democracy and ideological perceptions of reality, it was a shift in tone (DRA 1974). The BBC reported about modernisation in East Berlin and appreciated modern inventions in the East, but still compared them unfavourably with the standards and freedoms of West Germany.

A prominent example of this changed messaging, which connected reports about the East and West, is the "Brief aus Berlin" ("Letter from Berlin"). It reported on events and special places in East *and* West Berlin, including culture, politics, and everyday life. For instance, it reported about a design exhibition in East Berlin, which showed East and West German products as an "interesting and good compilation" (DRA 1984f), East German art exhibitions (DRA 1984d) or about the permanent exhibition, "GDR – Socialist Fatherland" of the "Museum für deutsche Geschichte". The report went on to say that "The exhibition offers, despite many deficits, many objects which present a fascinating impression of the former Soviet zone and current GDR" (DRA 1984c). Other episodes of "Letter from Berlin" reported about Western innovations in East Berlin, such as "American Square Dances" with live music (DRA 1984e), shopping streets and concrete high-rises ("Plattenbauten") (DRA 1984b), or the big shopping centre in East Berlin, which offered many goods from the West, although they were evaluated as very overpriced and of low quality (DRA 1984a). In general, these features mentioned the achievements of the GDR, while criticising the deficits of socialism. The condescending Cold War style of the BBC German Service was turning into much more balanced reporting that still presented the superiority of the Western model. West Berlin was not only presented as a modern counterpart, but also as a historical site. Many reports about West Berlin covered themes connected with the Second World War, such as the Jewish Ghetto, unexploded munitions in the ground, or the ninetieth birthday of Rudolf Heß. Despite the different focus on East and West Berlin, the BBC presented Berlin as *one* exciting metropolis – its reports connected both sides of the Wall.

This transformation of the BBC German Service could not stop the decline of listeners and the decrease of audience share. Why did the BBC continue its German Service? In a television interview with SWR in 1959, Lindley Fraser, head of German programmes at the time, responded to this question: "To keep relations with Germany on good terms"; moreover for the sake of the "zone" (Fraser 1959). He also campaigned in lectures and interviews for overcoming misunderstandings, for example, the belief among Germans that the British did not want German unification or that the British were afraid of an armed Germany. In consequence, the German Service was not just about the GDR; it was also about influencing the opinion of West Germans. In the more peaceful period of the 1970/80s, these efforts to support Anglo-German relations constituted one major reason for continuing the German Service.

After 1989 it became evident that the German Service was part of a now defunct Cold War constellation. In 1990, after the fall of the Wall, the BBC exploited its new-found freedom in East Berlin, but started to historicise its role. In the spring of 1990 it organised a discussion with East German intellectuals and presented an exhibition in East Berlin and Leipzig about the "BBC auf Deutsch" (DRA 1990a). For the last time, it received an intense reaction from East Germany. While the BBC German Service received only 100 letters from the GDR in the first six months of 1989, it received 1,900 letters in the first six months of 1990. Many people expressed their thanks for the broadcaster, asked for contacts and expressed political views, because writing such letters no longer posed a risk (DRA 1990b). However, these letters of thanks also struck a valedictory note.

By the end of the 1990s, the worldwide audience for the BBC World Service had dropped to just five million listeners. With the spread of English, the BBC had evolved into a language course and programme for speakers and lovers of English in Germany. As the BBC stated in the 1990s, only a quarter of its German listeners listened to its German programme, but 75% listened to regular English-language BBC stations. As a result, the German programme was closed down in 1998.

4 Conclusions

The BBC German Service had a remarkable impact on German broadcasting after 1945. The invention of public broadcasting was more than a mere transfer of an organisational structure from Britain to Germany. The staff of the BBC German Service and its mode of perceiving and reporting on current affairs influenced the self-conception, programme content and style of German journalism. Its programming before 1945 was a school for émigrés returning from London to Germany, as well as for British journalists in post-war Germany, and for Germans joining the BBC for the first time.

The German BBC's broadcasting during the war was closely connected with that of the Cold War period. Many concepts, ideas and thoughts were taken up and transformed to reach an East German audience. From the perspective of the 1950s and early 1960s, the German BBC Service was a success story. The BBC became an important bridge between East and West Germany, reaching an educated audience and becoming a role model for other new German broadcasters, such as Deutschlandfunk and Deutsche Welle, which took up elements of the BBC, eventually eclipsing their mentor. The BBC had become a victim of its own success.

References

Arnim, Tim von. 2012. *„Und dann werde ich das größte Zeitungshaus Europas bauen". Der Unternehmer Axel Springer.* Frankfurt: Campus.

Baumann, Lutz. 2014. „Der Beat und die Westsender". https://www.hdg.de/lemo/zeitzeugen/lutz-baumann-der-beat-und-die-westsender.html Accessed 1 May 2024.

Becker, Ernst Wolfgang and Frank Bösch. Eds. 2024. *Partizipation per Post. Bürgerbriefe an Politiker in Diktatur und Demokratie.* Stuttgart: Franz Steiner Verlag.

Biermann, Wolf. 2017. *Warte nicht auf bessre Zeiten!* Berlin: Ullstein.

Bösch, Frank. 2012. „Politische Macht und gesellschaftliche Gestaltung. Wege zur Einführung des privaten Rundfunks in den 1970/80er Jahren". *Archiv für Sozialgeschichte* 52: 191–210.

Bösch, Frank. 2024. *Deals mit Diktaturen. Eine andere Geschichte der Bundesrepublik.* Munich: C.H. Beck.

Blatz, Merete. 2003. „Tips für Touristen (1972–1999): Das Programm und dessen Rolle als Botschafter Großbritanniens und Fenster zum Westen". *"Stimme der Wahrheit." German-Language Broadcasting by the BBC.* Eds. Charmian Brinson and Richard Dove. Amsterdam and New York: Rodopi: 221–43.

Boll, Monika. 2004. *Nachtprogramm. Intellektuelle Gründungsdebatten in der frühen Bundesrepublik.* Münster: LIT Verlag.

Brinitzer, Carl. 1969. *Hier spricht London. Von einem, der dabei war.* Hamburg: Hoffmann und Campe.

Brinson, Charmian and Richard Dove. 2003. "Introduction". *"Stimme der Wahrheit". German-Language Broadcasting by the BBC.* Eds. Charmian Brinson and Richard Dove, Amsterdam and New York: Rodopi: ix–xv.

Cannon, Gunda. 1988. *"Hier ist England – Live aus London". 50 Jahre Deutsches Programm.* London: BBC External Services.

Classen, Christoph. 2013. "Captive Audience? GDR Radio in the Mirror of Listeners' Mail." *Cold War History* 13.2: 239–54.

DRA. 1958. "Letters without Signature". 14 November. DRA A 33/168. Deutsches Rundfunkarchiv (DRA). Potsdam-Babelsberg.

DRA. 1961. "Zwei Genossen". 21 August. DRA A33/165. Deutsches Rundfunkarchiv. Potsdam-Babelsberg, Germany.

DRA. 1963. "Zwei Genossen". 28 October. DRA A33/165. Deutsches Rundfunkarchiv, Potsdam-Babelsberg, Germany.

DRA. 1964. Printed schedules (April). DRA A33/167. Deutsches Rundfunkarchiv, Potsdam-Babelsberg, Germany.

DRA. 1968. "Zwei Genossen". 28 August. DRA A33/1659. Deutsches Rundfunkarchiv, Potsdam-Babelsberg, Germany.

DRA. 1972. Printed programme: "BBC-Londoner Rundfunk März/April 1972". DRA A33/166. Deutsches Rundfunkarchiv, Potsdam-Babelsberg, Germany.

DRA. 1974. "Sondersendung 25 Jahre DDR". 7 October. DRA A33/165. Deutsches Rundfunkarchiv, Potsdam-Babelsberg, Germany.

DRA. 1984a. "Berlin Letter". 1 February. DRA A33/35/3. Deutsches Rundfunkarchiv, Potsdam-Babelsberg, Germany.

DRA. 1984b. "Berlin Letter". 31 August. DRA A33/35/3. Deutsches Rundfunkarchiv, Potsdam-Babelsberg, Germany.

DRA. 1984c. "Berlin Letter". 20 October. DRA A33/35/3. Deutsches Rundfunkarchiv, Potsdam-Babelsberg, Germany.

DRA. 1984d. "Berlin Letter". 23 October. DRA A33/35/3. Deutsches Rundfunkarchiv, Potsdam-Babelsberg, Germany.

DRA. 1984e. "Berlin Letter". 15 November. DRA A33/35/3. Deutsches Rundfunkarchiv, Potsdam-Babelsberg, Germany.

DRA. 1984f. "Berlin Letter". 22 December. DRA A33/35/3. Deutsches Rundfunkarchiv, Potsdam-Babelsberg, Germany.

DRA. 1990a. "BBC Deutsches Programm" (1990). DRA A33/167. Deutsches Rundfunkarchiv, Potsdam-Babelsberg, Germany.

DRA. 1990b. "Danke BBC 1990!". DRA A33/167. Deutsches Rundfunkarchiv, Potsdam-Babelsberg, Germany.

DRA. 1988. Hinter 1984 (chronologisch). "50 Jahre BBC in Berlin". DRA A33/164. Deutsches Rundfunkarchiv, Potsdam-Babelsberg, Germany.

DRA. 1998a. "60 Jahre BBC auf Deutsch". s.16. DRA A33/1669. Deutsches Rundfunkarchiv, Potsdam-Babelsberg, Germany.

DRA. 1998b. Regine Hildebrandt 13 March. DRA A33/1649. Deutsches Rundfunkarchiv, Potsdam-Babelsberg, Germany.

Dussel, Konrad. 2022. *Deutsche Rundfunkgeschichte*. 4th edn. Cologne: Herbert von Halem Verlag.

Fraser 1959. "Interview Lindley Fraser". *SWR Retro*. 1 October. (Video), https://www.ardmediathek.de/video/swr-retro-abendschau/interview-lindley-fraser/swr/Y3JpZDovL3N3ci5kZS9hZXgvbzEyMDY4MjY. Accessed 1 October 2024.

Greene, Hugh Carleton. 1947. „Hugh Carleton Greene zur Kritik der Parteien am NWDR". https://www.ndr.de/der_ndr/unternehmen/chronik/Rede-zur-Kritik-der-Parteien-am-NWDR-von-Hugh-Carleton-Greene-,audio50095.html Accessed 1 May 2024.

Hagedorn, Anke. 2016. *Die Deutsche Welle und die Politik. Deutscher Auslandsrundfunk 1953–2013*. Konstanz: UVK.

Hickethier, Knut and Peter Hoff. 1998. *Geschichte des deutschen Fernsehens*. Berlin and Heidelberg: Springer Verlag.

Hilgert, Christoph. 2015. *Die unerhörte Generation. Jugend im westdeutschen und britischen Hörfunk, 1945–1963*. Göttingen: Wallstein Verlag.

Hixson, Walter L. 1997. *Parting the Curtain: Propaganda, Culture, and the Cold War, 1945–1961*. New York: St. Martin's Press.

Hodenberg, Christina von. 2006. *Konsens und Krise. Eine Geschichte der westdeutschen Medienöffentlichkeit 1945–1973*. Göttingen: Wallstein Verlag.

Hodenberg, Christina von. 2015. *Television's Moment. Sitcom Audiences and the Sixties Cultural Revolution*. Oxford: Berghahn.

Holzweißig, Gunter. 2018. *Agitator und Bourgeois: Karl-Eduard von Schnitzler*. Berlin: Berliner Wissenschafts-Verlag.

Johnson, Peter B. 2003. "Working as the BBC's German Service Representative and News Correspondent in West Berlin, 1965–1970". *"Stimme der Wahrheit." German-Language Broadcasting by the BBC*. Eds. Charmian Brinson and Richard Dove. Amsterdam and New York: Rodopi: 207–19.

Johnston, Gordon and Emma Robertson. 2019. Eds. *BBC World Service. Overseas Broadcasting, 1932–2018*. London: Palgrave Macmillan.

Korbik, Mikko. 2017. "Guitars Galore #197". 3 October. https://www.radiostonefm.de/naechste-sendungen/4408-171003-gg-197 Accessed 1 May 2024.

Kutsch, Arnulf. 1991. „Unter britischer Kontrolle". *Der NDR: Zwischen Programm und Politik*. Ed. Wolfram Köhler. Hannover: Schlütersche Verlagsanstalt: 116–9.

Lampe, Gerhard. 2000. *Panorama, Report und Monitor. Geschichte der politischen Fernsehmagazine 1957–1990*, Konstanz: UVK.

Lawrie, Steven. 2003. "Erich Fried at the BBC." *"Stimme der Wahrheit." German-Language Broadcasting by the BBC*. Eds. Charmian Brinson and Richard Dove. Amsterdam and New York: Rodopi: 117–37.

Major, Patrick. 2013. "Listening Behind the Curtain: BBC Broadcasting to East Germany and its Cold War Echo." *Cold War History* 13:2: 255–75.

Marchal, Peter. 2004. *Kultur- und Programmgeschichte des öffentlich-rechtlichen Hörfunks in der Bundesrepublik Deutschland*. Ein Handbuch Bd.1: Grundlegung und Vorgeschichte. Munich: Kopaed.

Oliver, Emily. 2020. "Tuning into Germany. The BBC Occupation Service and the British Occupation." *German and the World. The Transnational and Global Contexts of German Studies*. Eds. James R. Hodkinson and Benedict Schofield. Rochester, NY: Camden House. 236–53.

Ostrogorski, Wladimir. 2003. „Der bewunderte Rivale oder der Londoner Rundfunk als heimliches Vorbild". *"Stimme der Wahrheit." German-Language Broadcasting by the BBC*. Eds. Charmian Brinson and Richard Dove. Amsterdam and New York: Rodopi, 185–95.

Palm, Stefanie. 2023. *Fördern und Zensieren. Die Medienpolitik des Bundesinnenministeriums nach dem Nationalsozialismus*. Göttingen: Wallstein-Verlag.

Peel, John and Sheila Ravenscroft. 2006. *John Peel. Memoiren des einflussreichsten DJs der Welt.* Berlin and Leipzig: Rogner & Bernhard bei Zweitausendeins.

Potschka, Christian. 2012. "Transnational Relations Between the BBC and the WDR (1960–1969): The Central Roles of Hugh Greene and Klaus Von Bismarck". *VIEW Journal of European Television History and Culture* 1.2: 71–78.

Puddington, Arch. 2003. *Broadcasting Freedom. The Cold War Triumph of Radio Free Europe and Radio Liberty.* Lexington: University Press of Kentucky.

Rebien, Kristin. 2003. "The Rise and Fall of Karl-Eduard von Schnitzler." *"Stimme der Wahrheit." German-Language Broadcasting by the BBC.* Eds. Charmian Brinson and Richard Dove. Amsterdam and New York: Rodopi: 159–77.

Ritter, Gerhard A. (ed.). 2006. *Friedrich Meinecke. Akademischer Lehrer und emigrierte Schüler. Briefe und Aufzeichnungen 1910–1977.* Biographische Quellen zur Zeitgeschichte, Vol. 23, Munich: Oldenbourg.

Rüden, Peter von and Hans-Ulrich Wagner (eds). 2005. *Die Geschichte des Nordwestdeutschen Rundfunks.* Hamburg: Hoffmann und Campe.

Rumpf, Wolfgang. *Music in the Air. AFN, BFBS, Ö3, Radio Luxemburg und die Radiokultur in Deutschland.* Münster: LIT Verlag, 2007.

Schädlich, Susanne. 2017. *„Briefe ohne Unterschrift": Wie eine BBC-Sendung die DDR herausforderte.* Munich: Albrecht Knaus Verlag.

Schäfers, Anja. 2005. "'In Berlin war eben überhaupt nichts unpolitisch': Der NWDR-Berlin bis zur Gründung des SFB." *Die Geschichte des Nordwestdeutschen Rundfunks*, Bd. 1. Eds. Peter von Rüden and Hans-Ulrich Wagner. Hamburg: Hoffmann und Campe: 355–74.

Schwarzkopf, Dietrich. 2007. "Ausbildung und Vertrauensbildung. Die Rundfunkschule des NWDR". *Nordwestdeutsche Hefte zur Rundfunkgeschichte*, 6.

Siegfried, Detlef. 2017. *Time is on my Side: Konsum und Politik in der westdeutschen Jugendkultur der 60er Jahre.* Göttingen: Wallstein Verlag.

Sösemann, Bernd (ed.). 2001. *Fritz Eberhard. Rückblicke auf Biographie und Werk.* Beiträge zur Kommunikationsgeschichte, Vol. 9. Stuttgart: Franz Steiner Verlag.

Starkmann, Alfred. 2003. "Changing the Guard: The Transition from Emigrés to Recruits on the Staff of the BBC's German Service". *"Stimme der Wahrheit." German-Language Broadcasting by the BBC.* Eds. Charmian Brinson and Richard Dove. Amsterdam and New York: Rodopi. 185–95.

Thacker, Toby. 2003. "German Musical Life". *"Stimme der Wahrheit." German-Language Broadcasting by the BBC.* Eds. Charmian Brinson and Richard Dove. Amsterdam and New York: Rodopi: 77–92.

Tracey, Michael. *Das unerreichte Wunschbild: Ein Versuch über Hugh Greene und die Neugründung des Rundfunks in Westdeutschland nach 1945*. Stuttgart: Kohlhammer-Grote, 1983.

Wagner, Hans-Ulrich. 2003. "Über alle Hindernisse hinweg: London-Remigranten in der westdeutschen Rundfunkgeschichte. " *"Stimme der Wahrheit." German-Language Broadcasting by the BBC*. Eds. Charmian Brinson and Richard Dove. Amsterdam and New York: Rodopi: 139–57.

Wagner, Hans-Ulrich. 2005. „Das Ringen um einen neuen Rundfunk: Der NWDR unter der Kontrolle der britischen Besatzungsmacht". *Die Geschichte des Nordwestdeutschen Rundfunks*, Bd. 1. Eds. Peter von Rüden and Hans-Ulrich Wagner. Hamburg: Hoffmann und Campe. 13–84.

Wagner, Hans-Ulrich (ed.). 2008. *Die Geschichte des Nordwestdeutschen Rundfunks*. Band 2. Hamburg: Hoffmann und Campe.

Wagner, Hans-Ulrich. 2015. "Repatriated Germans and 'British Spirit'. The Transfer of Public Service Broadcasting to Northern Post-War Germany (1945–1950)". *Media History* 21.4: 443–58.

CHAPTER 11

Dancing at the Edge of the Crossroads/Abyss: *Panorama* Goes to Berlin, 1959–61

Mark Fenemore

This is not a chapter about the BBC broadcasting to Berliners but rather about that august corporation's broadcasting from Berlin to a British audience. In particular, it looks at live outside broadcasts by the BBC's investigative, television, current-affairs flagship. From 1955 to the present, *Panorama*'s reporters have roamed the world's trouble-spots, covering crises and witnessing upheavals. Today, 24-hour rolling television news has a crucial role in framing debates and spinning messages. Bolstered by the internet, TV plays a crucial role in projecting soft power and in securing psychological-warfare objectives. Some of the executives who shaped *Panorama* had direct experience of this field during World War Two. Its first editor, Dennis Bardens (1953–54), had worked at the Press Office of the Ministry of Information. He had been responsible for broadcasting propaganda material designed to confuse and disrupt the enemy (McQueen 2010, 338). As well as transmitting codes to resistance fighters, in the event of invasion, it was his task to keep a clandestine press running (Press Gazette 2004).

1 Berlin in the Period 1958–61

In 1945, the victorious Allies agreed to administer Berlin through four-power government. Although they aimed to cooperate, relations between the various allies were uneasy from the start. Trigger-happy American soldiers had shot marauding Soviet "comrades" dead within hours of arriving in the city. The strained honeymoon period lasted nearly three more years before the irrevocable breakdown of relations in the spring of 1948 (Fenemore 2023). Henceforth, the two sides abandoned the pretence of joint, four-power governance and waged no-holds-barred cold war. An island-enclave 120 miles from West Germany, the city was the cornerstone of a divided Germany which, in turn, was at the heart of a divided Europe (Gaddis 1997, 115). 1958 came at the end of a decade-long campaign of deliberate destabilisation of East Germany by the Western powers. The system of would-be utopian communism was vulnerable

 | HTTPS://DOI.ORG/10.1515/9783111302508-011

to infiltration and subversion because of the open border. A combination of Marshall and Federal German Aid had made West Berlin irresistibly attractive both to business magnates and teenagers. In terms of mass culture as well as of consumerism, the western sectors came to symbolise affluence and untrammelled freedom. West Berlin was not just an outpost of free speech; it was also an island of temptation. In the burgeoning cold war, Berlin became a key arena for brinkmanship. Although demonstrating the fragility of communist rule and sparking waves of mass flight, much of it through Berlin, the 1953 and 1956 uprisings also pointed to the dangers of an overly aggressive "Rollback" policy (Fenemore 2020, 236). Nevertheless, the GDR's woes continued. The fact that many of those fleeing were young and skilled meant that their defection was especially damaging. In his 1958 ultimatum, Soviet premier Nikita Khrushchev threatened to sign a separate peace treaty with East Germany. He sought, unilaterally, to scare Washington and London with a warning that, without their cooperation, he would end the four-power occupation of Berlin.

2 *Panorama*: The Ordinary Man and Woman's Window on the World

TV was a novel medium with an unprecedented ability to transmit news of events rapidly and directly, with greater resonance and impact on the receiver than either radio or the press could muster. In Britain, Queen Elizabeth II's Coronation, on 2 June 1953, had led to a huge jump in TV ownership, with the new device taking pride of place in the living room. Examining the way it allowed viewers to experience a powerful sense of immediacy and intimacy, feminist historian Janet Thumim investigates the invention of television culture. She sees a triangular relationship between men, women and "the Box" (Thumim 2004). TV pioneers saw women as central to their project of lodging television right at the heart of the home. This new and untested technology soon found ways to alter the domestic spaces, habits and routines it invaded. Nevertheless, executives were careful to contain the presence of women on the screen, lest it disrupt prevailing norms and mores (Thumim 1998, 91).

In November 1953, *Panorama* started out as a fortnightly, half-hour, current-affairs and arts magazine. Initially, the programme's remit was to cover domestic issues, including investigative reporting of social and consumer affairs. Before evolving to cover major international, geopolitical events, it provided book reviews together with highbrow theatre and film criticism. In part, this mixed format was designed to address and include female audience members. Recreating the atmosphere and imperatives is difficult; we only have fragments in the form of internal memos. Often what happened to be recorded were the budget items rather than the office politics. Few of the broadcasters had the time to jot down their innermost thoughts, whether about gender or about diplomacy. To his chagrin, in 1958, editor Rex Moorfoot (1958–60) did lament that they had managed to put out a programme without "a single woman's face" in it (Thumim 2004, 93–4).

By 1955, *Panorama* had established itself as a high-profile, current-affairs programme and the BBC's flagship in terms of values and integrity. In competition with its commercial rivals (Independent Television, ITV, and Independent Television News, ITN), it represented the gold standard of public-service broadcasting. For their part, international news organisations rated the programme's demonstration of the BBC's authority and accuracy. Quality journalism was a mark of British values (of sportsmanship, fair play and stiff-upper-lipped objectivity). Despite the onset of decolonisation, in this arena, Britain gave the appearance of continuing to punch above its weight. *Panorama*'s discussions of major topics and international events were often so credible and authoritative that the programme became must-see broadcasting. On 13 April 1954, for example, it held a lively debate on the implications of the hydrogen bomb, during which mathematician and philosopher Bertrand Russell, representing the Campaign for Nuclear Disarmament (CND), traded moral arguments with the Archbishop of York (Jones 2018, 631).

The revamped version of *Panorama* was born out of an epic struggle that is the subject of this chapter. Not that between capitalism and communism, dictatorship or democracy, or even between men and women, but one between the BBC and ITV. This cut-throat arms race was shaped above all by the personalities of three men and one woman. At the forefront of this no-holds-barred attack on the BBC's news monopoly were the harshly bespectacled and abrasive Robin Day and his mentor, all-round sportsman and good egg Aidan Crawley. Fighter pilot, wartime escaper and secret agent, the Old Harrovian had served as a Labour MP and went on to win a seat for the Conservatives, serving as a Minister of the Crown for both. As well as being President of the Marylebone Cricket Club, Crawley became the founding Editor of ITN. In the Second World War, he had been recaptured four times. He almost made it to the Swiss border, but his tiredness (rather than his forged papers) gave him away. "Action Man" was responsible for plucking Day from obscurity and putting him in front of a camera. It has to be said that this move was greeted with evident dismay by their new ITN colleagues (Day 1989, 75–6).

The new-look weekly *Panorama* was designed to combat ITN and went on air just days before its rival launched on 22 September 1955. Television journalism as we know it today had to be invented. At ITN, Robin Day in particular, represented a new, brash combative style of reporting and interviewing. While at St. Edmund Hall, he had been President of the Oxford Union. There, he rubbed shoulders with "aesthetes and athletes, playboys and poets, scholars and sportsmen. There were entertainers, egg-heads, wits and war heroes (Day 1989, 29)." With Crawley's encouragement, he became UK television's first "newscaster". The brisk and pugnacious former pupil barrister was much "less sycophantic" to his guests than they were used to, preferring to take them apart with forensic rigour. His non-deferential, rapid-fire persona was later dubbed the "Grand Inquisitor" style. At the time, viewers were thoroughly repelled, seeing him as "overbearing", with a marked tendency rudely to interrupt (Thumim 2004, 97).

Ironically, the ITN challenge, spearheaded by Day and Crawley, helped to revitalise a flagging *Panorama*. Reviewing its approach, the BBC stalked the upstart by becoming more aggressive and partisan. Executives realised that the programme needed a "sharper, less stuffy and deferential approach" (McQueen 2011, 681). Having helped to revolutionise TV journalism, Day's David-like potshots helped to transform Richard Dimbleby, and his vehicle, into an overpowering Goliath. Having been rattled by the competition, the BBC hit back boldly, both revamping their current affairs and poaching some of ITN's star reporters. In 1959, Head of Television Talks, Leonard Miall, succeeded in headhunting Day for *Panorama*, blatantly using his trademark vim to lure viewers away from his rival (McQueen 2011, 97). Aggrieved at cutbacks that he felt undermined the undertakings that had been made to him, Crawley also jumped ship. The new approach seemed to work: Chris Chataway, also poached from ITN, developed his own form of hard-hitting, investigative, social-affairs reporting. In the use of "on-location interviews" with ordinary members of the public, *Panorama* took its inspiration from Columbia Broadcasting System (CBS)'s *See It Now* (Jones 2018, 636).

3 Taking the Helm: Richard Dimbleby

Behind the public face of *Panorama*, and surreptitiously setting its agenda, stood a formidable woman, albeit one conspicuously uninterested in promoting the interests of her gender. If Richard Dimbleby was the face of the revamp, the driving force was Grace Wyndham Goldie. Educated at Cheltenham Ladies' College, Bristol University and Somerville College, Oxford, she had become Miall's assistant at Talks. She was utterly convinced that, with his reputation for "journalistic integrity" together with his unique knowledge and authority, Dimbleby could single-handedly transform *Panorama* into an unbeatable "heavy-weight", current-affairs programme (McQueen 2011, 338; Thumim 2004, 272). Convinced by his expert handling of the BBC's 1955 Election Results Programme that he was the man for the job, she was ready to pay him the princely sum of 100 guineas per programme to do so. Thanks to her encouragement, he thus became Britain's first recognisable "anchorman", a concept borrowed from North American broadcasting, where Walter Cronkite and Edward R. Murrow excelled. Wyndham Goldie's stated aim was to make the programme more serious and meaningful (in her words "consequential"). She was cognisant that they were forming "something quite new", for which no name yet existed. The rationale for the new format only emerged in retrospect. As early as 1950, Dimbleby had proposed a new form of televised current-affairs programme, existing somewhere between the immediacy of news and the permanence of documentary (Dimbleby 1975, 267). This was precisely the niche that *Panorama* went on to fill.

Dimbleby had a reputation for being respectful but searching. He managed to combine urbanity with gravitas, drama with poetry. To Rachmaninov's Symphony No. 1, he opened a window for his viewers to the world. A tall, bulky man, with a calming voice and courteous manners, he had a natural authority. This helped him, quickly and often permanently, to establish a rapport with his audience. His mere presence created a tremendous sense of excitement and occasion. Covering state ceremonies such as the Opening of Parliament, Dimbleby gave the appearance of knowing "every jewel in the Imperial Crown, and every stitch in a Herald's tabard" (Day 1989, 112). The peculiar balance between razzamatazz and integrity turned the show into an undisputed and prestigious, investigative flagship. Before the war, Lord Reith's BBC had cultivated an "Olympian tone of detachment", aimed at educating and informing the public. In such a mindset, entertaining them only ever appeared as an afterthought. The tone was even but ponderous. As a radio broadcaster during the war, Dimbleby had done much to overcome and banish such snobbish and isolating didacticism (Jones 2018, 635). With Dimbleby, Chataway, Crawley and Day on the same side, *Panorama* managed to become a potent behemoth and by far the BBC's most popular programme.

Dimbleby regarded editor Paul Fox (1961–63) as his one true friend in television. Neither having been to university, the two men shared a sense of intellectual insecurity. Nevertheless, their lack of conventional laurels provided them with an important emotional, instinctive, populist feel for what the audience actually wanted and needed. With or without a script, inside or outside the studio, Dimbleby delivered his lines with the same unhurried, relaxed authority. If *Panorama* became the conscience of the BBC, Dimbleby was its calm, reasoned expression. His viewers grew not only to trust his judgement completely, but to look to him for reassurance. During the Cuban Missile Crisis, one viewer telephoned the BBC to seek assurances from Mr. Dimbleby that there would be no war. Only then could she feel safe enough to consider sending her children to school (Wheen 1985, 73). With *Panorama* setting the nation's political agenda every Monday night at 8pm, Prime Ministers and Ministers of the Crown nervously tuned in to find out what issues they might have to face, at the Despatch Box in the House of Commons, later in the week. If he was unquestionably authoritative and empathetic as an anchor, Dimbleby could also be a bit portentous and self-important. Privately, he was conservative and, in the eyes of some critics, especially younger liberals within the BBC, somewhat reactionary (Dimbleby 1975, 357–8). Under his helm, *Panorama* now had a central place in the weekly schedule and, with it, a dominant position from which to help shape the cultural and political development of the nation. The standard format was five disparate domestic items with at least one foreign-affairs story.

4 *Panorama*'s Office (and Gender) Politics

In giving the flagship programme more heft and depth, Grace Wyndham Goldie inadvertently reshaped *Panorama*'s expression of gender (Jones 2018, 637). She saw it as her task to cultivate male talent in current-affairs broadcasting. The men that she encouraged and promoted became known as "Grace's boys" (Thumim 1998, 94). To underline its seriousness and centrality as hub of national life, *Panorama* visibly stressed the maleness of its gravitas. Women presenters could only distract from this message. The stars who faced the nation on Wyndham Goldie's behalf were all "big egos" who had to be well looked after, whether in the form of first-class air travel or a well-stocked drinks trolley. Although socially liberal and technologically (and thereby culturally) innovative, the BBC at this time represented a "stronghold of the masculine" (Thumim 1998, 94). *Panorama* constituted "a deeply male preserve", where the "masculine beasts of the jungle" could prowl and posture. Their audience, according to foreign correspondent Richard Lindley, consisted of "a few self-effacing secretaries" and female researchers willing to indulge their chest-thumping grunts (Lindley 2003, 263). Unlike later generations of reporters, the "*Panorama* boys" were all men of some maturity and experience. They had commonly seen war service or had worked in professions beyond television. Such experiences made them trust their judgement and their instincts. Intellectually, words and ideas came first and the pictures a distant second.

Day also admits that such strong-minded males could also sometimes be a tad temperamental (Day 1989, 129, 135.)

Behind the scenes a generational shift was taking place. A graduate of the London School of Economics, the aptly named Michael Peacock (1955–58, 1960–61), was one of the BBC's cleverest young men: able and tough, he was more than "a little arrogant" (Dimbleby 1975, 273). Ludovic Kennedy (known to his colleagues as "Ludo") had been a pupil at Eton and a member of the Bullingdon Club. An author and a playwright, later campaigning prominently against capital punishment, Kennedy did not need *Panorama* to achieve celebrity. At times, viewers felt that he could appear overly serious and "somewhat indifferent" to the people he was talking to (Thumim 2004, 97). In terms of their self-understandings, there was something of the atmosphere of the gentleman's club. A number of ideas for programmes began as relaxed conversations over a glass of single malt (WAC 1961f). The tone of the interviews was establishment chaps talking with tact, but also authority, to other establishment chaps. Unquestioned privilege rubbed shoulders with a grandiose sense of mission. *Panorama* was such a household name that a company proposed creating a board game based on it. Nevertheless, the idea of his star presenters being subject to the vagaries of "up-ladders and down-snakes" left Moorfoot, ex-Fleet Air Arm, feeling queasy (WAC 1959b).

Although the tone had become more thrusting and virile, elements of the old magazine format persisted. Heavyweight topics were thus mixed with lighter fare, in the hopes of appealing to multiple demographics. On April Fool's Day 1957, for example, *Panorama* broadcast a report on spaghetti harvesting from the trees of Switzerland, which angered some viewers. On occasion, Dimbleby could be viewed engaging in an ice cream-eating contest, swallowing a transmitter or jumping from a balloon. As a legacy of its original format, the programme remained a "bizarre cocktail of the trivial and the significant" (Dimbleby 1975, 356, 277). The programme was not unopposed. The Bacon Curers of Kent were not alone in finding an interviewer "extremely hostile", his every question "completely loaded". Day brought his trademark, courtroom-style mode of questioning (as if conducting a cross-examination) over from ITN. This was a skill men were assumed to be better at embodying and manifesting. A woman who dared to adopt the same tone or demeanour was unthinkable. She would quickly be denounced as shrill, overly aggressive and thus inherently unladylike. Because of its coverage of international affairs, the BBC also received angry missives from a slew of embassies and governments. Director-General Hugh Carleton Greene (1960–69) judged it wise not to fulfil a request from the Czechoslovakian Embassy to receive a copy of the *Panorama* script (WAC 1962–63). Lawyers representing local-government officials or trade associations often also sporadically threatened litigation. The pharmaceutical industry, individual Anglican vicars, Dutch homosexuals and psychics all felt misrepresented by the BBC's distorting mirror. Both the left and the right in Germany felt that *Panorama* was slanted against them and inherently anti-German. Feeling misrepresented, the government of the less mighty or belligerent Isle of Man was equally vexed.

5 On the Spot for Geopolitical Crises

With Dimbleby at its helm, *Panorama* took some breath-taking calculated risks. International crises, like the tensions surrounding Berlin, created an appetite for an entirely new form of journalism. Peacock looked back on the Hungarian Uprising and overlapping Suez Crisis as the moment when *Panorama* truly came of age (Miall 1966, 96). He did not feel that it was the "proper function of journalism" to remain neutral (Dimbleby 1975, 282). While allowing an increased global purview, Wyndham Goldie did not want the programme to focus exclusively on diplomacy or international affairs, for fear of alienating the audience, not least the female part (Thumim 2004, 95). Viewers also seemed opposed to sacrificing the magazine format to single-item, documentary-style reporting. Nevertheless, one viewer found that the template was getting distinctly stale: "Man-on-the-spot, woman-on-the-spot, pro, anti, uneducated, accent, posh accent. Usually in that order." Their conclusion was surprisingly meta: "Take a look at yourselves and have a *Panorama* programme on *Panorama*" (Thumim 2004, 95–6).

6 The German Crisis of May 1959

The Berlin crisis appeared to be at its "most delicate" and thorny stage in May 1959 (WAC 1961e). The BBC's flagship investigative programme saw it as part of its mission to provide an illustrated on-the-spot report, explaining the complex situation to British viewers. The goal was to set out the intricate issues, happening in an unfamiliar place, using evocative visual material. Before the advent of affordable package holidays, such treatment allowed those people, who could afford a TV and a licence, to travel the world, at least vicariously. The May 1959 broadcast was timed to coincide with the opening of the Foreign Ministers' Conference. The Geneva Summit underlined that Berlin represented the meeting point of two immense ideological, tectonic plates. With its open border, the city represented a crucial gap in the

Iron Curtain, where daily hundreds and even thousands of skilled workers were escaping.

Broadcasting footage from Berlin the very day that the Foreign Ministers met in Geneva was a considerable feat. More than the stern demeanour of Andrei Gromyko, it underlined the risks of the tiniest of missteps. One false move could easily plunge Europe into war. In the global arms race, it was very important for President Eisenhower to demonstrate a credible deterrent. *Panorama* asked what it was like to live in the encircled city in such days of crisis. The whole future of the Western world appeared to be dangling by a single, flimsy, fraying thread. Plans for a Berlin film stressed the topicality of a story set in the city at this tense moment. At this time, *Panorama* was at the zenith of its influence and status. With other news reporting largely confined to the studio, its thrusting, nomadic reporters could see themselves as an indispensable source of immediate local colour and drama. Although thunder clouds loomed, there was still some residual German hope of a miracle in their fortunes, in the form of reunification.

7 Forging White Heat amid the White Noise

On the cusp of the 1960s, technology was striding forward in leaps and bounds. Such innovations permitted a rethink of how to cover major international events. Up to 1960, BBC audience research figures recorded that it routinely secured 25 per cent of total viewers. In this period, television appeared to be developing hourly. Filming from the very heart of the divided city was bold and dramatic. Reporter Robert Kee nimbly steps from West to East Berlin, with consummate grace, like a dancer, demonstrating the border's invisibility and hence porosity. In clipped tones, he annunciates: "Through it runs the invisible boundary between West and East Berlin. It is astonishingly easy to go from one to the other." His insouciance about getting run over adds an element of risk and tension to his address to camera. With a series of vignettes, Kee peels off layers of the Berlin onion, to create a psychogram of the patient. He expertly alludes to different parts of the divided psyche and suggests the atmosphere of the city, caught on the crossroads / crosshairs of the cold war. "You can still get 25 years in Siberia on this side of the line. You can't over here ... yet." (BBC 1959).

Kee's broadcast involved cooperation with a German TV company, Sender Freies Berlin. German cameramen thus provided the vivid, black-and-white footage, taken by a 16mm Arriflex with synchronised sound. Although he only spent ten days in the city, Kee appeared completely at home, giving arresting and intense impressions of life in the divided former capital. The vox pops were mainly with English-speaking West Berliners or recently arrived refugees from East Germany. The report addressed a range of issues, from leisure, consumerism and ideological differences to smuggling, asylum-seeking and policing of the border. The scenes in the nightclub evinced the gay liveliness of the seductive, sinful city hinted at by 1920s visitors Christopher Isherwood and Harold Nicolson. Flitting about the vibrant metropolis like a voyeuristic flaneur, Kee appears utterly at ease in his surroundings. Hand rakishly on his hip, he suavely demonstrates the nightclub-telephone's operation, calling a blonde lady at another table. Nevertheless, he insisted that the city's gaiety belied and concealed the state of unrelenting crisis it was caught up in. Connecting the human to the political, he asked a teenage interviewee: "Do you know any girls who have boyfriends in the East Sector of Berlin?" (BBC 1959).

Day described Kee's strength as his "romantic intensity", which he contrasted with Ludovic Kennedy's fierce and unremitting integrity (Day 1989, 129). Nevertheless, *The Times* saw his mellow attitude as having a distinct edge. As his much-lauded report from Algiers showed, he had the exceptional ability to make viewers feel that he was directly talking to them (*Times* 2013). Although on the cusp of just forty, Kee could boast a wealth of experience. A. J. P. Taylor had been his mentor in pre-war Oxford. The high-profile don continued to have affection for his favourite student even after his younger wife, Margaret, became completely besotted with the 19-year-old. Although this infatuation eventually led the couple to divorce, Taylor chose not to blame Kee, seeing him as having behaved honourably. Clever and handsome, he was, after all, irresistible to both sexes. In part, Kee joined the RAF to escape Margaret's attentions. He had to warn the guards at his training camp not to let her in.

Shot down laying mines over the North Sea, Kee twice tunnelled out of Stalag Luft III. On one run, his false papers and rudimentary German allowed him to get as far as Cologne. Looking back, he said that public school had been quite good training for camp life. Planning escapes and outwitting the "goons", it had all been "rather fun" (*Irish Times*, 2013). In a subsequent broadcast, he managed to give some viewers the impression that he was anti-German. His producers argued that his summing up may have been a little blunt, but this was because "nerve-racking" technical issues had impacted on his delivery (WAC 1961a). At no point during his Berlin report did he show any signs of nerves. Stressing the dystopian oddity of the breeches and jackboots of the East German border guards, Kee viewed them with humour rather than hatred.

Flown back to London, the film reels had to clear customs and then be hustled through editing and magically released into the ether. Part of the programme was specially shot in East Berlin, but without the "man-in-the street" interviews proposed for the western side of the city border. *Panorama* producers saw no point in tedious interviews with communist officials. No fee was necessary for the use of "old zither music" (WAC 1959c). As a consequence, presenter fees represented the principal cost of shooting. Kee earned the lavish sum of £70. Otherwise, the Berlin trip (facilities and general expenses) came to £200. *Panorama* simultaneously made a version for Sender Freies Berlin called "Berlin through English Eyes" (WAC 1959a). Producing versions in different languages was incredibly complex. We do not have a gender breakdown of the production and research assistants, cameramen, film editors, secretaries or graphics staff (Jones 2018, 635). Nevertheless, we do know that studio floor manager Joan Marsden and production secretary Margaret Douglas constituted female exceptions. In the case of Kee's film, the memos record that Wendy Cheetham, a personal assistant, was specially flown over. She played a crucial role in coordinating the shooting and listing of shots. Her rapid, on-the-spot transcription of two separate scripts, one in English, the other in German, made the ambitious joint project possible.

Although Kee had boundless chutzpah and charisma as a presenter, he was not the editors' first choice. He only got the gig because Aidan Crawley was unavailable. Kee was not only free but keen to take part. The nonchalant way he strides into the busy intersection at the border is remarkable, almost as if he has nine lives. There were inherent risks in reporting from an ideological frontline during a period of heightened international tension. Even without soldiers with guns, reporting from a fraught border situation is risky. In 2014, foreign correspondent Saima Mohsin was run over by a two-ton jeep reporting from the border in Gaza. She has not fully recovered.

8 Panorama Goes to Berlin (Again), 1961

Between May 1959 and July 1961 much had changed both in Berlin and with *Panorama*. By this point, Khrushchev had threatened to sign a separate peace treaty with East Germany three times. Over three million people had left that country (*Panorama* rounded the figure up to four). This was an untenable situation for the communist leadership. The broadcast came just a week after the new President, John F. Kennedy (JFK)'s televised speech on the Berlin crisis, on

FIGURE 11.1 Richard Dimbleby (1913–65) presenter of "Panorama". (© BBC)

25 July 1961. By good fortune, however, technological innovations not only heightened the threat of world annihilation, but increased the scope of what was possible to achieve with television. *Panorama* was at the forefront of developing the brand-new, international, live outside broadcast. Also, unbeknown to viewers, Richard Dimbleby (see Figure 11.1) had survived an "attempted Palace putsch". Behind the scenes, some of his colleagues had sought to dethrone the host and, with him, the magazine format. Both Kee and Day had been at a party in 1960 where such a move was mooted. On this occasion, the BBC defended their anchorman. As far as they were concerned, "Dimbleby was *Panorama*". The feeling nevertheless remained that the great man was, in some sense, "too big" for the show. He complained to Day that the BBC hierarchy was trying to turn him into a "bloody announcer". He saw the scripted voice-overs they wanted from him as work more suited to a "human parrot" (Dimbleby 1975, 368, 359–60, 396). Desperate to get out of the studio routine, he was helped by having his friend Paul Fox as editor. Kee's report had demonstrated how much drama and impact footage on and from Berlin could have. *Panorama* wanted to scoop the competition with high-profile stories. In so doing, they managed to extend the range and possibilities of television as a medium. Two years earlier, a live broadcast from Potsdamer Platz would have appeared miraculous. Now, in 1961, anything was possible. Three months earlier, Dimbleby had made the first ever live TV broadcast from the Soviet Union. Broadcasting the May Day Parade in 1961 was a major feat, both on technical and political grounds. Instead of officials, he had interviewed ordinary Muscovites in the streets. All were full of pride at Yuri Gagarin's recent achievement on 12 April.

The soundtrack of the "*Panorama* Goes to Berlin" special was the Vienna Philharmonic Orchestra's rendition of Richard Strauss's *Also sprach Zarathustra*. The theme is better known as the opening to Stanley Kubrick's *2001: A Space Odyssey* (Metro-Goldwyn-Mayer, 1968). Here, it accompanied an aerial shot, from a helicopter, zooming in on the Brandenburg Gate. Using live, in-situ broadcasts from the heart of the divided city, *Panorama* sought to become the "definitive" source on geopolitics in the ripped apart *Frontstadt* (WAC 1961c). With Potsdamer Platz providing a "sombre flashpoint", the programme was designed to sign the series off with a bang. Panning shots showed the whole border, allowing viewers to peep into the forbidden city of East Berlin.

Potsdamer Platz is busier with street furniture and signage than Kee's intersection. Dimbleby is sturdier, stiffer and slightly out of focus. "'The endangered frontier of freedom.' That's what President Kennedy calls the dividing line between East and West that runs through the heart of Berlin. A frontier that it's no exaggeration to say could be the flashpoint of a third and perhaps a final World War." Having been liberated from the confines of the studio and brought back to his old stomping ground of postwar Berlin, he appeared in his element. Possibly nudged by Kee's earlier report from the city, he sought to appear both salient and striking. If Kee's report had been quite coquettish, in its nimble fluidity, Dimbleby's performance was rather more stolid and stentorian: "This nail driven into the cobble. On this side of it, a man dare not speak his mind, on that side of it, a man is free. Two worlds separated, here in the Potsdamer Platz, at any rate, by a single nail." His evaluation of the crisis was balanced, but not by any means neutral. Compared to 1959, Dimbleby was safely away from oncoming traffic, but experienced the full rush of live, international, seat-of-his-pants broadcasting. Faced with constant near-disasters in the studio and outside, the natural broadcaster handled such difficult situations with aplomb. Dimbleby did not let himself become "chained to the electronic gadgetry of the medium". He was its master rather than its servant (Dimbleby 1975, 353). As Lord Home opined later in the programme, "Whatever other faults we have in Britain, we don't lose our nerve." (BBC 1961). The footage from Berlin was transmitted live by Eurovision terrestrial microwave link, spanning the 593 miles between Berlin and London in seconds. This was truly revolutionary and game changing TV.

Operating under such conditions required complete assurance and savoir faire. With more than twenty years of experience in conducting live outside broadcasts, Dimbleby had both in bucket loads. In his days as a radio broadcaster, he had developed the ability to speak live without notes. He had been present, reporting on events as they unfolded, at Dunkirk, El Alamein and D-Day. In 1945, he not only flew over Berlin with Bomber Command, but was also present at the liberation of Bergen-Belsen. He was always ready to switch to a standby routine if the transmission circuits should happen to fail. Reacting to unseen telerecordings or unforeseen events, "He hit cue after cue as he promised he would" (Dimbleby 1975, 274). It was his friend Paul Fox who had persuaded the veteran broadcaster to cease playing the role of mere announcer or link man. The two men shared an obsession with outside broadcasting, believing that it lent the programme a crucial sense of urgency.

The focus of the special was more on formal geopolitics, jurisdictions and dystopian juxtapositioning. There was less of an attempt to put oneself in Berliners' shoes or to show their pursuit of escape and fun, as a way of relieving the tension. Both Dimbleby and his fellow presenter Kee could "remember those savage closing days of the war" when the "last tattered stronghold of Hitler" (BBC 1961) disintegrated into a maelstrom of flames and rubble. Both reporters recognised the fact that the retribution, wrought "for the terrible things the Germans had done in Europe" (WAC 1961g), was itself cruel and terrible. Kee always distinguished between the Wehrmacht soldiers, who had saluted him and treated him humanely in Stalag Luft III, and the SS, who were liable to brutalise prisoners or to shoot them at dawn (Kee 1982, 178). Given the fate meted out to the fifty Great Escapers, his willingness to forgive was remarkable.

Peacock later argued that, in 1961, *Panorama* had assembled a brilliantly effective dream-team of reporters (Day 1989, 146). Although Dimbleby was the central anchor and master of ceremonies, he showed his collegiality by switching (or segueing) to reports by Kee and "Ludo". These more in-depth reports seemed to collapse the "geographical and political barriers" separating their British audience from the events (Dimbleby 1975, 370). In his report, Kee openly sided with the freely elected (and capitalist) government of West Berlin: "The Russians cannot allow the flow of refugees to go on. Can the West afford to have this exodus stopped?" For *Panorama*'s reporter, the options for the Western Allies and for the sober-minded diplomats in Washington and London appeared to be surrender or suicide: the risk of a nuclear war starting by accident was all too real. Compared to 1953, however, East Berlin appeared "deceptively calm and peaceful". Asking if another popular uprising was possible, he pointed to the anomalies created by "this strange half-open frontier" (BBC 1961).

The map they had commissioned was designed to emphasise that West Berlin was an outpost, entirely surrounded by East German territory, at a distance of some 120 miles from the East-West German border. A chauffeur-driven Mercedes 220S had allowed "Ludo" to cover nearly a thousand kilometres in a week, most of it taking him on a trip down the Autobahn to the border crossing at Helmstedt. The map's shading was supposed to link West Berlin to West Germany, while underscoring the (political and economic) contrast with East Germany (WAC 1959a). Openly siding with the Western Allies, *Panorama* insisted that they were in West Berlin because West Berliners wanted them to stay. The "freedom of two million West Berliners" was intrinsically connected to "the survival of the rest of us". Nevertheless, they recognised that the Allied garrison mostly had a symbolic function. "They couldn't save Berlin against 200 Russian divisions." (BBC 1961).

Dimbleby emphatically presented newspaper kiosks on the western side of the border as bastions of "free and unfettered comment". How long could Walter Ulbricht permit his population to carry on "voting with their feet"? Multi-location, with vox pops in Marienfelde and New York City, "Panorama Goes To Berlin" was followed by a live studio debate in Bristol. Several of the New Yorkers linked Berlin to Laos and Cuba and saw this as a bluff by Khrushchev. However, a young black man identified the Berliners as people who were "fighting for freedom just as we are." A uniformed cop said, "We've got a guy in the White House who don't take no guff." A woman disagreed, saying that Berlin was not worth "getting into a war over". On the other side of the Atlantic, a Scottish woman thought the sabre-rattling was foolish and that German division was both "unnatural" and "ridiculous". Canvassing public opinion simultaneously in North America, Britain and Germany was a remarkable feat. In its Berlin specials, the programme excelled at linking social and human issues to the geopolitics. "Women weep for joy every day, just because they've moved from one district of the city to another." Rolf Menzel of *Sender Freies Berlin* had managed to find a suitably telegenic, English-speaking family for Dimbleby to interview. The British broadcasters had stressed that they wanted one with a child at university and another still at school. They awkwardly cluster around Dimbleby, the two young women looking at the ground. "You're still at school. How much talk is there at school about the Berlin crisis?" (BBC 1961), he demanded. Initially, they had proposed a studio interview with the family, with Dimbleby seated at a desk. Although somewhat stilted, the interview in the open air was much more atmospheric.

Just two weeks before the Wall went up, Ludo opined that the Soviets could not interfere with cross-border transit "without throwing" the entire economic life and functioning of the city "into confusion". He also perceptively stated that those seeking asylum in Marienfelde were "not the traditional sort of destitute refugees who have been rotting in camps in Europe since the end of the war". By contrast to the situation in 1945, 1953 or 1956, many of them were choosing to leave perfectly adequate jobs and homes. In his view, they were not seeking material goods so much as political freedom. They desperately sought free "air in which to breathe and speak their thoughts." (BBC 1961) The script had "without fear of the knock on the door at midnight" but it was crossed out. (WAC 1961h). Looking back to a time when received pronunciation was de rigueur, "Ludo's" timbre and intonation is less natural, but more dramatic. Whether dynamic (Kee) or stentorian (Dimbleby and Kennedy), the BBC was still in a battle for ratings with its in-house and commercial rivals. This explains the razzamatazz.

9 Reception

Seven million Britons from all demographics tuned in to the 1959 broadcast. Eight million sat rapt through that of 1961. This was deemed particularly impressive because *Panorama* was going up against *Wagon Train*. As ever, the other channel was pulling out all the stops to lure in the lower classes. Three quarters of the sample audience fully supported *Panorama*'s handling of the topic. 83 out of a possible 100 was 10 points higher than their previous high score. Viewers praised the broadcast as an unblinking look at one of the most burning questions of the day. In bringing home the desperate tension and importance of the international situation, a building contractor believed that these edifying stories would matter to every single soul on the planet. A gas fitter felt that the programme illustrated the anomaly of splitting a single, cohesive city in two. He was most taken by the analogy of dividing London down the middle from King's Cross to Camberwell. A retiree imagined that any thinking person would be stirred by the drama of the situation. A quarryman argued that the presenters represented the "best five" the BBC could have picked for the job. Others emphasised their urgency, diplomacy and flair in getting to the nub of the issue (WAC 1961d).

Dimbleby and Kee could tread political minefields like no others. But it was the anchor's sureness of touch, in broadcasting live from the border, that was truly exceptional. His feat in dominating the central Berlin real estate was so brilliant that it provoked awe in the audience. Viewers loved his "nail in the cobbles" illustration, viewing the scenes near the Brandenburg Gate as "beautifully picturesque" (WAC 1961d). "Ludo's" patience, in helping his interviewees when they stumbled over English words, appeared demonstrative of innate British diplomacy and tact. The quality of the pictures and sound were second to none, painting the grim reality of two disparate and hostile worlds lying side by side. Those who critiqued the programme said that it offered standard common knowledge about the German situation and little that was new. A Post Office engineer felt that *Panorama* was helping the world's leaders to talk themselves into a crisis. Others insisted that the lively and opinionated New Yorkers should not have been allowed to talk over one another (WAC 1961d).

In Berlin, *Panorama* was taking considerable risks to extend the medium. In part, technological innovations created new possibilities. But we can easily lose sight of the multiple "intuitive leaps" and "laborious negotiations" that went into creating such a successful (and internationally admired) format (Thumim 2004, 98). Although the two reports from the border of Berlin were judged a tremendous success, there were some dark clouds on the horizon. The day after the Wall went up, Panorama's editor, Paul Fox, lamented that the show's budget was inadequate to support standard foreign travel. Routinely having to beg for extra funds was both "demoralizing and frustrating". In his view, Monday night was "operationally the worst night of the week." Editing staff routinely had to work at weekends while the presenters blithely went away to the country (WAC 1961e). Ominously, executives deemed the dubbing time required for each show excessive. A week later, Fox could nevertheless write to Rolf Menzel of Sender Freies Berlin: "Right now, I'm off on holiday. If Macmillan can go, so can I! See you at the Summit?" (WAC 1961b).

Politically, within the BBC, the ground was shifting. By the early 1960s, critics had begun to condemn the Corporation's subservient attitudes to the status quo. With its "pontifical airs", the pompous and stuffy Old Boys' Club seemed hopelessly shackled to Establishment views and "middlebrow morality". Despite his innovativeness and intellectual substance, Dimbleby did not escape that critique (Dimbleby 1975, 337). He feared that television could easily sink into the trivial and lurid gutter of Westerns and gameshows promoted by ITV. With high-profile, gripping live international broadcasts that set the agenda, his *Panorama* was a way of staving off that threat. With it, the BBC had somehow managed to create a factual programme that could outstrip *Wagon Train*. With Dimbleby at its helm, from 1955 to 1963, *Panorama* dominated the nation's cultural, political and intellectual life. The programme not only helped ordinary viewers to keep abreast of current affairs; it also formed their opinions and shaped their perspectives.

Nevertheless, if television sought to shape the national culture, the political elite in turn sought to influence the new medium. On 12 May 1960, Lord Teviot, a member of the House of Lords, Britain's unelected upper chamber, had opined that the BBC was exceeding its remit, by allowing *Panorama* to investigate and discuss affairs that were properly the concern of Ministers of the Crown. With the explicit goal of influencing public opinion, the BBC was going too far. Despite the received pronunciation, in his view, it was a dangerous and demotic medium. Such a nefarious and sinister policy on the part of *Pano-*

rama – of permitting Africans to criticise Ministers – could only be designed to manipulate ordinary citizens into becoming supine minions for a malign, external agenda. Defending the BBC in this culture war, Labour's Lord Stonham asked whether ITV programmes were somehow cleaner thanks to being interspersed with detergent advertisements. Just because "one or two interviewers do not know their job and manners", this was no cause for censorship. He added: "Just think of the questions that Mr. Khrushchev could ask Mr. Macmillan at the Summit Conference: 'Why have you closed your Window on the World? Is *Panorama* too revealing?'" (*Hansard* 1962). Looking back, Richard Lindley summed up his fifty-year history of the programme with the words "Pride" and "Paranoia" (Lindley 2003). If part of the Cold War was cultural and psychological, as a state-funded public broadcaster, the BBC could easily find itself a target.

Though, at times, he found the Corporation's bureaucracy clumsy, Dimbleby believed the BBC could offer "a tortured world ... a beacon of good sense and sound values". For others to refuse "to lift up their eyes", and witness the miraculous effects of such a prodigy, was deeply offensive to him (Dimbleby 1975, 336–7). The outside broadcast technology, on which live foreign broadcasts depended, remained fickle and unreliable. Sometimes the circuits and wires simply failed to work. Commentating live on the Queen's visit to the Wall, during a trip to West Berlin in 1965, Dimbleby was faced with a monitor without pictures and no voice from London. Just when things appeared to be back on plan, he heard: "We're not on the air. London isn't getting us." Exasperated and exhausted, Dimbleby uttered the words "Jesus wept". Unfortunately, London had been receiving him loud and clear. Within minutes, hundreds of aggrieved viewers had rung the BBC to protest at his blasphemy (Dimbleby 1975, 393). The *Daily Mirror* mocked: "So he *is* human after all." Mortified, he had to suffer the condemnation of the illustrious *Bradford Telegraph* for having momentarily lost his calm and shown his irritation. He was more annoyed that the BBC had subsequently chosen to cut their coverage of the monarch's visit short before she had actually reached the Wall. This was not only an insult to Her Majesty, but also an affront to his core beliefs about broadcasting. For him, outside broadcasts, with their majesty and theatre, were sacrosanct and inviolable.

His son describes him as a patriarch who sought to lead the public, gently and reassuringly, "through the muddle" of a tense and bipolar world. Fiercely patriotic, devoted both to the monarch and to the values she represented, he feared challenges to the status quo. By 1965, everything he cared for was under attack. "The humiliation of Suez" had yielded to "the shame of Rhodesia – and no-one cared." (Dimbleby 1975, 397) In retrospect, he appears not just as the "voice of the BBC", but the unique variant of British masculinity that characterised his generation. He feared that, if dumbed down, television would become indistinguishable from wallpaper. When he died later that year, a part of what made British broadcasting exceptional and unbeatable went with him. So too did some unchallenged and largely unspoken patriarchal assumptions about national, class and gender superiority.

In the hands of Dimbleby and Kee, "Auntie" made no pretence at being neutral. In the face of tyranny, the BBC was clearly in favour of freedom. Nevertheless, by interviewing ordinary people on the streets of New York and in the Bristol studio, *Panorama* showed that views were divided about the best way forward. Kee's smooth urbanity fitted Berlin's reputation as a city of sin dedicated to decadent pleasures. The handsome and dapper (still young) man, sauntering insouciantly into a busy intersection, does nothing to betray the depths and viscerality of his experiences in the Third Reich. This was an age in which presenters happened to have tunnelled their way to freedom. While amply demonstrating the perilous proximity of the two hostile systems, at the same time, he unmistakably had a spot of fun. Supported behind the scenes by the likes of Wendy Cheetham, he looks very much like the right man in the right place at the right time. With its dream team of male reporters, *Panorama* offered British viewers a priceless (but historically situated and politically loaded) window on the world.

References

BBC. 1959. "Panorama: Berlin". Broadcast 11 May. Introduced by Richard Dimbleby. Ed. Rex Moorfoot. Associate Producers David Wheeler and Kenneth Lamb. Reporter Robert Kee. https://www.bbc.co.uk/programmes/p015q9h9 Accessed 1 January 2025

BBC. 1961. "Panorama goes to Berlin 1961". Broadcast 31 July. Presented by Robin Day, Robert Kee, Ludovic Kennedy, John Morgan. Directed in Berlin by Bryan Cowgill. Ed. Paul Fox. https://www.bbc.co.uk/webarchive/ Accessed 1 January 2025.

Hansard. 1960. House of Lords Debates. 223, 12 May: 825.

Day, Robin. 1989. *Grand Inquisitor: Memoirs*. London: Weidenfeld and Nicolson.

Dimbleby, Jonathan. 1975. *Richard Dimbleby: A Biography*. London: Book Club Associates.

Fenemore, Mark. 2020. *Fighting the Cold War in Post-Blockade, Pre-Wall Berlin. Behind Enemy Lines*. New York: Routledge.

Fenemore, Mark. 2023. *Dismembered Policing in Postwar Berlin: The Limits of Four-Power Government*. London: Bloomsbury.

Gaddis, John Lewis. 1997. *We Now Know: Rethinking Cold War History*. Oxford: Oxford University Press.

Irish Times. 2013. "Renowned Historian and Journalist". 19 January.

Jones, Khaleelah. 2018. "Making the Political Popular: the Early Days of the BBC's Panorama." *Historical Journal of Film, Radio and Television* 38.3: 622–41.

Kee, Robert. 1982. *A Crowd is not Company*. London: J. Cape.

Lindley, Richard. 2003. *Panorama: Fifty Years of Pride and Paranoia*. London: Politicos.

McQueen, David. 2010. "Panorama, Conflict Coverage and the 'Westminster Consensus'". (Bournemouth University, unpublished PhD thesis).

McQueen, David. 2011. "A Very Conscientious Brand: A Case Study of the BBC's Current Affairs Series Panorama". *Journal of Brand Management*. 18: 677–87.

Miall, Leonard (ed.). 1966. *Richard Dimbleby, Broadcaster by His Colleagues*. London: BBC.

Press Gazette. 2004. "Dennis Bardens: Prolific Journalist, Author and Secret Agent", 18 March.

Thumim, Janet. 1998. "'Mrs Knight Must Be Balanced': Methodological Problems in Researching Early British Television". *News, Gender and Power*. Eds. Stuart Allan, Gill Branston and Cynthia Carter. New York: Routledge: 91–104.

Thumim, Janet. 2004. *Inventing Television Culture. Men, Women and the Box*. Oxford: Oxford University Press.

Times. 2013. "Robert Kee". 12 January.

Wheen, Francis. 1985. *Television: A History*. London: Century.

WAC. 1959a. "Panorama". T32/1,240/1. BBC Written Archives Centre, Caversham, UK.

WAC. 1959b. Rex Moorfoot. "Panorama: Proposal for a Game". 6 May. T32/1,191/6. BBC Written Archives Centre, Caversham, UK.

WAC. 1959c. Rex Moorfoot. "Panorama". 11 May. T32/1,240/1. BBC Written Archives Centre, Caversham, UK.

WAC. 1961a. "Panorama". BBC Legal (Germany). T16/716/1. BBC Written Archives Centre, Caversham, UK.

WAC. 1961b. "Panorama". T32/1,282/1. BBC Written Archives Centre, Caversham, UK.

WAC. 1961c. "Panorama General". T32/1,191/9. BBC Written Archives Centre, Caversham, UK.

WAC. 1961d. "Audience Research Report: Panorama Goes to Berlin", 31 July. T32/1,282/1. BBC Written Archives Centre, Caversham, UK.

WAC. 1961e. Paul Fox (Editor). "Panorama". Article for the *Radio Times*, 17 July. T32/1,282/1. BBC Written Archives Centre, Caversham, UK.

WAC. 1961f. Paul Fox (Editor). "Panorama". 14 August. T32/1,191/8. BBC Written Archives Centre, Caversham, UK.

WAC. 1961g. "Panorama. Berlin". n d. T32/1,282/1. BBC Written Archives Centre, Caversham, UK.

WAC 1961h. "Panorama. Refugees". n.d. T32/1,282/1.BBC Written Archives Centre, Caversham, UK.

WAC. 1962–23. "Panorama".T16/716/3. BBC Written Archives Centre, Caversham, UK.

CHAPTER 12

Rocking the Stasi

Chris Bowlby

During the Cold War the BBC sensed the significance of its role in making popular Western culture as well as credible news accessible across the Iron Curtain. Once the Curtain had collapsed there was then a new role for the BBC – discovering and telling the stories of those who had sustained that culture under enormous pressure and exploring what effect all this might have had in undermining communist rule.

One programme I was especially keen to make for BBC radio focused on music. I had first begun to wonder about its cross-border power when living in a divided Berlin as a teenager in 1980. My understanding of Cold War geography was distinctly hazy when I arrived in the city and moved into a room in the West Berlin suburb of Tempelhof. Due to start work at an old people's home in the Wedding district the following week I looked at a map of the underground system and saw that the most direct route for me appeared to go through East Berlin. Impossible, I assumed, until my landlady explained that, under one of the many pragmatic arrangements made in defiance of ideological hostility, Western trains were indeed allowed to run under the Berlin Wall and out the other side – but without stopping.

And so every work-day morning at around 6am I sat in a yellow West Berlin underground train as it trundled through so-called "ghost stations" in the East with crumbling interiors, evocative old signage and spookily dim lighting. Before the building of the Wall the station platforms would have been thronged with Berliners. Now the only people there were armed border guards, patrolling to ensure that no East Berliners attempted to escape onto these tantalising Western trains. I would have headphones on listening to music during these journeys, and one morning as my train slowed I glanced up to see a guard peering into my carriage who also had headphones. What, I remembered wondering, was he able to listen to? Was it the same music as me, or was that completely *verboten* and inaccessible?

On time off from the old people's home I began to make day trips as a tourist to East Berlin. And one day I caught sight of a couple of teenage punk rockers walking around quite close to a group of East German schoolchildren dressed in the disciplined uniforms and red scarves of the communist youth organisation, the *Freie Deutsche Jugend*. Punk in the West meant rebellion of a

 | HTTPS://DOI.ORG/10.1515/9783111302508-012

kind. But in the East, I thought, that kind of rebellion must have been especially hard to sustain.

After the end of the Cold War I found myself thinking about those individuals and what had become of them now. And as research began to emerge from sources such as the archives of the East German secret police, the Stasi, it became clear to me that music had indeed been a significant battleground behind the Iron Curtain, with the communist authorities devoting much energy to trying to restrict its influence. It seemed a story well worth telling and eventually became a BBC radio documentary, "Rocking the Stasi", on which the following chapter is based.

The building of the Berlin Wall in 1961 happened to coincide with the early stages of a golden era in global popular music. And while the leadership of the German Democratic Republic (GDR) could seal their people off from physical contact with the West using barbed wire and concrete, when it came to Western music, the border was far more porous. Broadcasters' radio waves spread above the Wall; individuals posting or smuggling Western records and tapes could also penetrate the Wall's defences, provided they escaped the GDR authorities' attempts at detection and confiscation.

An indication of the East German leadership's unease about this came in a famous speech by the Politburo leader Walter Ulbricht in 1965, in which he questioned whether the GDR should copy "every kind of filth that comes from the West". "Dear Comrades" he continued, displaying his speechwriter's diligent research into corrupting Beatles lyrics, "we should put an end to the monotony of Yeah Yeah Yeah and everything that goes with it".

In some ways this was just a local version of the outrage with which many in older generations around the world greeted rock and roll. But the irony of a leader fond of making lengthy tedious speeches about communist ideology denouncing the Beatles as "monotonous" was an especially choice example of the GDR leadership's ignorance and angst.

As always, it was assumed that the state could and should regain cultural control. GDR leaders feared that love of Western music would lead to love of Western politics, so they desperately tried to develop their own top-down communist youth culture to go with the compulsory Russian taught in schools instead of English. Among the counter measures devised by Ulbricht and his colleagues was a futile attempt to restrict the playing of Western music at parties with a ludicrous quota system. There was also the offer of supposedly attractive alternatives to GDR youngsters such as a state-sponsored dancestep. Dagmar Hovestädt was part of the team which researched this for the Stasi Records Office in Berlin.

> They came up with something called the Lipsi, which was a very strange concocted brain child of coming up with something that would look like a cool youth culture. But you can't organise and strategise a youth culture, that's not how it works. It comes from people picking up in a society on vibes, on things that are there. They want to express themselves and they don't express themselves according to some 70-year old Politburo member in his fantasy.

Instead of practising the Lipsi young East Germans were glued to their radios, trying to catch the latest tunes beamed in by Western stations. And the regime's greatest fear was that this listening could corrupt even their elites – such as soldiers and border guards.

Gift aus dem Äther, "Poison from the airwaves", was the alarming headline from one propaganda programme made for the East German military, a copy of which is in the Stasi archives. It included a recording of a young soldier put on trial by the GDR authorities after confessing how Western music had led him astray. "At first it was just music, beat, pop, hits exchanged with friends. I discussed the lyrics with my friends" began the supposed confession. But the moral of this story – hammered home at the end of the programme in suitably forbidding tones – showed how fearful the GDR regime now was about music's subversive power.

> Just listening once to a Western broadcaster is once too many. You expose yourself to the enemy's poison, lose your class consciousness and put yourself – consciously or unconsciously – on the other side of the barricades.

The regime had form when fearing infection from Western airspace. I was once told by an enthusiastic Communist party member in Dresden that in her 1950s childhood she had obeyed party orders and gone out into local fields to collect Colorado beetles dropped by US aircraft to destroy the GDR's potato crop. Now in the 1960s the GDR and its Soviet ally tried jamming Western broadcasts to prevent musical infection.

There was also great anxiety about Western musicians performing within earshot of the East. If there is one story that symbolises the GDR regime's paranoia about music – and the tragedy of being a young music fan there – it is the story of a Rolling Stones concert that never happened.

It all began in 1969 with a throwaway comment by a DJ on the radio station RIAS – based in West Berlin but much listened to on the other side of the Berlin Wall. The Beatles had earlier that year played on the roof of a London recording studio. Imagine, the DJ mused, if the new publishing house built by entrepreneur and newspaper owner Axel Springer in West Berlin, right next to the Wall, staged a concert featuring, say, the Stones on its roof so Easterners could come and listen too.

In the GDR the DJ's notion quickly moved from rumour to widely believed "fact". Thousands of young East Germans convinced themselves that the Stones really would play. And, what's more, the concert would happen on the same day their rulers were planning a day of celebrations in East Berlin to mark the 20th anniversary of the GDR's founding.

Cue panic among the Stasi. They hated Springer – seen as a capitalist ogre bent on luring young people away from the Communist faith – so assumed the rumoured concert was part of a sophisticated Western plot. Their files from the time are full of items like photographs of slogans chalked on roads in East German towns telling Stones fans to come to Berlin – and reports detailing how the Stasi then tracked down and arrested the subversive sloganisers.

But hundreds did still come to Berlin on the day. I met Eckart Mann, then a 16-year-old, at the same spot opposite the Springer building where he'd waited in 1969. He'd heard the rumour, and thought, "Stones, play here. Wow, wow, wow!"

In fact, the Stones never appeared, but the GDR authorities did. As the crowd moved towards the Brandenburg Gate the policed arrived, and Mann was beaten and arrested. He was convicted of being an "anti-socialist element". In his files I discovered that the Minister of State Security and head of the Stasi, Erich Mielke, had taken a personal interest in his case. Mann was given two years in prison, then expelled to the West, and cut off from his family who remained in the East. "What was prison like?" I asked. He shrugged. "Not OK, but what could I do?" And so a teenager paid a bitter price for his love of music. That Rolling Stones concert might have been a myth. But the courage and enterprise of many individuals ensured that music of all kinds did still reach into every corner of the GDR.

As a teenager, Alexander Kühne was desperate to bring more music into his life in a remote village, Lugau, hours from Berlin. When we revisited his childhood home, he showed me his bedroom. "In this corner was my bed, here is my record player. And out of this window I saw the whole world".

And yet for a music lover that world could seem frustratingly inaccessible. He was desperate to bring as much of its music as possible to his village. One way was to give your Grannie a shopping list of recordings to obtain from travel to the West – pensioners were allowed by the GDR regime to visit the West, as they weren't seen as vital citizens. But if you didn't make sure Grannie knew exactly which records to bring back, it could all go terribly wrong. "Once I ordered a Clash album from 1982 and she came back with a Johnny Cash album" he recalled. "And that was a huge nightmare". You could still see the pain on his face.

So instead Alexander decided to turn his village into a major music venue. It happened to be near a major rail junction, and he persuaded all kinds of music fans and bands to head for the room behind the village pub. "This place is where we made the biggest parties in East Germany", he said proudly, as he showed me round. Farmers at the bar would look on bemused as hundreds of New Wave fans or Glam rockers headed past them – with up to 1,000 packing a hall meant, according to police regulations, to hold only 100. The pub owner, Alexander recalled, enjoyed all the extra revenue, becoming a member of the GDR economic elite by swapping his Trabant car for a Mazda. As it was so remote the police and Stasi were slow to react to these huge gatherings – apart from on one occasion when Alexander was arrested, taken to a police station and told the Stasi would come for him the next day. "I was very frightened", he recalled. Luckily for him his mother, a teacher and Communist party member, had once taught the local police officer. She insisted the pub concert was merely a birthday party, ordered him to release her son, and then dealt with the Stasi when they arrived at her school. She never told her son exactly what happened. "She's my hero" is all he says now, with quiet admiration.

But back in the big cities pressure from the Stasi was relentless on music fans seen as "subversive" and "anti-social". What they needed were spaces in which to gather and perform or listen to music free as far as possible from interference by the authorities. As they would rarely if ever be allowed to create their own spaces, that led to some fascinating and unlikely alliances with other institutions seeking autonomy. Some punk rockers, for example, began to share space with the East German Evangelical church, parts of which had maintained some independence from the most intrusive state control, acting as a significant forum for various kinds of dissent from the GDR regime. Dirk Kalinowski from the punk band Zerfall told me how he began to visit the Galiläa church in Berlin.

> It was all about the possibility to meet without state control which in your private life was always difficult with repression, visits (from the authorities). Here was a protected space. They could arrest you as you arrived in front of the door or as you left. But here inside you were safe. This wasn't like the youth clubs under state control. Here you could meet twice a week and make music.

And make your music, what's more, in the middle of church services. Halfway through a time of quiet Sunday contemplation, pastor Gerhard Cyrus would pause and then ask his mostly elderly congregation to listen to something just a bit different.

> It was mad – as front man I could see right into the faces of the congregation who were completely shocked. And Pastor Cyrus would explain – we've got some young people here, they've made a group, they'd like to perform and off we went. And the whole place rocked with so much noise and we were shouting. The only ones who were laid back about it were the children who jumped up straight away. I'll never forget it – one old couple covered their ears and then walked out. They were completely shocked.

The Stasi were shocked too, alarmed by the idea of a punk or any other subculture spreading. They used to make recordings of all their top-level meetings, now preserved in the archives. In one, the veteran Minister of State Security Erich Mielke can be heard trying to get his head – and his tongue – round such baffling things as punks, skinheads and fans of heavy metal.

But how could the secret police deal with or even understand something like punk? I managed to track down Jürgen Breski, then a Stasi officer trying to monitor and infiltrate what was seen as the anti-state, subversive punk scene. He agreed, eventually, to an interview about what he and his Stasi colleagues had been trying to achieve.

> JB: The aim was to control "the scene" as it expanded, to stop it from becoming too well known. In the end we wanted to remove it completely but the question was how to do it.
>
> CB: Was one of your main jobs with punks to find out where they were going, what they were doing and recruit some to give you information?
>
> JB: Yes of course there were the so-called IMs, Inoffizielle Mitarbeiter or informers. Nothing would have worked without them. There were various opportunities to recruit them. They were young, they all lacked life experience. So you would get to them with pressure. Some were persuaded to really work with us so you said "well, go there and try to infiltrate there and there". But often these informers didn't realise they were being used as informers.
>
> CB: So you said to them "oh we'll just have a conversation from time to time" but they didn't realise they were informers?
>
> JB: Yes, exactly.

> CB: And you talked about applying pressure – what did you do?
>
> JB: Well, you'd forbid them from going to certain areas or say that if you don't do such and such you'll go to prison. They didn't have the experience to know whether that threat was real or a bluff. There were some other nice ideas. For example, military service. You knew about certain illegal bands. A couple of times a year members would be called in for individual meetings. And you'd have them called up for military service and spread them around the country. Suddenly the band had no musicians and couldn't get back together again quickly.

It could be a bit tricky, Herr Breski admitted, to follow the Stasi rulebook. It was hard to stay undercover taking a young punk informer for a secret meeting in a Stasi safe house when the informer was sporting a large red Mohican haircut. Among those the Stasi also attempted to recruit was musician Dirk Kalinowski.

> There were various scenarios. The classic one was arrest. You'd be arrested maybe at a concert or party, and threatened with punishment. Then there'd be the offer – it doesn't have to be like this, we don't have to punish you if you'll work with us.
>
> Or you'd be tracked down – for example when I was at college the director came into the classroom one day and told me to come to her office as "my uncle" was there. "Uncle" – what's going on I wondered? So I came into the office and a Stasi officer was sitting there and he began along the lines of: Herr Kalinowski we're very interested (in working with you), it would be very good for you, save a lot of trouble. And I stopped and said, hold on, I'm not doing that. But they kept trying until I think 1988 when I put in an application to leave the GDR. I wanted it clear I'm not working with you, I want out.

Others were less defiant. After the GDR had collapsed and Germany reunified Stasi files were opened to the public. Dirk and the rest of the band were shocked to discover their drummer, someone they had seen as a close and trusted friend, had in fact been a very thorough Stasi informer.

Where local bands were unavailable due to state harassment venues could occasionally be filled by bands that had been smuggled across the Berlin Wall from the West. The West German punk rock band Die Toten Hosen managed to cross without arousing suspicion among the East German authorities by wearing conventional clothes, combing their hair and leaving their instruments behind. Armed with borrowed instruments they then played concerts in several venues. Lead singer Campino told me he was impressed by a local youth culture with great originality, resilience and depth.

> We were on a long train ride across the GDR and there was an East German school class on the same train. And they realised it was Die Toten Hosen from West Germany and so they all came to us. And we had a long talk as the journey was 12 hours or so. And it was so nice for us to speak to the "other" Germans. They had a certain kind of pride, and a belief even though they loved rock and roll and our kind of music. They said you in the West have got the best clothing and fashion and those sort of things but we have got friendship and solidarity. We help each other and we're not superficial.
>
> CB: That's really interesting. A lot of people might have the idea that they were like robots living under a dictatorship but actually they had a spirit and a culture just because they were living under a dictatorship.
>
> C: Absolutely. And they were having these friendships amongst each other and they meant more than in our world because they had to pay a bigger price for everything that went wrong.

Regimes could impose all kinds of restrictions. But still music fans created free spaces with that strong sense of solidarity, a unique state of mind across communist-ruled Europe.

By the later 1980s the groups operating outside state control in the GDR were growing in confidence. The tectonic plates behind the Iron Curtain were beginning to shift, though few if any could foresee how rapidly it would lead to the revolutionary earthquake of 1989. Mikhail Gorbachev's reforms in the Soviet Union were beginning to pose very difficult questions for ageing Communist regimes such as that in East Berlin. And the regimes also felt new pressure from the West, cultural as well as political.

In June 1987 US President Ronald Reagan visited West Berlin, stood in front of the Brandenburg Gate and uttered one of the most famous Cold War soundbites: "Mr Gorbachev, tear down this Wall!" But another event by the Brandenburg Gate that month was of far more interest to many East German young people. David Bowie gave a concert, which was clearly audible across parts of the city's east. Bowie was a global star who had lived in Berlin and knew well its surreal Cold War atmosphere and musical energy. He'd recorded some of his most famous albums there – like Heroes. While the Rolling Stones concert in 1969 had turned out to be merely a rumour, now there was a real musical challenge for the GDR authorities to face. And the response showed how those authorities were becoming more divided. I spoke to Dieter Dietze who was the youthful deputy head of East Berlin's police when the Bowie concert (see figure 12.1) was played. As before, the authorities feared that enthusiasm for Western music was, for some at least, being used as cover for growing political dissent.

> DD: It had become more and more common for young people from the East to come and try to listen to the music in the original (so to speak) and to come as close to the Wall as possible. The flashpoint was on the street Unter den Linden where rock fans gathered. We believed the majority just wanted to listen to the music. But of course there were others who wanted to misuse the situation for other things.
>
> CB: Did you feel as policeman it was your job to stop these people from listening to the music, to keep order, keep them away from the Wall but as a young man, a rock fan yourself you knew how much it would mean to listen to these bands?
>
> DD: Yes that's absolutely right. I had no problem with those who just wanted to listen to the music. There was no need I thought for the police to intervene. But in 1987 particular situations developed where some of the rock fans tried to break through police formations and that became difficult.
>
> CB: Was that an important time as people became more confident in challenging the regime. Did you feel this is pointless, we can't stop people from wanting to listen to this music, it's going to undermine the regime?
>
> DD: It wasn't quite so straightforward. But it was clear to me that music, rock music belonged to young people, that there was no way you could deny that to young people. So I and a couple of others began to argue – why don't we do something like this?
>
> CB: But there must have been people high up in the Communist party or the Stasi who said 'we should not do this. We must not have large groups of young people coming to concerts by Western bands. That will be a bad influence'?
>
> DD: Yes that was definitely the case. But those with responsibility in the GDR weren't just those in the older generation. There were people like me in my mid 30s who had their own opinions. So yes it was completely unthinkable for some

> in the leadership to stage big events in the GDR with the likes of Bob Dylan, Joe Cocker and Bruce Springsteen. But for my generation it was simply great.

FIGURE 12.1 The stage is set for a David Bowie concert in front of the Reichstag and near to the Berlin Wall in June, 1987. (© Alamy)

Whatever the scepticism among the GDR gerontocracy, they now sought a safety valve and agreed to invite Western stars to perform in the east with Bruce Springsteen giving one of the biggest concerts ever seen in East Berlin in 1988. But as Dagmar Hovestädt of the Stasi archives authority points out, that and other concerts by Western stars quickly came to stand for much more than musical enjoyment.

> These concerts become a rallying point for the demands for human rights, access to travel, freedom to express yourself. Imagine a hundred thousand East German youths singing "Born in the USA" – what does that do to a society where the leaders all in their 70s and 80s are saying we have a Wall which will stand for another 100 years? So these cracks in society have a long history – the Wall didn't open in one day, the music builds up to it. They invited it in because they need the pressure releasing with young people because they know they

> kind of lose them. But at the same time it reinforces the desire to go out. And in contrast to the kids in the late 60s who tried to go to a fantasy Rolling Stones concert and paid dearly with gaol and persecution in the 80s that fear has gone, the state has lost control.

Springsteen even made a statement in German during his concert expressing the hope that "all barriers would be torn down". He did not mention "the Wall" but East Germans, so practised in a totalitarian state at reading subversively between the lines, knew exactly what he really meant.

Within eighteen months the Berlin Wall had been torn down, East Germany was disappearing, the Cold War was coming to an end. The free spaces first created for music had also become free spaces for unrestricted democratic debate. And the mighty Ministry of State Security with its huge army of informers was in meltdown. Elite Stasi officers like Jürgen Breski were suddenly and humiliatingly out of a job. He has had plenty of time since to reflect on how the Stasi once thought it could and should try to control virtually everything.

> JB: Do I have regrets? Yes and no. From today's perspective much seems pointless, a waste of effort. It wasn't only the Ministry of State Security that was too concerned with attempting to control a society completely. Firstly, it was pointless and secondly it didn't achieve much. As for the punks – sometimes we had influence, but in the end there were no results. In that respect it was pointless.
>
> CB: People were sent to prison because of the actions of you and your colleagues. How do you feel about that now?
>
> JB: Nowadays things are seen in terms of freedom of expression which didn't exist in public life then. In a society that aims to be better that has no place. Today I'd be against doing something like that. But you grow up in a society, grow with this society's norms, you profit from them. And when later you have the chance to see that from a different perspective you say: ok that was a mistake, it shouldn't have been that way.

The Stasi archives bear witness to the huge amount of time and effort the secret police devoted to trying to control the GDR's musical scene. As well as files full of reports on those involved and the often dubious testimony of its thousands of informers, there is a collection of confiscated Western musical material, including records and tapes taken from Western travellers or intercepted from postal deliveries. Ironically enough, many of those tapes were then reused by Stasi officers short of equipment to tape their own surveillance of dissidents' phone calls or domestic conversations.

It is of course impossible to gauge just how significant music was in contributing to the undermining of the GDR regime. But the broadcasting of popular culture by the BBC and others from the 1960s onwards undoubtedly influenced the generations growing up after the country's ageing political leadership. It sustained a sense of free association and contact with the West in defiance of the authorities' attempts to demonise their Cold War opponents. The end of the Cold War was due to all kinds of factors and trends, political and economic as well as cultural, some within countries like the GDR, some external such as the change in Soviet policy under Mikhail Gorbachev. But in the late 1980s music fans – as well as others in the GDR – could sense the authorities' growing loss of confidence and control. The more or less free spaces they had created for performance could now be used for much more overt discussion of alternatives to communist rule. And the experience of joining in ever larger audiences listening to all kinds of music added to the sense of solidarity and civil courage that was highly significant as crowds came out into the streets to demand change in late 1989, overcoming fear of a violent response by the regime and its backers.

"Music comes into your spirit" was how Dagmar Hovestädt put it to me. The history of music in the GDR reminded her of an old German proverb *Die Gedanken sind frei* (thoughts are free). "So the music that can't be stopped by borders of anything reminds you constantly that there is joy in self-expression".

I still find myself wondering about that border guard I observed from an underground train in 1980. Was he influenced by listening to what the horrified authorities called "poison from the airwaves"? What has become of him now, with guards like him redundant after the Wall's disappearance and the Berlin underground and all its stations, east and west, open to all as people travel to work or, say, to the many music concerts now freely accessible across the city? There can be no nostalgia for a Cold War era when so many in the GDR and elsewhere suffered so much for their independence of mind and enthusiasms. But I do feel grateful for having witnessed the extraordinary cultural spirit sustained by music, with the BBC and others reaching almost every corner of places that otherwise felt so brutally cut off from the rest of the world. Such broadcasting could even help sustain the morale of a teenager like Alexander Kühne, whose Grannie catastrophically confused Johnny Cash with The Clash, and who decided to become a musical entrepreneur in the most unexpected of places. When I asked Alexander what he was thinking as he returned to the improvised concert hall behind a village pub in Lugau where thousands came to enjoy all kinds of music he replied simply, with a wistful grin, “I am waiting for the party to start”.

References

The BBC radio documentary “Rocking the Stasi”, presented by Chris Bowlby and produced by Jim Frank, is available here: https://www.bbc.co.uk/programmes/p057dydf Accessed 31 December 2024.

An accompanying Online piece by Chris Bowlby is here: https://www.bbc.co.uk/news/magazine-40447191 Accessed 31 December 2024.

A Stasi archives publication on the Rolling Stones concert that never happened is available at https://www.stasi-unterlagen-archiv.de/informationen-zur-stasi/publikationen/publikation/gefaengnis-statt-rolling-stones/ Accessed 31 December 2024.

Walter Ulbricht’s comments on “Yeah Yeah Yeah” can he heard here: https://youtu.be/Q55mQpAGNMc Accessed 31 December 2024.

The GDR’s state-sponsored dance step the Lipsi can be seen here: https://www.youtube.com/watch?v=0Qbc9VUBy_8 Accessed 31 December 2024.

CHAPTER 13

Punk Rock in a Cold Climate: John Peel and East Berlin Sub-culture in the 1980s

Will Studdert

In the 1996 documentary *Autobahn Blues*, John Peel remembered:

> When I was a child (...) we were always taught to hate Germans, still are by some politicians. But I couldn't really believe in the wickedness of an entire nation. So, years ago when I was asked to do radio programmes here, it seemed like a chance to make a small contribution to a healing process. (Peel 1996)

While his contribution to an Anglo-German healing process is difficult to gauge, Peel's broadcasts undoubtedly made a major cultural impact in both East and West Germany from the late 1970s onwards. Broadcasting on stations such as BBC World Service, British Forces Broadcasting Service (BFBS), and Radio Bremen throughout the 1980s, the *Süddeutsche Zeitung*'s description of Peel as "arguably the most influential radio DJ of all time" reflects his continued popularity in the country (Kedves 2012). His wife Sheila Ravenscroft recalls that there were endless "swarms of leather-clad Germans pulling into our driveway in under-sized cars" until his death in 2004, and afterwards as well. For Peel – who is generally credited for having coined the tongue-in-cheek phrase "Krautrock" in 1968 – the German programmes were "a source of pride", and he noted with amusement that he was voted "Top DJ in Europe" in the country in spite of barely speaking a word of German (Peel and Ravenscroft 2005, 413).

Due to radio's ability to transcend national and political boundaries, John Peel also – more or less inadvertently – cultivated a large audience in the German Democratic Republic (GDR) from 1976 onwards. This chapter will explore his role in introducing punk to the GDR and his subsequent influence on subcultural developments in East Berlin, examining the impact that his musically eclectic broadcasts exerted on the city's underground scene, which had a high degree of cross-pollination between musical genres and artistic fields from the outset. It will also draw on materials including files from the Robert Havemann Gesellschaft's Archive of the GDR Opposition to trace the gradual entrenchment of the punk scene within alternative structures such as

 | HTTPS://DOI.ORG/10.1515/9783111302508-013

the Evangelical Church's Offene Arbeit and grassroots activist groups, and argue that punk's do-it-yourself ethic empowered young people in the GDR to participate in other forms of cultural production, as well as oppositional politics and organised antifascism. The aim of the chapter is to show the ways in which the broadcasts of John Peel – "the Pope of punk music, noise music, weird music, and avant-garde" (Francke 1992) – directly and indirectly impacted upon the East German cultural, social, and political landscape in the final decade of the GDR.

1 John Peel and "Ostpunk"

Born John Robert Parker Ravenscroft in Heswall on the Wirral Peninsula in 1939, John Peel initially worked as a DJ in the United States before returning to Britain in 1967, taking the midnight to 2 a.m. shift on the pirate station Radio London and developing the music programme "The Perfumed Garden", which brought the sounds of Britain's musical underground to the airwaves. When he realised that the Radio London station managers were not listening, he omitted the weather reports and the advertisements and played whatever he wanted, which made him amongst other things the only DJ at the time to play the debut albums of Jimi Hendrix and Pink Floyd (Peel and Ravenscroft 2006, 283). Radio London went off the air in August 1967, and the following month Peel was employed by the BBC's new station Radio 1, which replaced the BBC Light Programme, where he continued to develop his eclectic format. The same year, the first Peel Sessions were recorded, originally as a means of circumventing Musicians' Union rules on the amount of "needle to vinyl" time, but which would go on to become an international cultural institution in their own right as an important outlet for new and unusual bands.

In September 1976, Peel made his debut on the BBC World Service with a programme that was broadcast every Saturday night at 11.30p.m, GMT, and around the same time he started presenting a weekly programme, "Rock Today", for the British Forces Broadcasting Service in Germany. Peel was an early convert to punk music, which found its way onto his programmes from Spring 1976 onwards; punk also allowed the veteran DJ, who was approaching his fortieth birthday, to "toughen up" his image, cutting his hair, adopting a "proletarian, Midlands-infected growl that had little to do with his previous accent", and give his programmes a sense of danger (Cavanagh 2015, 14). On 10 December 1976 on Radio 1, nine days after the Sex Pistols had caused a national scandal with their televised volley of obscenities on the Bill Grundy Show – which resulted in their being banned by Radio 1 and John Peel being warned not to broadcast any punk music on his show – Peel responded with a dedicated sixty-minute "Punk Special", closing with the Pistols' "Anarchy in the UK".

This enthusiasm for the burgeoning punk movement also found its way onto his "Rock Today" broadcasts – which were rebranded "John Peel's Music on BFBS" in January 1980 – and started to find a receptive audience in the GDR. While the Sex Pistols' refrain of "No Future" resonated with young people in unemployment-hit Britain, in East Germany the problem was "Too Much Future". For the writer and musician Ronald Galenza, East German society demanded "the nationalisation of emotions (...) The absence of any perspectives was exhausting. There were no utopias, no visions, and there was no hope." (Galenza 2023a, 19–20) Another former punk, the writer and gallerist Henryk Gericke, asserts that the punks were rebelling against a system that denied them the right to have "fantasies, dreams, and perspectives", and directed their contempt against a "model utopia that codified the future for eternity". (Gericke 2018, 16) These stifling social conditions and the accompanying feeling of alienation – of being "a stranger in your own home" (Gericke 2018, 16) – created fertile soil for punk to take root in the GDR.

Punks in East Berlin and elsewhere in the country were initially so isolated that some, like Britta Bergmann, who first discovered the Sex Pistols in 1977 aged fifteen through a black-and-white photograph in a smuggled West German magazine, were unaware that any others existed in the GDR beside themselves (Mohr 2019, 10–17). When the first punks were sighted on East Berlin's streets around 1979, it was a "micro-cultural scene of approximately 20 activists", as well as satellite groups of "outsiders of all stripes" (Gericke 2018, 17). Indeed, from its inception the East German punk scene existed in a heterogeneous cultural context, exerting influence upon and drawing inspiration from other social groups and artistic fields. Gericke notes that

> the GDR underground scene resembled a Hydra, a constellation of musicians, poets, painters, photographers, and filmmakers. The artists embraced the energy of punk rock, the genres collided, the dissolution of forms sought a shape. In the middle of it all, punks romped through the apartments of poets, bands made rackets in ateliers. (Gericke 2018, 17)

The numbers were also slowly growing, and the subcultural phenomenon that John Peel had helped to initiate began to manifest itself in the GDR's public sphere. There was safety to be found in numbers from wilful police harassment, controls and arrest, and East Berlin began attracting punks from around the Republic, not least because the provinces were more isolated and dangerous (Biedowicz 2022). Due to their highly distinctive appearance and behaviour, there were also frequent clashes not only with the authorities but with other citizens. As Michael Horschig of the East Berlin band Namenlos recalls, in 1979 and 1980 the "previously isolated, scattered punks began gathering in discotheques", gravitating towards large dancehalls in southern Berlin such as the Trinksäle Plänterwald and the KWO Klubhaus, where they "drank beer, danced pogo and ska (…) discussed our ideals and then often got in brawls with the entire discotheque." (Horschig 1999, 17–18).

2 John Peel's East German Audience

By 1981, the Stasi estimated that there were approximately 1,000 punks and an additional 10,000 youths who qualified as "punk sympathisers" across the GDR (Michael 1999, 74). In East Berlin, the exponential growth of the punk scene was aided by the fact that listeners could easily pick up all radio stations from the western half of the city on the FM dial (Biedowicz 2022). Hauptabteilung XX of the Ministry for State Security (Stasi), which was responsible amongst other things for the monitoring the media, churches, and the political underground, surmised that repeated listening to the BBC and other "enemy" musical broadcasts would inevitably bring young East Germans "into contradiction with social conditions in the GDR and the social organisations of the GDR" (BSTU n.d.). The idea that these contradictions may have been pre-existing and not the work of malign external powers was beyond the imagination of the Stasi, but it was certainly true that "John Peel's Music" and other popular programmes such as RIAS Treffpunkt (Rundfunk im amerikanischen Sektor [RIAS]) and SFBeat (Sender Freies Berlin) helped to further broaden the chasm between the regime and its disaffected youth.

Indeed, his BFBS broadcasts soon had a cult following among young East Germans. Henryk Gericke recalls that "John Peel's Music on BFBS remained (…) one of the most important sources [of music], and there was hardly a punk or even someone interested in independent music who didn't sit by the radio as if attached to a drip every Saturday night." (Gericke 1999, 100) Officially, the main target for Peel's British Forces broadcasts was British soldiers stationed in West Germany, but he was aware that his real audience was primarily "German teenagers" in East and West (Peel 1996). However, while elsewhere the Foreign Office exerted pressure on the BBC to broadcast popular music programmes such as "Eine kleine Beatmusik" in order to attract younger listeners in the East (Major 2013, 265), the subversive success of Peel's broadcasts in the GDR seems to have been something of an accident, not least because East

Germans were not the intended audience of BFBS. There appear to have been no official efforts made on the British side to monitor or gauge the size of his German listenership, and Peel himself received little feedback from listeners in the GDR, probably due to the risks attached to writing to western broadcasters and the Stasi's regular interception of mail. Nonetheless, in 1995 he recalled that "I used to get, not a lot of letters, but enough letters. (…) But the main thing was you knew that each letter you got, people had gone to some trouble to get it to you, because they would (…) send it themselves when they were on holiday in a slightly more benign country like Poland or Hungary." (Katzorke and Schneider 1996). The following year, he said of his East German audience, "I suppose that I was aware almost from the start that people [in the GDR] were going to be listening (…) I was always aware of them being there but you didn't really get much response from them, except from two or three bolder spirits who would write from time to time." (Peel 1996).

If his East German listeners remained an enigma to John Peel until after the fall of the Berlin Wall, the music he played was initially just as much of a mystery to his listeners in the GDR. Michael Horschig states that he "heard two Sex Pistols songs on the radio at a friend's place. The next months were spent gathering what sparse information was available and trying to find out what [punk] was. (…) For years, John Peel's Music on the BBC was the only place where a young person who rejected the FDJ [Free German Youth] could get new music, new wave and punk, as well as two-tone ska and reggae." (Horschig 1999, 17). Moreover, once over the Wall the broadcasts led a strange afterlife of their own. Listeners habitually taped John Peel's programmes off the radio onto the ubiquitous Stern Recorders – a standard gift for the coming-of-age Jugendweihe celebration in the GDR – reproduced them in small numbers, and passed them on; ironically, the act of repeated listening to this cultural contraband was itself a subcultural rite of passage. In the words of Bernd Jestram of the East Berlin bands Rosa Extra and Aufruhr zur Liebe, "Punk was like a bomb for me. I sat at home and taped John Peel, and then listened to the tape at least ten times a day. For me, that was my revolution." (Galenza 1999b, 42).

As the first East German punk bands emerged, cassettes also provided both recording and distribution possibilities away from the monopoly of the state record label AMIGA. Like other countries in the Eastern Bloc, the GDR had a thriving culture of samizdat literature; while self-publishing newspapers and booklets was "generally suicidal" (Schneider and Friedrich 1999, 143), it was possible to do so under the auspices of the church, which possessed limited printing and duplicating capacities. For listeners, the process of producing audio samizdat (*magnetizdat*) was far simpler and could be done independently from one's own home. Songs were recorded straight onto cassette, and in spite of the inevitably raw sound, bands "had a finished product as soon as the last note had subsided." (Mohr 2019, 327). Over the course of the 1980s, numerous underground cassette labels sprang up across the Republic, with the tapes often accompanied by handmade magazines or creative DIY graphics. In 1984, together with his bandmate Roland Lippok, Bernd Jestram started the cassette label Assorted Nuts, which was initially intended as an outlet for recordings of their bands Aufruhr zur Liebe and Ornament und Verbrechen. Assorted Nuts was possibly the first cassette label in the GDR, and the cassettes were initially dubbed by connecting Stern Recorders together with a diode cable. As Lippok recalls, "the moment of self-control was very important, we could decide everything for ourselves. The technical quality was lousy, but one had a fantastic feeling of self-determination." (Galenza 1999a, 134).

3 Broadening Horizons

If punk's arrival in the GDR was imparting a liberating do-it-yourself ethic to the country's disenfranchised youth, the fact that Peel's broadcasts were never limited to one particular style also served to provide young East Germans with an unorthodox and eclectic musical education. The writer David Cavanagh points out that, for John Peel, "genre juxtaposition was a prerequisite, a sine qua non and a flat-out non-negotiable imperative. (…) Listeners in 1978 hoping to hear an exclusive taste of the new Clash album would have to wait while Peel played a selection of Morris dances by the Albion Band". (Cavanagh 2015, 8). In the 1970s his enthusiasm for reggae earned him the nickname "Jah Peel" in the British music press (Cavanagh 2015, 8), and over the course of his career he would be an early advocate of a variety of new musical styles including two-tone ska, hip-hop, post-punk, krautrock, jungle, and drum 'n' bass.

This open-mindedness also directly impacted early punk bands in the GDR, some of whom began to evolve in different musical directions whilst ostensibly remaining within the punk scene's orbit. While punk may have been the catalyst for the personal revolutions taking place across the Republic in the late 1970s and early 1980s, for many listeners it was not the final destination but a gateway to a broader world of musical ideas and forms of artistic expression. Furthermore, East Berlin's underground culture was defined by the cross-pollination of ideas, and genre-defying collaborations emerged between punk and other nonconformist bands with "filmmakers, poets, puppeteers, and rogues", with whom they made "art, racket, and nonsense". As Bernd Jestram recalls with regard to Rosa Extra, which operated within the punk scene but deviated aesthetically and exhibited strong "no-wave" tendencies, "We were influenced by the energy of punk and John Peel. Later, punk became uniformed and static. That was not the spirit that John Peel spread, and which inspired us." (Galenza 2023b, 70).

Indeed, whereas some bands remained firmly rooted in punk music and aesthetics, other early protagonists of the scene were moving on but applying punk's do-it-yourself ethic to other musical or cultural fields. For the photographer and journalist Michael Biedowicz, who both participated in and documented the GDR's punk and underground scenes during the 1980s, the experience instilled a self-confidence that helped him to start his career:

> It was a form of empowerment. In punk you can do it yourself, you don't have to know how to play your instrument. If you apply this approach to other things, you can also become an artist, whether or not you've studied art. Just do it. I internalised that from the punk movement. (Biedowicz 2022)

Biedowicz also emphasises the fact that John Peel's eclectic broadcasts quickly turned listeners on to other radical sounds and genres:

> Through listening to his programme I discovered hundreds of weird bands. A whole cosmos opened for me. (…) His credo was always "absorb everything possible", don't get stuck on one musical direction. Be aware of how wide the musical horizon is. (Biedowicz 2022)

As the GDR's musical underground diversified and evolved over the course of the 1980s, the authorities attempted to co-opt critical groups from a variety of genres including punk, electronic, New Wave, and experimental under the label *Die anderen Bands* (The Other Bands). If they made the necessary lyrical or artistic compromises, bands could apply for an *Einstufung* (rating) that would allow them to perform at officially sanctioned gigs, charge admission fees, and earn a living from their music (Gericke 2023, 19). Some bands rejected entering into a Faustian bargain with the state, choosing to remain "resolute in the totality of their illegality" until the collapse of the GDR (Galenza 2018, 19). Nonetheless, the fact that independent bands such as Die Art, Die Vision, and Sandow were able to reach a larger audience on the national stage was also empowering for some listeners, such as the writer Sascha Lange, who "realised that we shouldn't just idolise the western stars (…) but that one could also try to make music oneself." (Lange 2007, 139).

Another avenue for *Die anderen Bands* to reach an audience was provided in March 1986, when the GDR state radio launched a new dedicated youth radio station Jugendradio DT64, which featured a programme that was explicitly inspired by "John Peel's Music" on BFBS. *Parocktikum* was presented by the East German journalist Lutz Schramm, who by the following year was broadcasting from midnight to 5am, playing punk, indie and hard rock, as well as the first East German hip-hop bands. Schramm saw his remit as "similar to John Peel, namely to publicise music that was unknown at that time." (Galenza 1999c, 295). His playlists also included Anglophone groups such as The Clash, Dead Kennedys, Billy Bragg, as well as two of Peel's favourite British bands, The Fall and Half Man Half Biscuit. At the end of each year, Parockticum conducted an annual listeners' poll in the style of American and British music magazines; in 1987, for example, listeners voted in the Californian punk band Dead Kennedys' anthemic "Nazi Punks Fuck Off" at No. 1. (Kowasch 1999, 339).

From September 1987, Schramm also organised the *Parockticum* Sessions, directly modelled upon the BBC's legendary Peel Sessions. In his own words, "I clearly wanted to develop [the Sessions] along the lines of John Peel (but I didn't succeed)". The goal was to provide bands with the opportunity to make live or studio recordings paid for by DT64 to be broadcast on air, circumventing the GDR's cumbersome radio bureaucracy and censorship. However, the recordings suffered from poor sound quality, due to sound engineers who lacked experience with the type of music played. Moreover, Schramm was soon falling foul of the censors, with whom he engaged in a protracted dispute after the Dresden post-punk band Kaltfront was rejected for a session on both lyrical and musical grounds, even though the lyrics were "hard, decisive, honest, and just depressive" rather than political (Galenza 1999c, 294).

Nonetheless, *Parocktikum* provided many East German bands with an opportunity to avoid bureaucratic hurdles and make it onto the airwaves. In Schramm's assessment, some of the more unusual groups such as D.A.M. from Rathenow may not have existed without the opportunity to broadcast on *Parocktikum*:

> They wanted to be a band. But they didn't make any music, they just made a racket in the cellar along the lines of "now we're going to test out our great-grandmother's washing machine". They probably only functioned because they had a medial echo. (Galenza 1999c, 294–5).

Indeed, while some underground bands had no interest in having their music broadcast by a state institution, Schramm found himself – like John Peel – inundated with tapes from "all possible corners", musically speaking (Binas 1999, 248). The importance of *Parocktikum* in providing a platform for underground bands – who did not necessarily have an *Einstufung* – has also been highlighted by the musicologist Susanne Binas, a member of the East Berlin avant-garde band Der Expander des Fortschritts. Binas points out that "when Lutz Schramm started playing tapes (…) that he had only just received yesterday from someone or other, it was actually absurd. Bypassing the censors, with no sign-off." (Binas 1999, 248).

4 Politics and Society

The fact that John Peel's broadcasts were so indelibly connected with the birth of the East German punk scene means that they also – albeit indirectly – had political repercussions in the GDR. Although the punks were initially largely apolitical, the harshness of their treatment at the hands of the state led to a rapid politicisation within the scene; while the repeated listening to tapes of Peel's broadcasts and other *magnetizdat* constituted a musical radicalisation process, state-sponsored aggression or outright violence against the punks forced them by default into political opposition. Initially, their brushes with authority had been with the Volkspolizei and the Kriminalpolizei, but in early 1981 the Stasi assumed responsibility for combatting the punk scene. In mid-1983 Erich Mielke, the Minister for State Security, initiated a campaign of *Härte gegen Punk* (severity against punk), employing various tools of physical and psychological violence, and enacting a wave of "arrests, preventative detention, prison sentences, military impressments, and, in a few cases, expulsion from the GDR". (Howes 2017, 29).

The punks' growing hostility toward the state was reflected in the increasingly political nature of bands' songs (Horschig 1999, 37), and succinctly expressed by the East Berlin band Betonromantik in the lyric "DDR Terrorstaat/Wir haben deine Scheiße satt". In 1983, another group from East Berlin, Namenlos, attacked the GDR's nascent neo-Nazi skinhead scene – which had its origins in the punk movement – in the song "Nazis in Ostberlin". In a further unambiguous missive, this time aimed at the Stasi, Namenlos singer Jana Schlosser compared the state security apparatus with Heinrich Himmler's SS. As part of the *Härte gegen Punk* crackdown, each of the band members received prison sentences of up to 18 months, only for Horschig and Schlosser to resume their musical and political activities upon release (Preuß 1999, 61). Ironically, these two songs also provided the authorities' dubious rationale for banning a church-organised event in 1983, which was intended to foster dialogue between punks and other youths, because "at this event, as in Berlin and previously in Halle, songs that are hostile to the state will be sung, namely

'Nazischweine in Ostberlin' and 'MfSss [sic.]'. The event would thereby have a fascist character and (…) could not take place." (RHG 1983c).

The politics of GDR punk also found its way onto the broadcasts of John Peel, who periodically received and played music from East German bands. He gave airplay to the split LP eNDe: DDR von unten (GDR from below), featuring Thüringen punk band Schleim-Keim, whose "bleak lyrics [aimed] critical blows specifically at an East German establishment", alongside the avant-garde poetics of the Dresden art-punk group Zwitschermaschine (Howes 2013, 584). While eNDe was the GDR's first "tamizdat" record, smuggled out and published in West Berlin by the punk label Aggressive Rockproduktionen, and therefore readily available in the west, other bands in the GDR used whatever limited channels were available to them to send tapes to Peel, who sometimes broadcast them in spite of musical misgivings. In 1995 he admitted that, to his "great embarrassment", the political content and the broader context of the lyrics had been completely lost on him:

> When I started doing programmes for BFBS I spoke no German at all, and I still don't. (…) And of course, the lyrics to the song are much more important, I mean, the music is usually terrible, really. But the lyrics, obviously (…) Something that sounds to me like, 'Hey baby, let's do it one more time tonight' will mean like, it will have something about Brezhnev or the repeal [of] legislation (…) Even if I could speak the language, the real meaning is buried several layers deep in the language. (…) So even if I spoke German, it would be western European German, so I wouldn't have understood what was really being said. (Katzorke and Schneider 1995).

Nonetheless, by broadcasting the sounds of the East German underground back into the GDR, Peel was emphatically closing the broadcaster-listener loop. Schleim-Keim's singer Dieter "Otze" Ehrlich, for example, had stumbled across Peel's broadcasts by chance whilst turning the medium-wave dial in 1979 (Papenfuß 1999, 62); now his own idiosyncratic East German variant of punk was being broadcast back into the country by the same DJ several years later.

If the specific East German context was lost on Peel, it was also becoming increasingly complicated as the decade wore on. With the GDR's cultural establishment becoming ever more aware that it was fighting a losing battle against its own youth, the Stasi's draconian tactics began to diverge from official cultural policy. By 1985, as the historian Seth Howes notes, the "open repression exemplified by the arrests, impressments, and expulsions during *Härte gegen Punk* had given way to the cultivation of informants in punk bands, the dogged compilation of lists of attendees' names at punk concerts, and the careful perusal of GDR punk lyrics and Western fanzines intercepted in the mail." (Howes 2017, 32). Moreover, as Henryk Gericke argues, the Stasi was increasingly out of its depth with grassroots youth subcultures, which continued to multiply and splinter into opaque sub-genres:

> The Stasi was already completely disoriented and groping its way through a counterculture that had long-since split into sub-scenes such as booze punks, anarcho-punks, hardcore punks, and skins. Metal kids and hooligans made the whole thing even more confusing. Then came New Romantic. The guardians of the System could no longer understand it. Gothic? By then they had already completely lost track. (Gericke 2018, 19).

To make matters worse for the Ministry, this bewildering subterranean menagerie was also afforded a degree of protection by the Evangelical Church's Offene Arbeit, which supported marginalised groups in the GDR and played an important role in providing facilities and even mediation in conflict situations with the authorities. While the unlikely collaboration between the church and punks had its vociferous critics on both sides, the majority of punk concerts in the GDR took place on church premises, which constituted "a sort of extraterritorial space". The assembled punks had to "tolerate a prayer now and then" before the start of the concert (Gericke 1999, 99), but concerts in churches – unlike events in private apartments – were safe from police or Stasi intervention, albeit not from the presence of Stasi informants recruited from both the punk community and church circles.

Certain church social workers, such as Deacon Lorenz Postler of the Erlöserkirche in Berlin-Rummelsburg, worked tirelessly on behalf of the punks. Postler, for example, organised a representative Punk Council (Punkrat) within the church, communal countryside hikes, and regular punk evenings (RHG 1983a). In a 1983 letter to two senior church figures, Bishop Gottfried Forck and Generalsuperindendant Günther Krusche (the latter, it later emerged, was a Stasi informant), Postler argued that punks were being habitually subjected to "disproportionate and brutal" police raids, frequent arbitrary summons to police stations, the forced cutting of hair and the confiscation of jewellery, while independent observers such as church youth workers were barred from attending court proceedings under pretexts of a lack of space, facilitated by the deliberate selection of the smallest courtrooms. He also noted that the vocabulary of the insults which he had heard used both by officials and members of the public against the punks "often resorted to a vocabulary that reminds one of darker times," for example with references to gas chambers, work camps, and euthanasia (RHG 1983b, 1983c).

From 1980 onwards, the Erlöserkirche was the site of regular Blues Masses, large festival-like events attended by a diverse range of interest groups, advocating everything from religious freedom, gay and lesbian rights, the demilitarisation of East German society, and environmentalism. Punk bands such as Namenlos also performed at the Blues Masses, which went into steep decline from 1985 onwards, with the various interest groups fragmenting and consolidating themselves elsewhere, and ceased altogether in 1987. The Erlöserkirche events became more secular and punk-oriented, with the annual Alösa Spring Festival – A-lös-a being a Berlin jargon wordplay on Erlöser (Redeemer), referring to the 'a' in 'anarchy' – constituting one of the few international punk gatherings in the GDR (See Figure 13.1). The festival on 21–22 April 1988 attracted 2,500 visitors – including many from Poland – and featured sixteen bands from the GDR, Czechoslovakia, Poland, Hungary, Italy, and West Germany (Friedlich and Schneider 1999, 118).

Another important location for East Berlin's punks was the Umweltbibliothek (Environment Library), which was established in 1986 and located in two basement rooms of the Zionskirche Gemeindehaus in Berlin-Mitte, serving variously as a library, samizdat publishing house, event space, and a meeting place for the GDR opposition. Together with the church's Offene Arbeit, the *Initiative, Frieden und Menschenrechte* (Initiative for Peace and Human Rights) and local Peace Circles, the Umweltbibliothek co-organised the first grassroots Kirchentag von Unten (Church Day from Below) on 24–26 June 1987, which was held in opposition to the official church celebration to commemorate Berlin's 750th anniversary, drawing up to 6,000 attendees (Furlong 2013, 457), and attracting a mix of "left-wing dissidents, punks, and anarchists". (Friedlich and Schneider 1999, 116).

Motivated by the large number of attendees, the groups co-founded the Kirche von Unten (Church from Below [KvU] in "a direct challenge to the Church hierarchy" (Furlong 2013, 457). As the ethnomusicologist Alison Furlong notes:

> The KvU became a way for these groups to advance their agenda without going through a hierarchy that they increasingly viewed as corrupt. In this way, each of the diverse groups that had coalesced into a single Blues-Mass public could continue to pursue its own goals, whether sacred or secular. (Furlong 2013, 457).

In the words of "Speiche", a prominent East Berlin punk and KvU activist, it was "a sort of networking between punks and artists and gay groups and peo-

FIGURE 13.1 Punks in Berlin at the Alösa Spring Festival, April 1988. (© Michael Biedowicz)

ple who wanted to leave the country and people who didn't want to leave the country and people who said they wanted to change the country." (Bernt and Wolf 1999). From November 1988, the KvU also had its own rooms in the St. Elisabeth parish community centre in Berlin-Mitte, which came to house a library and a printing press, and was used by groups such as Rahman Satti's initiative *Schwarze Deutsche in der DDR* (Black Germans in the GDR), as well as for punk concerts. As one of the few alternative spaces in East Berlin that stayed open all night on Fridays, it became a magnet for more politically-minded punks, and regularly drew crowds of two hundred at weekends.

5 Antifascism in the Late GDR

While elements of the punk community were increasingly becoming intertwined with oppositional church, civil rights, and environmental groups, not all countercultural developments that resulted from punk were benign. From 1983 onwards, individual skinheads had been appearing on the punk scene, which "at that time had nothing much new to offer" (Gericke 1999, 97). The initial GDR skinhead scene largely comprised former punks who orientated themselves towards Oi! music – a British subgenre of punk – but, increasingly, also to the White Power movement (Gericke 1999, 97), which soon also attracted youths from other demographics such as football hooligans and the military (Brück 1991, 21). Conversely, as the historian and former KvU activist Dirk Moldt has demonstrated at length, the skinheads' militant tendencies, hatred of "asocials" and intellectuals, perceived work ethic, and clean-cut image were utterly relatable to the Stasi, and in spite of their embrace of neo-Nazi ideology and violent behaviour they were never considered a threat to anything like the degree that punks were (Moldt 2002, 24–5). As late as 1988/89, the city of Dresden banned punks – whose "unaesthetic appearance injures human dignity and endangers order and security" – from the city centre, pubs, and in some instances even public transport, and issued (sometimes multiple) fines for transgressions (RHG 1988a, 1988b, 1988c). Meanwhile, neo-Nazi skinheads in Berlin successfully had an FDJ youth club ban for threatening behaviour and the singing of the Nazi "Horst-Wessel-Lied" overturned on the grounds that it constituted discrimination (RHG 1989). Unsurprisingly, a January 1989 government analysis still identified punks as the country's biggest youth problem (Mohr 2019, 299).

The government was at least finally forced to acknowledge the problem of neo-Nazism following an incident in October 1987, when a concert organised by KvU activists at the Zionskirche – featuring the bands Element of Crime (West Berlin) and Die Firma (East Berlin) – was attacked by around thirty neo-Nazi skinheads shouting anti-Semitic and anti-communist insults (Galenza 1999, 270). Due to the extremely violent nature of the incident and the severity of the injuries to the victims, who were punched, kicked, and trampled on as the large numbers of Volkspolizisten outside the church stood by and watched, it was widely reported in the West German media, and the KvU played an important role in bringing it to national attention in the GDR, where it also had a muted media echo in the party newspaper *Neues Deutschland* (Gericke 1999, 98). The attack forced GDR society to rethink its complacency regarding homegrown neo-Nazism – a public outcry at the lenient suspended sentences for the perpetrators caused them to be revoked – and pushed the ruling Socialist Unity Party (SED) to instigate a working group, "AG Skinhead", within the Kriminalpolizei to study the phenomenon.

However, the "Findings of the criminal investigation department on neo-fascist activities in the GDR" made grim reading for the regime, and were kept top secret until the fall of the Wall. The criminologist Bernd Wagner, who led "AG Skinhead", recalls:

> Anti-fascist groups active in the church milieu at the time analysed the situation very aptly, and (…) recognised a connection between the GDR dictatorship, its despotic character, Nazism, and rampant nationalism among the population. However, the Stasi did not primarily focus on the neo-Nazis, but rather on the church Antifa groups, which it accused of having a "hostile-negative", anti-state attitude. (Wagner 2018).

One such church Antifa group was established in Berlin under the auspices of the KvU, and published the regular samizdat *Antifa-Infoblatt* (RHG 1989) to document neo-Nazi activities and violence against foreigners, punks, and others – the subjective nature of the writing and the recurring eyewitness reports of incidents and court cases involving punks strongly indicate that they played an active role in its production. The final page of the edition dated 2 November 1989 (one week before the fall of the Wall) is a call to arms for the demonstration at Berlin's Alexanderplatz on 4 November, which would become a seminal event in the looming collapse of the GDR. With pro-democracy demonstrations gathering traction, the *Infoblatt* warned that organised neo-Nazis were infiltrating the "independent demos of responsible and reform-oriented citizens", and attempting to give the demonstrations and slogans an explicitly nationalist character. Accordingly, they called for a united antifascist bloc at the Alexanderplatz demonstration on 4 November, "silencing nationalists and fascists" and preventing them from hijacking the demonstration (RHG 1989).

In retrospect, such messages – which add problematic nuance to the "peaceful revolution" narrative – were prescient, and foresaw the major problems that the new federal states on the territory of the former GDR were to have with neo-Nazi violence and murders into the 1990s and beyond.[1] After the fall of the Wall, Bernd Wagner, too, sought to raise the alarm by publicising the previously-suppressed findings of AG Skinhead, as well as newly-available Stasi and police files documenting neo-Nazi activities in the GDR. However,

1 For example, the murder of Angolan worker Amadeu Antonio in Eberswalde in 1990, and the former *Umweltbibliothek* and KvU activist Silvio Meier in Berlin in 1992.

he was largely ignored by both the public and the West German Bundeskriminalamt (Wagner 2018). By January 1990, neo-Nazis at the weekly Monday demonstrations in Leipzig were in "festive spirits", openly performing the Hitler salute and shouting anti-communist slogans (Lange 2007, 173–74). The warnings of resurgent right-wing extremism were drowned out in the euphoria of *die Wende*.

6 Conclusion

On 24 September 1995, nearly five years after German reunification, a large group consisting of members of the early GDR punk scene, as well as a camera crew, boarded the boat MS *Kreuz As* on the bank of the River Spree in former West Berlin. The punks and ex-punks had been rounded up for a reunion by the filmmakers to participate in the documentary *Störung Ost*, and bribed with an on-board buffet, a DJ playing punk records, and "hard-won" coupons for beer and schnapps. (Gericke 1999, 94) A number of other guests with various connections to the GDR punk scene had been invited. Bernd Wagner, who had studied the punks as well as neo-Nazis for the Kriminalpolizei, had agreed to participate in a discussion but failed to appear. Deacon Lorenz Postler of the Erlöserkirche, warmly remembered by many for his engagement on behalf of the punks in East Berlin, was on board. Another special guest also accepted the invitation and travelled from England to meet his former listeners – who were surprised to find out that the man behind the iconic voice was "small and somewhat chubby" (Gericke 1999, 100) – John Peel.

While it is notoriously difficult to gauge the impact of a particular broadcaster or programme, by all accounts John Peel's broadcasts played an important role in bringing punk – and then everything else imaginable – to the GDR. This had implications that went far beyond music and subculture. Looking back, Henryk Gericke has stated:

> Today, the period between 1981 and 1983, for all the emotion, appears to me to be akin to a transit space. In retrospect, it is striking how many of those who haunted the initial punk scene later became painters, musicians, writers, actors, directors, DJs etc. They, but also many others, had to go through it if they wanted to get somewhere else. At the time, punk was an effective way to give in to one's own need to express oneself and to become sure of it before later taking on more concrete forms behind the camera, on the stage, on the screen or even as a cook at the pots in the kitchen of a restaurant. Whether you went on to become an artist or not, punk was a crash course. (Gericke 1999, 100).

On the East Berlin underground scene, where the boundaries between musical genres, art forms, subcultures, and radical politics were at best extremely blurred, punk had been a starting point for myriad personal journeys, heading in every conceivable direction.

It was also continuing to exert an influence on the city itself. The writer and DJ Tim Mohr, arriving in Berlin in 1992, found a colourful and creative scene unfolding behind the grey, run-down pockmarked facades of the old East:

> Hidden behind unmarked doors, down ladders in empty lots, nestled among the crumbling bricks of a candlelit basement or a disused cistern, in the attics of half-destroyed buildings, even in abandoned bunkers and bank vaults, a kaleidoscopic new city was taking shape. (…) [East German punks] ran or worked at most of the places I hung out at, they had set up nearly all the first bars and clubs in the East and established in the process the ethos of the fledgling new society being built almost from scratch after the fall of the Berlin Wall. (Mohr 2019, xv–xvi)

The chain of events that had started with a few East German teenagers stumbling across strange, raucous new music on western radio stations in the late 1970s had played its own part in the demise of the old regime. In newly united Berlin, it was now shaping the beginnings of what was to come next.

References

Biedowicz, Michael. 2022. Interview with William Studdert. Berlin, 2 November.

Binas, Susanne. 1999. "Kassetten als Kassiber". *Wir wollen immer artig sein. Punk, New Wave, HipHop und Independent-Szene in der DDR 1980–1990*. Eds. Ronald Galenza and Heinz Havemeister. Berlin: Schwarzkopf & Schwarzkopf.

Bernt, Matthias and Dietmar Wolf. 1999. "Speiche, Speiche, wir wollen deine Leiche". *telegraph* #3. https://telegraph.cc/archiv/telegraph-3-1999/speiche-speiche-wir-wollen-deine-leiche/. Accessed 7 January 2024.

Boehlke, Michael and Carsten Fiebeler. 2006. *Ostpunk! Too Much Future*. Rundfunk Berlin-Brandenburg/Egoli Tossell Films.

Brück, Wolfgang. 1991. "Skinheads vor und nach der Wende in der DDR". "Minderheiten". *Sicherheit und Frieden (S+F)/Security and Peace*. 9:1: 18–22.

BStU n.d. Feindtätig unter Jugendlichen [westlicher Sender]. MfS HA XX 10067, Bundesarchiv Stasi-Unterlagen-Archiv [BStU]. Berlin, Germany.

Cavanagh, David, 2015. *Good Night and Good Riddance: How Thirty-Five Years of John Peel Helped to Shape Modern Life*. London: Faber & Faber.

Francke, Jürgen. 1992. 9 January. "Radio Bremen feuert Indie-Guru John Peel". *Die Tageszeitung*. https://taz.de/Radio-Bremen-4-feuert-Indie-Guru-Peel/!1687910/ Accessed 11 January 2024.

Friedrich, Jasper André and Ray Schneider. 1999. "Leipzig von Unten: Punk- und Independent-Szene, Aktionen, Zeitschrifen und Bands". *Wir wollen immer artig sein. Punk, New Wave, HipHop und Independent-Szene in der DDR 1980–1990*. Eds. Ronald Galenza and Heinz Havemeister. Berlin: Schwarzkopf & Schwarzkopf. 102–45.

Furlong, Alison. 2013. "Politics, Faith, and the East German Blues." *Colloquia Germanica, Themenheft: Sound Studies in German Contexts* 46.4: 433–461.

Galenza, Ronald. 1999. "Assorted Nuts: Eine Label Geschichte (Roland Lippok und Bernd Jestram im Interview)". *Magnetizdat DDR. Magnetbanduntergrund Ost 1979–1990*. Eds. Alexander Pehlemann, Ronald Galenza and Robert Miessner. Berlin: Verbrecher Verlag. 131–8.

Galenza, Ronald. 1999a. "Wimpelgrab & Gegentanz: Berlin". *Wir wollen immer artig sein. Punk, New Wave, HipHop und Independent-Szene in der DDR 1980–1990*. Eds. Ronald Galenza and Heinz Havemeister. Berlin: Schwarzkopf & Schwarzkopf. 260–87.

Galenza 1999b. "Provokation, Paranoia, und Parties: Interview mit Bert Papenfuß, Aljoscha Rompe, Ronald Lippok, und Bernd Jestram 1999". *Wir wollen immer artig sein. Punk, New Wave, HipHop und Independent-Szene in der DDR 1980–1990*. Eds. Ronald Galenza and Heinz Havemeister. Berlin: Schwarzkopf & Schwarzkopf. 41–50.

Galenza, Roland. 1999c. "Spule, Feedback, und Zensur: Interview mit Lutz Schramm (DT64). 1999". *Wir wollen immer artig sein. Punk, New Wave, HipHop und Independent-Szene in der DDR 1980–1990*. Eds. Ronald Galenza and Heinz Havemeister. Berlin: Schwarzkopf & Schwarzkopf. 288–95.

Galenza, Ronald. 2023a. "Diskurs-Pogo oder: Fluide Dissonanzen". *Magnetizdat DDR. Magnetbanduntergrund Ost 1979–1990*. Eds. Alexander Pehlemann, Ronald Galenza and Robert Miessner. Berlin: Verbrecher Verlag. 17–24.

Galenza, Ronald. 2023b. "Was Mir deine Schleuder ist Dir meine Waschmaschine: Von Rosa Extra bis Hard Pop". *Magnetizdat DDR: Magnetbanduntergrund Ost 1979–1990*. Eds. Alexander Pehlemann, Ronald Galenza and Robert Miessner. Berlin: Verbrecher Verlag. 67–92.

Gericke, Henryk. 1999. "Schatten voraus! Punk, im Jahr zwölf nach Punk". *Wir wollen immer artig sein. Punk, New Wave, HipHop und Independent-Szene in der DDR 1980–1990*. Eds. Ronald Galenza and Heinz Havemeister. Berlin: Schwarzkopf & Schwarzkopf. 94–101.

Gericke, Henryk. 2023. "Subkultur und Diktatur: Punk Rock DDR". *Warschauer Punk Pakt*. Ed. Alexander Pehlemann. Mainz: Ventil Verlag. 13–18.

Garner, Ken. 1993. *In Session Tonight: The Complete Radio One Recordings*. London: BBC Books.

Horschig, Michael (1999). "In der DDR hat es nie Punks gegeben." *Wir wollen immer artig sein. Punk, New Wave, HipHop und Independent-Szene in der DDR 1980–1990*. Eds. Ronald Galenza and Heinz Havemeister. Berlin: Schwarzkopf & Schwarzkopf. 17–40.

Howes, Seth (2013) 'Killersatellit' and Randerscheinung: Punk and the Prenzlauer Berg, German Studies Review, 36(3), 579–601.

Howes, Seth (2017) 'DIY, im Eigenverlag: East German Tomizdat LPs', German Politics & Society, 35(2), 26–47.

Katzorke, Mechthild and Cornelia Schneider. 1996. "Störung Ost: Punks in Ostberlin 1980–1983". ZDF.

Kedves, Jan. 2012. "Neues Album von F.S.K.: Überwältigend routiniertes Rumpeln". *Süddeutsche Zeitung*. 30 May. https://www.sueddeutsche.de/kultur/neues-album-der-avantgarde-pop-band-f-s-k-autobiografische-doppelgaenger-1.1369309. Accessed 26 December 2023.

Kowalczuk, Ilko-Sascha. 2002. *Freiheit und Öffentlichkeit. Politischer Samisdat in der DDR 1985–1989, Eine Dokumentation*. Berlin: Schriftenreihe der Robert-Havemann-Gesellschaft (Band 7).

Kowasch, Fred. 1999. "Radio Glasnost: ein Feindsender als Medium der DDR-Opposition". *Wir wollen immer artig sein. Punk, New Wave, HipHop und Independent-Szene in der DDR 1980–1990*. Eds. Ronald Galenza and Heinz Havemeister. Berlin: Schwarzkopf & Schwarzkopf. 336–340.

Lange, Sascha. 2007. *DJ Westradio*. Berlin: Aufbau Verlag.

Major, Patrick. 2013. "Listening Behind the Curtain: BBC Broadcasting to East Germany and its Cold War Echo". *Cold War History*, 13:2: 255–75.

Mohr, Tim. 2019. *Burning Down the Haus: Punk Rock, Freedom, and the Fall of the Berlin Wall*. Chapel Hill: Algonquin Books.

Moldt, Dirk. 2002. "Keine Confrontation! Die Rolle des MfS im Zusammenhang mit dem Überfall von Skinheads auf ein Konzert in der Berliner Zionskirche am 17. Oktober 1987". *Horch und Guck*. 40: 14–25.

Papenfuß, Bert. 1999. "Eine stürmische Landjugend: Interview mit Dieter 'Otze' Ehrlich (Schleim-Keim)". *Wir wollen immer artig sein. Punk, New Wave, HipHop und Independent-Szene in der DDR 1980–1990*. Eds. Ronald Galenza and Heinz Havemeister. Berlin: Schwarzkopf & Schwarzkopf. 62–5.

Peel, John. 1996. *Travels with my Camera: Autobahn Blues*. Uden Associates/Channel 4.

Peel, John and Sheila Ravenscroft. 2005. *Margrave of the Marshes: His Autobiography*. London: Corgi.

Michael, Klaus. 1999. “Macht aus diesem Staat Gurkensalat: Punk und die Exerzitien der Macht”. *Wir wollen immer artig sein. Punk, New Wave, HipHop und Independent-Szene in der DDR 1980–1990*. Eds. Ronald Galenza and Heinz Havemeister. Berlin: Schwarzkopf & Schwarzkopf. 72–93.

Pehlemann, Alexander. 2023. “Kein Ende mit ‘eNDe’: Zur Geschichte von ‘DDR von Unten’. In den Worten von Dimitri Hegemann und Karl-Ulrich Walterbach, sowie des MfS”. *Magnetizdat DDR: Magnetbanduntergrund Ost 1979–1990*. Eds. Alexander Pehlemann, Ronald Galenza and Robert Miessner. Berlin: Verbrecher Verlag. 93–106.

Preuß, Thorsten. 1999. “Stasi, Spaß, und E-Gitarren: Die Geschichte der Berliner Punkband Namenlos”. *Wir wollen immer artig sein. Punk, New Wave, HipHop und Independent-Szene in der DDR 1980–1990*. Eds. Ronald Galenza and Heinz Havemeister. Berlin: Schwarzkopf & Schwarzkopf. 51–61.

RHG 1983a. Lorenz Postler, “Kurze innerkirchliche Information über die wichtigsten Geschehnisse der Punkarbeit/KKR-Friedrichshain aus der Sicht des angestellten Mitarbeiters”. (March). Ki 12/1/71. Robert-Havemann-Gesellschaft, Berlin.

RHG 1983b. Lorenz Postler, Uwe Kühlisch, Gerd Jäger. “Information an den Bischof Dr. Forck und den Generalsuperindendent Dr. Krusche mit der Bitte, ein Gespräch mit entsprechenden staatlichen Stellen zu suchen”. 29 March. Ki 12/1/82. Robert-Havemann-Gesellschaft, Berlin.

RHG 1983c. Lorenz Postler an Laudien, Passauer,Krusche, und Kulisch. “Zusammenfassung von Berichten über Halle / 22.10.83 in Stichpunkten”. 30 October 1983. Ki 12/1. Robert-Havemann-Gesellschaft, Berlin.

RHG 1988a. “Dresdner Polizei: Will-Kür statt Pflicht”. *Umweltblätter*. 1988. Nr. 10, 7–8. PS 107/26. Robert-Havemann-Gesellschaft, Berlin.

RHG 1988b. “Aktion und Spenden für diskriminierte Punks”. *Umweltblätter*. 1988. Nr. 12, 9. PS 107/27. Robert-Havemann-Gesellschaft, Berlin.

RHG 1988c. “Protesterklärung der Kirche von Unten (DDR-weite Vollversammlung) zu den Repressionen gegen Punks in Dresden”. *Umweltblätter*. 1988. Nr. 12, 8–9. PS 107/27. Robert-Havemann-Gesellschaft, Berlin.

RHG 1989. *Antifa-Infoblatt*. 2 November 1989. PS 4/2 OA KvU. Robert-Havemann-Gesellschaft, Berlin.

Schönian, Valerie and Michael Schlieben. 2017. “Wie war es im Osten? Punk in der DDR: Das hat mich ziemlich angekotzt. Interview with Namenlos singer Jana Schlosser”. *Zeit Online*. 4 June. https://www.zeit.de/gesellschaft/zeitgeschehen/2019-05/punk-wie-war-das-im-osten-ddr-podcast. Accessed 7 December 2023.

Wagner, Bernd. 2018. “Vertuschte Gefahr: Die Stasi & Neonazis.” https://www.bpb.de/themen/deutsche-teilung/stasi/218421/vertuschte-gefahr-die-stasi-neonazis/. Accessed 31 December 2023.

CHAPTER 14

'You Have Become a Citizen of No Man's Land – I Send you my Greetings': Screening Berlin in the BBC's John le Carré Adaptations

Joseph Oldham

1 Introduction

On Monday, 25 October 1982 millions of UK viewers tuned in to watch the sixth and final episode of the BBC dramatisation of John le Carré's novel *Smiley's People* (BBC 2, 1982). Over the course of the serial, veteran British spymaster George Smiley (Alec Guinness) has uncovered proof that his nemesis, the KGB chief known by the codename "Karla" (Patrick Stewart), had misappropriated Soviet funds to have his sick daughter cared for in a Swiss clinic. Now, with the ruthlessness he had once ascribed to his rival, Smiley uses this information to blackmail Karla into a defection to the West. Receiving a coded telephone call informing him that Karla has accepted his terms and will be defecting in Berlin, Smiley remarks, "Well, that's where he would choose, I suppose. Yes, it's natural." Sure enough, a few days later Smiley and his allies travel to the world capital of espionage where they intercept Karla at the end of his long walk across the Oberbaum Bridge disguised as a workman (see Figure 14.1). It was indeed a natural setting for this encounter, for as Sam Goodman writes, "of all the occupied spaces of post-war Europe it was Berlin that captured the imagination of spy authors and the general public alike most securely" (Goodman 2016, 28). In the *oeuvre* of le Carré, this sequence was also a callback to a memorable less successful attempted escape from the East in his earlier breakthrough novel *The Spy Who Came in from the Cold* (1963). Yet the road which had led these two Cold War opponents, Smiley and Karla, to this point was a long and twisting one in which, appropriately, not everything was as it appeared.

This chapter will examine the representations of Berlin in the BBC's le Carré adaptations, of which the climax of *Smiley's People* is only the best-known. Firstly, I explore the earliest interest from the BBC in adapting le Carré, including an unsuccessful attempt to adapt *The Spy* in 1963. I then examine le Carré's first television adaptation, Rediffusion-London's production of his short story *Dare I Weep, Dare I Mourn* (1967), arguing that a popular

 | HTTPS://DOI.ORG/10.1515/9783111302508-014

FIGURE 14.1 George Smiley meets KGB chief "Karla" at the Oberbaumbrücke in Berlin at the climax of the BBC's 1982 adaptation of John le Carre's *Smiley's People*. In fact the scene was filmed in Nottingham, UK. (© Everett Collection)

association of le Carré with Berlin led the production team to add an original Berlin sequence but logistical problems forced them to find alternatives to shooting in the city itself, foreshadowing a problem that recurred across subsequent BBC adaptations. Following this, I explore how le Carré's famous Karla trilogy of the 1970s, two books of which were adapted into the acclaimed BBC serials *Tinker Tailor Soldier Spy* (BBC 2, 1979) and *Smiley's People*, constituted the author's effort to break from German settings in favour of a more global conception of the Cold War, yet Berlin still retained its allure when it came to concluding the sequence. I then consider how a brief revisiting of early 1960s Berlin in le Carré's semi-autobiographical novel *A Perfect Spy* (1986) was expanded into a significant episode of the BBC's 1987 serialisation, which for the first time explored the city's interest value as a period setting. Finally, I trace the history of a long-delayed new BBC adaptation of *The Spy* in which le Carré was keenly involved over the last few years of his life, and how this even fed back into his prose writing, inspiring two new books in which he revisited the landscapes of Cold War Berlin.

2 "Not Interested in Anything to do with Berlin Wall": The BBC's Earliest Interest in John le Carré (1961–63)

"An interesting 'who-dun-it' with the background of modern Russian spies, but not of sufficient merit to make a dramatisation worth while." This was the verdict of television scriptwriter Michael Voysey on the merits of adapting le Carré's debut novel *Call for the Dead* (1961) for television in a report dated 8 August 1961 (WAC 1961). Set in London, the story followed the investigation of veteran spymaster George Smiley into the mysterious suicide of a civil servant, leading him to uncover the penetration of the UK Foreign Office by a ring of enemy agents. But Voysey had evidently not paid close attention, for le Carré's enemy spies were not Russian, but in fact agents of the German Democratic Republic (GDR). At a time when much spy fiction, such as Ian Fleming's early James Bond novels (prior to the introduction of SPECTRE in 1961), imagined a Cold War in which Britain was locked in conflict with Moscow, this was an unconventional move. But this was an early sign of le Carré's longstanding passion for German culture and the German language, and the "German soul" that many commentators have identified in his novels. Indeed, although le Carré had written the novel whilst in the employ of Britain's domestic Security Service (MI5), by the time it was published he had transferred to the Secret Intelligence Service (SIS, commonly known as MI6) and been posted to Germany, working under-cover as a diplomat in Bonn.

There is no evidence that le Carré's second novel, *A Murder of Quality* (1962) was considered for adaptation by the BBC at the time of publication, though his third novel would be a different matter. With Smiley relegated to a supporting role, *The Spy Who Came in from the Cold* centred on a new protagonist, Alec Leamas, who undertakes a staged defection to the GDR, ostensibly with the aim of planting misinformation that will discredit Hans-Dieter Mundt, a major Stasi officer. Le Carré's decision to focus on the GDR rather than the Soviet Union is thus carried forward from *Call for the Dead*, quite directly in the form of Mundt who had previously appeared as a member of the spy ring in the first novel. Here, however, a new advantage of setting a Cold War narrative in Germany becomes apparent: the representation of a literal Cold War frontier. Since he had completed writing *Call for the Dead*, the GDR had commenced construction of the Berlin Wall on 13 August 1961, and le Carré would later describe this as a major spur for the novel, recalling how "I watched the Wall's progress from barbed wire to breeze block; I watched the ramparts of the cold war going up on the still-warm ashes of the hot one" (Le Carré 2013).

The Wall bookends the novel, which opens with the last survivor of Leamas's East German network gunned down whilst trying to escape at Checkpoint Charlie, and concludes bleakly with Leamas himself and his girlfriend Liz Gold shot whilst trying to effect their own escape over the Wall. In its exploitation of the dramatic and symbolic potential of this Cold War frontier, *The Spy* was a trailblazer. As Toby Manning writes, "it both channelled and *made* history, helping to inscribe the Wall into the cultural imagination", influencing a wave of subsequent Berlin-set spy novels including Len Deighton's *Funeral in Berlin* and Adam Hall's *The Berlin Memorandum* (Manning 2018, 51). Given both its inspiration and influence, it is perhaps surprising how little of *The Spy* actually takes place in Berlin, beyond its memorable beginning and end; before Leamas's crossing into the East the novel is largely set in the UK and the Netherlands, whilst afterwards the setting is mostly unspecified locations deeper into the GDR. Nonetheless, part of the novel's acclaimed verisimilitude was flashback material exploring Leamas's more everyday intelligence work of running of the Berlin station.

By the time of *The Spy*'s UK publication in September 1963, the BBC television drama department was undergoing a shake-up, with new Head of Drama Sydney Newman aiming to produce more drama engaged with contemporary social realities. One outcome was *Story Parade*, a flagship anthology series of modern novel adaptations for the soon-to-be-launched second channel BBC2. One novel considered for adaptation was *The Spy*, with Story Editor Irene Shubik requesting a report on its potential. The report by Lorna Hemingway, dated 5 November 1963, was effusive. "The plot is full of suspense all the time," she wrote. "The characters are brilliantly drawn and the dialogue powerful and convincing ... Motivation is excellent throughout; there is no false sentiment ascribed to these men, they are entirely convincing." In the final analysis, "there would seem to be ample material for a seventy-five minute play". One curious feature of the surviving copy of this report is a handwritten comment stating, "not interested in anything to do with Berlin Wall", also dated 5 November (WAC 1961–80). (It appears next to a tick acknowledging Shubik's receipt of the report, suggesting that it might have been hers.) It is hard to account for this position, as the topic would remain extremely topical for the next few years and had not (yet) been exhaustively mined by fiction.

Nonetheless, a serious inquiry about acquiring the rights for *The Spy* did, in fact, follow, with Shubik sending a brief to the Copyright Department on 5 December and James Doran proposed to script the adaptation (WAC 1961–80). This proved unsuccessful, however, with Doran writing to Shubik on 30 December to say "I'm sorry 'The Spy Who Came In From The Cold' isn't available, but I'm not surprised" (WAC 1961–80). Doran does not state why he was not surprised, but presumably this was because, in the three months since its publication, *The Spy* had undergone a meteoric rise in the

British bestseller charts, becoming the surprise UK publishing phenomenon of 1963, a feat which would be replicated in the USA and more widely in early 1964. In fact, the screen rights were already unavailable even by the date of publication, with American film director Martin Ritt having bought the rights at manuscript stage.

What would the proposed television play of *The Spy* for *Story Parade* have been like? The key word is "play". British television was still only a few years on from the point where most drama was transmitted live, and productions were still largely recorded continuously in a studio using a multi-camera set-up. Lez Cooke describes how "the whole production schedule was organised so as to build up to 'the big night', with two or three weeks of rehearsals for the cast leading up to two days of camera rehearsals in the studio and then a final dress rehearsal in the studio on the afternoon before the evening ... recording" (Cooke 2015, 47). Notably, amidst a host of artistic merits listed in Hemingway's report on *The Spy*, she also highlights the practical advantage that "settings would be reasonable in number and mainly interior" (WAC 1961–80). Although some location inserts may have been incorporated, it is very unlikely that this would have entailed any filming in Berlin, or indeed anywhere outside of south-eastern England. Furthermore, given the archival practices of the time, it is likely that, even if the play had been produced, the tape would have been wiped and we would be unable to view it today.

With backing from Paramount Pictures, Ritt's film of *The Spy* was made with far higher production resources than a BBC television play, with location filming in Germany and the Netherlands. Yet with its long dialogue scenes, drab settings, claustrophobic interior spaces and stark monochrome cinematography, in some ways the film may not have been so different from a hypothetical BBC play adaptation, and indeed was likely shaped by Ritt's own background of directing in live American television drama. Still, one major location proved impractical for filming, perhaps inevitably considering the violent action required to take place there. The Berlin Wall featured at key dramatic moments was, in fact, a replica, constructed in a floodlit square in Dublin, whilst the then-undeveloped London Docklands provided the backdrop for sequences in East Berlin (Sisman 2015, 278). Subsequent spy films of the era would also employ "the liminal divide of the Wall" to serve "as the supreme symbolic setting for the East-West conflict" including the film adaptation of *Funeral in Berlin* (1966) which, unlike *The Spy*, featured filming at the real Wall (Burton 2018, 347). For le Carré's subsequent television adaptations, however, the artificial setting of Ritt's film would provide a more enduring template.

3 "We'd have Probably been Shot if we had as much as Turned a Camera on the Actual Wall": Bringing le Carré's Berlin to Television in *Dare I Weep, Dare I Mourn* (ITV, 1967)

When *Call for the Dead* was eventually adapted for screen, retitled *The Deadly Affair* (Sidney Lumet, 1967), it too was for cinematic release. Indeed, with his work now attracting attention from major Hollywood studios, le Carré's rapid rise to global prominence seems to have placed his novels out of the reach of television at this point. Le Carré himself was apparently sceptical about the medium, writing in a letter to his stepmother Jean Cornwell circa 15 October 1963 that Associated Television (ATV), one of the coalition of regional broadcasting companies that then made up Britain's commercial television service ITV, "wanted to do a Smiley serial with J le C writing it, but that I really couldn't do. Can you imagine it?" (le Carré 2023, 125). Le Carré's uncredited role providing minor rewrites on Ritt's *The Spy* instead spurred a keen interest in filmmaking. Having become successful enough as a writer to leave his job at SIS, le Carré would spend large portions of the late 1960s working on screenplay adaptations of his next two novels, *The Looking Glass War* (1965) and *A Small Town in Germany* (1968).

In fact, it was another ITV company that made the first le Carré production for television, when Rediffusion-London produced a standalone adaptation of le Carré's short story *Dare I Weep, Dare I Mourn*. Something of an oddity from an author who otherwise seldom wrote short stories during this period, *Dare I Weep* centres on Dieter Koorp, a grocer from Lübeck, who travels to the GDR to mourn the death of his domineering father, only to find that the old man is very much alive and determined to enlist his son in a mission to smuggle him over the frontier into the West. Although now largely forgotten, Rediffusion's adaptation was a prestigious and ground-breaking production, directed by Ted Kotcheff, a leading UK television director who had recently transferred to feature films with *Tiara Tahiti* (1962) and *Life at the Top* (1965). Unlike the studio-based television play described above, this was a pioneering effort to create a television *film*, shot on 35mm film with substantial location filming in and around Hamburg. Producer Anthony Perry described how "we managed to find an East German setting in a West German medieval town," the team even securing police permission to furnish the buildings with "East German posters, banners and political portraits" for filming purposes (Rediffusion Facts 1966a). The film was budgeted specifically for sale to the ABC network in America, which first transmitted it in colour as part of their *Stage 67* anthology series on 21 September 1966, with a black-and-white UK transmission following on ITV (which had not yet adapted to colour) on 28 September. In fact, both transmissions predated the publication of le Carré's original story in the *Saturday Evening Post* on 28 January 1967.

In hindsight, Perry suggested that "we paid an unreasonably large fee" for le Carré's slender tale (Perry 2006), and we might infer that Rediffusion were purchasing less the contents of le Carré's story than the prestige and connotations of his name. Certainly, Stanley Mann's script hugely expands le Carré's narrative, changing Koorp into a neurotic businessman called Otto Hoffmann (James Mason), and adding a new plot twist at the end. Indeed, the story seems to have been adjusted to better fit a popular image of le Carré's oeuvre, notably with the insertion of a Berlin Wall sequence, when Berlin had not even appeared in the original story. (Indeed, le Carré had similarly avoided reusing Berlin as a setting in *The Looking-Glass War* and *Small Town*, despite both novels featuring other significant German locations.) In the television version of *Dare I Weep*, Hoffmann is shown to work in a West Berlin office with a clear view of the Wall. In the opening sequence, whilst arranging for the transportation of his father's body by telephone, he is horrified to witness a botched attempt to climb over the Wall from East to West by a nameless young man, who is shot dead by East German police during the attempt whilst his waiting girlfriend on the Western side screams with terror. Again, however, there were the problems of how to enact such a sequence, and a research trip to Berlin left Perry with the impression "we'd have probably been shot if we had as much as turned a camera on the actual Wall" (Rediffusion Facts 1966a). Instead, the production team followed the same approach as Ritt on *The Spy* and constructed their own replica. Rediffusion's Senior Designer Fred Pusey, a veteran of Second World War camouflage operations, found an open space in the Paddington area of London, then being redeveloped, where the production could take advantage of "the differing backgrounds of half-pulled-down houses and railway lines – for East Berlin – and new flats – for West Berlin" (Rediffusion Facts 1966b). The 150-foot-long artificial Wall, made of a lightweight material, was topped with barbed wire made of nylon for reasons of safety.

Meanwhile, le Carré's initially promising involvement in filmmaking was turning sour. The eventual film of *The Looking-Glass War* (1970) disregarded le Carré's work on the screenplay entirely and was disowned by the author, whilst the projected film of *Small Town* never entered production at all (Sisman 2015, 328–29). It is perhaps no coincidence that this was the point when le Carré began taking a more serious interest in television as a vehicle for his work, although his first direct pitch for the medium was not an adaptation, but an original play. *The End of the Line* was a two-hander set almost entirely in the carriage of a train from Edinburgh to London, in which an atomic spy in a state of psychological disintegration encounters a mysterious clergyman who offers him a chance to confess. This was rejected by the BBC in July 1969, and was instead taken up by Thames Television, a new ITV company which had taken over Rediffusion's franchise, for their anthology series *Armchair Theatre* (broadcast 29 June 1970) (Oldham 2020, 314–17). Although the British Rail setting had no overt connection to Berlin, a German connection would later emerge when the play was remade in the German language for West German television under the title of *Endstation* (ARD, 23 January 1973). Although it was not uncommon for British television plays to enjoy foreign language remakes, it seems likely that this was in some way facilitated by le Carré's own German interests and connections.

Part of the problem of adapting le Carré's novels for television was that, since *The Spy*, they had grown considerably in both length and narrative scope. This is well-illustrated by the response to a 1974 proposal from Kenneth Ross to adapt le Carré's non-genre novel *The Naïve and Sentimental Lover* (1971) as a 90-minute BBC television play. In a letter to Ross's agent Douglas Rae, dated 13 March 1974, Graeme MacDonald, producer of the *Play for Today* anthology series, commented that the book was likely "outside our scale of operations" due to its "fairly epic scale" with locations in Paris and Switzerland, also suggesting that "too many of the good things about it would be lost in bringing it down to 90'" (WAC 1961–80). Thus, even this rare departure by le Carré from espionage was beyond the scope of the television play, for reasons equally applicable to his post-1963 spy novels. It was not until later in the 1970s that le Carré's work finally found a television form to accommodate both axes of expansion.

4 "An Espionage *Comédie humaine*": Le Carré's Global Cold War at the BBC

When le Carré's work finally came to the BBC, it would not be as a play but instead as seven-part serialised adaptation of his seventh novel, *Tinker Tailor Soldier Spy* (1974). *Tinker Tailor* had relaunched the Smiley series with a "whodunit" plot in which the spymaster works to uncover a high-level penetration agent within his own service. That this story initially ended up on television rather than the cinema arose from le Carré's discomfort with the film offers he received; as he later commented, "I was very leery, then, of the short form and I thought that *Tinker, Tailor* would work far better in long form" (Wootton 2002). That he had overcome his earlier scepticism towards "a Smiley serial" for television is perhaps indicative of how the multi-part serial or "miniseries" was now growing in prominence as the major form for prestige drama (eventually supplanting the single play), offering more potential to convey the complex, multi-stranded plot of *Tinker Tailor*.

After an earlier attempt at adapting the novel by London Weekend Television stalled, it was picked up by the BBC on the initiative of Jonathan Powell, producer of the BBC 2 classic serial strand. This was part of a drive to incorporate some contemporary literature alongside the established literary canon to keep the strand fresh, and featured Alec Guinness playing the role of Smiley for the first time. Stylistically too it was a ground-breaking production. Whilst most classic serials up to that point had been largely produced in the studio in a manner akin to the television play, *Tinker Tailor* (BBC 2, 1979) was filmed almost entirely on location with single camera in a style more akin to *Dare I Weep* (Oldham 2017b, 79–86). Certainly, Powell considered the practice of location filming to be integral for communicating the "connection between landscape and theme", noting that "all the locations are filmed pretty nearly in the places they are written about in the book" (interviewed by the author, 26 July 2012).

But this was not to be the point where Berlin finally appeared in a BBC le Carré adaptation, for this novel was in fact the point where le Carré decisively broke from the longstanding focus on Germany that had run across his 1960s novels. *Tinker Tailor* was designed as the start of a new sequence of novels reframing the Cold War as a stand-off between the UK and USSR, as epitomised by the introduction of the Soviet spymaster Karla as Smiley's longstanding nemesis. In parallel, by increasingly incorporating locations outside of Europe, le Carré opened "a new and expansive geographical vista on what by then had come to represent a global Cold War" (McGarr 2023, 275). As the author himself later recalled, alluding to the influence of Honoré de Balzac on his work during this period, "I had originally intended to do an espionage *Comédie humaine* of the Smiley-Karla stand off, and take it all over the world. Make it a kind of fool's guide to the Cold War" (quoted in Wootton 2002). Thus, whilst the core mole-hunt narrative of *Tinker Tailor* takes place in England, a sense of a wider narrative scope is suggested by flashback sequences set in locations around the globe.

Yet in practice these often seemed to be places offering similar narrative possibilities to Germany in le Carré's 1960s novels. One sequence, presented in flashback in the novel but relocated to the start of Part One of the adaptation to seize audience attention, sees the agent Jim Prideaux cross into Czechoslovakia to meet a potential defector, only to fall into a trap. Here Czechoslovakia rather than Germany provides another iteration of what Douglas McNaughton terms "the Iron Curtain discursive unconscious" of British popular culture which "revolves around an iconographic shorthand of checkpoints, blockhouses, watchtowers, Eastern European cars, pine forests and urban wastelands; liminal boundary sites reflecting the Cold War's border crossings and moral ambiguities" (McNaughton 2018, 383–4). Drawing on interviews with key personnel, McNaughton describes how production designer Austen Spriggs travelled to Czechoslovakia to take reference photographs and was briefly arrested, although later a team including cameraman Tony Pierce-Roberts were able to shoot some background plates in the real location. Nonetheless, most of the sequence, including everything featuring actor Ian Bannen (Prideaux), was shot in similar-looking locations in Scotland to circumvent these logistical problems.

In another flashback sequence, agent Ricki Tarr discovers the mole's existence through his affair with a Soviet diplomat's wife in Hong Kong, another location offering familiar dramatic possibilities. As Manning writes, "during the Cold War, Hong Kong's role in Asia resembled that of West Berlin in Europe: an isolated Western island in a vast Eastern sea, a capitalist showroom in an anti-capitalist 'desert' and both a Cold-War buffer and a Cold-War provocation" (Manning 2018, 133). Indeed, le Carré found this location sufficiently interesting to make it the central setting of the second novel in the Smiley-Karla sequence, *The Honourable Schoolboy* (1977). For the production resources of the BBC adapting *Tinker Tailor* in 1978, however, attempting to represent Hong Kong was considered impractical, and the Ricki Tarr (Hywel Bennett) flashback sequence was transplanted to Lisbon where overseas filming took place. Finally, another flashback shows the younger Smiley's brief encounter with Karla in a prison cell in Delhi in the 1950s. Originally planned for the Lisbon shoot, this was ultimately filmed on a set in Ealing Studios, London.[1]

Meanwhile, le Carré had decided to conclude the Smiley-Karla sequence, later declaring that "I began to become intensely bored with this stand-off. The Cold War was over long before it was officially declared dead" (Wootton 2002). Accordingly, his next novel, *Smiley's People* (1979), written during the filming of *Tinker Tailor*, was the final entry in what was now a trilogy. For this, le Carré returned to the spaces of his 1960s novels, with Smiley investigating Karla's Achilles heel through a range of northern European settings. With the televised *Tinker Tailor* a critical and popular success, the BBC elected to produce a sequel. *The Honourable Schoolboy* was dismissed due to the impracticality of representing its east Asian locations, and so the BBC skipped straight to *Smi-*

1 A letter from Jonathan Powell to David Cornwell (le Carré's real name) dated 13 September 1978 outlines these planned filming locations (WAC 1977–82a).

ley's People, with Powell again producing and le Carré himself rewriting problematic scripts by John Hopkins (Sisman 2015, 423). One notable change is that the contents of Smiley's blackmail letter to Karla, withheld from the reader in the novel, is explicitly conveyed through a voice-over by Guinness, with a memorable sign-off, situating both Smiley and Karla in the liminal space for which the Berlin Wall had become such a potent physical metaphor: "You have become a citizen of no man's land – I send you my greetings."

This was another generously resourced production, and with the novel's main overseas settings – France, Switzerland and West Germany – proving generally more accessible to the BBC than Czechoslovakia, India and Hong Kong, there was far less need for artistic licence over locations this time. There was, however, inevitably one exception, when a request to film on the Oberbaum Bridge was declined by the GDR authorities. After an extensive search, Lady Bay Bridge in Nottingham, England was deemed a credible enough substitute. "With German signs on the local office blocks and checkpoints specially built," said Powell, "it looks amazingly real" (Billington 1981, 29).

5 "A Garrison of Spies": Reconstructing Early 1960s Berlin in *A Perfect Spy* (BBC 2, 1987)

Le Carré's purported boredom with the Cold War would, in fact, prove short-lived. Whilst his next novel, *The Little Drummer Girl* (1983), did indeed break with this framework to focus on the Arab-Israeli conflict, by the mid-1980s he was back in more familiar terrain, albeit now without the expansive "espionage *Comédie humaine*" serialisation. *A Perfect Spy* (1986) emerged from le Carré's desire to write a semi-autobiographical novel in which he would imagine the circumstances which could have led someone from his background to become a long-term penetration agent and traitor. Accordingly, Magnus Pym, le Carré's alter ego in the novel, is shaped by similar encounters with the secret world as those of the author in the 1950s and early 1960s, making this inevitably another Cold War novel, albeit one that delved far more extensively into the conflict's history than any previous le Carré works.

Tracing Pym's life and career across Europe and America from the 1930s to the 1980s, the novel has a particularly expansive scope. Berlin, home to "a garrison of spies", features briefly when Pym is posted there by "the Firm" (a fictionalised SIS) to develop his career as an intelligence officer in the early 1960s, although his employers are unaware that Pym has now fully committed to a lifetime of collaboration with Axel, his friend and controller in Czech intelligence. This sequence sees le Carré revisiting not only the setting but also the era of *The Spy*, yet the most dramatic images of Wall-crossings and shootings are absent in favour of a more "everyday" Berlin spying, le Carré painting the city as "a playground for every alchemist, miracle-worker and rat-piper that ever took up the cloak" (le Carré 1987, 563). The most dramatic incident here comes when Pym, living in an East Berlin flat under diplomatic cover, is visited by two police officers in the middle of the night and escorted to a police station. Pym (and the reader) is briefly wrongfooted into thinking that his espionage activities been exposed, before it is revealed that the police have in fact arrested his disreputable father Rick Pym following one of his dubious financial schemes. Rick was closely based on le Carré's own conman father Ronnie Cornwell, with this sequence inspired by real incidents in which the author had to bail his father from prison in Austria and Switzerland (Sisman 2015, 309, 323).

A Perfect Spy (BBC 2, 1987) would be the third BBC le Carré adaptation, and the last before a long hiatus. Arthur Hopcraft, who had previously adapted *Tinker Tailor*, returned to script the new production, and one feature that proved divisive was his decision to radically restructure the novel's complex intercutting of past and present into a more linear, chronological telling of Pym's (Peter Egan) life story (Oldham, 2017a, 290). Hopcraft described how, in structuring the re-ordered material for serialisation, "the story has to be told in episodes, and you have to balance it so that each episode carries the story forward, with a series of minor climaxes leading up to the final one" (Caudwell 1988, 36). The brief Berlin sequence from the novel was developed into the climactic final third of Part Four, encompassing Pym's courting of fellow service employee Mary (Jane Booker) to advance his career at the urging of Axel (Rüdiger Weigang). For the first time in a le Carré adaptation, Berlin was to be a historical setting (the date specified as 1962 in the script), requiring some element of period dressing.

Powell would later praise Hopcraft for his ability to hone le Carré's material "down to diamond-like clarity" (Atkin et al. 2004), and in contrast to the novel Hopcraft's adaptation has a far more precise sense of place. His script for Part Four clearly specifies a range of locations in the city by name.[2] Some of these are in the West, such as a cafe terrace on Kurfürstendamm where Pym meets his superior Jack Brotherhood (Alan Howard), or a montage sequence in which a Czech photographer tries to capture images of Mary in Tiergarten,

2 The copy of this script in Hopcraft's archive is titled "Episode Three" due to the abandonment of an earlier plan to transmit the first two hours as a double-length special (Hopcraft 1985–6).

Charlottenburg and Kreuzberg. Others are in the East, including Pym's apartment, the police headquarters where Rick is detained, and the Soviet War Memorial where Pym discusses his plans for Mary with Brotherhood as the episode concludes (Hopcraft 1985–86).

Whether Hopcraft thought the production likely to film in these locations is unclear. However, when a contemporaneous report in the *New York Times* described how "apart from the American scenes, the film was shot entirely on location, using 216 different locations in England, Austria, Switzerland and Corfu", one name was again conspicuously missing (Caudwell 1988, 36). Indeed, even the potentially more accessible West Berlin locations were not used, with the proposed montage centring on Mary not appearing in the completed episode. The lack of filming in Berlin, of course, made little difference to largely interior scenes in Pym's apartment or the police station, although one notable change from script-to-screen was the moving of Pym and Brotherhood's final conversation from the Soviet War Memorial to an ordinary street. Behind them, held in a lingering shot before the final fade-to-black, is the Berlin Wall, with the prominently displayed graffiti "13000 Frauen von ihren Männern getrennt! Wie lange noch?" ("13,000 women separated from their men! For how much longer?"). In an example of the serial's attention to detail, this is a recreation of some authentic graffiti which had been displayed on the real Wall in 1962, as captured by photojournalist Erich Andres on 1 March.

By the time of *A Perfect Spy*'s transmission, it would not take much longer for the question of Berlin's separation to be resolved, with the Berlin Wall finally falling on 9 November 1989. When this occurred, le Carré had already begun writing another book which looked back over the history of the Cold War, albeit in a far looser form. *The Secret Pilgrim* (1990) was a collection of interlinked short stories in which, inspired by an informal dinner talk delivered by Smiley, the protagonist Ned reminiscences on his own long career in Cold War intelligence. Writing most of the book in early 1990, Le Carré was able to use the present-day framing narrative to offer a reflective coda on the end of this period in world history. Berlin's only appearance in the book, however, is once again confined to the "golden age" of the 1960s, when Ned remembers how his one-time best friend suffered catastrophe through accidentally losing a crib sheet with the names and contact procedures for his network of agents whilst in East Berlin. With this book completed, le Carré thereafter proceeded to a new phase of his career, turning emphatically away from the Cold War to new sites of global intrigue. It would not be until the late 2010s that le Carré returned to his formative ground of Cold War Berlin, and this would, in fact, be inspired by a new interest in his work from the BBC.

6 "The Past Coming Back to Accuse the Present": Revisiting Cold War Berlin in le Carré's Final Projects (2016–20)

In 2016 le Carré made a high-profile return to the BBC with a six-part adaptation of his 1993 novel about the international arms trade, *The Night Manager* (BBC 1, 2016). Unlike previous adaptations, this was not an in-house production, the leading role instead taken by The Ink Factory, an independent production company established by le Carré's sons Stephen and Simon Cornwell (Oldham 2017a, 297–8). Following the critical and popular success of this serial, the company announced that its follow-up would be a new six-part television adaptation of a far better-known novel, *The Spy Who Came in from the Cold*, again for transmission by the BBC. And whilst *The Night Manager* had been updated from its original early 1990s setting to the 2010s, there was no question that this classic Cold War text would be removed from its early 1960s period. Not only would Berlin be a period setting again, but filming at the Wall would now be doubly impossible due to its demolition 27 years earlier. As with *The Night Manager*, le Carré would serve as Executive Producer (formalising his uncredited advisory role on earlier adaptations) whilst initial reports named Simon Beaufoy as screenwriter (Schwindt 2016).

Over the decades, the six or seven-part serial had proven an effective form for the complex narratives of *Tinker Tailor*, *Smiley's People*, *A Perfect Spy* and now *The Night Manager*. But *The Spy* was, in some ways, a strange choice for this treatment, as a far tighter and slenderer novel than those that followed; indeed, back in 1963 Hemingway had considered it ideal source material for a 75-minute play. And so, the team behind the new adaptation found the original novel insufficient in scope and complexity to support their intended six episodes. Le Carré himself was enlisted to help solve the problem and, as the *Sydney Morning Herald* reported, "to expand the narrative he started building a new superstructure around it: background to the main characters, children and parents, extra facets to their secret lives" (Miller 2017). And in addition to the original 1960s setting, the expanded story would include material set in the present day, le Carré describing how "I went on developing the notion of the past coming back to accuse the present in these people" (Miller 2017). The process of developing this idea launched an obsession which would haunt the last few years of his life and career.

For the immediate adaptation of *The Spy*, however, this introduced a new problem of how to structure the past and present timeframes in relation to each other. Unable to immediately resolve this, The Ink Factory changed course, instead prioritising a new adaptation, *The Little Drummer Girl* (BBC 1, 2018). Le Carré, however, elected to use the superstructure as the basis for a new novel, which he described in a letter to writer Al Alvarez and his wife Anne on 16 September 2016 as "my Ur-novel, a kind of Rosenkranz & Guildenstern version of the 'Spy Who … '" (le Carré 2023, 567). To add authentic texture to his new depiction of early 1960s Berlin, le Carré undertook research that would have been impossible at the time he originally wrote *The Spy*, visiting the former Stasi headquarters in Berlin and investigating old files, including his own. Indeed, the BBC had been a catalyst for this as, whilst preparing an ultimately unmade television documentary on the book, the corporation had applied for le Carré's file. This turned out to be heavily redacted; as he wrote in a letter to fellow novelist Alan Judd on 18 May 2019, "it had four German press cuttings in it, & nothing else" (le Carré 2023, 589). However, le Carré took the opportunity to look up his father's file and found that Ronnie Cornwell had indeed been active in Cold War Berlin, possibly even attempting to con the Stasi, making the Berlin episode of *A Perfect Spy* apparently closer to the truth than he could have known when he first wrote it (Miller 2017). The resulting new novel, *A Legacy of Spies* (2017), re-examines events depicted in *The Spy* from different perspectives, adding new backstory, showing the previously elided role of Smiley, and depicting his protégé Peter Guillam coming under investigation in the present day for his part in Leamas's demise, providing an "oblique reappraisal of the Cold War past as both a diametrical contrast to and formative matrix of the present era" (Snyder 2020, 17). But whilst early 1960s Berlin dominates once again, the post-1989 Berlin makes a rare appearance, in a brief flashback where Guillam finally visits Leamas's grave after the fall of the Wall.

As the first book to feature Smiley in 27 years, the 2017 publication of *Legacy* attracted considerable attention, but this did not displace the new adaptation of *The Spy*. In a letter to John and Mary James of the Aldeburgh Literary Festival on 25 May 2018, le Carré mentioned an impending visit to the set of *The Little Drummer Girl* in Prague where he would "discuss earnestly the adaptation of 'Spy Who … ' plus 'Legacy of Spies in a joined-up TV series for the Beeb", then projected to film the following winter (although ultimately this did not go ahead) (le Carré 2023, 589). It seems that at some stage le Carré assumed scriptwriting duties himself, as hinted in an email to Jonny Geller on 8 June 2020, in which he noted that "the six hours of SPY/LEGACY screenplay, however imperfect they turned out to be, took their toll" (le Carré 2023, 621). As the octogenarian le Carré had not scripted any of his adaptations since *The Tailor of Panama* (2001), this indicates how personal the project of revisiting his breakthrough novel had become, although still the adaptation process was proving problematic.

By the time of his email to Geller, le Carré was writing yet another Smiley book in COVID lockdown, in a further example of the curiously generative effect of the long-delayed television adaptation of *The Spy*. This was to be another series of linked short stories like *The Secret Pilgrim*, provisionally entitled *The George Smiley Years*. Once again, le Carré had returned to the early 1960s, trying to write a story set in Trieste or Vienna in 1961, but it was the moment at the other end of the Wall's lifespan that now proved more compelling. In a letter to the playwright Tom Stoppard on 1 July 2020, le Carré described being absorbed by a scene:

> Set in 1989, with the Wall just down, when Smiley finally decides he is ready to meet his old nemesis, Karla, settled under another name with his mentally sick daughter in a village not far from yours. What vision, if any, do they now have in common? Who will be the leading voice in the (theoretically) post-ideology world, what is do-able, what is pie in the sky?

But for all the attempt to recapture the utopian moment of 1989, this is counterpointed by le Carré's gloom about the world that had latterly emerged from the triumph of capitalism, particularly the recent developments of Trumpism and Brexit. 1989 now seemed a rare moment "when the world could have been usefully re-ordered" but was squandered "when no voice, no leader, & no real inclination towards a world united manifested itself" (le Carré 2023, 622).

The proposed adaptation of *The Spy* (combined with *Legacy*) would eventually evolve into the first season of the ongoing television series *Legacy of Spies* (2027-). Long before this commenced filming, however, its long and troubled development seems to have had a profound impact on the novel's original author, inspiring new books both complete (*Legacy*) and incomplete (*The George Smiley Years*). This has encompassed the revisiting of Berlin at crucial historical moments, with a new perspective on the early years of the Wall which had inspired *The Spy*, and a new melancholic engagement with the fall of the Wall as a moment of lost promise for remaking the world.

7 Conclusion

In a 1993 interview le Carré acknowledged the significance of Berlin to his output to date, even though its appearances in his novels had often been irregular and fleeting. Defending himself against criticism for continuing to write genre fiction about espionage, he remarked that "I saw the [Berlin]

Wall go up when I was 30 and saw it come down when I was 60", and in the years in between "spying was the genre of the cold war" (Coleman 1993, 25). This significance is evident in the le Carré adaptations broadcast on the BBC, as well as the secret history of unmade projects, and how they sometimes even fed back to influence le Carré's writing. The BBC's first serious interest in bringing le Carré's work to television came with a failed attempt to adapt his foundational Berlin tale *The Spy* as a television play in 1963. When his work was first successfully adapted for television with *Dare I Weep* three years later, the source material was heavily amended to feature the city and the Wall, indicating how integral these elements had become to his authorial profile at this time. However, despite pioneering a style of production based around substantial overseas location filming, later taken up by the BBC adaptations, the Rediffusion team proved unable to film at the real Wall, beginning a cycle of doubles and replicas that ran across subsequent productions.

In the subsequent cycle of BBC classic serial adaptations of le Carré, Berlin's appearances tended to be fleeting, with the source novels attempting to expand the scope of le Carré's spying world to the broader canvas of a global Cold War, although there were memorable evocations of the city for Karla's final defection at the end of *Smiley's People*, and a more developed period re-enactment of the "classic" early 1960s Berlin for *A Perfect Spy*. And even in recent years, long after the fall of the Wall, a long-delayed project to produce a new serialised adaptation of *The Spy* for the BBC would prove profoundly influential on le Carré, motivating him to revisit the city in both the crisis years of the early 1960s and also, for the first time, to reflect on the city as a foundational site for the reconstruction of the post-Cold War world, whose utopian possibilities seemed ever more distant and intangible.

References

Atkin, Ronald, Peter Preston and David Lacey. 2004. "Arthur Hopcraft". *Guardian*. 26 November.

Billington, Michael. 1981. "Alec Guinness does a Second Tour of Duty as le Carré's Spy." *New York Times* 20 December. https://www.nytimes.com/1981/12/20/movies/alec-guinness-does-a-second-tour-of-duty-as-lecarre-s-spy.html Accessed 31 December 2024.

Burton, Alan. 2018. "'Jumping on the Bondwagon': The Spy Cycle in British Cinema in the 1960s". *Journal of British Cinema and Television* 15.3: 328–56.

Caudwell, Sarah. 1988. "One of le Carré's Spies is Missing." *New York Times* 9 October https://www.nytimes.com/1988/10/09/arts/the-curtains-part-on-murder-most-british-one-of-le-carres-spies-is.html Accessed 31 December 2024.

Coleman, Terry. 1993. "Carré on Writing." *Guardian.* 17 July.

Cooke Lez. 2015. *British Television Drama: A History.* 2nd ed. London: BFI/Palgrave.

Goodman, Sam. 2016. *British Spy Fiction and the End of Empire.* New York and London: Routledge.

Hopcraft, Arthur. 1985–86. *A Perfect Spy* (10 December 1985 – 23 June 1986). 1/20/ii Script. AHP120, Arthur Hopcraft Papers, University of Salford Archives and Special Collections, Salford, UK.

Le Carré, John. 2013. "I was a Secret Even to Myself". *Guardian.* 12 April.

Le Carré, John. 1987 [1986]. *A Perfect Spy.* London: Coronet.

Le Carré, John, with Tim Cornwell (ed.). 2023. *A Private Spy: The Letters of John le Carré.* London: Penguin.

McGarr, Paul M. 2023. "The Neo-Imperialism of Decolonisation: John le Carré and Cold War India." *Intelligence and National Security* 38.2: 271–84.

McNaughton, Douglas. 2018. "Cold War Spaces: *Tinker Tailor Soldier Spy* in Television and Cinema." *Journal of British Cinema and Television* 15.3: 375–95

Manning, Toby. 2018. *John le Carré and the Cold War.* London: Bloomsbury.

Miller, Nick. 2017. "John le Carré: Why I brought back Guillam, Smiley and the Cold War." *Sydney Morning Herald.* 12 September.

Oldham, Joseph. 2017a. "From Reverential to 'Radical' Adaptation: Reframing John le Carré as 'Quality' Television Brand from *A Perfect Spy* (BBC 2, 1987) to *The Night Manager* (BBC 1, 2016)". *Adaptation* 10.3: 285–304.

Oldham, Joseph. 2017b. *Paranoid Visions: Spies, Conspiracies and the Secret State in British Television Drama.* Manchester: Manchester University Press.

Oldham, Joseph. 2020. "'Don't Let the Side Down, Old Boy': Interrogating the Traitor in the 'Radical' Television Dramas of John le Carré and Dennis Potter". *Cold War History* 20.3: 311–27.

Perry, Anthony. 2006. "An Interesting Film of the Cold War Era." IMDb. https://www.imdb.com/review/rw1311879/?ref_=tt_urv (Accessed 31 December 2024)

Rediffusion Facts. 1966a. Producing "Dare I Weep, Dare I Mourn" (press release).

Rediffusion Facts. 1966b. Building the Berlin Wall in London (press release).

Schwindt, Oriana. 2016. "John le Carre's 'The Spy Who Came in from the Cold' to be Adapted for TV by Paramount TV, The Ink Factory." *Variety.* 20 July. https://variety.com/2016/tv/news/john-le-carre-the-spy-who-came-in-from-the-cold-paramount-tv-the-ink-factory-the-night-manager-amc-1201818497/ Accessed 31 December 2024.

Sisman, Adam. 2015. *John Le Carré: The Biography.* London: Bloomsbury.

Snyder, Robert Lance. 2020. "Secret Cold Warriors: John le Carré's *A Legacy of Spies*". *Orbis Litterarum* 75.1: 15–23.

Wootton, Adrian. 2002. 'John le Carré at the NFT'. *Guardian*. 5 October.

WAC. 1961–80. Writer's File: John le Carré. T48/368/1. BBC Written Archives Centre, Caversham, UK.

WAC. 1977–82a. *Tinker Tailor Soldier Spy* Producer's File T65/38/1. BBC Written Archives Centre, Caversham, UK.

PART 3

Since 1989

∴

CHAPTER 15

Traces of the Berlin Wall in the Radio Archive: Reportage, Resistance and Retrospectives

Kate Lacey

1 Introduction

Many histories of the BBC's relationship to the Berlin Wall could be told, and no single essay could encompass them all. Such is the significance of the Wall to Cold War history and its after effects, and so powerful is its place in the cultural imaginary, that to single out any one aspect or to focus on any one period would leave too much unsaid. Similarly, even with a focus just on radio, the BBC is a singular institution in its complexity – a national public service broadcaster with global reach, enjoined to inform, educate and entertain via multiple platforms and modes of engagement, and constantly navigating its relationship to government alongside its claims to independence and objectivity. In an attempt, then, to survey some of the manifold connections that can be traced between the BBC and the Berlin Wall over the last 60 years, this chapter offers four vignettes to evoke the Corporation's work in monitoring international broadcasts, making programmes for different publics, reporting the present and documenting the past.

Following the life story of the Wall, the chapter begins with radio reports of the Wall's sudden construction in August 1961, moves on to radio's relationship to listeners in a divided city at the height of the Cold War, and then considers the implications for institutional policy at the World Service with the collapse of the Wall in 1989. Finally, the chapter surveys reconstructions of the Berlin Wall in anniversary and other retrospective radio programming. Each vignette is tied to a specific archive as a way to offer different glimpses of the complex and dynamic roles that the BBC has played in relation to reporting, reaching over and remembering the Berlin Wall. Together, they construct a mosaic made up of the interplay of institutional and diplomatic politics, the personalities and practices of programme-makers, the construction of schedules and soundscapes, questions of representation and identity, and the experiences of the listening publics. Key to much of it is the understanding that disembodied radio voices could carry across the solid concrete wall that segregated the city. The selections are framed by my perspective as a

 | HTTPS://DOI.ORG/10.1515/9783111302508-015

radio historian and media theorist but are also coloured by my own relationship to this history as a former resident of Berlin in the years before and after the Wall came down.

The first vignette takes us back to August 1961 and the building of the Berlin Wall.

2 Building the Berlin Wall

By August 1961, the "Berlin Question" was reaching another major crisis point. The city was located deep within the territory of the communist German Democratic Republic but West Berlin, still formally under Allied supervision, had to all intents and purposes become part of the Federal Republic. Inevitably, it become a city freighted with symbolism on either side in the icy tensions of the Cold War. Nevertheless, despite the border between the two Germanies having been closed since 1952, the border between East and West Berlin, while guarded, remained open. This allowed Berliners to commute between the different sectors of the city with relative ease, but temporary exit visas also afforded citizens of the GDR the opportunity to defect to the West, for reasons personal, political or economic. It was an opportunity they were taking up in their tens of thousands by the summer of 1961 in the so-called *Republikflucht* (Major 2002). To halt this haemorrhaging of the population (while publicly claiming it was a security measure against Western infiltration), the border around West Berlin was closed without warning in the early hours of 13 August, a ring of barbed wire and barricades ahead of the more permanent construction of the "anti-fascist protection barrier", better known as the Berlin Wall (Wilke 2014; Stiftung, n.d.).

Of course, the BBC covered the story at the time, as did every other news organisation as a major international crisis unfolded (BBC Archive 2024). But it is not the BBC's own coverage of events that is the focus here, but rather the insights that can be gained by exploring the archive of the BBC Monitoring Service.

BBC Monitoring had been set up during the Second World War to monitor, transcribe and translate international radio broadcasts for feeding real-time information into the gathering of foreign intelligence for the government and for the BBC's own journalism (Webb 2023). Such was its value that its operations continued throughout the Cold War and beyond, albeit its connections with the intelligence services have not been without controversy over the years. The service, originally funded directly by government, remains a major multimedia provider of open source news and information to a range of clients as part of the BBC World Service Group, funded through the license fee and subscriptions since 2013 (Bardgett et al. 2019; BBC Monitoring 2024).

In 2015, I was invited to participate in a project, led by Suzanne Bardgett of the Imperial War Museum, to test the interdisciplinary research possibilities of the BBC Monitoring Service Collection, then stored by the Museum in a former RAF building at Duxford Airfield (IWM 2015). Though the historical daily summaries had long been available to researchers via the BBC Written Archives at Caversham, the treasure trove of some 15 million pages of verbatim transcripts, in English, of programmes from all over the world, was at the time little used. The "Listening to the World" project invited scholars from a range of disciplines to explore the collection for a series of five themed workshops, including one on the Cold War, to help make the case for opening up the archive. The archive has since been moved to Caversham and the daily summaries up to 2001 made available as a digital resource (Readex 2024).

My foray into the archive was to examine transcripts of broadcasts around the sudden closure of the German-German border in Berlin by the East German authorities on 13 August, 1961 (Lacey 2015). The disruptions to planned programming are well documented (DRA n.d.), though recordings of the day's coverage are incomplete. But the verbatim BBC Monitoring transcripts, simultaneously translated, offer English speakers the chance to access the coverage from many different countries, regardless of other language skills. Reading through the reports on East and West German radio, the differences in both style and ideology between the two sides come as no great surprise, but there is something nevertheless revealing about "hearing", albeit at one remove, the first draft of history. More even than daily press reports, they give a direct sense of the events developing by the hour – urgent, undetermined, and unsettling.

Throughout the summer of 1961, West German radio bulletins had been dominated by stories of East Germans fleeing the privations of communism across the Berlin border to the liberty of the prosperous West. The propaganda value of featuring high-status individuals, such as scientists and physicians, abandoning their posts in the East and seeking refuge in the Marienfelde emergency reception camp, was not lost on the broadcasters in the summer of 1961. (Lacey 2015, 5). East German radio reporting, meanwhile, was all about the bellicose West, its militarisation, its revanchism, its espionage, its refusal to work towards a German peace treaty, its role as inheritor of the fascist past. It too carried daily reports of citizens leaving for the West, but not of their own volition. A report on 2 August spoke of "dozens of slave trade HQs" run by the American secret service using "devilish means" (Lacey 2015, 7). In an interview the following day, President Walter Ulbricht described them as victims of the

West's "psychological warfare and sabotage", "human trafficking", "blackmail, coercion and forcible abduction" (Lacey 2015, 6). Despite growing tensions surrounding the exodus of East German citizens, the transcripts also show Ulbricht in early August repeatedly rebroadcasting his famous June statement to the press that, "No-one has the intention to build a Wall".

That all changed in the early hours of 13 August. From 4 a.m., and throughout the day, the East German station, the Berliner Rundfunk, carried the "Declaration of the Warsaw Pact States" announcing the need for "protective measures at the borders" in response to the failure of the Western powers to respond to the "peaceful initiatives" of the GDR and in order to "restore calm". They also carried information about the new travel restrictions in the city, interspersed with music to instil both calm and national pride (DRA n.d.). In the evening, as the BBC Monitoring transcripts show, political commentaries conveyed the action as a decisive and triumphant move against an enemy that had been both threatening and complacent. Hermann Ley, the First Chairman of the State Radio Committee, took to the airwaves to describe how, "shortly after midnight a tight cordon was thrown around the head-hunters' web in West Berlin [...] while the officers of the West Berlin occupation troops slept off their Saturday evening hangover... " (Lacey 2015, 8). The following day, more colourful metaphors followed, with the action being said to have "localised the tumour" and "closed the ratholes" used by the "bitter enemies of our Worker-Peasant regime" (Lacey 2015, 9).

Meanwhile in the West, the radio schedules on 13 August were given over to providing more on-the-spot reporting, beginning with a mid-morning newsflash listing how positions had been taken up at various points along the sector boundaries by double squads of the People's Police, units of the Soviet army erecting tents, soldiers of the People's Army with assault kits, gasmasks and bayonets fixed, while five tanks were reported at the Neukölln boundary. Reports describe holes being dug at the border "according to travellers", barbed wire blocking S-Bahn routes "according to railwaymen", and a passer-by reporting to police that tanks had been drawn up on the Alexanderplatz (Lacey 2015, 9). The tumbling series of eyewitness accounts only heightens the sense of crisis. There were also reports of violence that contrast directly with the description of calm propounded in the East Berlin commentaries. For example, there was a report at 15:45 that East Berlin frontier guards had used tear gas and smoke bombs against three hundred young West Berliners who had advanced to the barbed wire, and another where a policeman had reportedly bayonetted a West Berliner in the knee. And there continued to be stories of individual escapes, for example, a refugee swimming across the Teltow canal from the Soviet side to West Berlin, "carrying his 3 year old child on his back" (Lacey 2015, 10). The formal response by Willy Brandt, then Mayor of West Berlin, declaring the action in breach of international law and insisting on the right of self-determination, was carried in the evening news bulletins.

The BBC Monitoring reports would have provided the British government and its allies with valuable information to complement its secret intelligence (Omand 2015), and would have been a ready source of information for the BBC's journalists in reporting a volatile situation as it developed over the weeks and months. For historians and communications scholars, the reports – and especially the transcripts on which they were based – have bequeathed a way to explore the radio archive to reconstruct a sense of history being made in the present tense and, by extension, for a way of connecting geo-political history to everyday experience. For example, the struggle to find a consistent vocabulary for what was happening is one thing that the archives reveal, as the temporary crisis ossified into a new everyday reality and the language of barbed wire, barricades, sector boundaries and zonal frontiers gradually concretised, literally and symbolically, into the Berlin Wall. Although the transcripts rarely comment on the style or sound of the content they record (save for remarking on poor reception), and though it must be remembered that the output was selected and transcribed for specific purposes, in the absence of recordings they can nevertheless provide a vivid sense of the battle for hearts and minds and ears that was being fought in the airwaves above Berlin.

The BBC Monitoring service was hardly alone in tuning in to the multiple radio stations competing for the attention of Berliners. The listening public on either side of the divided city could and did continue to listen in to radio from both sides. Indeed, the frequencies were full of choice, including not just the German stations, but stations for the Allied forces in the Allied sectors and a whole array of international broadcasters, among them the BBC. Ulbricht famously complained that the aerials pointing to the West meant "the class enemy is sitting on the roof" (Marks 1983, 50). Jamming was hardly a sustainable option in such a confined and politically sensitive space. Indeed, so physically close were the opposing sides that it was not unknown for stations to set up loudspeakers at points along the Wall to "broadcast" directly to the other side (Nicholson 2014, 85–8). Nevertheless, there were plentiful attempts to cause interference (Classen 2014) and even a campaign to get members of the FDJ (Freie Deutsche Jugend), the youth organisation, to turn radio and television antennae physically "in the direction of Socialism" (Ross 2004, 40).

On the day the border was closed, BBC Monitoring transcribed the "commentary of the day" on East German radio which had fulminated on the influence of Western radio on young people gathering in anger at the closure of the Brandenburg Gate. The speaker was Manfred Klein, who was to become news editor-in-chief from 1970 to 1989, and served briefly as the very last Director of East German radio after the Wall fell (Müller 1995, 2317). In this piece to microphone, it is possible to discern how he seems to be addressing his ire and his warnings directly to the audience in the West, at the same time as celebrating the regime's decisive action to his listeners in the East:

> Some people, incited by RIAS [Radio in the American Sector] and the so-called 'Free Berlin' broadcasting station, spy and agents' organisations, indulged in provocative hooliganism on the West Berlin side. Now, heavy-armoured troop-carriers, police and factory fighting squads have been posted on our side. The Gate is closed. There is no shilly-shallying. The barkers have only themselves to blame. He who challenges the Worker-Peasant regime should beware. There will be discussions with provocateurs and there will certainly be no long discussions at the frontier. (Lacey 2015, 12–13)

Twenty years later, in an article in *The Listener* Malcolm Brown (1981), producer of a BBC1 documentary to mark the anniversary called *Checkpoint Berlin*, described someone who had perhaps been in the very crowd described by Manfred Klein that night. Wolfgang Wilde, by 1981 a lawyer in West Berlin, as an 18 year-old listening to breakfast radio on the morning of 13 August 1961, had heard that "something dramatic" was afoot. Deciding to take a look for himself, he joined a crowd of around two thousand at the Brandenburg Gate. The gathering was apparently peaceful until it became clear that the Western forces that had also gathered there were keeping the West Berliners away, rather than intervening to stop the barrier being constructed before their eyes. Wilde said the crowd then became "emotionally charged" and speculated that had "one determined man" taken the lead, the crowd would have pulled down the Wall themselves and perhaps the course of history "might have been different". It is a recollection of a single man from a walled-in city, perhaps a wistful and wishful account of a personal and historical path not taken, but it also serves here as a small reminder of how radio did not just report the events, nor simply have an impact as propaganda, but that it had its own part to play in listeners' lives and the part they played in the history unfolding.

3 Airwaves over the Berlin Wall

The recognition by broadcasters and listeners alike, that the concrete wall which brutally divided the city was no barrier in the ether – lies at the heart of the second vignette which speaks to the role of BBC not as a monitor, but as a programme-maker participating in the prosecution of Cold War public diplomacy and propaganda. The example comes from the BBC German Service, established in 1938, which had been broadcasting a mix of information, entertainment and English language lessons to the Eastern zone since April 1949, and would continue to do so until 1975, shortly after the UK recognised the GDR (Brinson and Dove 2003; Major 2013; Oliver 2019a). Hardly neutral – it was funded, after all, by the Foreign Office – the nightly "East Zone Programme" aimed to persuade listeners in the East of the moral and material superiority of the West and thus to counteract the messages being carried by their domestic radio stations, though it stopped short of advocating active resistance (Studdert 2023).

Throughout the period, albeit with increasing difficulty and risk, listeners in the Eastern zone would correspond with the BBC via its Berlin office at Savignyplatz, and these letters became the inspiration and substance for the most celebrated of the German Service's programmes, *Briefe ohne Unterschrift* (Letters without signature). Though the programme pre-dates the Wall, it grew in popularity and significance thereafter. Long neglected, it has in recent years been the subject of several academic and public histories of BBC broadcasting in the Cold War (Schädlich 2017; Oliver 2019a, 2019b; BBC 2019; Studdert n.d.; Museum 2021).

The Friday evening show would open with an invitation to its listeners to write in "wherever you are and with whatever is in your hearts" (Museum 2021). A selection of the anonymous correspondence they received would be read out each week and be commented on by Austin Harrison, the Deputy Head of the German Service who presented the programme in fluent German, albeit still heavily inflected by a clipped BBC English accent (Stasi 2021). Although the programme scripts do not survive, research has revealed the letters to be a fascinating insight into the everyday lives and varied opinions of East German citizens, at least among the self-selecting and largely dissident audience (Major 2013; Schädlich 2017). While many listeners would write in about their frustrations with shortages and restrictions in the East, or expressly write of their trust in the BBC, others would voice their support for the regime, or vent their frustration at how the scourge of a divided Germany had settled into a tolerable solution for both sides. It was certainly important to the BBC's reputation that the programme did not only broadcast letters from those who were critical of the regime, and it is significant that in performing a certain even-handedness in this way it provided a space for an exchange of views not normally available to citizens of the GDR. This was a perspective widely echoed in the BBC's External Services broadcasting across Eastern Europe through the Cold War, or at least was a position that many in the BBC, and certainly in the BBC German Service, sought to protect against intermittent attempts by the Foreign Office to influence its output (Major 2013, 264–65). Looking back at the BBC's influence in this regard, the Head of the Polish Service, Eugeniusz Smolar, put it like this:

> We represented the quality, the fairness, the openness and, most important, we represented the alternative. When the communists wanted to persuade everybody there is no alternative, there was. The alternative was us. (Smolar 2019, 77)

The BBC received around 40,000 letters over the programme's 25-year span and, having originally been dispatched via diplomatic bag from Savignyplatz to the production team in London, many of these letters are now held by the BBC Written Archives. Others, the ones that did not reach their destination because they were intercepted, are now to be found in the Stasi Documents Archive in the *Bundesarchiv*, along with the off-air recordings that formed part of the surveillance regime. The Stasi considered the BBC, and this programme in particular, as "a site of psychological warfare", and devoted huge resources into tracking Harrison's activities and intercepting the letters, in order to identify those who were treasonously interacting with the BBC, although also perhaps as a way to gauge the public mood (Major 2013, 268, 275). The BBC, even by the mid-1950s, was evidently anxious about the danger the programme could pose to its correspondents, despite the practice of using code names and excluding any traceable means of identification. In a move that could easily have lost it listeners, the show would openly acknowledge the risk its listeners were taking, with the following words:

> BBC – three dangerous letters. Dangerous for all those who fear the truth and especially dangerous for all those who want to hear the truth and actually hear it at great personal risk. (Major 2013, 269)

Once letters could no longer be posted directly in West Berlin, the situation became only more precarious. Harrison would give out a contact address each week, either frequently updated postbox numbers or fake addresses leading to bombed out buildings, in an attempt to keep one step ahead of the surveillance and protect their correspondents as much as possible.

The programme was not without its casualties, although it is not clear that the BBC recognised quite the lengths that the Stasi would go to in order to deter, detect and punish its listeners. A BBC documentary on the subject, *London Calling: Cold War Letters*, includes the oral testimony of Karl-Heinz Borchardt, who in 1968 at the age of sixteen was inspired by the Prague Spring to write to the programme (BBC 2019). He describes how he had begun actively to listen out for different programmes from the West – Radio Luxembourg and Radio Saarland for the music, RIAS and the BBC for speech. This, despite the risk of fines and censure, was reasonably common practice across the GDR – it has been estimated that up to half of all East Europeans were tuned in regularly to Western radio (Ross, Johnson and Parta 2010, 345). But Borchardt's letter was intercepted by the Stasi who were able to see it had been written by a schoolboy. Astonishingly, they then organised a school essay competition in order to identify the letter-writer by his handwriting. Borchardt was convicted and spent 2 years in incarceration. Despite this experience, Borchardt does not blame the BBC, but rather credits the programme with having inspired him to find his voice.

By the early 1970s, there were fewer letters, perhaps because of ever closer surveillance, perhaps because of the radio's decline as a source of information and propaganda in the television age or the ready availability of radio output more appealing to the younger generations of East Germans. But what this snapshot illuminates, apart from the role of the BBC in treading a contradictory line between non-intervention and offering a space of resistance, is the heightened political valuation of the act of listening during this period. When historians follow the archives and focus on a particular programme or broadcaster, it is easy to forget the placelessness of the radio spectrum, and that listeners on both sides of the Wall did actively and deliberately, or even just casually, tune in to multiple channels at different times (Major 2013; Kuschel 2016). There are also many different reasons that audiences might listen out for sounds that cross borders, not all to do with narrow informational or political incentives (Roth-Ey 2020). Music radio was certainly widely used by young East Berliners to engage in sub-cultural sonic border-crossing, for example (Stahl 2016). But what is so poignant in the example of *Briefe ohne Unterschift* is that at the precise moment when radio listeners, so often caricatured as passive consumers of radio wares, seem to be most actively engaged in listening as an act of resistance and writing back in a form of interactive co-production, they are at the same time unwitting pawns in a much bigger play for power.

4 The Fall of the Wall

The third vignette takes us to 1989 and the fall of the Wall (see Figure 15.1), an event it is probably fair to say that conjures up visual rather than audio iconography, except, perhaps, for US President Reagan's famous words during his visit to West Berlin on 12 June 1987: "Mr. Gorbachev, tear down this Wall!" (Robinson 2007), or perhaps, for those like me who gathered along the now diminished Wall in those momentous November days, the constant sound of the so-called "*Mauerspechte*", people "pecking" away at the Wall with pickaxes and chisels, fuelled by pent-up anger and jubilation.

Once again, rather than exploring the BBC reportage of the time, this section takes a more oblique approach to this world-historical moment by looking for traces in a specific archive, in this case the recently published BBC Connected Histories database (Hendy et al. 2022). This collection of seven digitised archives, curated by colleagues at the University of Sussex in collaboration with BBC History, includes the BBC Oral History archive (BBC History, "Origins" n.d.). This began as a large collection of "exit interviews" with BBC employees, recorded over many years for internal purposes, and until recently not publicly available. The value of the collection, beyond any particular revelation, is in hearing the voices of a whole range of different players within the BBC, often talking remarkably candidly in interviews intended not for immediate broadcast or circulation, but as contributions to the BBC's longstanding tradition of recording its own history for posterity. Drawing on these archives and supplementing the original oral history archive with new interviews, project members also produced themed packages for the BBC website, originally under the rubric "100 Voices" to mark the Corporation's centenary, but now presented simply as "Voices of the BBC" (BBC History "Voices" 2023).

The collection includes several interviews with journalists and others recalling some aspect of working for the BBC through those tumultuous days in November 1989 or recalling how important the BBC World Service coverage had been to politicians and journalists in Eastern Europe struggling to keep up with the fast-moving events. The Managing Director of the World Service during this period (1986–93), John Tusa, was interviewed on his departure by veteran broadcaster and former Director of BBC Radio (1964–69), Frank Gillard. Gillard had not only instigated the restructuring of BBC radio stations in 1967, introducing both pop music radio and local radio to the UK, but in 1972 had also instigated the oral history archive itself. Like Gillard, Tusa had been a reforming Director. He insisted, for example, that new investment in the infrastructures of transmission was matched with investments in programme making, a modernisation of how the World Service sounded and bringing all the BBC external services under the World Service name. This all helped to shore up the World Service against political antipathy from the Thatcher government – the latest iteration of a long-standing "attritional consensus" (Webb 2014, 185) between the Corporation and the state.

In a wide-ranging interview, Tusa describes the fall of the Wall as "one of those wonderful journalistic and personal experiences" that no-one had seen coming. While there was clearly a momentum for change since Gorbachev had come to power in the USSR, and it seemed as if a more benign political system might emerge, the sudden collapse and "total wipe out of one half of the political system that we had worked with", he said was something that, "nobody at all could foresee" (Tusa 1993, 4). But if the BBC was hardly alone in failing to predict the imminent breaching of the Wall and the seismic events that followed across the Soviet Bloc, Tusa maintained that World Service journalism carried on pretty much unchanged, even as the Cold War came to an end, saying,

> … we had, though we didn't know why we were doing it, we had in place a theory of how we broadcast internationally which was valid both in the cold war world and from the post-cold war world. (Tusa 1993, 5)

This was the same ethos referred to above, the sense that the BBC had developed a model of international broadcasting that stood for fairness and trustworthiness and sought to answer "a universal need" for information rather than to target specific propaganda messages to audiences behind the Iron Curtain. For this reason, Tusa maintained, the BBC World Service had no need to "re-theorise" its raison d'être nor alter its operations greatly when the Cold War came to an end.

Now, there will of course be different interpretations and analyses of the BBC's coverage of the fall of the Wall and the extent to which it played into the emerging – and problematic – concept of a new world order (McLaughlin 2016, 178; Seaton 2016). Indeed, Tusa acknowledges in this interview that there were at least two camps even within Bush House at this juncture, largely divided by generation, with the older "cold warriors" being more antagonistic towards the Warsaw Pact regimes. But in terms of the BBC's own sense of mission, the Corporation's peculiar mix of public service values in the national interest on the global stage, honed through its Cold War experience, remained

FIGURE 15.1 Journalists reporting on the fall of the Berlin Wall in front of the Reichstag, 13 November 1989 (copyright Kate Lacey)

largely unchallenged, even as the fall of the Wall shattered the geopolitical status quo.

5 Remembering the Wall

And so to the final vignette, which sets out to trace how the Wall has been remembered in BBC radio programming in the thirty and more years since it fell. Here, it is the public-facing BBC website that is the featured archive, acknowledging the role that the BBC plays in constructing cultural memory in the UK, which it does through its daily broadcasting operations of course, but also through its role in curating an increasingly rich online archive of programme recordings and contextual materials. Some of this curatorial work has already been referenced, for example, the pages of the 100 Voices project devoted to a collection on "The BBC and the Cold War" (BBC History 2023). In addition to embedded clips and interviews from the BBC Oral History project, the site includes a list of direct links to select radio programmes on the topic available to listen on via BBC Sounds, the "home for audio from across the BBC" (BBC Sounds 2018). Of the fifteen programmes or series listed, three are exclusively about the Berlin Wall, which is some indication of how it still carries a great deal of symbolic weight in the BBC's representation of the Cold War which, after all, was conducted across the globe.

But what of the coverage of the Wall in BBC output as a whole? For that, I turned to the BBC's Programme Index (BBC Programme 2023). Formerly known as the BBC Genome Project, the Programme Index is a publicly accessible record of the BBC's programme listings, from 1922 onwards (including facsimile scans of *The Radio Times* from 1923 to 1959). It is only a record of what programmes were due for broadcast, but despite its limitations – no detailed record of news coverage, for example, and relatively few links to programme recordings – it does provide a near complete searchable database. A simple keyword search produces up to 608 results for radio programmes referencing the Berlin Wall in their metadata. Only 19 of these appear in the data through the 28 years of the Wall's existence, although it must be said that such results also indicate the limitations of undertaking a content analysis with a database that does not include the actual content, and for which there are more channels and more detailed programme descriptions, and therefore greater hit rates, as the years go by. Nevertheless, it is still possible to glean something of the flavour and discern some patterns in the coverage, not least in the frequency and variety of the retrospective material produced to mark the recurrent anniversaries of events associated with Wall.

The first programme dedicated entirely to the Wall was broadcast in June 1963: a "radio study" of East Germany, called *Behind the Berlin Wall* (Home Service, 18 June 1963, 20:30). The first radio drama on the subject was *Over the Wall,* a serial in seven episodes by Val Gielgud, broadcast in 1965 (Light Programme, 6–20 June 1965, 19:00). There were intermittent treatments of life in the divided city, and especially stories of escape, as in *The Wall,* a programme that focused on families kept apart by the Wall (Radio 4, 25 May 1971, 20:30), or as another programme called it, "the squalid, preposterous wall" (*Germany Calling,* Radio 4, 10 August 1972, 22:45). To mark the 20th anniversary, the arts series *Kaleidoscope* considered the effect "this division of a city has had on its writers and its artists" (Radio 4, 13 August 1981, 21:30), while in 1987, the flagship news programme, *Today,* broadcast live from East and West Berlin on the occasion of the city's 750th anniversary (Radio 4, 25 May 1987, 06:30), followed that evening by a study of the East German capital in a programme called *The Price of Peace* (20:25). Finally, in a sign of the momentum for change that was beginning to build as the 1980s drew to a close, Radio 3 broadcast an international youth orchestra performing Britten's "War Requiem" on either side of the Wall (1

April 1988). Here already the Wall is being featured across a whole range of genres – documentaries, discussions, news and arts programming.

In the first few years after 1989, various programmes recounted the extraordinary events surrounding the fall of the Wall, alongside others which interrogated the new European landscape in terms of intellectual and artistic life, or invited journalists, diplomats and dissidents to share their recollections. The first drama of the post-89 period seems to have been another drama with the title *Over the Wall,* this one by Adrian Bean about a bid for freedom by two high-wire artists (Radio 4, 20 September 1995 at 8.30pm).

Though there were a handful of programmes to mark the 5th anniversary, by the 10th Radio 4 would dedicate a whole day of programmes to *The Day the Wall Came Down,* including special episodes of regular shows like *Today, Woman's Hour, Front Row* and a special debate, chaired by Misha Glenny, on the implications for European unity (Radio 4, 9 November 1999, 06:00; 10:00; 19:15; 20.00). Alistair Cooke broadcast his reflections on that first decade a few days later in an episode of *Letter from America* (Radio 4, 12 November 1999, 21:00). Another ten years on, Radio 4 ran a whole 1989 season to mark the twentieth anniversary, including a daily 5 minute dose from the archives, introduced by John Tusa. *1989: Day by Day* ran for 91 episodes from 5 October 2009 (BBC 2024). Tusa also led a discussion programme with political figures from the time, *1989: How the Wall Fell* (Radio 4, 27 October 2009, 20:00). It was not only the view from the major players that made it to air, however. The regular World Service programme dedicated to listeners' points of view, *Over to You,* for example, interviewed a listener about his recollections of radio and television in Berlin and East Germany at the time, recalling the complex transnational media landscape of the city in a time before satellite TV or the internet (World Service, 31 October 2009, 11.40). *Witness History* told the story of a family's experience of the morning the Wall went up (World Service, 9 November 2009, 00:50).

Thus far, the retrospective work of radio, as revealed through the programme listings at least, has been dominated by documentary, drama and discussion programmes on the speech-based channels of Radio 4 and the World Service. But the 20th anniversary was certainly marked across other stations, too. On Radio 2, Jeremy Vine hosted *The Day the Wall Fell,* a show from various locations in Berlin, interviewing people about their memories (Radio 2, 3 November 2009, 22:30). There was also an "irreverent" documentary entitled *How David Hasselhof Brought Down the Wall* (10 November 2009, 22:30). Radio 3 had special themed performances across its output, including, for example, a focus on the orchestras of the former East Germany (*Performance on 3,* 5 and 9 November 2009, 19:00), and on the Jazz scene before and after the Wall (*Jazz*

Line-up, 8 November 2009, 23:30). It also had a feature on the new music scene in Berlin (*Hear and Now,* 7 November 2009, 22:30) and on the repercussions across the arts of losing "the muse of censorship" (*Sunday Feature,* 8 November 2009, 21:30). Radio 5 Live invited veteran journalists into Kate Silverton's studio to reminisce on covering the story (8 November 2009, 9:30), and *5 Live Breakfast* was live from Berlin on 9 November. Indeed, even Radio Devon broadcast live from the Brandenburg Gate that day (9 November, 14:00). The music stations no doubt also marked the anniversary in their own way, but the Programme listings of the period of course leave no trace.

Across the BBC there were some 70 radio programmes, including repeats, that explicitly marked the 20th anniversary, and the reverberations of the Wall's collapse were explored in relation to myriad aspects of life. Beyond the worlds of news, diplomacy and music mentioned above, there were programmes about the impact on football (*World Football,* World Service, 7 November 2009, 02:32), the economic impact of "*Ostalgie*" (*Business Daily,* BBC World Service, 6 November 2009, 08:32), a review of post-1989 German literature (*The Verb,* Radio 3, 6 November 2009, 21:15), the question of different health outcomes in unified Germany (*Health Check,* World Service, 9 November 2009, 10:32), the impact of the rise and fall of communism on vocabulary and dialect (*Word of Mouth,* Radio 4, 17 November 2009, 16:00), the opportunities and debates about architecture in the city since the Wall was opened (*The Strand Archive,* World Service, 17 November 2009, 22:32), and the practical challenges of reuniting the city's infrastructure (*1989: Restitching the City,* Radio 4, 24 November, 11.00).

Of course there are also plenty of programmes about the Wall in the listings that are not tied to anniversaries – among the more idiosyncratic ones are a comic imagining of how social media might have covered the story (*History Retweeted: The Fall of the Berlin Wall,* Radio 4, 12 March 2014, 23:00), a dramatisation of how the Stasi came to let Bruce Springsteen play East Berlin in 1988 (*Born in the DDR,* Radio 4, 20 June 2015, 14:30), a nature walk along the borderlands (*Costing the Earth: Iron Curtain Turns Green,* Radio 4, 29 October 29 2019, 15:30), and a treasure hunt for "Norfolk's bits of the Berlin Wall" (Radio Norfolk, *Treasure Quest,* 7 March 2021, 13:00). Another programme worthy of mention in the context of this chapter is an edition of *The Archive Hour* that explored "whether the power of radio had helped to bring down the Wall" (*The War of the Airwaves,* Radio 4, 20 November 1999: 20:00).

But modern media scheduling does love an anniversary, and so again there was intense coverage for the 30th anniversary, though this time characterised by a particular interest in presenting individual life stories. There were programmes, for example, about people who worked for or were watched by the Stasi (*Stasiland,* Radio 4, 4–8 November 2019, 14:00), a family who sought refuge in Czechoslovakia in the summer of 1989 (*Witness History: East German Refugees in the Prague Embassy,* World Service, 23 October 2019, 08:50), inhabitants who collected their *Begrüßungsgeld* in the first few weeks after the Wall was opened (*Welcome Money,* Radio 4, 4 November 2019, 20:00) and young Berliners who came together in the clubs and cultural scene (*The Cultural Frontline: How Germany Reunified on the Dance Floor,* World Service, 9 November 2019, 02:32). Most prominent was the award-winning series, *Tunnel 29,* by Helena Merriman, which over ten episodes told the remarkable story of a tunnel, built by students with financial support from the American broadcaster, NBC, and through which 29 East Berliners eventually escaped to the West (Radio 4, 21 October – 1 November 1 2019, 13:45). The story, illustrated with photographs and documents, is also presented on an accompanying news webpage (BBC News, 2019).

Media retrospectives are always at least as much about the present day as they are about the past, and much of this 30th anniversary programming is framed by the unavoidable resonances with President Trump's rhetoric of "Build the Wall" and the emergence of new divisions in Europe, post-Brexit. As migration issues and new nationalisms rose up the political agenda in the United States, Europe and elsewhere, the question of building barriers to keep other people in or out inspired further retrospection on the Berlin Wall. *Free Thinking,* for example, asked "why we build walls rather than bridges" (*Walls,* Radio 4, 15 January 2019, 22:00), *Thinking Allowed* looked at the social history of human barriers (*Walls,* Radio 4, 13 February 2019, 16:00) while *Archive on 4* explored the modern history of border walls around the world (*Build the Wall!* Radio 4, 9 November 2019). Perhaps for that reason, there was more interest around the 60th anniversary of building the Wall in 2021 than in all the previous decades put together.

6 Conclusion

Long after the concrete blocks and lookout towers have gone, the Berlin Wall survives in symbolic form through representations like those described here, embedded into the cultural memory with each iteration and its meaning shifting with the generations and within ever-changing political landscapes. The BBC is just one site where this cultural memory work happens, but it is certainly a significant one, not least in the way it can draw on its own extensive archive to tell stories about the Wall. It is also significant in its commitment to telling these stories in ways that inform, educate and entertain and in ways that reach multiple publics. In other words, tracing the echoes of the Berlin Wall through the radio archives in all these various ways, also reveals something of how the Corporation adapts through political and historical change and in relation to changes in the public moods and tastes. Part of the story here is the way that the BBC has collaborated with public institutions and universities in developing publicly accessible archives about its own role in the history as well as in its representations of that history and collation of witness testimonies. The wealth of stories, the range of connections and the reflection of so many aspects of human experience through the BBC's many engagements with the Berlin Wall surely confirm the importance of public history and of public service broadcasting in telling those histories and keeping the lessons of the past in the public eye and, indeed, the public ear.

References

Bardgett, Suzanne, Friederike Kind-Kovács and Vincent Kuitenbrouwer. 2019. "The Act of Listening: Radio Monitoring, 1930–1990." *Media History* 25.4: 391–99.

BBC. 2019. *London Calling: Cold War Letters. 17 November* at 20.00, BBC, 60 mins. https://www.bbc.co.uk/programmes/m000b1h0 Accessed 16 January 2024.

BBC. 2024. *1989: Day by Day*. Episodes. https://www.bbc.co.uk/programmes/b00nd2p5/episodes/guide Accessed 16 January 2024.

BBC Archive. 2024. "The Berlin Crisis." https://www.bbc.co.uk/archive/the-berlin-crisis/zrt6kmn Accessed 9 January 2024.

BBC History. 2023. "Origins of the BBC Oral History Collection." https://www.bbc.com/historyofthebbc/100-voices/bbc-memories/frank-gillard/ Accessed 11 January 2024.

BBC History. 2023. "Voices of the BBC." https://www.bbc.co.uk/historyofthebbc/100-voices/ Accessed 11 January 2024.

BBC Monitoring. 2024. https://monitoring.bbc.co.uk/ Accessed 9 January 2024.

BBC News. 2019. "The Story of Tunnel 29." https://www.bbc.co.uk/news/extra/Od4dL9Lip2/tunnel_29#group-The-End-md7MusCaGi Accessed 16 January 2024.

BBC Sounds. 2018. "This is BBC Sounds." https://www.bbc.co.uk/programmes/p06q9h6q Accessed 16 January 2024.

Brinson, Charmian and Richard Dove (eds). 2003. *"Stimme der Wahrheit": German-language Broadcasting by the BBC*. Amsterdam: Rodopi.

Brown, Malcolm. 1981. "The Berlin Wall." *The Listener*, 106, no. 2722, August 13: 130–2.

Classen, Christoph. 2014. "'Um die Empfangsmöglichkeiten ... des Senders RIAS völlig auszuschalten ... .' Störsender in der DDR 1952 bis 1988." *Rundfunk und Geschichte* 40, 3–4: 25–40.

DRA [Deutsches Rundfunkarchiv – the German Radio Archive]. n.d. "Der Mauerbau1961 im Rundfunk der DDR.". https://www.dra.de/de/mauerbau-1961 Accessed 9 January 2024

Hendy, David, Margaretta Jolly, Tim Hitchcock, Denice Penrose, Alban Webb, Ben Jackson, Mike Hammond and Anna-Maria Sichani. 2022. *Connected Histories of the BBC* [CHBBC]. https://connectedhistoriesofthebbc.org Accessed 11 January 2024.

IWM [Imperial War Museum]. 2015. "Listening to the World: BBC Monitoring Collection." https://www.iwm.org.uk/research/research-projects/listening-to-the-world-bbc-monitoring-collection-ahrc-research-network. Accessed 9 January 2024.

Kuschel, Franziska. 2016. *Schwarzhörer, Schwarzseher und heimliche Leser: die DDR und die Westmedien.* Vol. 6. Göttingen: Wallstein Verlag.

Lacey, Kate. 2015. "The Wall of Words: Radio and the Construction of the Berlin Wall." *Listening to the World: Academic Papers.* https://www.iwm.org.uk/research/research-projects/listening-to-the-world-bbc-monitoring-collection-ahrc-research-network/academic-papers. Accessed 9 January 2024.

Major, Patrick. 2002. "Going West: The Open Border and the Problems of *Republikflucht.*" *The Workers' and Peasants' State: Communism and Society in East Germany under Ulbricht, 1945–71.* Eds. Patrick Major and Jonathan Osmond. Manchester: Manchester University Press. 190–209.

Major, Patrick. 2013. "Listening Behind the Curtain: BBC Broadcasting to East Germany and its Cold War Echo". *Cold War History* 13.2: 255–75.

Marks, David. 1983. "Broadcasting Across the Wall: The Free Flow of Information Between East and West Germany". *Journal of Communication* 33.1: 46–55.

McLaughlin, Greg. 2016. *The War Correspondent.* 2nd edn. London: Pluto Press.

Müller, Silvia. 1995. "Der Rundfunk als Herrschaftsinstrument der SED". *Materialien der Enquete-Kommission: Aufarbeitung von Geschichte und Folgen der SED-Diktatur in Deutschland.* Frankfurt: Nomos, Suhrkamp: 2287–2326.

Museum für Kommunikation Frankfurt. 2021. "'Briefe ohne Unterschrift': DDR-Geschichte(n) auf BBC Radio." Exhibition March 4 to September 5. https://briefe-ohne-unterschrift.museumsstiftung.de/. Accessed 9 January 2024.

Nicholson, Esme Joan. 2014. "Hier Spricht Berlin: Radio, Space and Voice in Divided Berlin, 1961–1989." PhD. Dissertation., University of Exeter.

Oliver, Emily. 2019a. "A Voice for East Germany: Developing the BBC German Service's East Zone Programme." *Historical Journal of Film, Radio and Television* 39.3: 568–83.

Oliver, Emily. 2019b. "Listening Through the Iron Curtain." https://www.bbc.co.uk/historyofthebbc/researchers/listening-through-the-iron-curtain. Accessed 9 January 2024.

Omand, David. 2015. "The Importance of BBC Monitoring for Intelligence." *Listening to the World: Academic Papers*. https://www.iwm.org.uk/research/research-projects/listening-to-the-world-bbc-monitoring-collection-ahrc-research-network/blogs Accessed 9 January 2024.

Readex. 2024. "BBC Monitoring: Summary of World Broadcasts. Essential Global Media, 1939–2001." https://www.readex.com/products/bbc-monitoring-summary-world-broadcasts Accessed 9 January 2024.

Robinson, Peter. 2007. "Tear Down This Wall" *Prologue Magazine*, 39.2. https://www.archives.gov/publications/prologue/2007/summer/berlin.html Accessed 16 January 2024

Ross, Corey. 2004. "East Germans and the Berlin Wall: Popular Opinion and Social Change Before and After the Border Closure of August 1961." *Journal of Contemporary History* 39.1: 25–43.

Ross Johnson, Alexander and Eugene R. Parta. 2010. "Cold War International Broadcasting and the Road to Democracy." *Cold War Broadcasting: Impact on the Soviet Union and Eastern Europe*. Eds. Alexander Ross Johnson and Eugene R. Parta. Budapest: Central European Press. 345–50.

Roth-Ey, Kristin. 2020. "Listening Out, Listening For, Listening In: Cold War Radio Broadcasting and the Late Soviet Audience." *The Russian Review* 79.4: 556–77.

Schädlich, Susanne. 2017. *"Briefe ohne Unterschrift": Wie eine BBC-Sendung die DDR herausforderte*. Munich: Albrecht Knaus Verlag.

Seaton, Jean. 2016. "The New Architecture of Communications." *Journalism Studies* 17.7: 808–16.

Smolar, Eugeniusz. 2019. "Interview SxMs186/8. Transcript". BBC Oral History Collection, *Connected Histories of the BBC*. https://connectedhistoriesofthebbc.org/data/sxnew/EugeniuszSmolar/interview1/SxEugeniuszSmolarTranscripts1.pdf Accessed 11 January 2024.

Stahl, Heiner. 2016. "A Border-Crossing Soundscape of Pop: The Auditory Traces of Subcultural Practices in 1960s Berlin." *Countercultures and Popular Music*. Eds. Sheila Whitely and Jedediah Sklower. New York: Routledge. 223–35.

Stasi Unterlagen Archiv. 2021. "Podcast – Anonyme Briefe an der BBC". Folge 31, 14 April. https://www.stasi-unterlagen-archiv.de/informationen-zur-stasi/themen/beitrag/anonyme-briefe-an-die-bbc/ Accessed 9 January 2024.

Stiftung Berliner Mauer [Berlin Wall Foundation]. n.d. https://www.stiftung-berliner-mauer.de/en/node/125 Accessed 9 January 2024.

Studdert, Will. 2023. "Letters Without Signature". https://www.bbc.com/historyofthebbc/100-voices/coldwar/letters-without-signatures/ Accessed 9 January 2024.

Tusa, John. 1993. "Interview" BBC Oral History Collection, *Connected Histories of the BBC*. https://connectedhistoriesofthebbc.org/play/?id=209mode=doc#document-view. Accessed 11 January 2024.

Webb, Alban. 2014. *London Calling: Britain, the BBC World Service and the Cold War*. London: Bloomsbury.

Webb, Alban. 2023. "BBC Monitoring in Wartime." *History of the BBC*. https://www.bbc.com/historyofthebbc/100-voices/coldwar/monitoring/ Accessed 9 January 2024.

Wilke, Manfred. 2014. *The Path to the Berlin Wall: Critical Stages in the History of Divided Germany*. Oxford: Berghahn.

CHAPTER 16

The BBC and Berlin Beats: Creating Cultural Heritage and Techno Tourism

Beate Peter

1 Introduction

When young Brits are asked what they associate with Berlin, their response will often be techno and clubbing. Clubbing to the sound of electronic music is part of the city's nightlife, defined through music, clubs, DJs and rituals. All of these contribute to an image of Berlin as being young, creative, dynamic and worth a visit. Such an image needs to be permanently updated so that new political, social, cultural developments and trends can be responded to. As a result, contemporary nightlife in Berlin is flexible, constantly changing and rejuvenating itself. At the same time, however, there is a notion that techno in Berlin has to be protected and preserved because it is in danger of becoming extinct. This is most evident in the application that was made in 2021 to UNESCO to have techno in Berlin officially acknowledged as intangible cultural heritage (ICH) and be safeguarded through "measures aimed at ensuring the viability of the intangible cultural heritage, including the identification, documentation, research, preservation, protection, promotion, enhancement, transmission, particularly through formal and non-formal education, as well as the revitalization of the various aspects of such heritage" (UNESCO 2022, 6). In early 2024 Berlin's techno culture was added to the German list of ICH, evidencing the importance of that cultural practice to be preserved, continued but also further developed (Deutsche UNESCO-Kommission n.d.). On the one hand, techno culture in Berlin is defined by constant change, on the other it is argued that it needs conserving. The city's club culture is dynamic, ephemeral, evasive. Inside the clubs, cameras are mostly forbidden. Some of the clubs are infamous for their long queues and the difficulty in gaining entry. But how does this vibrancy square with the notion of heritage as something that has to be captured, defined and documented? How can a living culture be adequately identified and recorded as heritage? Using the UNESCO application as a starting point, the first part of the chapter discusses the relationship between techno as heritage and contemporary clubbing experiences for those coming from that very culture that they wish to preserve.

 | HTTPS://DOI.ORG/10.1515/9783111302508-016

The second part of the chapter is concerned with the ways in which Berlin's techno culture is mediated to an international audience. The number of tourists attending club nights in Berlin has increased over the last few years, and in 2018 tourists made up about a quarter of the audience in Berlin's nightclubs (Damm and Drevenstedt 2019, 39). Given that club tourism brings an estimated EUR 1.5 million annually to the city (Damm and Drevenstedt 2019, 28), it is important to analyse in which ways Berlin's techno heritage is presented to an audience that has potentially not been able to immerse itself in the lived culture of the city. Using an episode of the BBC's programme *Art of Now* on Berlin's nightlife, the discussion focuses on the narration of techno's history in order to establish how the gap is bridged between a historical understanding of techno and its current iteration. By considering processes of fossilisation and renewal it will become clear that it is possible to understand Berlin's club culture as heritage that can be preserved whilst staying flexible enough to update itself. Doing this work, the BBC becomes an important cultural commentator for Berlin, as it helps not only to identify and define techno as cultural heritage but also to create techno tourism.

2 Cultural Heritage

Berlin as the capital of techno seems to be manifested in a global cultural memory of electronic music (Nye 2013; Wright Hurley 2015). Events such as the Love Parade, clubs such as Tresor or Berghain, cultural figures such as Dimitri Hegemann (Tresor), Dr Motte (Love Parade, Rave the Planet) or Robert Henke (Ableton) – all contribute to a certain image of Berlin as a (perhaps *the*) cultural hub of Germany when it comes to techno. Although Berlin has not been the only city in which techno was played and became popular (Sicko 1999), the common narrative seems to have linked techno irrevocably with Berlin: its history, its spaces, its people. Connecting events, people and places with one another is a way of not only writing history but also creating cultural heritage. Graham (2002) asserts that heritage is "a social construction, imagined, defined and articulated within cultural and economic practice" (1003). He goes on to say that heritage "is concerned with the ways in which very selective material artefacts, mythologies, memories and traditions become resources for the present. The contents, interpretations and representations of the resource are selected according to the demands of the present" (1004). Through Graham's lens, the selection process is only one aspect of cultural heritage. A more important consideration is related to how these different components of heritage are related to one another. Similarly, with regard to popular music, Cantillon et al. (2018) state that "if history is a record of the past, heritage is those aspects of the past that are important in creating a sense of identity among a particular group of people, whether a nation, a city or a neighbourhood" (5). They admit that "heritage is, therefore, highly contested and always changing" (5). Through the creation of heritage as a process of selection, contemporary hegemonic power relations become visible (Graham 2002). They come to the fore when "reflecting who is given authority to speak more broadly in society" (Cantillon et al. 2018, 2). With regard to the techno heritage of Berlin, there is a question about the power of definition: what is Berlin techno as a cultural form? What is part of it? What is not? A fixed definition of Berlin techno through sound exclusively would lead to the fossilisation of this heritage without the option to be "recreated by communities and groups in response to their environment, their interaction with nature and their history" (UNESCO 2022). Yet, mythologised stories (or histories) are important hegemonic tools to confirm the position of those who are part of the narrative. An understanding of heritage as a hegemonic social construction that is defined as much through a process of selection as it is through a process of establishing relations between selected tangible and intangible components, is conducive to the discussion of techno culture as intangible cultural heritage.

In 2020, members and supporters of Berlin's techno community organised themselves under the umbrella organisation *Rave the Planet*, and in 2021 they applied for techno culture in Berlin to be recognised by UNESCO as intangible cultural heritage. UNESCO defines this as "practices, representations, expressions, knowledge, skills – as well as the instruments, objects, artefacts and cultural spaces associated therewith – that communities, groups and, in some cases, individuals recognise as part of their cultural heritage" (UNESCO 2022). The application included a video (Rave the Planet 2019b), in which Dimitri Hegemann, considered one of the founding fathers of Berlin's techno culture, identifies four particular conditions that have turned the city's techno into heritage which needs to be protected: the euphoria people felt as a result of the fall of the Berlin Wall, the hands-off approach by the police and law enforcement services, the historic absence of a curfew; and the music itself. In the following section I am going to critically discuss these four conditions in light of Graham's (2002) notion of heritage as a social construction and focus on the links that are made between the different elements.

Hegemann situates Berlin techno historically and geographically by referring to the fall of the Berlin Wall and the prevalence of a particular affect: euphoria. The common narrative of the fall of the Wall as being unanimously welcomed and causing collective euphoria is perhaps a little too simple, ignoring rather complex collective-affective states. Euphoria will have been experienced in combination with a range of other emotions, very often dependent on geography and demographic. Gook, for example, argues that the historical situation in 1989 Berlin was marked by both pain and hope (2016, 171). As an East German structure was abolished (including educational systems and employment structures) young people in particular were faced with uncertainties/opportunities. Coupled with West Berlin's young demographic consisting of squatters, conscientious objectors[1] and hippies, which created a unique attitude to life (Henkel and Wolff 1996, 162), the mood of the city altogether has to be taken into account. Biehl and vom Lehn (2016) describe this as an aesthetic that they call "Berliner Luft". They argue that techno's aesthetic practices in Germany's capital are defined by an interaction of architecture, DJing, dance and music. For Hegemann to downplay the complexity of emotions means that he is fossilising the already popular narrative of the fall of the Berlin Wall.

What might indeed be more useful is a reference to a generally affective state of German people at that time, one that allowed the younger population to recognise and respond to affective affordances in techno spaces. A contextualisation of affect among Germans helps much better to explain why electronic dance music in particular started to flourish in Berlin: the spaces and practices facilitate the production of affect through the dancing body. In doing so, they emphasise a specific aesthetic experience. This is especially relevant since scholarship on electronic dance music cultures has started to establish them as affective cultures (Solberg 2014; Garcia 2020; Garcia-Mispireta 2023; Gook 2016; Pope 2011). Accepting that there existed a heightened state of affect in Germany, one which also translated into a particular receptibility of music and dancing, facilitates a discussion on Berlin's electronic music as inclusive and diverse: dynamic and encompassing different musical styles. To focus on just one musical style is not only evidence of a judgement of taste but also of a hegemonic reading of electronic music from Berlin. Understood through Graham (2002), such narrow focus evidences the "demands of the present" (1004) on the city's heritage. In the UNESCO application, focus is placed on a recognisable Berlin sound rather than aesthetic practices, and as we shall see later, this sound is far from being euphoric.

The second condition mentioned by Hegemann relates to the absence of hegemonic control in the form of the police or law enforcement agencies. The use of empty spaces in the built environment was possible in Berlin, as oftentimes ownership of buildings or land was unclear. Such an appropriation of

1 Young men living in Berlin were exempt from mandatory military service.

unoccupied urban space is not particular to Berlin. Dutch *gabber* or British acid house are musical genres that became popular through a similar use of space. What is, however, unique to Berlin, is the creative ways in which these spaces were managed. Gutmair (2021) argues that the relative disinterest in the unused spaces by local government was met with a high interest by artists. He states that the anarchic period of occupying space for parties was superseded by a period in which temporary licences were granted for the use of those spaces. Those licences would still define the spaces themselves as ephemeral and intangible because the future use and purpose of the buildings would be uncertain. Yet, they contributed to "silent urban development" (Gutmair 2021, 108) of the city in that the legal or semi-legal use of spaces would facilitate a continued hands-off approach by the police and law enforcement services. As a consequence, affective cultural practices taking place away from media attention could develop on the one hand, and a model of economic sustainability was developed on the other. Subsequently, the creation of a whole industry was based on the facilitation of affective experiences in temporary spaces (see Taylor and Peter, forthcoming).

Related to the development of economic sustainability is the fact that Germany's capital has not had a curfew for more than 70 years. In Berlin, the party will go on – for days and days. This is not new to the city or to techno, but the celebration of club culture as an everyday phenomenon makes it omnipresent in the city. It leads to club culture being normalised and becoming accepted as part of the city's tapestry. But there is more to the absence of a curfew. With the boundaries of night and day blurring, it is not just the perception of ordinary Berliners that is impacted when observing club culture and related practices 24/7 but also the perception of those who actively participate in techno's rituals. Returning to Biehl and vom Lehn's (2016) concept of "Berliner Luft", the connection between physical techno spaces, DJing, dancing and music have to be understood as something shaped by the expansion of time. As the social and cultural production of techno spaces is implicitly defined through the presence of bodies, the physical characteristics of those bodies have to be taken into consideration. In a city that facilitates the continuous engagement in techno practices, dynamics have to be marked by ebb and flow, by high energy phases that are superseded by phases of calm and relaxation. That has an impact on the social construction of space, on the DJing, the music and the dancing (Pascual 2022). To understand Berlin techno is to understand both the ubiquity of the culture and time as another constituting element of the space in which it operates.

The final component Hegemann refers to when discussing the popularity of techno culture in Berlin, is the music itself. It is perhaps the most difficult to describe. For a long time, Berlin techno was understood to exhibit a particular musical aesthetic – one that can be packaged and marketed to the world. In the promotional video for the UNESCO application, reference is made to the Berlin sound being loved all over the world, implying that it is also recognised. Nye (2013) contends that the Berlin sound as it existed as part of a minimal culture was emblematic of the early 2000s in Berlin and has since "become a central trope of the German techno scene and press" (156). At the same time, he suggests that the sound has changed and developed, exemplified through his concept of the minimal continuum. However, through his case studies, Nye also shows that "the dogma of minimal techno prevents innovation" (177). The Berlin sound, as soon as we attempt to define it, becomes static, too fixed and rigid, and it is denied its opportunity to develop and to be "constantly recreated by communities and groups in response to their environment, their interaction with nature and their history" (UNESCO 2022). The creation of a recognisable, marketable cultural product carries with it the inherent danger of fossilisation. To define the sound of Berlin through a particular minimal, moody and slow style would do an injustice to the great variety of electronic musics that cater for the audiences that come to delve into the city's clubs.

In the context of the UNESCO application, techno in Berlin is being fossilised to such an extent that it has no opportunity to develop. The techno heritage is not presented as a lived culture but as part of a particular moment in history. The argumentation of Rave the Planet seems to suggest that concurrent with the creation of a unified Germany was the birth of a Berlin-specific techno culture. The links that are made between a place-based event and the music culture point at only one particular moment in time: the demise of the GDR and the changes that occurred as a result. Hegemann's four aspects that he argues led to Berlin techno becoming a unique heritage are all linked to that moment of upheaval: the emotions, the absence of the police, the sudden availability of built environment that could be appropriated, and the emergence of the music itself. It is portrayed as the zero hour of both unified Germany and Berlin techno. By referring to a specifically historic musical aesthetic in addition to a political moment in history establishes the importance of a certain cultural heritage but also situates it firmly in the past without immediate connections to the present. What we see here, then, is a perhaps necessary simplification of the history of techno in Berlin, one that lends itself to mythologisation. Yet, the popularity of Berlin as a nightlife destination (Oktay 2014) suggests that clubbing is understood as a lived culture that is active and pulsating.

3 Techno Tourism

Berlin's techno tourism attracts visitors from all over the world. Rapp (2009) describes those people flocking to Germany's capital in order to submerge and immerse themselves in the city's electronic night life as the "Easyjetset". These people come to Berlin in order to party in a way that they cannot do at home (Rapp 2009, 78), suggesting that they are able to engage in cultural practices that are specific to Berlin. Rapp warns against understanding the "Easyjetset" as a homogenous cohort. It consists of people who love electronic music that they can dance to. They come together to co-create club culture: the immersion into what Wark (2023) calls techno time. But why Berlin? Rapp does not so much cite historical references but two unrelated economic reasons for the development of the "Easyjetset". First, the liberalisation of European air traffic led to the development of discount airlines that made flights affordable for a younger demographic that would not necessarily be in full-time employment. Second, the bankruptcy of the Berlin municipality meant that centrally located, and potentially lucrative empty spaces or buildings were not bought up as quickly as in other European capitals, thus continuing to be available for party organisers (Rapp 2009, 78–80). Although Gutmair's (2021) assessment of the availability of space is slightly more nuanced and points out the change from a free appropriation (anarchy) to "the era of temporary licence" (102), both authors hint at the fact that neoliberal capitalism did not advance as quickly in Berlin (see also Phillips and Pögün-Zander 2021). This is echoed by Färber's analysis of Berlin's simultaneity of a stagnating economic situation and a parallel growing sector of cultural production" (422). The reason that is given for this development is the specific character of Berlin's demographic, one that can very well be traced back to the city's political situation before the fall of the Berlin Wall. Bridges (2006) identifies the ethos of the people to be one of solidarity, Bader and Scharenberg describe it as subcultural flair (2009, 79). Similarly, Gutmair (2021) portrays early party organisers as lacking monetary motives. These concepts try to integrate cultural practices that are based on values diametrically opposed to the neoliberal city. They are part of the city's fabric in general and techno culture specifically. Ingham et al. (1999) provide the perhaps most useful theorisation through their concept of "sonorous geographies", which they define as "aural sensing of the environment in its social, political, economic, and cultural contexts" (283). By doing so they argue that sound is not perceived objectively but only ever in a geographical context, one that includes wider societal conditions. Returning to Graham's (2002) understanding of heritage not only being a process of selection but also one that establishes connections between the selected artefacts and practices, the city's history does indeed become part of contemporary club culture.

But how are the "social connotations beyond the musical" (Nye 2013, 154) experienced by young people today? Henkel and Wolff state that techno culture was created specifically with the aim of experiencing the world differently and to co-produce a particular feeling for a whole generation (1996, 163). What they refer to is to experience the world affectively, with an aesthetic that focuses on a collective experience in times of alienation. Consequently, affect can be seen not only as a constituting factor for techno culture but also as its aim. Reckwitz (2017) defines an aesthetic experience as stimulating the senses and resulting in affective responses. He situates such experience as only ever in relation to itself and only for the purpose of itself. Does such self-referential experience have to be considered as inherently a-historical? Not at all, as a tracing of aesthetic experiences would establish a history that can be partly defined through exactly those socially constructed spaces that techno culture utilises. For example, the policy to have no photos taken inside Berlin's nightclubs is a known practice. It has an impact on the experience on the dance floor and is part of what is sought by visitors. To document the experience through means of one's own body instead is a fundamental criterion of club culture. It leads to the accumulation of experiential knowledge (Peter 2021). As a result, the lived culture in which one is to participate rather than to observe thematises the body and its being in and interacting with space: space that is geographically, culturally, politically and socially situated.

Berlin's umbrella organisation representing its nightclubs and events, Clubcommission, states that "Berlin has a pioneering role to play due to its position as the home to a diverse and extremely lively club culture" (n.d.). Just as the people who make up the participants of Berlin's club culture are diverse, so are their experiences. This portrayal of culture is somehow difficult to advocate in light of UNESCO's reasoning as to why intangible cultural heritage needs to be protected: "while fragile, intangible cultural heritage is an important factor in maintaining cultural diversity in the face of growing globalization" (UNESCO 2023). Such understanding of intangible Berlin's club-cultural heritage as being in danger of extinction and needing protection from the globalised world stands in opposition to the globally recognised culture that every year attracts more than three million visitors to Berlin (Damm and Drevenstedt 2019). On the one hand, the heritage is understood to be identifiable and clearly defined, on the other it is in itself diverse. In other words, it needs protecting against external forces while, at the same time, opening up to be shaped by them. This oxymoron can be defined as including two diametrical processes: fossilisation and renewal.

One way of reconciling these supposedly conflicting positions is to consider the perspectives through which club culture in Berlin is understood and mediated. Rave the Planet is an organisation that "was founded in 2020 by Dr Motte, the father of the Berlin Love Parade, and a few other enthusiasts who have been longterm involved in the techno scene" (Rave the Planet 2019a). Rave the Planet represents techno culture's producers and their insider perspective. Their experience of Berlin as a cultural space and their personal investment in the history of techno culture is recognisable in their treatment of techno culture as heritage. Its values appear to directly oppose neoliberal principles, and the UNESCO application highlights the need to be protected from capitalist engulfment. This portrayal of techno culture as an independent ecosystem ignores the fact that the marketing of club culture to an international tourist audience, even if presented as a subculture or alternative culture, is part of the current night time economy. Furthermore, it also turns a blind eye to the fact that, in response to cultural, societal and political changes, club culture has diversified. Diverse line-ups, inclusive audiences, safe spaces and accessible venues are the result of recently adopted principles and codes of behaviour. This reluctance to acknowledge change could be linked to a discussion on hegemonic power relations *within* a culture and the sense of identity that is created among those who are personally invested in said culture.

If the former perspective is one from within, it is worth considering a perspective from the outside. Foreign programmes reporting on the city's nightlife are an example of such a perspective, as they mediate an image to those who have not experienced Berlin's clubs. Moreover, a personal investment might not be as high, so narration is not necessarily informed by a person's role in a culture. That techno's self-conception might be fundamentally different to a techno tourist's idea of Berlin's clubs seems likely (Nardi 2014). For the former, techno is part of belonging, everyday ubiquitous practices, also often a source of income. For the latter, a weekend visit to Berlin's clubs is the opposite: something out of the ordinary, special, to be tried as part of a foreign culture. In the following section, a radio programme is discussed in order to show how the history of techno in Berlin is narrated from the outside. The discussion focuses on the ways in which techno's history is narrated to include the current landscape, and how, as a result, practices of fossilisation and renewal are combined.

4 BBC Radio 4. Art of Now: Berlin's Nightlife

Since its founding in 1922, the British Broadcasting Corporation has had strong connections with Germany, in particular with Berlin. It has reported and commented on the city's political, social and cultural life ever since, and this volume is testament to the ways in which the BBC has shaped the image of both Germany and its capital. With most international tourists coming from the UK (Berlin Tourismus & Kongress GmbH 2023), the BBC is crucial for the creation and delivery of an image of Berlin that piques potential tourists' curiosity. The chosen programme conveys the unique characteristics of Berlin techno and combines a historical perspective with the notion of Berlin techno as being lived heritage that people are welcome to immerse themselves into. It is then compared with the presentation of techno as heritage as part of the UNESCO application to highlight those elements of the narrative that allow for both fossilisation and renewal to contribute to an understanding of Berlin' club culture.

BBC Radio has numerous national and regional stations, all of which serve specific audiences. Radio 1, for example, is aimed at 15–29 year olds, and "is to entertain and engage a broad range of young listeners with a distinctive mix of contemporary music and speech" (BBC 2020a). Radio 4's target audience is mature and provides "a mixed speech service, offering in-depth news and current affairs and a wide range of other speech output including drama, readings, comedy, factual and magazine programmes. The service should appeal to listeners seeking intelligent programmes in many genres which inform, educate and entertain" (BBC 2020b). Given the remit of the radio services, one would assume that a programme on Berlin's nightlife would air on Radio 1, but instead it ran on Radio 4. As part of the regular schedule, *Art of Now* is a programme in the form of "documentaries exploring the latest worldwide cultural issues, trends, celebrations and rebellions" (BBC 2024a). On 14 May 2020, DJ Emily Dust presented an episode on "Berlin's Nightlife" (BBC 2024b).[2] For a mature audience, as the BBC defines the Radio 4 listeners, one could imagine that Berlin's nightlife is defined through opera, theatre or literature. But in this episode, Berlin's nightlife is equated with club culture.

Unsurprisingly, the programme is presented by Emily Dust, herself a DJ and producer. She refers to DJing in Berlin as a rite of passage. From the very outset it is made clear that the programme is narrated by somebody who possesses the factual knowledge of the city's culture but is not immersed in it. Dust's

2 See https://www.bbc.co.uk/programmes/m000j1j7 (accessed 1 April 2025).

stakes are low in the city's music history, which allows her to employ a slightly removed perspective. The reason for the programme is the so-called *Klubsterben* in the city, an acceleration of clubs needing to relocate or shut down because of real estate competing for and claiming urban club spaces. Although this phenomenon is not unique to Berlin, Dust describes not only the city's club life as inimitable but also the ways in which both organisers and the local government seek to prevent the dying of nightclubs. When Dust sets the scene for the programme, she does that by describing urban club spaces: "Berlin's nightlife exists in dark concrete rooms in fiercely joyous reclamation of buildings" (01:10). She makes reference to the built environment while also hinting at cultural practices and the ephemeral spaces that are specific to clubbing. This treatment of space as being both material and immaterial gains importance as the programme progresses.

The episode continues by confirming techno's mythologised history of young creatives with an entrepreneurial spirit living in West Berlin needing space for their self-actualisation, and getting that when the Berlin Wall falls and empty buildings become available. Although Dust allows Dimitri Hegemann, one of the instrumental cultural managers in the city, to frame Berlin's techno history as starting with the fall of the Berlin Wall, the focus on the built-up environment makes it possible for her to link Berlin's political history, in particular its Nazi history, with contemporary culture. Doing so, Dust goes a step beyond the celebrated zero hour of Berlin techno. It is significant because putting club culture into a wider historical context means becoming attuned to cultural changes and trends over time and, more importantly, accepting them as part of culture. Through a historisation that is defined by the changing purposes of buildings and the recognition that "Berlin's clubs are in buildings layered with history", Dust joins material and immaterial aspects of club culture. Both the physicality and the atmosphere of a club space are important and echo Biehl and vom Lehn's (2016) recognition of the impact that buildings have on the culture that is practised inside.

One of the aims of the programme is to showcase the diversity of Berlin's nightlife with regard to both musical styles and audiences. For that reason, Dust stays clear of the definition of a Berlin sound. When techno is referred to, it is done with a critical view. Dust lets her interview partners state that at some point the music in clubs seemed to be conformist with its minimal tracks. The people contributing to this episode counter the idea that contemporary Berlin can be defined by a particular sound. This is not to say that the programme does not use popular musical references to Detroit DJs and their music as heavily influencing the sound culture in Berlin. But Dust also acknowledges the current musical landscape as diverse, multicultural and inclusive. Both the formative years of techno culture and its current form are discussed, but little is said about the transition from the minimal sound that used to characterise Berlin's clubs in the early 2000s (Nye 2013) to the diverse musical styles that are representative of Berlin today. Dust uses the clubs' architecture to provide the continuity that is needed to narrate a cultural history of Berlin's nightlife. This focus on both the material and immaterial qualities of the buildings allows her to link the past with the present in a way that Rave the Planet do not. In Dust's version, intangible cultural heritage is situated in history and also allowed to develop and adapt to an ever-changing environment.

As indicated earlier, the reason for the programme to be made was the threat of many clubs needing to relocate and shut down because of real estate claiming their spaces. Many of them are located on private land, and an increase in its value presents a challenge to those who are renting. According to Knight Frank (Locke 2018), in 2018 rents in Berlin increased by 11%, whilst property prices increased by almost 15%. Related to such a change in numbers is a demographic shift towards an increase in higher income groups populating the city. In other words, the character of the people frequenting nightclubs changes, which has an impact on the way in which club spaces are socially constructed. But there is more to it. As Dust finds out, Berlin's unique position is partly based on the fact that the club scene was never created to last. Spaces were temporary, and the aesthetics that came with this notion heavily informed the clubbing experience. But Berlin's nightclubs are a stable source of income for the city. What Dust carves out beautifully in this discussion on property is that the buildings are the residue of former cultures, regimes, economies or societies. They are partly defined by their ephemeral character and the fact that nobody knows how long they will exist. Yet, they are one of the characteristics of Berlin's nightlife; they provide what Ingham (1999) calls "the experience of virtual sound worlds" and "audio technology, combined with certain musical genres and arrangements of physical space" (81). Dust manages to develop a much stronger argument for the protection of physical space than Rave the Planet do. Dust's presentation of the issue is more nuanced, yet the links she forges between places, spaces and cultural practices and the need for protection is very strong. For example, if rising rents translate into the need to sell more tickets, which in turn means creating a more "mainstream" line-up, then musical risk-taking is jeopardised. As argued by Biehl and vom Lehn (2016), "Berliner Luft" will change, as its components change: its architecture, its music and DJing, as well as its dancing (as a different demographic is starting to explore club culture).

Through her interview partners, Dust suggests two, seemingly contradictory, things. On the one hand, the techno spaces benefit from deregulation: little state interference, a continued laissez-faire approach and a sense of the community possessing full agency, for the state "not to care". On the other hand, such spaces need protection because if the physical spaces are gone, the culture will change altogether. Throughout this programme, Dust focuses less on the *selection* of material and immaterial heritage and more on the *connections* that are made between them (Graham 2002). Yet, having accepted the changing nature of culture at the beginning of the programme, Dust does not advocate for the protection of club spaces to be the only solution to the current challenge. For young people to appropriate available physical spaces does not have to happen in Berlin's city centre. According to Hegemann, who is being interviewed on the programme, that can happen in rural areas or other places outside of Berlin, for as long as young people have a certain autonomy to work with these spaces. The renewal of a culture does, as a result, not have to be fixed to one specific geography. One could consider the development of real estate in Berlin as one of the changes that communities have to take into consideration when recreating their heritage (see UNESCO 2003), and real estate will continue to have an impact on cultural urban heritage. However, where there is gentrification, there is also desolation – even if temporarily. Club culture in Berlin will survive, but it depends on how much we allow it to renew itself (Peter 2014).

5 Conclusion

This chapter discussed Berlin's club culture as intangible cultural heritage and a lived experience. It used as its starting point the successful application that was made to UNESCO in order for Berlin techno to be recognised as intangible cultural heritage. The narration of the UNESCO application was juxtaposed with that of a BBC radio programme on Berlin's nightlife. The very different narratives that emerged might partly be explained by the different lenses through which Berlin's nightlife is viewed. Rave the Planet present the heritage as theirs to be protected, and personal stakes are high. Advocating a definitive history of techno in Berlin, Rave the Planet fossilise a culture that is meant to breathe, to develop, to adjust to changes in its environment. Yet, there might be reasons for trying to permanently inscribe particular values and ideologies into Berlin's club culture, and that is linked to the status of those who write the history. To present an insider perspective means to assign cultural capital to oneself; capital which increases the commercial value of people, their practices and their spaces (see Bauer and Hosek 2015, 294). The selection of dates, times, locations and events is considered to be more important than the connection between selected material and immaterial heritage. That is because a focus on the interdependence of heritage artefacts and practices might enable a shift away from the importance of individual DJs or cultural figures towards the facilitation of an aesthetic experience. Writing oneself out of history might be difficult for those who not only consider themselves part of it but also assign themselves important roles.

The perspective of an outsider, one who is not personally invested in the writing of the club culture history of Berlin, is sometimes necessary to facilitate a more objective interpretation of a cultural condition and to make connections that seem less obvious. The distance that the BBC have through their role as observer and commentator of rather than as active participant in the cultural life of Berlin, positions them well to elaborate on Berlin's *Klubsterben*. They are able to respect the view of all invested parties, which is obvious in the programme through, for example, the portrayal of a specific sound (Berlin techno) as oppressive and restrictive. That take on the capital's techno is in stark contrast to the UNESCO application and highlights the tension between the fossilisation and renewal of a culture through narration.

Where the UNESCO application could be read as the desperate plea of an established industry to indirectly ask for property to be protected, the BBC programme on Berlin's nightlife establishes a more obvious connection between the material and immaterial quality of buildings and their impact on cultural practices. As a result, the need to save buildings and club spaces appears more urgent. However, equally important is the programme's outlook on the changes of Berlin's nightlife. Focusing on renewal rather than fossilisation, a case is made for the finding and exploration of new physical spaces so that club culture can continue to strive, albeit in different ways.

Regardless of future changes to club culture in Berlin, the BBC present it as a lived culture, one that people can immerse themselves in. Moreover, by establishing the connections between the city's architecture, its music and its cultural practices, Berlin's nightlife is indeed presented as having a unique flair, one that is co-created on the dance floor and felt through the body. Techno tourism greatly benefits from the portrayal of Berlin's club culture as being in the here and now, as ephemeral and temporary, susceptible to change and evolving – all without severing the link to its own history. That history can be felt in the spaces that, for now, still exist. To be part of that affective culture, even if just for a visit, warrants a visit to Berlin's capital and its clubs.

References

Bader, Ingo and Albert Scharenberg. 2010. "The Sound of Berlin: Subculture and the Global Music Industry". *International Journal of Urban and Regional Research* 34.1: 76–91.

Bauer, Karin and Jennifer Ruth Hosek. 2015. "Introduction: Narrating the new Berlin: Site, Sound, Image, Word". *Seminar* 51.4: 293–300.

BBC. 2024a. Radio 4: Art of Now. https://www.bbc.co.uk/programmes/b09w07c4 Accessed 31 December 2024.

BBC. 2024b. BBC Sounds. Art of Now: Berlin's Nightlife. https://www.bbc.co.uk/sounds/play/m000j1j7 Accessed 31 December 2024.

BBC. 2020a. BBC Trust: BBC Radio 1. https://www.bbc.co.uk/bbctrust/our_work/services/radio/service_licences/bbc_radio_1.html Accessed 31 December 2024.

BBC. 2020b. BBC Trust: BBC Radio 4. https://www.bbc.co.uk/bbctrust/our_work/services/radio/service_licences/bbc_radio_4.html Accesses 31 December 2024.

Berlin Tourismus und Kongress GmbH. 2023. "Tourism Statistics January to June 2023". https://about.visitberlin.de/sites/default/files/2023-08/guests-overnights-berlin-jan-jun-2023.pdf. Accessed 31 December 2024.

Biehl, Brigitte and Dirk vom Lehn. 2016. "Four-to-the-Floor: The Techno Discourse and Aesthetic Work in Berlin". *Society.* 53: 608–13.

Bridges, Elizabeth. 2006. "Berlin™: Techno and the Ambient Politics of Venue". *Mediating Germany: Popular Culture between Tradition and Innovation.* Ed. Gerd Bayer. Newcastle: Cambridge Scholars Press. 92–106.

Cantillon, Zelmarie, Catherine Strong, Lauren Istvandity and Sarah Baker. 2018. "Framing the Field of Popular Music History and Heritage Studies". *The Routledge Companion to Popular Music History and Heritage.* Eds. Sarah Baker, Catherine Strong, Lauren Istvandity and Zelmarie Cantillon. Abingdon and New York: Routledge. 1–10.

Damm, Steffen and Lukas Drevenstedt. 2019. *Club Culture Berlin.* Berlin: Clubcommission e.V.

Deutsche UNESCO-Kommission. n.d. "Bundesweites Verzeichnis des Immateriellen Kulturerbes". https://www.unesco.de/kultur-und-natur/immaterielles-kulturerbe/immaterielles-kulturerbe-deutschland/verzeichnis-ike. Accessed 31 December 2024.

Färber, Alexa. 2008. "Flourishing Cultural Production in Economic Wasteland: Three Ways of Making Sense of a Cultural Economy in Berlin at the Beginning of the Twenty First Century". *Creative Urban Milieus: Historical Perspectives on Culture, Economy, and the City.* Eds. Martina Heßler and Clemens Zimmermann. Frankfurt: Campus Verlag: 421–40.

Garcia, Luis-Manuel. 2020. "Feeling the Vibe: Sound, Vibration, and Affective Attunement in Electronic Dance Music Scenes". *Ethnomusicology Forum*, 29.1: 21–39.

Garcia-Mispireta, Luis Manuel. 2023. *Together, Somehow: Music, Affect, and Intimacy on the Dancefloor*. Durham: Duke University Press.

Gook, Ben. 2016. "Berlin and Detroit: An Alien Techno Alliance. Cultural Politics and Social Transformation after the Fall of the Wall'. *LIMBUS: Australisches Jahrbuch für germanistische Literatur- und Kulturwissenschaft*. Eds. Franz-Josef Deiters, Axel Fliethmann, Brigit Lang, Alison Lewis and Christiane Weller. Freiburg: Rombach Verlag. 171–201.

Graham, Brian. 2002. "Heritage as Knowledge: Capital or Culture?". *Urban Studies* 39. 5–6: 1003–17.

Gutmair, Ulrich. 2021. *The First Days of Berlin*. Cambridge and Medford, OR: Polity Press.

Henkel, Oliva and Karsten Wolff. 1996. *Berlin Underground: Techno und HipHop zwischen Mythos und Ausverkauf*. Berlin: FAB Verlag.

Ingham, James. 1999. "Listening Back from Blackburn: Virtual Sound Worlds and the Creation of Temporary Autonomy". *Living Through Pop*. Ed. Andrew Blake. London and New York: Routledge. 112–28.

Ingham, James, Martin Purvis and David B. Clarke. 1999. "Hearing Places, Making Spaces: Sonorous Geographies, Ephemeral Rhythms, and the Blackburn Warehouse Parties". *Environment and Planning D: Society and Space* 17.3: 283–305.

Locke, Claire. 2018. Berlin Insight. https://www.knightfrank.com/blog/2018/09/17/berlin-insight-2018-. Accessed 31 December 2024.

Nardi, Carlo. 2014. "The Scene of Scenes: Berlin Underground Parties, Neither Movement nor Institution". *Poor, But Sexy: Reflections on Berlin Scenes*. Ed. Geoff Stahl. Bern: Peter Lang: 83–93.

Nye, Sean. 2013. "Minimal Understandings: The Berlin Decade, The Minimal Continuum, and Debates on the Legacy of German Techno". *Journal of Popular Music Studies* 25: 154–84.

Oktay, Enis. 2014. "The Unbearable Hipness of Being Light: Welcome to Europe's New Nightlife Capital". *Poor, But Sexy. Reflections on Berlin Scenes*. Ed. Geoff Stahl. Bern: Peter Lang. 211–25.

Pascual, Luciano. 2022. "Technique, Experience and the Social Function of Techno Music: A Comparative Analysis of Theodor Adorno and Robert Fink". *Dancecult: Journal of Electronic Dance Music Culture* 14.1: 23–38.

Peter, Beate. 2014. "Breaching the Divide: Techno City Berlin". *Poor, But Sexy: Reflections on Berlin Scenes*. Ed. Geoff Stahl. Bern: Peter Lang. 173–89.

Peter, Beate. 2021. "Experiential Knowledge: Dance as Source for Popular Music Historiography". *Popular Music History* 12.3: 275–94.

Phillips, Mark Nicholas and Yüksel Pögün-Zander. 2021. "The Post-Wall–Era Club Culture of Berlin as Cultural Heritage: 'Where there was Jag, there is Art'". *Interior Provocations: History, Theory, and Practice of Autonomous Interiors*. Eds. Anca

I. Lasc, Deborah Schneiderman, Keena Suh, Karin Tehve, Alexa Griffith Winton and Karyn Zieve. London and New York: Routledge: 85–103.

Pope, Richard. 2011. "Hooked on an Affect: Detroit Techno and Dystopian Digital Culture". *Danceult* 2.1: 24–44.

Rapp, Tobias. 2009. *Lost and Sound. Berlin, Techno und der Easyjetset*. Frankfurt: Suhrkamp.

Rave the Planet. 2019a. About Us. https://www.ravetheplanet.com/en/info/about-us/#:~:text=Rave%20The%20Planet%20is%20a,and%20culture%20of%20electronic%20music. Accessed 31 December 2024.

Rave the Planet. 2019b. Techno goes UNESCO. https://www.ravetheplanet.com/en/techno-goes-unesco/. Accessed 31 December 2024.

Reckwitz, Andreas. 2017. *The Invention of Creativity*. Cambridge: Polity Press.

Sicko, Dan. 1999. *Techno Rebels: The Renegades of Electronic Funk*. New York: Billboard Books.

Solberg, Ragnhild Torvanger. 2014. "Waiting for the Bass to Drop": Correlations between Intense Emotional Experiences and Production Techniques in Build-up and Drop Sections of Electronic Dance Music". *Dancecult* 6.1: 61–82.

Taylor, Steve and Beate Peter. Forthcoming. "Differential Space and Collective Affect: A Spatial Politics of Electronic Dance Music". *Cultural Politics*.

UNESCO. 2022. "Basic Texts of the 2003 Convention for the Safeguarding of the Intangible Cultural Heritage". https://ich.unesco.org/doc/src/2003_Convention_Basic_Texts-_2022_version-EN_.pdf. Accessed 31 December 2024.

UNESCO. 2023. "What is Intangible Cultural Heritage?" https://ich.unesco.org/en/what-is-intangible-heritage-00003. Accessed 31 December 2024.

Wark, McKenzie. 2023. *Raving*. Durham, NC and London: Duke University Press.

Wright Hurley, Andrew. 2015. "Establishing Minimal Techno as Soundtrack to the Creative City: Hannes Stöhr's Berlin Calling". *Seminar* 51.4: 315–32.

CHAPTER 17

In Conversation: BBC Correspondents Past and Present

Katya Adler, Chris Bowlby, Ben Bradshaw, Mark Brayne, Jenny Hill, Frank Jahn, Johannes Riedel and Caroline Wyatt

CB: I'm Chris Bowlby, formerly BBC for some time. Never actually a BBC correspondent in Berlin. I was in Prague but made a lot of programmes about Germany. Let's start our discussion with Mark, who was here in the early 1980s and let's talk about the post of being a BBC correspondent, a slightly unusual one. I'm slightly tempted to address you as Lieutenant-Colonel (retired), which may mystify people. Tell us how that came about.

MB: The thing about Berlin was that the BBC came with Richard Dimbleby and others in 1945 in May, and nothing changed in Berlin in legal terms really until unification, until the end of the four-sector occupation of Berlin. So the BBC post in Berlin wasn't actually a BBC correspondent, it was a BBC representative. And as BBC German Service representative, representing the BBC and reporting for the German Service in German, but also tangentially in the English language as well for the rest of the BBC, we actually had the honorary status in terms of access to NAAFI[1] of Lieutenant-Colonel. But it didn't continue afterwards, and there was nothing military about that.

CB: No promotion if you were well behaved.

MB: No promotion. But that gave us accommodation in what was called a Type 4 house, I think. So we had a military house on the edge of the Grunewald and Ben also later lived there. The main thing was, we had an orange pass. So I'd done two years with Reuters in East Berlin first, in '77 and '78, so I was pretty embedded in East German society. Jutta, my wife, and I sang in the East Berlin Cathedral choir, the Domkantorei. Every Monday evening we would rehearse. We were good friends with Regine Hildebrandt[2] and her fam-

1 Navy, Army, and Air Force Institutes.

2 Regine Hildebrandt (1941–2001), a pharmacologist, later founded *Democracy Now* (1989), with her husband Jörg.

 | HTTPS://DOI.ORG/10.1515/9783111302508-017

ily, by virtue of being in the choir. We also had friends in Leipzig. I'd studied in Leipzig and I speak Russian as well, not that that was much relevance in East Germany in those days. And so, when I switched from East Berlin to West Berlin – defected from East Berlin to West Berlin as BBC correspondent – I still had all these connections in the east. So we would trundle backwards and forwards – I would also do the journalism – and we didn't have to come back, we didn't turn into pumpkins at 12 o'clock, we didn't have to do any Mindestumtausch[3] or anything like that. So we had access to the whole of actually occupied Berlin. We were part of the fabric of Berlin. We had a kind of status and acceptance, which was very rewarding both socially and professionally. And in a lot of East Germany, in East Berlin, although we weren't accredited and couldn't go to any of the official functions, we were very welcome. And reporting into the German Service with the *Briefe aus Berlin* every Saturday until quarter to twelve, we had a very dedicated, if not massive, audience in Berlin. If I got anything wrong I discovered it very quickly.

CB: So you had a strong sense of connection with your audience.

MB: A huge connection. Real sense of connection. We were local reporters, not just reporting for the BBC as I did from Beijing and from central Europe as well, after Berlin. There we were reporting out to the outside world. In Berlin we were local reporters and you had to get it right.

CB: And this relationship with the authorities here, the occupying authorities. Did they talk to you? Did they try to give you information? For example, the famous BRIXMIS[4] who were wandering around East Germany, monitoring what was going on there. Would they talk to you?

MB: It was a solid professional business, like normal relationship, but it was very handy having friends and sources in BRIXMIS at the time of Solidarity in Poland, which I covered from Berlin. I covered the British military dimension of that. Because the BRIXMIS knew that the Russians were manoeuvring around the eastern borders of Poland and putting pressure on the Poles to stop their Solidarity movement. So it was very useful to have those connections. I was approached once by MI6 and I did say no.

3 Currency exchange.
4 The British Commanders'-in-Chief Mission to the Soviet Forces in Germany.

CB: In terms of its prominence as a news story, obviously political coverage of Berlin in one sense, as far as the BBC was concerned, there was a lot coming out of Bonn. Were you concentrating in many ways on what one might call, more feature material, German language material, that kind of thing, rather than it being a constant news story?

MB: Graham Leach was BBC Bonn, so he definitely covered things there. I mean, I was very junior, I was only in my late 20s at that point. One of the things about being Reuters, then BBC in Berlin, was that there were 2700 pages of Stasi files on me, which was quite fun. Another interesting thing perhaps to observe is that when we were in East Berlin, my wife Jutta was studying at the Pädagogische Hochschule, which later joined up with the Freie Universität in West Berlin, was commuting from East Berlin to West Berlin to join her students. So we really did live Berlin in those days in a way that's difficult to reimagine. It was a real privilege to have been here at the time.

CB: Ben, if I could turn to you now. It sounds like you had an incredibly good sense of timing, arriving when you did in '89. Did you have a feeling that things were going to be moving – it's very easy to say with hindsight – when you arrived?

BB: I remember being asked at my interview, for what had been Mark's job the one before the guy before me, as a promising, up and coming, BBC journalist, why on earth I wanted to go to Berlin? Because the biggest, most high-profile story, my predecessor had, was when Rudolf Heß died in Spandau gaol, which kind of got him his moment of fame. And I said, "Well there's this Gorbachev thing going on at the moment and there are changes afoot in Poland, who knows? Something exciting might happen while I am there".

I'm not sure whether I convinced them, but anyway, as soon as I got here of course, in early Spring of '89 my feet had barely touched the ground. I famously actually missed the Berlin Wall coming down because I hadn't stopped working from the moment I arrived and I thought, "If I don't have a break now, I'm not going to have a break for 18 months", the speed the story was moving.

An anecdote about this absolutely invaluable allied pass that enabled us to go, drive to and fro through Checkpoint Charlie unchecked. There was a wonderful occasion where, and I was, you know, an ambitious young reporter, *Newsnight* rang me up and said, "Can you get us an interview with Jens Reich?", who was the founder of *Neues Forum*, the first kind of really serious guy who's fronting an East German opposition organisation. Well I said, I hadn't got a TV crew, it was very difficult for TV people, for people who are like Graham Leach, and others, Brian Hanrahan, to get accredited in East Berlin. The East German authorities were not exactly cooperative. But I said, can you find me a non-Berlin crew, who can come over for the day. They found me a Swiss camera crew. I smuggled in their camera equipment while they just travelled normally on the S-Bahn. We met at Jens Reich's apartment. We did what's called a "simul-rec". Those of you here who are broadcasters here will know. It's a technique where he held the phone below him and they recorded the sound and the pictures. They had to then fit it back together in London. The funny thing about this is that the next day I got a call from the BBC, saying "we've had a complaint from the East German embassy in London, because you didn't ask permission for this interview, and they don't know how you got it". And, of course, in theory we were, I was supposed to ask permission to interview people. In the end by then it was quite clear that the security apparatus of the East German regime was breaking down. And it was a free for all. And with this pass, if I had been given problems by the East Germans, which didn't really happen – there was an occasion when a couple of British correspondents were roughly handled on Alexanderplatz during a demonstration – all I needed to do was present this pass and say "I'm terribly sorry, you have to summon a Russian officer, I don't have to speak to you". So it was very valuable, very valuable indeed, at a time when it was very difficult for western journalists to come in and cover this massive story.

CB: It is interesting to remember that a lot of people assume that the Wall came down and almost immediately everything was peaceful and Germany reunified more or less the next day. There was in fact, an extraordinary period, for the following year or so, in the immediate aftermath of the Wall coming down a very uncertain situation, it wasn't at all clear that all was going to be peaceful.

BB: Very uncertain. Another famous memory was lying in bed, having been asked to do a two-way with the *Today* programme, following Mrs Thatcher's famous comments that German unification wouldn't be on the agenda for many years. And when this comment was put to me – I hadn't heard it before – I kind of spluttered before I replied, "I'm terribly sorry to have to tell you, but that's not the mood here and it's certainly not the mood in East Germany".

There was such a wealth of stories, not just the obvious ones, like how Germany was going to be unified, customs unions, all of those things, but kind of really interesting, sort of underneath stories: for example, restitutions of properties in the East. One that fascinated me as a young person who'd had a lot to do with Germany in the '70s and '80s as a teenager was the discovery of all these retired Baader-Meinhof terrorists who'd been settled in East Germany, working as plumbers and electricians and social workers, and you kind of, you'd heard rumours about that and also the role that East Germany had played in supporting the Red Army Faction, but there had been no proof. So many stories like that that came out and provided a wealth of content and broadcasting for months and years to come.

CB: And was it easy for you to say, "Look, these are the interesting stories". It was all such new territory, wasn't it? Or did you get a certain kind of story that appeared to be in demand from London and you had to sometimes resist that and say, "this is actually more interesting, more significant"?

BB: No, I was actually very free to suggest story ideas. I mean there were things that British audiences might be more interested in. I did a lot of extra work for American and Canadian broadcasters, because again, they didn't have anybody here. There was just a real thirst for anything about this process and how it was going to end. And it was very much up to me to decide what I wanted to do.

CB: I wanted to bring in Caroline Wyatt now, who first reported for the BBC from Berlin as business correspondent, because there was a big economic story to be told. What were the kind of business and economics stories, that were of interest then?

CW: There was a lot of interest in what reunification was going to mean for Germany, for the economy, for the coming together of east and west. Actually, the German business reporter came about as a post because of internal BBC politics, which were that, I think that we had something like seven correspondents based across Germany. BBC World Service spelled out that they weren't getting enough out of them and so they decided to smuggle in their own person via the back door and label it a business reporter. And while business formed the biggest part of what I did initially, it very rapidly morphed into a kind of generalised Germany. But very much looking at Eastern Germany and how reunification was working. Because I'd lived in West Berlin during the 1980s when my father was working with the British military government from '82 to '85, so I'd never had the chance to go to East Berlin. And then I suddenly found myself living, working, in the BBC bureau, the East Berlin bureau with Diana Goodman, who was there on Schadowstraße. And it was a wonderful time of the city flourishing, coming back together again. There was this incredible landscape of cranes everywhere, building sites, these deep holes that were being dug under Leipziger Platz, Alexanderplatz, all of the centre of Berlin. And it was that time of Helmut Kohl talking about the "blühende Landschaften",[5] that were going to evolve. "Ostalgie" was actually just beginning to come back, already then in 1993, '94, '95, where having had these vast waves of sort of joy and sort of ecstasy at reunion, people were starting, particularly in eastern Germany, in places like Magdeburg or Leipzig or Dresden, looking at the levels of unemployment, they were horrendous. And people were starting to say "we miss our old identity. We feel that we are being taken over." At the same time there were those stories that weren't business stories but were fascinating, as Ben was saying, about that sort of coming together again, where, for example, people who had been informal Stasi Mitarbeiter were suddenly being uncovered by people. So we went to talk to Vera Langsfeld, later a CDU deputy, whose husband it turned out had been spying on her throughout their marriage. We had all of those stories. The economy, the coming together. But also things like the first United Nations Climate Change conference (COP) in March 1995. It wasn't quite a fringe thing, but it was seen very much as a sort of Berlin thing of, you know, weird bicycles and photovoltaics, using solar power and wind energy and all of those things. So it was the most brilliant job I've ever been able to do.

CB: Lots of fascinating cultural life. Were you able to get a lot of that into your coverage as well?

CW: It wasn't just the politics, it wasn't just the city itself. It was also things like all of the artists who were visiting. So by that stage it was people like Vivienne Westwood was teaching at the fashion school, Marianne Faithfull came to do a series of cabarets. We went to film at the Travesti Schule, where people were learning how to be transvestites. It was the most staggering kind of flourishing of culture that I've ever seen in a city. You had the film festival, where I think we interviewed Til Schweiger, because I'd been to the cinema and had seen him and said, right, we have to do a series on Til Schweiger. Also I could meet him. We talked to Ute Lemper, who was singing at the time in the cabaret. We went down to Leipzig to do cabaret. We looked at how humour had helped undermine the Berlin Wall and undermine the Iron Curtain. And you know, at the same time, you went from covering cabaret in Leipzig to covering North Korean nuclear talks at the North Korean embassy in East Berlin. So it was the most fascinating time to be there.

5 Blooming landscapes.

CB: I would like to come back in a bit to you going back to Bonn and then back to Berlin, which sounds interesting. But now, Johannes Riedel from the BBC German language service, that's a really important part of this story from the BBC's point of view, and you span that period in a way, from the mid-1980s into the 1990s. You must have witnessed the enormous change in what the organisation felt it was doing then. Did you join what seems an organisation very much steeped in the Cold War, when it was the language service, was that very much its routine? Did it look as if that was going to go on forever? Taking in material from Berlin and broadcasting back to, in the German language, particularly to East Germany.

JR: Yes. When I started the position in '85 in the German service, that was still in the Cold War, we still had programmes like *Aus der kommunistischen Welt* (From the communist world) in the programme. And our news basically came from the central news room in Bush House, was translated and then broadcast.

CB: So it wasn't sort of on the ground reporting, it couldn't be by its very nature? It was more centralised?

JR: Yes, that's right. When the Wall fell, that took us quite by surprise. I still remember because I was presenting our newsreel. In the evening, we heard the news announcement by Schabowski[6] that the travel rules were relaxed. And everyone wondered what that meant.

CB: He sort of shrugged his shoulders, didn't he, and said "ab sofort", immediately, but then what did "immediately" mean? Nobody knew.

JR: Exactly. So we more or less went home bemused, and the expectation was that something would happen the next day, that they would explain what it meant or that something would transpire. And I went to bed and when I woke up the next morning, switched on the TV and I saw people dancing on the Wall. I couldn't believe it, I must say, I was in tears when I saw that.

CB: So it's easy to forget, isn't it, even for those who were professionally involved day by day with all the developments – and they had been huge –

6 Günter Schabowski (1929–2015), member of the Sozialistische Einheitspartei Deutschlands Politbüro.

with Gorbachev and East German leadership, no one imagined that that Wall would just disappear overnight.

JR: No, it really was completely surprising. Well, I immediately went to work and we prepared the afternoon broadcast, the evening broadcast. And I remember still that one of the priests from the civil rights movement, who went to the Berlin office the evening before, he had managed to drive by car to London and turned up for our newsreel, and we could interview him that evening, which was amazing really.

CB: Because there must have been a frustrating sense of distance in a way. This would have been the East, this closed society that you'd been commenting on from outside. Suddenly it was all opening up and that must have just transformed the nature of your potential journalism.

JR: Exactly. And he just took the opportunity, went by car, just straight driving over to England.

CB: But was there an immediate feeling of, "Ah, everything is going to be very different. The whole way we organise our journalism is going to be very different. What is it going to mean for us?"

JR: It did indeed, yes. We had a focus more on the role of presenting news as a step back from Germany, having the edit quality of having, not the German perspective, but more the international perspective and reflecting that back to Germany.

CB: Because suddenly your audience had all kinds of new media possibilities, if you like, so you had to think about what can make us still distinctive.

JR: Exactly, yes. We didn't have the task any more of enlightening, you know, the suppressed citizens of East Germany. But we had to find a new role. There we could come back to the BBC's objectivity, reflecting back to Germany a different angle from what they were used to from the German media. And it was at the time, also quite asked after. There were more radio stations which took our programme, our news, our international news, because the BBC had such a good name.

CB: And this being the World Service and funded by the government, there was also the decision about what was considered to be the government's priorities in terms of broadcasting, which eventually meant that the service closed, in the '90s.

JR: Yes. And it was still surprising that it survived ten years after the fall of the Wall. It was closed in 1999, a lot later than, for example, the French Continental Service and also some Eastern European services and so on. So it was surprising that it survived that long.

CB: Frank, let me ask you now, perhaps as someone who might have been a consumer of the BBC in those days, whether growing up you might have been aware of BBC journalism? Did it stand for something as you took on a journalistic career? What did it mean to you? Did it have a history or tradition?

FJ: The BBC? Yes, obviously, it was a role model. But can I just say, how interesting I found the stories you just told us. Because I'm a journalist: how you felt when the Wall came down and what your professional view of it was as well. But being East German too, it's also fascinating for me as well to hear what you thought in these days about us, my people, the East Germans, and what your stories were. I'm glad we could provide some stories for you in these days.

CB: So tell us what you were up to, let's say in the '90s, in this extraordinary period?

FJ: Obviously I was quite young at that stage. I was in school and then in the army, in those days. So I had to do my mandatory service in the army when the wall came down. I was reminded of that when Ben told us about the uncertainty in those days. I felt that quite strongly in those days, being young. We were all afraid. It could all end in civil war, in East Germany. Yes, we were celebrating it of course, but besides that it was a very dangerous moment and we did not know then that it would not end in blood.

CB: And how long did that feeling last?

FJ: Fortunately not very long. I think that it quite soon became clear, that all was quiet and that peaceful. It was with great relief we saw that.

CB: And how did you find out what was going on? Did you read newspapers? Listen to TV news, radio? What do you remember about that time in the media?

FJ: Yeah, I remember that a friend of mine knocked on my door and said that "Well, the Wall came down". "Pull the other one", as we say. "But no, no, really it is". We couldn't believe it, I couldn't believe it, but obviously it was true. What a moment in time.

CB: And becoming a journalist and training as a journalist, what inspired you to do that?

FJ: Maybe these days inspired me. Because journalism in East Germany was not what it is now, for us in this society. Journalism had a different quality in East Germany. It wasn't actually journalism at all, I would say. But I was lucky enough to be young and just starting out in my professional career, so when I chose journalism as my profession, I had all these opportunities before me. And maybe those days, maybe the reunification sort of inspired me to do that, because so much was going on in Germany. And to be able not just to consume Western media but be able to join it, professionally, that was quite exciting. So I seized that opportunity and tried to work for ARD.

CB: Caroline, just to come back to you, because you moved. I think, you were in Berlin and then you went to Bonn, because a bit like the German government, the BBC media operation stayed in Bonn for a while and then you came back to Berlin. So was that frustrating for a while, to go to good old *gemütlich* (cosy) Bonn where nothing much ever happened, when you knew everything was going on in Berlin, desperate to get back presumably?

CW: Yes, well I went to Bonn because the job came up. I think William Horsley was my predecessor in Bonn, and it was one way to actually get a BBC staff job instead of being a perennial stringer or freelancer, which was quite an expensive way to be a journalist, because sometimes you wouldn't get paid for a year or two, while your invoices went through the BBC machine. So I went to Bonn, and I knew that the government was going to return to Berlin, and actually, at that period, it was about '97, '98, it was when the party funding scandals began to nibble away at the CDU, so Bonn actually was an interesting place to go to. But I missed Berlin desperately, because I found myself doing stories about the art gallery in Bonn or conferences happening in Bonn, or the Wuppertaler Schwebebahn,[7] that was one piece on the 10 o'clock news.

It was a period when the BBC was actually really outward looking, or maybe the UK audiences were really outward looking, because we did a lot of pieces

7 Wuppertal Suspension Railway.

comparing or looking at how Germany did things and what the UK could learn. I think it must have been the beginning of the Blair government, so we would get a call, you know once or twice a month, going, you know, "how does Germany do healthcare? How does Germany do social care for the elderly?" And that was a phenomenally fascinating time because it really opened my eyes to the ways that things could be done differently and also to the changes that Germany itself was having to make, to its system, in order to do that incredible thing of bringing together East and West without social unrest, or with as little social unrest as possible. Because of course one of the stories that was a thread throughout that period was that it was also things like attacks on asylum seekers' homes. And so we were looking at that, and looking at what was happening in, say Brandenburg, as well. And we were able to travel around the whole of Germany as part of that job.

But really for me the main aim was to get the BBC bureau back to Berlin as soon as humanly possible, which I think I finally managed in about 1998 and into early '99. And I was so delighted when we got back to Berlin. We had a whole new bureau by then. We'd moved out of Schadowstraße. We'd moved out of Savignyplatz. And now we had to look for a new bureau. And we went to Platz vor dem neuen Tor and set up a whole new BBC Berlin, all-singing, all-dancing, satellite on the roof, able to broadcast any time of day or night. And of course that changed the way we did things as well, so it wasn't necessarily an unmitigated good, the ability to be able broadcast very cheaply, any time of day or night.

BB: The *Hauptstadtdebatte*[8] was huge at the time and very close. People forget how close it was, and how contested it was. I almost sort of abandoned my BBC duty to impartiality and objectivity in this. Because I remember making very strongly the case that the *Hauptstadt* could come to Berlin. But it was very strongly contested, including by, I think, a lot of people in the British government, because of the fear of, you know, German revival and the image of Berlin in the past. But Germany would be so different today if the capital had stayed in Bonn, and I thought the exclusion of the Eastern experience – which, you know, was very keenly felt in the German media in East Germany: the Westerners are coming to invade and take over our media. So someone like Frank Jahn was probably a trailblazer, in terms of a young East German coming up and tipping the balance back towards having a media that also reflected the East German lived experience. Because at the beginning, that was much not the case. I had friends who worked in East German media who felt very much

8 The decision to move the capital of Germany from Bonn back to Berlin.

that they were being taken over, colonised if you like, by journalists from the West. Which you could understand, for political and democratic reasons, but it meant that the balance, that the coverage, was then not going to reflect the experience of East Germans accurately and fairly.

CB: So important to talk about these tensions. But also perhaps to be sensitive about new generations coming through? Including those like yourself, who'd grown up in the East, who were going to have a completely different approach and who were going to really change things, and we needed to reflect that. Probably didn't always succeed in reflecting that well in the media, do you think?

FJ: Yes, we needed people coming East from the West and bringing the professionalism, but I think, also we need the East going West. That's what I did. I went to Hamburg, and started to work in Hamburg, and that was quite necessary, to mingle, to get the experience.

CB: Thank you, let us hear now from Katya Adler.

KA: My reporting relationship with Berlin goes back a very long way. BBC News Gathering sent me to Berlin for five or six months back in 2002. It was an opportunity to report on Germany, but for me personally, in that stage of my career, I wanted to get known in foreign news. And before I went, I went round every one of BBC's new programmes and said to the editors "What is it that you want from Germany that you feel you haven't been getting of late?" And again and again, "Oh come on, you know Katya, it's a worthy story, an economic story, but it tends to be boring, so unless it's stories about the Second World War as apart from the economy, we don't really tend to be interested". And I thought, "I'm going to show you guys".

And John Hooper, who was then the *Guardian's* correspondent in Berlin, he and I knew each other, and he said, "What about tango?" And he told me that Berlin was the second largest tango capital of the world, after Buenos Aires. And I thought, "that is my story". And the huge voyage of discovery went on for me. Every night of the week, there were clubs, there were tourists coming to Berlin just for tango, so they would sleep during the day and dance throughout the night. And I was particularly fascinated that it was particularly East Berlin that was so interested. One woman told me, under communism, men and women were supposed to be the same but in tango, she said, "a man is a man and a woman is a woman". And I will never forget those snowy nights that winter in the tango clubs, when men and women in their big winter coats would come in, clutching a plastic bag, disappearing into the toilets basically, to get changed, and come out transformed, the women in their long skirts, the men in their black trousers. And not only did I report, across the BBC, on tango but I also became hooked myself, on the dance.

During that time, of course, there was the second war on Iraq. Of course Germany played a huge role there along with France in opposing the war, so that was a very busy and interesting time for me, as regards BBC coverage.

And also there was that story, you probably remember, of the German cannibal, who decided to eat – flambé – his partner's appendage. And I thought at the time, naïvely, "the BBC's not going to want to cover a story like that". But there was huge interest in that by the BBC, as there was by every other news outlet, so that taught me something about foreign news reporting as well.

Now, I'm Europe editor, and I have been for many years, and we of course have Jenny Hill in Berlin, who does an amazing job of covering German politics. I dip in and out, depending on the story, but for me also of course, Germany is that huge player on the European and the world stage. What Germany does and says matters. It is the biggest economy in EU and most influential player in the bloc – sorry France – so there is always a big eye on Germany. And after Brexit we still need to look at Germany. It's not just about cars. Of course, in the UK, I believe that our audiences remain really interested in what is going on in European countries. And the UK wants to work with Germany, of course, when it comes to Ukraine, trying to contain Iran's nuclear programme as well, and here, in Norway as well, the UK through NATO is offering a helping hand to safeguard underwater infrastructure. Of course, the UK, like the EU, very much depending on Norway for energy, in the middle of the crisis, that we are in. So Germany should remain front and centre of our international reporting at the BBC, I would argue, and it remains very much a passion of mine.

CB: Let's talk to Jenny now. Did you have strong sense, of the kind of stories you would be covering? Did you know Berlin well, before you came.

JH: I didn't, not at all. And actually, like some others who've said something similar, a colleague had said to me, "Germany, you know, it's business, it's a bit of politics, it's pretty stable, pretty boring really". And I thought, "you can't possibly be serious". And on arrival I found of course, that my gut instinct had been correct.

And reasonably soon after I arrived, I remember speaking to an editor in London and saying, "we've gone down to Munich, gone to visit a refugee camp down here. You know, there's quite a lot of people starting to come into this country". And my editor was sort of like, "yeah, yeah, yeah" in a bored tone. And my goodness, you know in months we had the full-blown refugee crisis, which of course changed so much about how Germany is today, made a lot of significant shifts politically, not just in Germany, but across Europe of course. But even when I look back now, to how those early years of my career in Germany were, I really see a huge amount of change. We had the refugee crisis, we, you know, had a real rise in populist politics across Europe, in Germany too, and then of course, we had Brexit, and I wonder if there's any other European country, actually, that took Brexit as personally as Germany did.

I remember the morning after the referendum decision, walking through the Bundestag and seeing an MP there, who I knew quite well, and I sort of greeted him, you know, with my usual smile and he just looked at me with tears in his eyes and said, "what have you done?" And, you know, I was sort of not sure whether I was able to reassure him that I hadn't done it personally. (Laughter). But it was a really, painful moment for so many people here, I think, and not just politically either. So that obviously dominated and has continued, I think, to dominate a lot of my time here. It's quite interesting actually when Caroline was talking about the comparisons with Britain and Germany. I found that those comparisons continue, and there's a real appetite for them, but they've started to take on a rather more competitive feel. So you know, during the pandemic we had, well, "are the Germans doing worse than us or better than us?", and "how quickly are we going to get that vaccine out?" And even now, you know, we've got a new rail ticket coming out here next year, which will be reasonably cheap on a monthly basis for people, helping them during the cost-of-living crisis. And you know, again I'm just bracing myself for the inevitable interest that's going to come, you know, "well, why can't we do that in England, if the Germans are doing it?'. So I get a lot of that too.

CB: And in terms of personalities, the end of the Merkel era. She was a figure, I mean British audiences are not necessarily familiar with lots of German politicians, but she really of course made a huge impact on people, so that must have been a huge story in itself.

JH: It was, and I think during my time here she really grew into that huge figure who really managed to capture the imagination – I hesitate to use the phrase – of ordinary people at home. But people who weren't necessarily interested at all in politics, they knew who she was and they knew by and large, I think, what she was about. And it's very interesting to see how her popularity, if you like, has been somewhat trashed as we've started to see some of the flaws of her Russia, perhaps even her China policy, be laid bare, because of, you know, what's happened in the Ukraine and so on. It's very interesting to see how the Merkel era really did coincide with a really massive change for Germany. And today, you know I've been spending a lot of the day watching Olaf Scholz meeting the Chinese president and talking a lot about what Germany's relationship is going to be with China. And we're still not really sure what the current chancellor makes of China and what he really thinks Germany should be doing with China. There's a lot of suspicion around that, both here and across Europe, as you know. But I think, Germany is now once again at a time of really substantial change, and I think it's going to be really fascinating to see what the new Germany looks like. Not necessarily just under Olaf Scholz, you know he's talked about this *Zeitenwende*, Germany's shift in, well pretty much everything, but foreign policy, defence policy, in particular. These great big profound shifts in what people think about war and peace and their own place within that. There is a sense here I think, that we have seen a lot of those historical shifts that you all have been talking about, but in my view, those are just continuing now, and we are in a very exciting time.

CB: Yes, and some might feel, turning full circle, and Berlin again being at the centre of a lot of international tensions and relationships with the wider world, and threat and security, and all those questions being talked about and needing to be reported from Berlin again.

JH: Right, absolutely. And people are waiting to find out what Olaf Scholz really feels about what's happening. And the joy, as we all know, most of us know, of reporting on a coalition government is that it's never very clear cut. But as it's exactly as I say, we see what Germany will do militarily, and that will have a huge impact. We saw the real soul searching here over what Germany's responsibilities should be.

That's one of the things that I enjoy most about this job, I think, is the historical depth to decisions that are made today and you can really trace that palpably. You know, talking to anyone here in the wake of the invasion of Ukraine and people were desperately uncomfortable about what their country should do in this particular moment, what was the right thing to do? And I think that weighed more upon Germans than any other European country in many respects.

CB: Now I want quickly, before we get to questions, go round the panel, picking up that very point, of what are going to be the dominant stories out of Berlin coming up soon. Frank, do you want to start off? What will BBC correspondents be reporting particularly out of Berlin in the next few years, do you think? What's your instinct?

FJ: I can just strongly empathise with what Jenny just said, that Germany is at a turning point, it is at a crossroads. She mentioned Merkel and the change of guard to Scholz and we have this Ukraine war and that puts everything in question, of what was there so far. I mean, all the certainties, and our policies are now in question. Three major topics. First, it's defence. As Jenny mentioned, German politics always relied on discussing and debating things with other countries for stability. And now we have to see, well we have to put up defence so we have to put money into defence. That was a major mistake, I think, of Merkel's time, that she didn't see that and so our defence system, I mean there was no money for defence, I mean Germany was just hardly able to defend itself. And two other points of change where I see lots of change: energy and economics. I mean we were relying on Russia for energy and that is obviously now, it was a big mistake, so we need to sort that out. And the economy, I mean Jenny's just mentioned the visit to China, that's all the prosperity in the German economics depends on China, I mean most of it.

CB: Mark, what are your instincts? Anything particularly strike you at the moment?

MB: I think there's a Germany-shaped hole in sort of conceiving where we're going. Germany is a very grown-up country, a very cautious country. And I've got a lot of time for Scholz and masses of time for Merkel, obviously. Climate change is much, much worse. And there's lots coming up now in the run up to COP27 in Egypt. Climate change is coming down the track much faster than most people realise and it's going to present the international community with the most extraordinary challenges. It will put Ukraine into a very different perspective. I mean Germany had the experience last year of Ahrweiler, the main street was just full of debris and cars.[9] I mean, that is the shape of a lot of the stuff that's coming down the line.

And the way the international community works with China in particular, and needless to say the Americans, who goodness knows need grownups alongside them to keep the Americans on track. So I think, Germany is going to be more and more important. And coming out of Brexit Britain – I mean, let's not talk at great length about what's happening in Britain at the moment.

9 Ahrweiler district, in the western state of Rhineland-Palatinate, experienced the worst of the floods in July 2021, with 135 deaths.

We're going through a kind of – and I'm now a psychotherapist having left journalism – a kind of breakdown. I talk about Brexit as being sort of Britain's *Stunde Null* (zero hour), this point where the past suddenly stops. A bit like 1945 for Germany, thankfully with less violence. No, but Germany is a hugely important country, and I'm quite hopeful for the role that Germany might find itself playing, as very grown-up country compared to others we could think of here.

CB: Johannes, what's your instincts?

JR: I think Germany has also recognised that it can't play this laid-back role that has been done in the past. There were so many things now, the refugee crisis, the shock of the Brexit, Donald Trump in the United States, now the Ukraine crisis. And Germany knows more or less now that it can't stand back, that it has to change its policies.

I changed from the BBC German Service to Deutsche Welle, which is Germany's international broadcaster, and when I joined it, you know it had to take cuts nearly every year and that changed quite dramatically over the past five years, you know. More funding was poured into it, the main broadcast language changed, in the TV, international programmes changed from German to English, because English is the language you can make yourself understood. So the programme was expanded. Of course, the BBC was also partly what, Deutsche Welle aimed for and the other big competitor. That was a sign also that German politics understood that something had to be done and that Germany also has to do something on the media level to present itself.

CB: Ben, thoughts on that.

BB: Yes, just a couple of things to add. Now I'm afraid Jenny, that you're going to have to do more stories about Germany, as the prospect or possibility of a Labour government approaches. This is a Labour government that's very much modelling itself on Scholz and Scholz's victory. The contacts between the Labour party and the SPD are really growing again in importance and significance, and I expect that your editors back home will want you to do pieces about, you know, what is the Labour party going to do that Germany's done, etc. And I think, we can't get away from the collective national nervous breakdown of Brexit either, and I think, casting my imagination forward, to what will probably be a Labour government, I think that'll open up a fresh debate in the UK which is not possible at the moment. I mean, the conspiracy of silence is beginning to break down, including in the BBC, on Brexit, but I think that'll become an avalanche if you get the licence of a new government, that is interested in recalibrating, I'm not going to put it any more strongly than that, our relationship with the rest of Europe. In that context, Germany will be a massive player and incredibly important, if the European Union is going to be at all open to any suggestion from the UK point of view that we might try to creep a little bit closer to the EU again, economically and in terms of institutional structures.

CB: Your thoughts, Caroline. For example, the military question, Germany as a military power, as a former defence correspondent yourself, is that something which strikes you as a really interesting story?

CW: I think that is one of the most interesting stories of the last twenty to thirty years and of the next 20–30 years, because I remember reporting from Kosovo in, I can't remember if it was '98 or '99, but watching as the first German troops were deployed outside Germany, in a place where they were coming as peacekeepers and Kosovo Albanians threw flowers, welcomed them. You could see the kind of relief on the faces of the soldiers as they went in. And I thought that was a real watershed. But it didn't somehow flow forwards, you know, we saw what happened in Iraq with Germany and France, saying "Nope, not taking part". Where I think German leadership will be absolutely vital will be is on that defence front, as well as continuing to be absolutely vital on the international politics front, where, as Ben and Jenny were saying, the relationship with China, the relationship with Russia, will need careful, thoughtful leadership on the world stage, which Germany is very well placed to do. And I hope for all of our sakes, that the next 10–20 years, the next decade is a very dull decade of politics, because it has been far too exciting for a very long time.

APPENDIX

List of BBC Berlin Correspondents

*Vernon Bartlett 1929–34
Norman MacDonald 1945–48
Patrick Smith 1948–51
Charles Wheeler 1951–53
Ian MacDougall 1953–55
Guy Hadley 1955–58
Ivor Jones 1958–63
Peter Sewell 1964–66
Peter Johnson 1966–71
Bill Treharne Jones 1971–79
Eddie Vickers 1979–80
Mark Brayne 1980–82
Martyn Bond 1982–84
David Blow 1984–86
Tony Paterson 1986–88
Vivien Marsh 1988–89
Ben Bradshaw 1989–91
**Diana Goodman 1990–93
Martin Bell 1989–93
Caroline Wyatt 1993–96
Janet Barrie 1997–98
Katya Adler 1999–2000
Rob Broomby 2000–02
Tristana Moore 2002–03
Ray Furlong 2003–06
Steve Rosenberg 2006–10
Stephen Evans 2010–14
Jenny Hill 2014–23
Jessica Parker 2023–

*"Foreign Correspondent", 1932–34
**East Berlin correspondent

 | HTTPS://DOI.ORG/10.1515/9783111302508-018

Index

 | HTTPS://DOI.ORG/10.1515/9783111302508-019